Traffic
Management
and
Collision
Investigation

Traffic Management and Collision Investigation

WARREN E. CLARK
Golden West College
University of California—Longbeach

PRENTICE HALL CAREER &TECHNOLOGY. Upper Saddle River, NJ 07458

Library of Congress Cataloging in Publication Data

Clark, Warren E.
  Traffic management and collision investigation.

  Bibliography: p.
  Includes index.
  1. Traffic accident investigation. 2. Traffic
accidents—Research—United States. 3. Traffic
police—United States. I. Title.
HV8079.55.C55   364.1'47   81-12072
ISBN 0-13-926162-1   AACR2

Editorial/production supervision and interior design by Steven Young
Cover design by Miriam Recio
Manufacturing buyer: Ed O'Dougherty

Prentice-Hall Series in Criminal Justice
James D. Stinchcomb, Editor

Printed in the United States of America

10   9   8   7   6

ISBN 0-13-926162-1

Prentice-Hall International (UK) Limited, London
Prentice-Hall of Australia Pty. Limited, Sydney
Prentice-Hall Canada Inc., Toronto
Prentice-Hall Hispanoamericana, S.A., Mexico
Prentice-Hall of India Private Limited, New Delhi
Prentice-Hall of Japan, Inc., Tokyo
Pearson Education Asia Pte. Ltd., Singapore
Editoria Prentice-Hall do Brasil, Ltda., Rio De Janeiro

To
Dolly, Toni, and Heather,
and to
all peoples of good will who envision
synergism as the key to living in a
world community
and to
the Don Quixote philosophy
in all of us

Little difference does it make . . .
What shape our form or place
How light or hued our countenance
or what image lies upon our face
For it is that invisible vapour
That is our soul, which will win,
Or lose the race . . .

Contents

Preface

Traffic Management and Collision Investigation is designed to be more than a mere introduction to traffic. It is a source document that can be used by anyone involved in the traffic equation. The material is relevant for administration of justice students, sworn police officers, engineers, administrators, court attorneys, insurance investigators, corporate directors, and transportation safety directors. I have been impressed with the interest shown in this material and have, on occasion, taught many people involved with traffic from the public and private sectors.

There is no reason why an interested student cannot grasp collision reconstruction, even those for whom mathematics is as lost as Atlantis. Basic skill in addition, subtraction, division, and multiplication is all that is required. The mathematics can be further simplified by the student's use of a pocket calculator. Within a semester's work, the student will develop the skills to effectively complete a court-ready collision investigation, arrest report, and reconstruction that will defy challenge and offer a reasonable approach to understanding what happened at the collision scene, the speed of the participating vehicles, and a method for analysis to prevent a recurrence.

The book begins with an historical overview followed by terms unique to the study. From collision scene management through reporting and prevalent collision factors, the student learns the mechanics of the officer's responsibilities. Specific vehicle code sections are not studied and enumerated. I am convinced, after a decade of presenting the material, that teaching specific sections or code numbers is a waste of the student's time and an insult to his or her intelligence. It is far more important to grasp the concepts in understanding the prevalent collision factors. Every state and country offers a vehicle code book of law, which enumerates the specific section numbers to which the student can equate the concepts learned in this text.

Other chapters give special attention to the problems of arresting and reporting the drinking driver and to the reporting skills necessary to take a case to a successful conclusion. Human factors are explained so that the reader will understand how they figure into the driving equation. Following that is a composite picture of collision reconstruction, from feet per second to speed from skid marks. There is also a section for advanced students who want to develop a further insight as to how skid mark formulas are derived from Newton's Second Law of Motion and the Pythagorean Theorem. Due to the advent of world-wide metric utilization, the various formulas are worked and explained in both miles per hour and kilometers per hour. Unusual conditions are also covered, such as speed determinations from launching over ditch banks. Another chapter deals with wet weather driving and the phenomenon of hydroplaning. To acquaint students with the total traffic picture, a later chapter deals with traffic records, volume studies, and characteristics.

Final chapters deal with collecting, quantifying, and recording collision evidence; traffic supervision; unusual occurrence collisions, such as hit and run and vehicle arson; and the future of collision investigation. A complete collision investigation guide to translating numerical squares and conversion tables is included in the appendices, followed by a subject index for ready reference.

Traffic
Management
and
Collision
Investigation

1 Historical Development

The first human steps were designed to facilitate and speed movement as efficiently as possible from one point to another. Following animal trails and river banks, early humans soon found that their journeys placed them in direct conflict with animals and other Homo sapiens whom they did not wish to confront. It is possible that when meeting on narrow mountain trails, primitive people soon learned to establish the first rules of right-of-way. It is also possible that the most prestigious, heavily armed, or imposing individual on a collision course with another individual, soon learned to take control of the path, much in the same way that, in the present time, the larger vehicle often intimidates the smaller one, both in speed and size.

With the domestication of animals for beasts of burden came the necessity for the first recorded rules of the road and of parking. Camels were situated around the oasis according to the established hierarchy of their owners. The more favored or powerful the owner, the closer the campsite was to the water and the shade. This must have created the world's first parking lot congestion problem.

THE PHYSICAL ORGANIZATION OF SOCIETY

The Arabic Design

The Eastern cultures gave us the first recognizable form of traffic control, engineering, rules of the road, and street design. The center of this design was the town well or water supply, since water was paramount to survival. The cities

1

FIGURE 1-1.   Recognizing the Need for Traffic Rules

sprang up around the water, much in the same way early humans who traveled in the desert settled near an oasis. The city streets were, at first, no more than paths around tents pitched in a circle around the water supply. The tents gave way to structures built of sunbaked mud. Wood was in short supply in this area. With the advent of structures the paths became streets. The design was at first an accident. The most prestigious people of the community were allowed to live near the water in the first circle around the water supply. Those next in the hierarchy inhabited the second circle, and so on. The streets formed in concentric circles. A maze effect was created when the buildings were constructed, offsetting the paths which led from one row of buildings in the circle to the inner circle. In short, there was no direct path to the water supply.

With the well in the center, surrounded immediately by the local shiek's habitat,

2

FIGURE 1-2. The Arabic Design

the Arabic design served the towns' inhabitants very satisfactorily. The concentric circle of housing and shops with offset narrow streets complicated invader entrance. The design also made egress equally difficult. Each circle was protected by gates, further frustrating invaders and unwanted persons. Defenders lined the streets on rooftops. From their high vantage parapets, they successfully kept invaders at bay. The reader may be familiar with the several writings and recollections of "inner gates" found in the Old Testament of the Bible and in the Koran. Invading European crusaders found this design extremely difficult to breach. As the invaders finally scaled the outer perimeter and gained entrance, they had to repeat the feat over and over again before they could finally reach the precious water supply. With each breach, the perimeter of the circles became smaller and the defenders more concentrated upon the rooftops (See Fig. 1-2).

The European Influence

The cultures of Europe developed around another, equally valid, approach. In the beginning, societies recognized the necessity of banding together for their mutual protection from invaders. Being primarily agrarian, the farming community developed and relied upon a central fortress to which they could retreat in the event of an attack. The fortress concept expanded to include the creation of a military leader, a trained nucleus of soldiers, and a number of tradespeople to maintain the army and the fortress. Once again, the prestigious community members were protected within the confines of the fortress walls. The others, presumed to be protected, lived outside the walls and were connected by a system of road-ways to each other and to the fortress. The bastions were built around a common water supply, as in the early Eastern cultures. These stone monuments were a natural progression from the Arabic influence. A haven for mutual protection, access to potable water, and a safe place to store grain reserves was at stake. Most of the castles were built on the peripheries of lakes, rivers, and ocean shores, to facilitate transportation by water as well as conventional land routes.

The Development of Towns. It was the religious orders with their monks, nuns, and priests who were the catalysts for developing townships and eventually castle sites. The religions built their sanctuaries or havens a one-day ride or walk apart, that is from twenty to forty miles between sanctuaries, depending upon the terrain. Travel between sanctuaries gave rise to inns and rest stops for travelers.

With the developing transportation system of carriages came the related indus-tries which grew around the inns. Because few travelers could safely travel during the hours of darkness, the inns became havens. Walls and armed gatekeepers were soon to follow. With weapon sophistication came the necessity of higher walls, moats, drawbridges, and a regular company of defenders. With a continued demand for security, the castle emerged as the ultimate haven and eventually the core of a city.

The Roman Influence

It was really the Roman influence which did more to promulgate the growth of rapid transportation and city design than all of the methods and systems devised up to that time. The Roman armies conceived the concept of *grid* construction for their cities and encampments. (See Fig. 1-3.) The principle is still in use today, only we commonly refer to the pattern as *blocks*.

Grid Construction. The streets are designed in straight lines with intersections which meet at approximate right angles. With a number of blocks established, the legions developed a pattern of location. The Roman leaders occupied the block nearest the center of the complex. Obviously the central block was the most well-protected from invasion from any given direction. Centurions situated themselves in adjacent blocks to be close to their commanders.

The horse-mounted troops were located outside the blocks occupied by the centurions. Peripheral blocks were taken by the army proper. Outside, support cultures and camp followers took up residence in blocks beyond the troops.

The Romans built a very good network of streets between the blocks to provide a quick access to their respective staging areas. Bear in mind that a Roman encamp-ment might be in the same location for a number of years. Tents gave way to buildings and cities evolved, with the city founders occupying the central district.

This pattern design was still in vogue in the twentieth century and has certainly survived the test of time and practicality. The city hall has replaced the generals

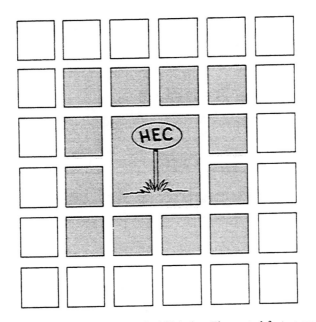

FIGURE 1-3. The Roman camp or "grid" design. The central feature was a large block reserved for the Roman generals. Adjacent blocks served as a base of operations for the Centurians and administrators. Outer blocks were relegated for armies, camp followers, and merchants.

in the central square. Shopping centers, courthouses, fire stations, and various institutions surround the central locale. Residential areas surround the core of the cities. Note that rail, heavy-duty transportation, and air facilities must be located outward, away from the central area, complicating access.

The Highway Concept. City planning is not the only engineering feat attributed to our Roman ancestors. They were the first to conceive of the super-highway. The armies needed mobility to maintain an empire that encompassed the then-known world. With the advancing armies came the corps of engineers who designed roadways still in use 2,000 years later. They developed roadbeds of large rocks, and covered these with finer grades of stones and sealant to hold everything in place. They graded the roadways and banked the turns to allow higher speeds of travel, such as with chariots. They also developed a number of laws which governed the use of the roadways, and issued encroachment permits for vendors who were allowed to transact business adjacent to the highways in specific locations. The engineers built storm drains to protect their roads, and ditches to allow for water runoff and irrigation. Traffic collisions did occur, and by law, were investigated. Violators were prosecuted and steps were taken to prevent recurrence of the infractions. To maintain the quality of the highways, weight laws were invoked, limiting the size of non-military loads which could be transported over the roads. To provide water for the cities, the Romans continued their engineering efforts and developed the aqueducts for which they are perhaps best remembered.

"All roads lead to Rome" was the truism of the age. Rome's roads spanned from Rome to England, traversing much of Southern Europe. Their highways also went eastward to the Holy Land and were later used in the Crusades.

GROWTH OF TRANSPORTATION PHILOSOPHIES

The Romans developed the principles of "Engineering, Education and Enforcement." The "Three E's" of traffic are still the basis for government institutions charged with the responsibility of moving vehicles, property, and people. The sophistication in application has probably never been more exacting than today. There is a National Highway Traffic Safety Administration, whose primary responsibility is one of research, statistical analysis, and education. Its subcommittees and commissions affect organizations at the most local level of municipal government. Automobile insurance carriers are also deeply involved in these areas, as well as police agencies to a lesser degree. Mass media has been attentive to the subject of collision-free transportation. Universities have expanded their curriculum to include highway engineering as a major course of study: the course work is a multi-faceted approach covering such topics as electrical engineering, the testing of roadway materials, and the appreciation of those human factors which influence our use of the highways. The police are empowered to enforce the laws which are designed to prevent collisions. Through proper education and engineering, it is conceivable that there would be no need for enforcement. However, the human is still an ancestor of the first person to climb down from the trees, and through neglect, carelessness, distraction, physical impairment, wanton disregard and mechanical malfunctions he will still exercise his prerogative to intimidate others and become involved in collisions.

Ever since human beings have stood erect, they have been trying to go faster than each other whether it is for escape, work, or sport. The propensity for speed led to what was surely the first camel race. When they found they could ride a horse, they began to breed a still faster horse. The Arabian is the undisputed race horse. The Clydesdale from Scotland is a fine example of a work horse and the Quarterhorse, the famous cow pony of the West, is fast for the first quarter-mile. With a physical limitation on what breeding could do for an identifiable strain of animal used as a beast of burden, the world settled back and enjoyed a steady pace of life, accepting the limitations of mobility. The late 1800s gave birth to what became a way of life, and ultimately, a necessity: the automobile. The six mile per hour pace of the horse-drawn carriage gave way to a machine which could propel people at sustained rates up to fifty miles per hour.

The Horseless Carriage

The automobile changed an entire world community, providing undreamed mobility. With the horseless carriage came the age-old quest for speed. The fascination with moving at twice the speed of the fastest horse became an obsession. It was not long before the horse was left behind as a mode of transportation. It is readily understood then, why the first traffic officers were known as "speed cops." With the advent of mass mobility and a car in every garage, it was evident that controls would have to be legislated and enforced. Drivers would have to be examined and duly licensed in the concept that driving a motor vehicle is not a right, but a privilege which could be suspended or revoked for infractions of the rules of the road.

Standardization of Laws. Beyond the issuing of citations for breaking the law, police agencies were given the responsibility of recording the collisions and developing a history of reporting and preserving the collision documents. With time and experience, this collision reporting became standardized on a form rather than just a page from the officer's notebook. There is a growing movement to standardize the laws pertinent to the operation of a motor vehicle. The Uniform Vehicle Control Act has been developed to serve as just such a guide and is published by the federal government. An example of the disparity which exists is the law enacted by several states concerning driving under the influence of alcohol. Most state laws regulate the level at which a driver is presumed to be under the influence at 0.10 percent Blood Alcohol. Other states regulate this downward to 0.08 percent, and still others feel that 0.15 percent is the cut-off level. The difference between the high and the low levels, depending on a person's body weight, could be as much as six drinks, or six ounces of 85 proof whiskey.

Another common disparity between the states is the law restricting the load limits on commercial vehicles; yet another is found in licensing requirements. The list goes on and on, adding to driver confusion when driving from one state to the next. Perhaps the single biggest disparity is found not in the enforcement of the law, but in the administration of justice within the court systems.

The Construction of Surfaced Highways. When World War I took our servicemen to Europe, they were impressed with the ease with which the German army could move from battle zone to battle zone on paved highways. At this time, America was just beginning to grow out of the horse and buggy days. For the most part, our highways which interlinked the cities were constructed from gravel with a rock roadbed. With the help of the U.S. Government, states began a vigorous campaign to build hard surfaced highways. As the network of highways grew, remote towns grew into cities and industry moved from the highly urban areas closer to their source of raw material for manufacture.

The Ribbon City Design. Again because of environmental factors, a third city design was born: The Ribbon City Concept (see Fig. 1.4). Ideally, the highway is a multi-laned super highway with controlled access on- and off-ramps with no cross-traffic. A railroad line runs along the highway to service heavy industry located in juxtaposition along the highway. The light industry and shopping centers are located to the outside of the industrial area, with residential homes and churches located to the outside of the shopping centers. Ideally the strip has an airport

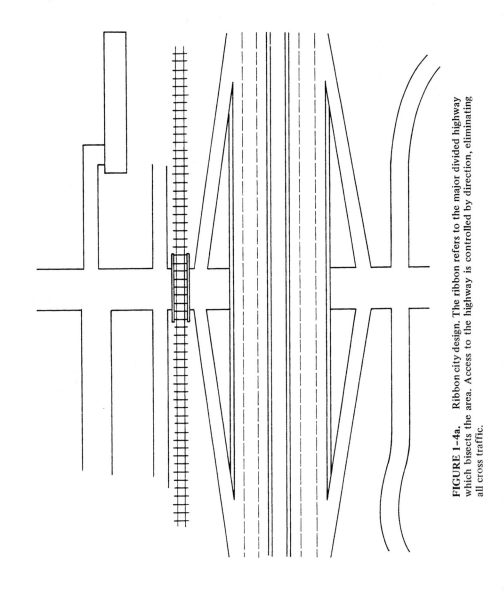

FIGURE 1-4a. Ribbon city design. The ribbon refers to the major divided highway which bisects the area. Access to the highway is controlled by direction, eliminating all cross traffic.

FIGURE 1-4b. This aerial photograph demonstrates the ribbon city concepts of controlled access to and from the major highway onto the arterial highway that runs top to bottom through the picture. Observe the clean appearance of the landscaped ramps, the office and light industrial area at the top, and the residential areas to the left. Trees are used by the landscape engineers to serve as sound and pollution barriers between the highway and homes.

FIGURE 1-4c. Design engineering often encompasses more than traffic. In this aerial photograph a drainage facility that bisects two major highways. The railroad to the right services the industrial area. The residential area to the left is remote from both the highway and industrial noise and pollution. Although out of the photograph, there is an airport to the upper left that services the area.

9

located at one end of the city with residential growth restricted away from the airport. The residential streets may follow the contour of the natural terrain, esthetically blending into the setting, sufficiently remote from the noise and contaminant pollution of the highway, railroad, and manufacturing area. A prime example of just such a community is to be found in and around Mission Viejo, California, south of Los Angeles and north of the San Diego on Interstate 5.

TWENTIETH CENTURY TRANSPORTATION

The Automobile

In 1898 the French first placed a motor on a carriage, inserted a front wheel guidance lever called a tiller, and began the era of the automobile. In 1899, the American-made "Locomobile" was on the streets of the United States. Its cost was a modest $600, but it took three months to obtain delivery. The Locomobile was also guided by a tiller and had the engine mounted in the rear. It was an open two-place carriage.

In 1899, the nation's first fatal automobile-involved collision occurred in New York City. The driver of the horseless carriage struck a horse and buggy at the dizzying speed of ten miles per hour. It was in this same year that counties, cities, and townships began to sell automobile registrations, although licensing was not mandatory.

In 1904 the British introduced their first horseless carriage, the Rolls-Royce. It had two cylinders which developed ten horsepower and was reported to have traveled the distance of 220 miles in one day without a breakdown. Two years later, in 1906, the Wayne Motor Car Company developed a fifty horsepower, four cylinder automobile in Detroit. The Wayne sold for $3,500. In this developmental period, it was the Ford Motor Company which ultimately triumphed through the advent of mass production, making the horseless carriage affordable.

Knowing little of what we call modern day ecology, gasoline was also at a premium in the earlier days. To beat this problem, the 1914 Saxon boasted 30 miles to the gallon with a four cylinder, fifteen horsepower Continental engine. The price was a reasonable $395.

By 1915, the automobile was here to stay. The mechanized cavalry of World War I had proven this point beyond a shadow of a doubt. The auto was the wave of the future on an uncertain sea.

The Highway

The British coined the word "highway." The name for the roadway which was built at a higher level than the surrounding area grew to popularity, especially through the lowland areas of Great Britain. The lowlands would flood with the rising tides and leave the "ways" awash in sea and river water. When the roadbeds were built upon a rock foundation above the high water mark with necessary bridges to allow for the flow of the sea and river water, the "ways" became known as "highways." Residents could then travel the highways regardless of the tides without worrying about being stranded by the rising waters. The term highway grew to encompass the definition listed in Chapter Two of this text, "a way or place of whatever nature, publicly maintained and open to the use of the public for purposes of vehicular travel."

It was not long before it was discovered that vehicles upon the cobblestone and rock-covered roadbeds provided a most uncomfortable ride. The vehicles suffered from the rough roads, losing wheels, and breaking axles and other component parts. In the early 1800s, John L. MacAdam, a Scottish engineer, developed a method for crushing gravel and small rocks which he mixed with hot asphalt. When the composite mixture was poured over the highways, it would flow into the rocks of the roadbed. He then rolled the surface with a weighted cylinder drawn by a team of draft horses. When the asphalt and crushed gravel mixture hardened, a smooth surface was developed that enhanced vehicular travel. Named for the inventor, this system of rolling asphalt and crushed rock composite for a road surface is known as "macadam," and is in worldwide use today.

THE SCOPE OF THE TRAFFIC PROBLEM

Forty-seven thousand American service men and women gave their lives during the period of the Viet Nam conflict. During that same period of time, over 300,000 men, women, and children were fatally injured in motor vehicle collisions on American highways. Collisions account for over 50,000 deaths per year, and are the leading causes of death for all persons aged one to forty-five. Property damage annually runs in excess of six billion dollars exclusive of the doctor, hospital, and attorney fees for the eleven million injured every year.[1] There is no way to place a price tag on the grief, pain, displacement, psychological changes, lost families, and disfigurement suffered by the injured, and everyone is a victim. Even when a motor vehicle collision involves only property damage, or what is known in police circles as a "fender bender," there is at minimum the inconvenience and cost of having the damage repaired, reported, and paid for, and the incalculable loss in terms of having suffered a close call.

There has most recently been a programmed safety drive, promoted by the federal government, to make injury-free driving more of a reality. In the late 1920s, safety glass became mandated, and seat belts were introduced in the 1960s. Impact bumpers and headrest were a product of the 1970s. The 1980 generation of vehicles are less powerful, more fuel efficient, and they include seat restraints, air

[1] U.S. Department of Transportation, 1978 National Highway Traffic Safety Administration, "Accident Facts."

bag dashboards, and fewer protuberances in the passenger compartment to strike and injure an occupant.

The engineers of the world have also been at work to develop a safer roadway, to accommodate faster traffic in greater volumes, and to develop a system of standardized signing consistent with international logos of simple pictures, circles, and arrows. Because our improved highways encourage faster driving, the death rate has climbed as has the severity of the collisions. With mandated lower horsepower into the year 2000, the auto manufacturers are stripping away vehicle weight in an attempt to maintain the weight to horsepower ratio. This ratio affects such vehicle performance factors as speed, acceleration, and ecological efficiency. To reduce the weight of an automobile, steel is removed and light plastics and other products are substituted. There is a growing concern that the removal of the protective steel will leave the occupants of a collision vehicle more vulnerable to injury.

Since September of 1899, when Mr. H. H. Bliss was fatally injured when he stepped off the trolley and was struck by a horseless carriage, the unknown factor of this problem is the vacillating and unpredictable human being. Unable to control the variables of driver personality, we have established laws that apply to everyone operating a motor vehicle and sanctions for the violators. The laws which govern the operation of motor vehicles are written by elected officials who reflect the will of the governed who are, for the most part, drivers. Collision statistics fail to impress most drivers or have a lasting effect on a driver's memory. When the 55 mile per hour maximum speed law was imposed in the seventies for economic reasons, it

FIGURE 1-5.   A southbound view of Interstate Highway 5 on a Friday evening. Note the five lanes in each direction and the southbound density of passenger vehicles in comparison to the northbound commercial vehicles.

was met with mixed emotion and generally accepted as a step to conservation of fuel during a time of rising gasoline prices. As we moved into the 1980s, the lower limit became less and less a factor of conservation when supplies of fuel appeared to be increasing to former levels. The tendency to speed returned, and the death rate increased along with injury collisions as drivers once again drove more miles and increased their speed. It would appear from this that economics, and not lost lives nor collision potential, is the determining factor in the dirver equation.

Since the invention of the automobile, approximately two million people have lost their lives as a direct result of motor vehicle collisions in the United States alone. The reader can readily grasp the overwhelming scope of this problem of traffic management and the reason for expanding our understanding of the many facets of this discipline.

DISCUSSION QUESTIONS

1. Which of the three major city designs most closely describes the city in which you live or work? Is there room for improvement in terms of vehicular flow patterns?

2. If you have been involved in a motor vehicle collision, what factors of this experience have affected your driving habits? Did the experience of the collision influence you in your decision to study this subject?

3. Do you see the smaller fuel-efficient motor vehicles as the answer to the transportation needs of your area?

4. How do you feel about the safety record of the drivers in your area? Did the last fatal collision which occurred in your area receive publicity in the media and if so, did the media coverage seem to have impact on the way people drive through the area where the fatal collision occurred?

Basic Terms

DEFINITIONS

To appreciate the problems of collision investigation, we must share a common understanding of the basic terms involved. Most of the terminology can be found in the respective vehicle codes of the various states and countries.

The information provided herein is a composite of those terms found to be in general agreement. The competence of a collision investigator is gauged by his or her ability to express the facts based upon a knowledge of the appropriate terms. The following lexicon of definitions is by no means complete nor is it intended to meet the needs of every situation which will confront the investigator. It is rather a springboard into one of the most fascinating areas of law enforcement.

Highway

A *highway* is a way or place of whatever nature, publicly maintained and open to the use of the public for purposes of vehicular travel. This definition includes streets.

As seen by the definition, the legislators intended that any way or place open to the use of the public for purposes of vehicular travel which is publicly maintained is a highway, and subject to the laws pertinent thereto. For example, the parking lot of a state, county, or city-operated hospital would fall under the definition of highway. The grounds and parking facilities of a private hospital would not meet the criteria.

Vehicle

A *vehicle* is a device by which any person or property may be propelled, moved, or drawn upon a highway, excepting a device moved by human power or used exclusively upon stationary rails or tracks. A train or bicycle is not a vehicle; however, a horse-drawn cart or motor driven cycle is considered a vehicle.

Roadway

A *roadway* is that portion of a highway improved, designed, or ordinarily used for vehicular travel. This definition implies that the shoulder area of a highway is not a portion of the roadway, as it is not designed and ordinarily used for vehicular travel. The difference between a highway and a roadway is this: a *highway* encompasses all of the right-of-way upon which the roadway runs, including all of the easement, the landscaping, ditches, drainage facilities, and so on. A *roadway* is simply that portion upon which the vehicles normally operate.

Sidewalk

A *sidewalk* is that portion of a highway, other than the roadway, set apart by curbs, barriers, markings, or delineation for pedestrian travel.

Pedestrian

A *pedestrian* is any person who is afoot or who is using a means of conveyance propelled by human power other than a bicycle. Thus, a pedestrian may be afoot or upon a skateboard or roller skates. A child riding a tricycle is still a pedestrian.

Person

A *person* includes a natural person, firm, co-partnership, association, or corporation. Thus, a company may register a vehicle in the name of the company and not in the name of the owners.

Private Road or Driveway

A *private road or driveway* is a way or place in private ownership and used for vehicular travel by the owner and those with expressed or implied permission from the owner but not by other members of the public.

With a few exceptions such as "hit and run" and "drunk driving on private property," the rules of the various vehicle codes do not apply. Few laws apply to private property and the operation of a motor vehicle. Unlicensed drivers may drive on private property with impunity in most states. Some states give local authorities the right to invoke laws regulating the use of a motor vehicle on private property such as shopping center parking lots.

Motor Vehicle

A *motor vehicle* is a vehicle which is self propelled. This simplest of all definitions covers a great deal of devices ranging from the traditional automobile to a motorized skateboard.

Official Traffic Control Device

An *official traffic control device* is any sign, signal, marking, or device not inconsistent with the vehicle code, placed or erected by authority of a public body or official having jurisdiction, for the purpose of regulating warning or guiding traffic.

A painted curb indicating a no parking zone is an example of an official traffic control device as well as the traditional stop and yield signs, provided such markings and signs are placed by the appropriate authority. In one incident, an irate citizen hand-painted a red curb area in front of his home to prevent the neighbor's teenage son from utilizing the space, then called in a complaint to have the vehicle removed for being in violation of the red curb marking. Although well-conceived and intended to alleviate a problem, the marking was not official.

Official Traffic Control Signal

An *official traffic control signal* is any device, whether manually, electrically, or mechanically operated, by which traffic is alternately directed to stop and proceed, and which is erected by authority of a public body or official having jurisdiction.

This is the usual traffic light referred to by definitions, and covers those lights used by school crossing guards in the performance of their duties.

Stop or Stopping

Stop or *stopping* when prohibited shall mean any cessation of movement of a vehicle, whether occupied or not, except when necessary to avoid conflict with other traffic or in compliance with the direction of a police officer or official traffic control device or signal.

Traffic

The term *traffic* includes pedestrians, ridden animals, vehicles, street cars, and other conveyances, either singly or together, while using any highway for purposes of travel.

Therefore, even one pedestrian constitutes traffic. This becomes significant in those cases involving pedestrian-automobile right-of-way collisions.

Driver

A *driver* is a person who drives or is in actual physical control of a vehicle. The term driver does not include the tillerman or other person who, in an auxiliary capacity, assists the driver in the steering or operation of any articulated firefighting apparatus.

Thus, a person who has had too much to drink who pulls over to the shoulder of a roadway but leaves the engine running while he sleeps it off, is still a driver, and subject to the laws of driving while intoxicated. Some jurisdictions hold that in such cases if the keys are present in the ignition switch, the man is capable of driving and is, therefore, a driver. In one case, it was held that where a drunk driver was towing another vehicle behind his car by means of a tow cable and the second car being driven or controlled by yet a second drunk driver, *both* are guilty of driving while intoxicated.

Crosswalk

A *crosswalk* is either: (a) that portion of a roadway included within the prolongation or connection of the boundary lines of sidewalks at intersections where the intersecting roadways meet at approximately right angles, except the prolongation of such lines from an alley across a street, or (b) any portion of a roadway distinctly indicated for pedestrian crossing by lines or other markings on the surface.

It is easy to see where a misunderstanding could occur in this definition if we did not realize that no markings need exist. A crosswalk exists across an intersection on the prolongations of the sidewalks on either side. The second portion of the definition is quite clear concerning marked crosswalks. A number of drivers and pedestrians become confused over the unmarked crosswalk, and collisions occur. This definition is of particular importance in those states where pedestrians have the right-of-way over vehicles upon the roadway, and when investigating "auto-ped" collisions, wherein the pedestrian was in an unmarked crosswalk.

Lane of Reference

In the event the collision occurred on a roadway having two or more lanes in each direction of travel, the investigator will find it much easier to communicate the lane of reference if he or she will follow this simple rule: The number one lane is that lane nearest the center line of the roadway. If the roadway is a north-south highway and the collision occurred in the north-bound fast lane, the designation is simply shown as the N-1 lane. If the collision occurred in the slow lane of a roadway having four lanes in a northerly direction, the reference would be to the N-4 lane, and so on. If a collision occurs on a one-way multi-laned street, the lanes are numbered from the left as the investigator faces the direction in which the vehicular traffic is flowing.

Prolongation

The term *prolongation* means the imaginary extension of a line. For example, envision the curb lines of an intersection as if they actually cross that intersection to meet the curb lines on the other side, thus drawing an imaginary box which outlines the intersection. Collision measurements are quire often referred from the prolongation of a curb line. A mid-intersection collision report might read that the point of impact was 34 feet west of the east prolongation of the curb line of Oak Street, and 17 feet south of the north prolongation of the curb line of Main Avenue.

Berm

This is a term which tends to confuse recruits, courts, and the public. A *berm* is the narrow raised ledge which exists on the outer edge of the shoulders on our major super-highways. The berm forms the trimline which separates the landscaping from the shoulder. Berm is contrasted to curb in that a curb delineates the edge of a roadway and usually adjoins the sidewalk adjacent to a city street.

Road

Road is that portion of a highway which defines the area from curb to curb, including the shoulders. Roadway, you will recall, covers only the main traveled portion of the road, exclusive of the shoulders.

Linear Compression

From the diagram (Fig. 2-2), it can be seen that slow-moving southbound traffic ahead forces all traffic to decelerate. Drivers begin to jockey for a more advanta-

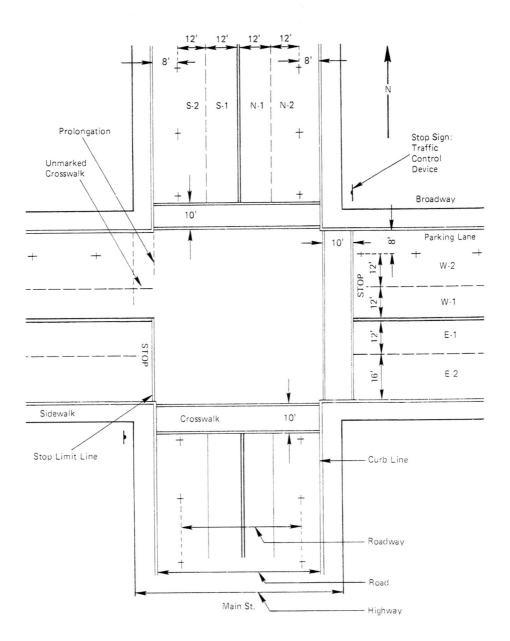

FIGURE 2-1. A Typical Intersection with Definitions and Measurements

19

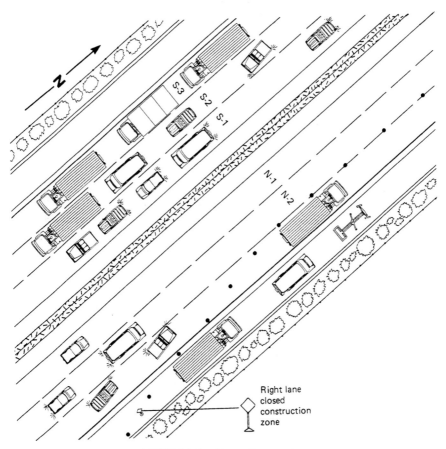

FIGURE 2-2. Linear Compression

geous position in order to drive around the slower vehicles. Linear compression causes the vehicles to "platoon" or group. This is readily observed as vehicles move in platoon fashion from one signal to the next in city or urban driving. The slow stop-and-go of linear compression creates an accordian effect in the distance between the vehicles, subsequently raising the probability of rear-end collisions.

Lateral Compression

Note (Fig. 2-2) that all northbound traffic is forced from three to two lanes. Lateral compression also occurs at the scene of traffic collisions, construction sites, in on and off ramp congestion, and in areas of right or left lane conflict with egress, merging, slowing and stalled disabled vehicles. A disabled vehicle completely off on the shoulder often presents a visual hazard which causes lateral compression as passing drivers swing wide of the potential area of conflict and the people standing by who are waiting for assistance. Lateral compression raises the probability of lane change violations.

FIGURE 2-3. Linear compression can result when a slow-moving vehicle pulls directly into the path of oncoming traffic. When the pick-up truck pulls along side the truck in the second lane, they will make a rolling roadblock in the second and third lanes.

COLLISION CLASSIFICATIONS

The following definitions and collision classifications are the standard interpretations and delimitations given and in accordance with the, "Manual on Classification of Motor Vehicle Traffic Accidents," Third Edition, published by the National Safety Council.

Accident or Collision

An *accident* or *collision* is an unintended event that produces damage or injury. The word "injury" includes "fatal injury." "Accident," "Collision," and "Crash" are synonymous, interchangeable words describing the event.

Motor Vehicle Traffic Accident

A *motor vehicle traffic accident* is any motor vehicle accident that occurs on a highway or that occurs after the motor vehicle runs off the road but before events are stabilized. Motor vehicle traffic accident includes collisions occurring on a highway involving:

1. a motor vehicle in transport setting in motion an object, such as the vehicle's occupants, load, or parts, without the motor vehicle itself doing the actual striking.
2. a motor vehicle in transport (in motion or in readiness for motion) involved in a noncollision event. A noncollision accident could be accidental poisoning from carbon monoxide generated by a motor vehicle or injury to a vehicle occupant from being thrown against some part of a motor vehicle or some object in the vehicle.

Motor Vehicle Nontraffic Accident

A *motor vehicle nontraffic accident* is any motor vehicle accident occurring entirely at a place other than on a highway.

The term *motor vehicle nontraffic accident* excludes off-highway accidents that do not involve a motor vehicle "in transport." The following are examples of this exclusion.

1. Property damage, personal injury, or death resulting from an organized racetrack or drag strip competition event.
2. Property damage, personal injury, or death sustained by a farmer due to a tractor overturning during an actual plowing operation.
3. Property damage, personal injury, or death resulting from operation of a forklift vehicle within an industrial plant or other building.

Off-highway accidents not involving a motor vehicle in transport, and events such as airplane crashes on highways and train accidents, which do not meet the definition of motor vehicle accident, are the responsibility of the sheriff, police department, coroner, Industrial Accident Commission, or appropriate federal authority.

In Transport

This describes the state or condition of a vehicle when it is in use *primarily* for moving persons or property (including the vehicle itself) from one place to another. *In transport* includes vehicles:

1. *In Motion.* This includes vehicles on or off a roadway.
2. *In Readiness for Motion.* This excludes vehicles in a designated parking area or on a shoulder. Motor vehicles in parking areas or on shoulders are not *in transport* unless they are in motion.

3. *On a Roadway but Not Parked in a Designated Parking Area.* Stalled, disabled, or abandoned motor vehicles on a roadway are considered to be in transport.[1]

Accidents after Stabilized Situations

A *stabilized situation* marks the end of an event. Nothing further will occur insofar as the event itself is concerned but other events may follow because of subsequent actions arising from the first event. The stabilized situation may be brief but definitely separates the end of one event from the beginning of another event. In some situations a temporary position of safety may be reached. This is a position in which a person would not be in jeopardy again were the position maintained until rescue or the hazard removed. In a collision where a stabilized situation can be identified, subsequent injury or damage-producing events are not considered a part of the original collision. The following examples are illustrative of stabilized situations.

1. After a motor vehicle accident, live electric wires fall on the involved vehicle, but there is no injury from the electric current because the occupants remain inside the motor vehicle. Subsequent injuries, which can be attributed to the electric current, that result from attempts to leave the motor vehicle or attempts to rescue are not a part of the original motor vehicle accident.
2. In a motor vehicle accident objects are loosened which remain in place until all occupants are removed from the area of risk from the loosened objects. Any subsequent injury or damage that can be attributed to the fall or roll of the loosened objects is not a part of the original motor vehicle accident.

Chain Reaction Accident

Occasionally, in the same area within a short period of time, several motor vehicles may be involved in collisions under hazardous driving conditions, such as reduced visibility due to fog. In a chain-reaction collision it may be difficult to determine whether the event was stabilized, or whether several collisions occurred with the situation stabilizing between separate collisions. Consequently, for the purposes of uniformity, such chain-reaction collisions should be considered single motor vehicle accidents.

Legal Intervention

Injury or damage caused by enforcement intervention (usually apprehension or attempt to apprehend) using a motor vehicle is not a motor vehicle accident insofar as the enforcing agency and violator relationship is concerned. If, when intentional

---

[1] A vehicle is considered to be on a roadway when any part of it is on the roadway and might be struck by a vehicle which is moving entirely on the roadway.

acts are committed, injury or damage occurs that goes beyond the original intent, the excessive acts are considered accidental and meet the specifications of a motor vehicle accident. To help distinguish between legal intervention and collision, some examples for each are provided below:

1. Legal Interventions
   a. A roadblock is set up to stop a law breaker, and the law breaker intentionally or unintentionally crashes into the roadblock.
   b. A police car cuts in front of a car to force the car to the curb or shoulder and, as a result, the two cars collide.
   c. A suspect vehicle crashes when bullets are fired into it from a police officer's gun.
2. Collisions
   a. A driver other than a law breaker crashes unintentionally into a roadblock.
   b. While eluding the police, a law breaker loses control of his vehicle and crashes into another vehicle.
   c. A police car skids and crashes while chasing a law breaker.

Deliberate Intent

Deliberate intent is an intentional act that directly or indirectly involves a motor vehicle in transport and purposely causes or tries to cause injury or damage to property. If the intended act results in injury or damage that goes beyond the

FIGURE 2-4a.   When traffic must converge from three to two lanes, the result is lateral compression.

FIGURE 2-4b. Even though lateral compression is evident as a road crew has blocked the far right lane, the Volkswagen makes an extra lane by straddling the line between the first and second lanes. Is this a traffic violation?

original intent, the additional event is accidental and considered a motor vehicle traffic accident. The following examples are *not* motor vehicle traffic accidents although a motor vehicle in transport is used to inflict injury or damage.

1. *Suicide or Self-Inflicted Injury.* A driver self-inflicts injury by driving a motor vehicle against a fixed object, into a body of water, or similarly misuses a motor vehicle in transport, *and* this intent is verified in some manner.

2. *Homicide, Injury, or Damage Purposely Inflicted.* A person deliberately intends to cause death, injury, or damage by driving a motor vehicle against persons, vehicles, or property.

3. *Staged Traffic Collision.* A collision intentionally planned or contrived for fraudulent purposes.

Succeeding chapters will include additional definitions which apply to the specific discussion such as with collision reporting and determination of speed from skid marks.

DISCUSSION QUESTIONS

1. A certain street comes to an end in a bulb-shaped turnaround and parking area adjacent to a public beach. Do the laws of your state relative to the operation of a motor vehicle apply to the parking lot area?

2. Is a Moped classified as a motor vehicle under the laws of your state?

3. A driver parks his automobile in his driveway adjacent to his home. The vehicle rolls forward, through a fence and strikes a neighbor's home. There are no injuries; however, there is a great deal of property damage. As the vehicle had been unoperated, and the collision occurred entirely on private property, is there a violation of law for failure to set the brakes on the automobile?

4. Can you develop examples of lateral and linear compression from your own driving experience?

3

Collision Scene Management

Collision scene management is the *raison d'être* or reason for being for the traffic collision investigator. The days when a police department could arbitrarily assign just anyone to handle the responsibilities of collision investigation are as much a thing of the past as horse and buggy transportation.

THE TRAFFIC COLLISION INVESTIGATOR

The investigator is primarily responsible for the welfare of the motoring public. The traffic officer's duty at a collision scene is to re-establish the uninterrupted flow of traffic with a minimum of delay, balancing his or her actions and decisions with due consideration for the participants and victims. Whenever a highway is temporarily blocked due to a traffic collision, there exists a high probability of additional collisions occurring in the stop-and-go accordion effect of vehicles stopping for, and trying to drive around, the confusion.

The investigator–reporter must possess the skills to administer life-saving first aid; preserve the scene; collect valuable evidence; photograph the area, the vehicles, the participants, and any evidence of a transient nature, such as skid marks; direct traffic; empathetically deal with victims; effect legal arrests; remove the damaged vehicles; clear the scene; and effectively compile an investigative report that encompasses the collision. The most important attribute of the traffic officer is the ability to deal with stress on a daily basis.

COLLISION MANAGEMENT

An attempt to put into priority the elements of collision scene management is a must for the investigator. The traffic officer must maintain flexibility, as each collision is different and may require a somewhat different approach. Generally speaking, the following list is an acceptable plan of action upon arrival of the officer and will efficiently cover most incidents.

Evaluation. Evaluate the assistance requirements necessary.
- a. Request assistance from the appropriate allied agencies, ambulance services, fire departments, coroner's office, and possible assistance for traffic control.
- b. Request the necessary tow service trucks and any specialized equipment.

First aid. Having made a quick assessment of the assistance required and having requested the proper agencies to respond, attend to the injured.

Protect the scene. Stabilize the scene as soon as possible following the care of the injured. Place flares or cones to warn oncoming traffic of the emergency which exists ahead.

Witnesses. Locate the witnesses and have them stand by until such time as they may be interviewed.

Evidence. Take the appropriate measurements, collect evidence, note the debris, and photograph as appropriate.

Vehicle removal. Direct the tow services into and out of the scene, giving them as much assistance as possible to expedite their presence in the area in a minimum amount of time.

Open the roadway. Effect the sweep and wash-down of the scene as soon as possible following the vehicle removal, and restore the normal traffic flow.

Statements. Obtain statements from witnesses and then drivers.

Arrests. Effect arrests as necessary.

Reporting. Compile the investigation report.

Evaluation

When the officer arrives on the scene, the evaluation process is already underway. Most officers know their beat and the idiosyncrasies of high collision areas. When a call is received to respond to a given scene, the officer already has a pretty fair idea what has happened and what will be needed to handle the situation from past experience. When the collision was reported, a good dispatcher will have ascertained not only the location but a rundown of collision severity, vehicles involved, injuries, and so on. The dispatcher can then advise the officer what additional assistance has been called. Each collision, however, has its own special requirements, and none should ever be considered routine. This is true for even the simplest fender-bender.

Special Equipment. Severe collisions will require specialized equipment to pry open doors or cut open passenger compartments to remove participants. Most fire departments maintain and train their personnel in the use of this equipment. When

28

calling for the fire department, be sure your dispatcher understands what you need the fire fighters to do, so that their dispatcher will order out the proper personnel and equipment. If you simply need a wash-down to clean the gasoline from a ruptured tank of a collision vehicle, the equipment needed is a pumper. If there are trapped victims, the tools necessary may well be on a paramedic unit or a ladder truck. It is well to remember that precious time lost in rolling the proper equipment may mean the difference between life and death.

Trained fire fighters are very adept at rigging lines to hold precariously balanced vehicles and they can also handle certain spilled loads that result from a collision. In this latter category, it is wise for an officer to call upon the services of the state department of transportation. State highway departments have crews trained to handle spilled loads. This is particularly important in the event of radiation hazards, chemical spills, and unknown gases which are transported over our highways.

Medical Help. When making the quick assessment of the scene upon arrival, the officer should call for an appropriate number of ambulances and if necessary, a deputy coronor. Here, too, it is wise to advise the dispatcher of special needs and requirements. In the event of trapped victims where there is going to be an obvious protraction of time in victim removal, you may want a doctor to ride in the ambulance and be present on the scene to assist in those cases where paramedics are not available. Persons with cardiac arrests and others with injured spines are two examples of instances where it is wise to notify your dispatcher to expedite and alert the proper rescue and ambulance personnel, as well as the hospital staff receiving the victims.

Towing Services. When calling for towing services, be specific. A regular tow truck will be at a loss to handle a big-rig roll-over. Many areas are fortunate in that they can call upon the tilt-bed or flat-bed tow trucks which can winch a disabled vehicle up onto the bed of the tow truck. These facilities are particularly practical with car fires as there are rarely any tires left on the disabled vehicle. They are also handy for the removal of vehicles constructed with a fiberglass exterior where traditional front-end hook-ups are difficult, if not impossible, without additionally damaging the body material.

In the event the collision clean-up will be extensive, requiring a lengthy process, it is wise to call for city street, county road, or state highway departments to assist in traffic control. They can erect barricades, place warning signs, provide for hazard removal, and generally provide traffic control, relieving much needed officers who are freed to assist at the collision scene.

First Aid

It is not intended to provide a course of emergency medical treatment procedures in this text. It is intended, however, to stress the importance of this skill. A traffic officer must know more than the basics, and be minimally trained in advanced first aid. It is not at all uncommon to read about an officer who is given credit for the saving of a life. Understanding the priorities of medical requirements at a collision scene are imperative. A broken femur is far down on the list of medical aid requirements compared with the attention required by a choking victim or a sucking chest wound punctured by a broken steering wheel or horn ring.

First aid is given second billing to the evaluation process and calls for assistance only because of the necessity to roll the proper assistance personnel and equipment to the scene. An officer may be outstanding in the art of first aid but without the proper medical attention given to expedite the victim to the hospital, the attentions will be quite useless in too many cases. So, take that extra minute to call for the assistance needed, then provide the first aid.

Protecting the Scene

Protection of the scene begins with your arrival at the scene of a major collision. The common device used is the patrol unit (Fig. 3-1). The flashing lights of the unit will serve as a temporary measure in the warning process of oncoming traffic. The unit will serve as a buffer between the officer and the injured victims. The close proximity of the unit also provides more immediate access to the first aid equip-

FIGURE 3-1. In the event of a collision, the police officer unlocks the control box and throws the right-hand switch from "automatic" to "flashing." When the intersection collision is cleared, the switch is returned to "automatic." In the event of a signal malfunction the officer can throw the switch to "flashing" and leave a note in the panel advising the repairman of the nature of the problem.

ment, a radio, and a facility in which to incarcerate a recalcitrant prisoner if an arrest is immediately necessary, such as with a fighting drunk driver or one who is attempting to flee the scene.

Once the first aid is completed and the wounds are sufficiently stabilized, the officer can break away to the unit, obtain the warning devices, and begin to lay a pattern to guide traffic around the collision scene. A number of departments are now utilizing reflective cones and flares for the hours of darkness. There are usually eight cones placed in the trunk of each traffic unit. Drivers are accustomed to observing cones and reacting to their restraints to traffic flow. The cones tend to provide a visual barrier of height. The flares by themselves appear to be simply unidimensional lights upon the surface of the roadway, so the combined use of flares and cones is effective.

Witnesses

One of the most important aspects of traffic investigation is often overlooked until it becomes too late. Witnesses will not usually stay at an accident scene once the ambulances are gone. Good witnesses are very difficult to locate. It is even more difficult to extract meaningful statements. An investigating officer will do well to remember these facts, and obtain his witnesses early in the process. One method is to ask the crowd that gathers, "Did anyone see what happened?" There are usually a few who will answer. Another approach is to state, "I'd like to have witnesses remain here, and the rest of you please leave or at least step back." Another method, and probably the most effective, is to watch the crowd as you are doing first aid and protecting the scene. A sixth sense will usually tell you who saw what by the way the person is pointing or explaining to other onlookers just what happened.

Having identified your witnesses, the experienced officer asks those persons if they have some form of identification with them. The officer will then collect driver's licenses or I.D. cards and ask the witnesses to please stand by until he or she can get back to them to write their statements; or, the officer may pass out summary sheets and ask the witnesses to write their own statements. The officer, nonetheless, retains the identifications. This process frees the officer to go on about his or her business, assured that the witnesses will stay at the scene at least long enough to have their driver's licenses returned to them. The driver's license is returned when the officer is satisfied that the witnesses have given an accurate account of what they saw, and from what position. The problem with having the witnesses write their own account of events is that much information is left out of the statement. When writing such a statement, people have a tendency to show a bias and use terms like "fast" or "speeding." As an officer, your statement of their recapitulation of events should be more specific. For example, "fast" to an older person could mean 55 or 65 miles per hour on a major highway, whereas a younger person might indicate that the speed was about normal for this stretch of roadway.

In addition to what they saw, it is important to know where they saw it from.

Was it possible to see all they say they observed? Few will actually have seen as much as they claim. Much of what they actually observed is supposition based on their prejudices, vehicle positions, skid marks, and so on, or something overheard in the crowd as they were waiting to be interviewed.

More intelligent people tend to be the most inattentive drivers, as well as the most unreliable witnesses.[1] The unqualified best witnesses tend to be the young people. As an observation based on experience, teenage boys will be the best with muffler sounds and cars, and quite good at gauging speeds and locations. Young ladies are astute observers in identifying the colors, driver identification and anything special about the vehicle. The poorest witnesses are generally doctors and attorneys. As professional people they tend, as a whole, to see very little and always appear to be in a hurry to leave the scene. One the other hand, nurses tend not only to be outstanding witnesses, but will most often assist with the first aid responsibilities.

Once the officer has identified and located the witnesses, obtained their identification, and asked them to stand by, he or she is ready to begin the search for evidence.

Evidence

The officer should begin with a full-sized sheet of paper on a clipboard. Draw a rough sketch of the intersection or roadway. In those collisions involving major injuries or fatalities, and in every instance wherein skid marks are present, the officer should use a steel tape measure to assure accuracy of the measurements. If other officers are not yet present on the scene to assist, you may want to elicit assistance from the crowd. Be sure you obtain the complete I.D. of the person who comes to your aid, and in your report be sure to list the person's name, address, and phone number. The court may want to call on this individual to attest that he or she held the tape measure in the position specified by you, the officer.

Note all evidence—vehicle debris, broken glass, a gouge mark in the pavement, a skidmark, a paint transfer, pieces of a spilled load or whatever may be present—on your rough sketch to be later transferred to your final drawing of the scene. Locate and measure the aforementioned items: Show them in your sketch and describe them in your report, as well.

You may wish to preserve the scene in photographs. Indicate on your rough sketch and final drawing your location and the photographs taken. Your photographs will not only maintain your integrity as a thorough investigator, they will show the locations of skid marks and other evidence that will disappear once the roadway is reopened and traffic obliterates the scene. Later chapters will deal with

[1] Kennedy, Norman, Kell, James H., and Homburger, Wolfgang S. *Fundamentals of Traffic Engineering.* (California: The Institute of Transportation and Traffic Engineering, University of California Press, 1978).

the subject of gathering evanescent evidence and the proper preservation of the material and information.

Vehicle Removal

The tow truck driver is an important member of the collision team. An experienced operator can save time and additional collisions by his or her expertise in clearing the scene quickly and with a minimum of confusion. An experienced operator can handle a multi-vehicle collision alone. The driver clears the scene by taking the disabled vehicles to the side of the road or an adjacent parking lot. By taking the first vehicle off the road, dropping it, and returning for the second, and so on, the operator can clear the area and take everything to a position of relative safety. It is much easier and considerably safer for an officer to make out a storage report on a vehicle while it is sitting in a parking lot than it is to constantly have to look over one's shoulder for traffic as the report is prepared in the middle of a roadway.

Assisting the Tow Truck Operator. An experienced officer can assist a tow truck operator in a number of ways. The officer knows how to rig the hookup in order to expedite vehicle removal once the tow truck is backed into position. The officer can direct oncoming traffic around the area of the pickup, alleviating the operator's anxiety over being struck by a passing motorist. By advising the police dispatcher of the types of vehicles involved in the collision, the experienced officer will have summoned the proper tow truck and operator. Finally, the officer may offer suggestions and direction to the operators to educate them in towing techniques used by other, more experienced operators. One such observation is the use of what is known as jack stands. At the scene of a collision where the rear tires of a vehicle to be towed are disabled, it is customary for an inexperienced tow truck operator to attempt to pick up the vehicle from the rear. This means stopping all traffic while the tow truck is U-turned in the roadway. Following the rear end hook-up, the tow truck with the disabled vehicle in tow will again have to be U-turned to send them on their way. This will necessitate stopping all traffic twice, a very dangerous proposition, as it engenders rear end collisions. Most tow trucks carry dollies. Dollies are a set of four small wheels which can be interconnected to lift the disabled vehicle from the ground by supporting the rear or front wheels. Operators are reluctant to utilize the dollies as the process is time-consuming. They will have to jack up the rear of the disabled vehicle to lift the rear wheels from the ground. They will then slide the dolly axles down either side of the rear wheels of the vehicle, make the connections for the dolly wheels, lower the jack, and let the disabled vehicle come to rest on the dolly. The process is not only time-consuming but dangerous in light of high-density, close-proximity traffic. A passing truck can cause a sufficient draft of wind to literally blow a disabled vehicle off a bumper jack. Also, it is difficult to find a median point on a rear bumper and a bumper jack that will support the disabled vehicle weight.

A simple solution to all of this is to have the tow operator carry two relatively inexpensive jack stands in the bed of the truck. The tow operator hooks up the disabled vehicle from the front in a normal manner, then lifts the front off the ground. The jack stands are then placed beneath the vehicle frame rails to the rear of the vehicle midpoint. The operator then lowers the disabled vehicle back to the ground, leaving the hookup in place. As the vehicle lowers, the weight pivots over the jack stands, like a child's teeter-totter or seesaw board. The front end of the disabled vehicle rests on the ground, the rear end lifts free of the ground, and the dollies can easily be slid beneath the rear wheels and quickly assembled. Firmly supported by the jack stands, there is little danger of the vehicle falling from a jack. The operator then picks up the front end of the disabled vehicle with the tow truck. The weight is relieved from the jack stands and the rear end of the disabled vehicle rests firmly on the dollies. The operator simply removes the jack stands and drives away, towing the disabled vehicle. This process avoids the double U-turn maneuver, the double shut-down of all traffic with the attendant rear end collisions, and the high probability of having a vehicle fall from a bumper jack and it expedites the entire process in a matter of a few minutes. (Fig. 3-2.)

An experienced tow truck operator is also a benefactor in assisting with the removal of trapped victims in a vehicle. When a person is trapped behind a collapsed steering post, on more than one occasion the windshield is cut away, and the tow cable is wrapped around the post, lifting the post upward and off the victim. The same process can effectively be utilized to open jammed doors.

A tow truck carries a variety of tools which can be most useful at the scene of a collision to pry fenders away from tires, cut battery cables, and so on. Most tow services carry push brooms, useful in cleaning up the broken glass and debris from the scene.

FIGURE 3-2. The "jack stand" procedure simplifies removal of a disabled vehicle without exposing the tow truck operator to unwarranted risk.

FIGURE 3-2. (*cont.*)

FIGURE 3-2. (cont.)

FIGURE 3-2. (*cont.*)

FIGURE 3-2. (*cont.*)

Completing the Storage Report

Whenever a driver has been taken from the scene of a collision to a hospital or other medical facility, the investigator is responsible for providing a thorough inventory of the vehicle and its contents prior to releasing the vehicle to the tow operator. Most departments have a prepared form which facilitates the recording of the various items to be listed. There are several items however that are often overlooked. People often carry a set of house keys in their glove box or a garage door opener. With these, an unscrupulous tow operator could easily rob the home of the collision victim. The only key which should go with the stored vehicle is the key to the ignition. An automatic garage door opener found in the glove box or clipped to the sun visor should be sent to the victim with other personal effects.

Before the ambulance leaves, the vehicle should be quickly scanned for personal items and articles of value. House keys should be removed from the key ring and included with other valuables.

A thorough inventory also precludes a victim's claim that valuable property in the vehicle was lost or stolen. An officer has little defense if he has not taken an inventory or if he completed the inventory in haste and overlooked obvious items.

It is recommended that items found in the passenger compartment of the vehicle be locked in the trunk of the car to prevent theft and exposure to weather. This is particularly true for clothing, books, and suitcases. Money and briefcases, like other valuables, should be sent with the victim.

Open the Roadway

Once the ambulances have departed, measurements and pictures taken, the involved vehicles safely out of the way, the patrol unit moved to a position of safety, and the roadway cleared of glass and debris, open the roadway.

This is no simple task. It requires forethought and coordination with other officers who may be involved in traffic control. Begin by removing the flares or cones closest to the scene of the collision. *Walk facing traffic.* Pick up the cones or flares as you come to them until you have reached the last or furthest warning device. *Remember—do not turn your back to traffic.* Remain in a position to observe traffic at all times through this process. You will be walking and standing adjacent to traffic and, at 55 miles per hour, those vehicles will be passing within inches of your body at the rate of nearly 81 feet per second. At 35 miles per hour the traffic will be moving at a rate of 51 feet per second as they pass. Drivers do not anticipate persons standing in an open roadway. Officers must be mindful of this fact and minimize their exposure to oncoming traffic.

Statements

Contact the witnesses who are now standing by in a safe, out-of-roadway area. Interview witnesses first. The drivers are interested parties and will undoubtedly be anxious to have the witnesses' statements taken as a priority.

Correct Form. When writing the statements of witnesses, use the third person in reporting. For example: Mr. Daniels (Witness 2) was standing at the curb on the southeast corner of the intersection of Main and Broadway. He observed the red Chevrolet (Vehicle 1) making a left turn from eastbound Broadway to north-bound Main. He was waiting for the light to change to walk across Broadway. His view was unobstructed as there were no other vehicles nor pedestrians in his line of sight. Mr. Daniels observed the Buick (Vehicle 2) westbound in the W-1 lane at approximately 35 miles per hour. The light facing Mr. Daniels was red, the light for both vehicles was green. He states the Chevrolet which had been stopped, made a sudden start, pulling into the path of the Buick, and so on.

Whenever a direct quote is used, place the statement of the witness within quotation marks. For example: Mr. Daniels states, "The Buick was not going over 35 miles per hour." When quoting a witness, spell out all the words. Do not use abbreviations, such as M.P.H. (miles per hour). For numbers 1 through 9, spell out in words (one, two, three, and so on). For numbers ten and above use the symbol (10, 11, 12, and so on).

Questions To Ask Witnesses. There are other questions which should be asked of a witness before taking stock of the gravity of the testimony. Where were they in relation to the collision? What obstructions existed to impair their view? How is their vision? Just what brought their attention to the imminent situation? Did they just happen to be looking in that direction, or did the sound of the crash cause them to look?

A witness who hears the crash and then sees the participating vehicles has little to offer in testimony as to what led up to the incident. An officer must be cautious that a witness offer only that statement which is relative to the facts he or she observed or heard. Avoid letting a witness make supposition, or worse, guessing as to what happened.

Witnesses Preparing Statements. If you have the witness prepare his or her own statement, have that witness write a signature immediately beneath the last sentence of the statement. Below the signature, have the witness print his or her name and date the entry adding the time below the data. The text of the statement should contain the name, address, age, and phone number of the witness. If your witnesses prepare their own statements, have each of them use a separate sheet of paper. Do not continue one statement following another on the same sheet. The second witness will have his testimony influenced by what he or she reads from the prior statement.

When allowing a witness to prepare their own statements, direct them to print. Much of what is in handwriting is illegible except to the writer. In the event of a serious injury collision, the case may well end in civil litigation. This civil process in many states may take three to ten years to be initiated in the courtroom. It is doubtful then, some years later, that the author of a handwritten report will be able to decipher his or her own writing.

Before accepting the report from a witness, verify by identification that the witness is one and the same purported in the statement. A crowd of witnesses particularly in a residential area will undoubtedly contain a friend or two of one of the participants. A friend may not only shave the truth but provide misinformation concerning identity in order to offset other statements.

Interviewing Drivers and Passengers. Once the witness information has been obtained and verified, thank the witnesses and release them, giving back their I.D. Then contact all drivers and passengers in the respective vehicles. Again, write the statements in the third person: he and she, Mr., Mrs., Ms., Miss, and so on.

Include in the statements such things as what happened prior to the collision and what they did or did not see before the crash. How fast were they going? What lane were they in? Were there any visual obstructions, such as fogged windows, sunrise, sunset, rain or glare, and so on? What was the mechanical condition of their vehicle prior to the collision? Are the brakes operative on the first application or must they be pumped? Does the horn work? Does the vehicle have good tires? Was the speedomoter operative? Were there any distractions (radio, heater, defroster, air conditioning, passenger conversations, crying children, or the sound of a siren)?

Having completed the statements, read them back to the individual, so that they may hear how their account reads and sounds. There may be a word or two they want to change to make it grammatically correct. Although it is not necessary to have the individual sign his or her signature to the statement prepared by the officer, it does tend to alleviate any problems which may arise in the future when the driver wishes to change the statement complaining that the information recorded by the officer was incorrect.

When a drinking driver is involved in a collision, it will serve the officer well to have the errant driver prepare a statement (and be explicit), and have the driver sign his signature. The statement often becomes "people's number one" as an exhibit in criminal court.

The officer must be particularly protective of young witnesses. Exercise a very low profile and be most empathetic when dealing with young people who have just witnessed one of the most traumatic scenes they may ever see in their lifetime. The officer's skill in this instance may very well effect how that child will react to the police for the rest of his or her life. The officer should remove his or her hat or cap while talking to the child, kneel down to be at eye level with them, and talk in low, understanding terms. Avoid police jargon, use simple words, and be specific. Do not badger, threaten, or offer some form of reward for talking with you. It is still the best form of interrogation to have your interview of the child in the presence of one of the parents. If one of the parents is not available, ask an adult neighbor or one of your fellow officers to stand by within listening distance. Obtain the neighbor's name, address, age, and phone number, and include this information in the statement text, or the officer's name and I.D. number if a parent or neighbor was unavailable.

Arrests

Primarily, the reference is to a physical arrest. For example: in the event of a collision involving a drinking driver, there is little to be gained by attempting to give the driver a field sobriety test and effect an arrest up to this point in time. Should you discern that the responsible driver is under the influence of alcohol or drugs during the course of your investigation process, you may wish to place the individual in your patrol unit in an in-custody status until you are ready to deal with the situation.

Once everything has been completed up to this juncture, provide the drinking driver with an opportunity to complete the field sobriety test. Chapter 6 deals with the testing of a suspected drinking driver in the field.

Having determined that the suspect is under the influence of alcoholic beverages or drugs, effect the necessary "in-custody" arrest, start the arrest report, provide the appropriate admonishments, and leave the scene of the collision and book the prisoner in your jail facility.

Up to the point of actually making the arrest, an officer should maintain a low-key approach to the suspect unless, that is, you suspect the individual may attempt to leave the scene. In any event, it is most advisable to have the individuals seated in your patrol unit cage or back seat until you are ready to talk to them as a witness. You can forestall their arrest anxiety and antagonism by having them prepare a statement as previously mentioned. Should the individual become violent or attempt to leave the scene, you will, of course, have no option but to restrain them.

In some instances, certain departments issue a citation or notice-to-appear to sober but errant drivers involved in a collision. The notice-to-appear is an arrest, and the arrested party is released upon providing their signature to the citation, thus giving their promise to appear to answer to the charges.

Most departments require the officers to investigate an incident, and submit the reports for review to a collision investigator. The court officer will then take the collision information to the city, township, or district attorney for a complaint to be filed. The complaint is then filed and the errant party notified by mail to appear in court to answer to the charges.

In all instances, it is the officer's responsibility to prepare the case for court.

Reporting

The officer has total responsibility for reporting the facts. Chapter 4 discusses the writing of the collision report. This is the last step in the collision management process, and without a doubt, the singularly most important. The report should be written in the officer's most professional manner. Not only is an officer known by the quality of his or her reports, but the department is under scrutiny as well. Copies of a collision report may be distributed to the following: the collision participants; owners of property damaged as a result of the collision; the respective attorneys; insurance companies; city, township or district attorneys; courts at all levels; road and highway departments of a city, township, county, or state; coronor's officers; federal departments concerned with collision investigations; and, quite often, media. As an investigator, your name appears on each page, and the reputation of your department depends on your skill. An investigation should be prepared as carefully as if a member of your family were involved.

The traffic officer must deal routinely with a great deal of stress. The officer cannot pick and choose the situations, nor the time, date, location, and participants. The next radio call may be a "fender-bender" or a triple fatality and it can come at any time. The officer must maintain flexibility to handle each unique situation.

DISCUSSION QUESTIONS

1. As the officer in charge of a collision scene, would you have reservations about asking a fire captain to move the fire truck to the shoulder of the road in order to expedite the movement of all lanes of traffic to avoid possible collisions due to lateral compression?

2. A seriously injured victim at a collision scene refuses medical aid based on religious grounds, and the paramedic on the scene advises you that the individual will die without immediate aid. You are in charge. What do you do?

3. If the person described in question 2 is a 13-year-old juvenile, what do you do?

4. A witness offers you a statement and identifies the driver who is responsible in a felony drunk-driver collision. The witness refuses to identify himself for fear of reprisal. What do you do?

5. What do you think about placing the signals on flashing red when working intersection collisions?

The Collision Investigation

The reporting of vehicle collisions is certainly nothing new. The Romans were the first to document this phenomenon and investigate the causes. In Chapter 3 we discussed the priorities to consider in collision scene management. In this chapter we will discuss how to organize the reporting of the investigation.

There are two basic kinds of collision recording: a report and a full investigation.

THE REPORT

A *collision report* consists of a face page which lists the names of the drivers and pertinent information: the kinds of vehicles involved, minimal information on the damage to the vehicles and other property; a location, date and time reference; occasionally a brief, hand-drawn sketch; and names, addresses, ages, and phone numbers of witnesses. There is often a coding box in which the officer checkmarks certain boxes showing the officer's opinion as to which driver was most at fault and for what violation; weather conditions; road conditions, and so on. (See the sample report at the end of this chapter.)

The officer then completes the report with a brief paragraph or two of explanation as to what happened. The report involves three steps: summary, point of impact and cause. Most departments will accept a report for minor collisions in which there are no injuries. Other departments state that whenever a vehicle is towed from the scene, a report is no longer sufficient, even if there are no injuries.

In any event, a report requires no special skill in the preparation. A report is usually taken for the benefit of the participants and their respective insurance carriers. Except for "hit-and-run," most states do not require that "fender-bender" or property damage collisions be recorded. As a result of this approach, some departments will neither respond to nor report a property damage collision. At most, they will have the participants prepare their own reports. In other departments, the officers are encouraged to simply have the participants exchange names, addresses, and other pertinent information, and report the collision to their respective insurance companies and the department of motor vehicles. Some drivers, particularly the uninsured, would rather not have a police report nor involve the other driver's insurance company and the department of motor vehicles. The department of motor vehicles in most states would then suspend the uninsured driver's privilege to drive, and in some instances, remove the registration plates from the uninsured motorist's vehicle. With no plates on the vehicle and a suspended privilege, the uninsured motorist will stop driving and soon become insured or face criminal sanctions. The officer might do well to remember that some collision participants do not want a report for this reason. If one of the participants does not have insurance to cover his liability, a report is one way to be sure the driver soon acquires insurance. This driver's next collision may involve injuries, and without insurance on the vehicle, the injured will have little chance for compensation.

In those states with no-fault insurance, the police report process is appreciably minimized. The participants of a property damage collision simply report the incident to the insurance company and the department of motor vehicles, and there is less police involvement. This is the way the system should work with no-fault or conventional insurance states. A traveler should discuss various laws with his insurance carrier, ascertaining what, if any, police reports will be required in the event of a collision.

THE INVESTIGATION

In the event a collision involves an injury, prosecution, or in some jurisdictions a towaway of any of the participating vehicles, there must be an *investigation.*

The face page of an investigation is similar to a report. (See the sample investigation at the end of this chapter.) The coding also remains the same. The difference is found in the format, which must follow a specific outline. This outline includes all of the facts surrounding the collision, and calls the officer's attention to the various aspects of the factual reporting of an investigation. The headings shown in the investigation should be as follows:

Notification
Scene
    a. Roadway description
    b. Traffic controls
    c. Weather conditions and lighting

Vehicles and participants
    a. Vehicle 1 P.O.R. (point of rest)
    b. Vehicle 2 P.O.R. (point of rest)
    c. Participants
Physical evidence
    a. Skid marks
    b. Gouge marks
    c. Debris
    d. Vehicle parts
    e. Other physical evidence
Injuries
    a. Victim 1
    b. Victim 2
Intoxication
    a. Field sobriety test
    b. Chemical test
Additional facts
Photographs
Other property damage
Secured evidence
Hit-and-run (if applicable)
Statements
Opinions and conclusions
Recommendations
Factual diagram

Notification

The notification entry is simply the time the officer was dispatched to the collision, and the time of his or her arrival on the scene. An officer should also note here the type of call that was dispatched. The dispatcher may have indicated a property-damage-only collision and upon the officer's arrival the collision is in fact found to be a multiple injury or fatal incident.

The officer should also explain any unusual time delays between call time and arrival time. It is not at all uncommon to be called from the scene of one collision to another. As a general rule, any delay over fifteen minutes should be explained.

Scene

Roadway Description. Describe the area of the collision. Is this a residential or business district, or perhaps an open area bounded by fields of grain or bordered by trees? Indicate the type of roadway: asphaltic, concrete, or gravel. Spell out the number and width of the lanes in each direction. Specify the directions of the roads: north, south, southwesterly, and so on. Include the locations, width, height, and specifics of curbs, shoulders, driveways, median areas, fences, loose materials, wet spots, oily deposits, and any fixed objects involved such as guard rails or bridge abutments.

If an engineering defect comes to light during the course of the investigation, a separate memo should be prepared and forwarded to the appropriate streets, roads, or highways department. The memo should include the nature of the problem: deep pot-holes, ruts, unrepaired cracks, unrepaired guard rail damage from a prior collision, and so on. Preface the memo with the collision report number and attach a copy of the investigation tying the collision investigation to the memo. Some jurisdictions also require a specialized form to be prepared by the officer in the event of an engineering or repair defect in a roadway. This special report is forwarded to the appropriate city, township, county, or state attorney's office in the event the collision litigation is culminated in civil court with a suit filed for liability against the jurisdiction involved.

Traffic Controls. Specifically describe any traffic controls present at the scene, whether it is a signal or a device. Indicate the location and type of control including visibility *from the driver's point-of-view.* The scenerio should include any temporary devices, flares, cones, traffic control persons, or officers that may have been present. Show where the devices or traffic control persons were located.

Weather Conditions and Lighting. Make notations such as dark, daylight, fog, rain, drizzling rain, snow, or whatever else is appropriate. Explain the positions of any overhead lighting or peripheral lighting from adjacent business buildings, and any other such relevant information.

Vehicles and Participants

Vehicle 1 at P.O.R. (Point of Rest). Locate and measure to permanent points of reference where the vehicle came to rest. The measurement process may indicate that the left front tire is 15 feet north of the south curb line of Main Street. The right rear tire is 21 feet north of the south curb line of Main Street. The left rear tire is 37 feet east of the east prolongation of the curb line of Broadway.

Describe the damage to the vehicle that occurred as an obvious result of the collision. Note old damage separately. Do not try to estimate the cost of repairs or specifically look for such things as cracked distributor caps, unless such a defect was a factor in causing the collision. Check the brakes and steering mechanisms. Pump the brakes and note if they are firm, or if they go to the floor upon the first application. Look for loose steering. If it requires a half turn of the wheel to obtain resistance to the steering, you may have located the mechanical defect that contributed to the cause of the collision. Glance at the windshields of the participating vehicles upon your arrival. A fogged windshield may also have been a contributing factor, and certainly worthy of an inquiry. A cursory look at the tires of the vehicles may also lead to a causation factor. Be sure to record that the mechanical soundness of the vehicles was checked. If there are no mechanical defects, simply indicate, "none noted."

Vehicle 2 at P.O.R. (Point of Rest).   Record in the same manner as shown with Vehicle 1. Do the same with other involved vehicles.

Participants

Note the position of the drivers and any passengers upon your arrival. Example: "Driver 1, Mr. Jones, was standing beside the left front quarter panel of his vehicle. No complaint of pain, no injuries noted." "Passenger Abrams, Victim 2, was located in the right front seat of Vehicle 2."

Physical Evidence

Skid Marks.   Identify by type of skid mark, origin, and termination. Measure with a steel tape or by using a wheeled measuring device, and not by pacing. Attempt to identify the skid mark with the tire of the vehicle leaving that mark. Measure any gaps, skips, and deviations that may have resulted from contact with another vehicle or outside influence. The skid marks will assist in locating the point of impact. If there are no skid marks visible, indicate, "None."

Gouge Marks.   Measure the length and indicate the direction of the marks. By viewing the paint, grease, oil, water, and residue around the gouge marks, identify the vehicle making the marks.

Debris.   Identify the debris by type and measure the location to which it is found. Identify the debris as headlamp glass, tail lamp assembly glass, windshield glass, fender dirt cake, radiator water, brake fluid, gasoline, and so on.

Vehicle Parts.   In addition to headlamps and tail lamps which normally break in collisions, there is a separate category of vehicle parts to describe any unusual pieces that may have been dislodged. The more unusual items include such things as bumpers, fenders, door handles, radio antennas, and those things attendant with holding a load in or on a vehicle. Those things attendant to a load are vehicle parts as described above and include such things as ropes, cables, chains, couplers, come-alongs, davits, and tie downs.

Other Physical Evidence.   Describe any evidence that does not fall within the definitions of any of the above categories. An example could be a load itself, such as suitcases released from the top of the car.

Other physical evidence might be a package being carried by a pedestrian crossing in a marked crosswalk when he was struck by a hit-and-run driver. The package fell to the ground, broke, and marked a point of impact with a small amount of escaping liquid.

Injuries

Identification of Victims. Identify each victim by name even though the name appears on the face page of the investigation next to the words Victim 1, and so on. This erases any possible error in reading the report.

Although it is not anticipated that the officer provide the same level of medical observation as a doctor, list the obvious injuries to the victim in as professional a manner as possible. To say the victim sustained a compound fracture of the right femur is far more explicit than stating he had a broken leg. There is nothing errone-ous about writing that a victim sustained multiple lacerations and abrasions over his entire facial area. Bear in mind that the report will have an audience and be read by a number of persons. Be as professional as possible.

Listing Fatalities. When listing a fatal victim, be sure to include such items as the name of the doctor pronouncing death and the hospital or facility with which the doctor is affiliated. Fatal victims must also be reported to the deputy coroner. At the time of reporting the case, the officer should obtain the coronor's case number, and enter that number in this portion of the report. If the officer is responsible for the notification of a fatality it is also necessary for the officer to list who was notified, where the notification was made, and the date and time in this portion of the report. Avoid letting the media have access to the name of the deceased until notification has been made to the next of kin. It is most unfortunate for a widow to hear about the change in her marital status on television or from other media prior to notification by the proper authorities, and it is embarrassing to both the officer and the department.

Every so often, an officer will have an injured victim that refuses medical aid either for personal or religious reasons. List the attendant circumstances surround-ing the refusal. Remember that an unconscious victim is not in a position to refuse emergency treatment, and must be treated until such time as they regain conscious-ness and can rationally object to further treatment. There are also those victims who are so completely traumatized by the collision that they cannot appreciate the gravity of their wounds. Stabilize these persons to calm them, and have them transported to a medical emergency facility before their body shock becomes irreversible.

List all the victims in the same manner, using the same format. For the purposes of the report, an injured driver is a victim, and should be numbered in order just like the rest of the victims. It often happens that Driver 2 becomes Victim 3 in the report. Victims 1 and 2 may have been the driver and a passenger in Vehicle 1. It is for this reason that the victim should be listed by name in this portion of the report.

Juveniles. In the event that juveniles were involved and injured to such an extent that emergency surgery is required, parental notification and consent is required. It is advisable to also list this information in the report. On rare occasions, parents cannot be located; where laws do not permit the doctors to continue, it may be necessary to locate a magistrate to assume temporary court custody. This action must be recorded in this victim scenerio.

One side note concerning military personnel who are fatally injured or disabled in a collision. Notification can be handled much more efficiently through the nearest military facility, even if that facility is no more than a recruiting office. The military offices are extremely helpful in providing a number of services to the police.

Intoxication

Whenever a collision involves a drinking driver, a driver under the influence of drugs, or a driver under the combined influence of alcohol and drugs, the officer must follow through with some form of testing to determine sobriety.

Field Sobriety Test. Chapter 6 will spell out the particulars of the various aspects and techniques of a field sobriety test. When the sobriety of a driver is in question and an officer administers such an examination, that fact should be noted in this portion of the report. Do not list all the specifics of the tests, simply note here that the driver had been drinking and passed or failed the field sobriety test. The arrest report will carry the details of the testing, interrogation, and incarceration. Do not include an opinion of sobriety in this portion of the report, as it is just an opinion or supposition to be proven in a court of law. The officer's opinion is to be written into the "Opinions and Conclusions" section of the investigation.

Chemical Test. When a driver is taken from the scene of the collision and provided an opportunity to complete a chemical test to determine his or her blood-alcohol concentration, that is a fact. To be included in this portion of the investigation is the following: location of the test; person administering the test; address, age, and phone number of the person administering the test; the type of test chosen; and the results of the test if known at the time of the writing of the report.

If none of the participating drivers in a collision show signs of intoxication indicate this fact in your report. This again provides the officer with legal protection. At some later date in court the officer can find in his report that he checked the drivers and found no objective symptoms of intoxication. This simple notation has saved a number of victims the embarrassment of having to go before a judge and jury in a civil trial to answer the sobriety question as posed by an attorney. Frequently, an attorney may plant a seed of doubt in a jury's mind and the reputation of an innocent driver–victim can be destroyed. In short, check for sobriety, and document your observations of fact.

Additional Facts

This is the portion of the report that covers the many extra notations that come to light during the course of an officer's investigation. If one of the participant drivers was restricted to driving while wearing corrective lenses, note the fact here, if he or she was driving in violation of that restriction. If one of the drivers has a physical impairment that may have contributed to the collision, write it down. For example, an epileptic that had a seizure and lost control of the vehicle, or a hearing- and speech-impaired driver who failed to see and hear an emergency vehicle, or a paraplegic whose adaptive control devices failed.

Note here any other discrepancies such as an invalid registration, an out-of-date operator's permit, health certificate, school bus, or ambulance operator's permit or certificate. Note, too, discrepancies in log books, explosive hauler permits, or special overload permits.

Some departments have ongoing studies of special classifications of collisions. If the department has such a program, the officer should be familiar with the ramifications and include the study information requested in this portion of the report.

Photographs

Major collisions require photographs to document the evanescent evidence which cannot be collected and preserved for a courtroom. Skid marks are an excellent example of an item for photography; vehicles at the scene are yet another. A good photographer is imaginative in his approach to obtain as much as possible with each click of the shutter. One officer took the elevator to the top of an office building and then went out on the roof to photograph the intersection and location of the participating vehicles at their points of rest. Another excellent approach is to photograph the area approaching the collision scene from the driver's point of view. The average driver's eyes are approximately three and a half feet from ground level, and there are often obstructions to vision not noted by a pedestrian.

Record the number of photos taken, the location, date, and time. If the photos are taken by someone other than the investigating officer, record the photographer's information. Television news teams often respond to a collision scene. Obtain the name of the lead person, the station identification, and address and record it in this segment of the report. Do the same with professional and newspaper photographers. Media personnel can be extremely valuable in the recording of the collision aftermath. With the officer's assistance and guidance, they will often provide excellent photos of evidence, vehicle locations, and participants. A friendly press is a valuable ally to the traffic officer.

Other Property Damage

If, during the aftermath of a collision, a vehicle has spun out of control, tearing out a residential fence, shrubs, or flowerbed, or striking public property and causing damage, explain the extent of the damage and obtain the owner's name, address, and phone number. This information should then be recorded under the heading "other property damage." The officer should make a reasonable effort to contact the owner of damaged property or to find someone who can reach the owner so they may contact your department for a copy of the collision report. In the event the property damaged is public property, a simple notification through the departmental dispatcher will normally suffice. Some departments prepare a damage tag and affix this tag to the damaged property. The owner then presents the tag to the department and obtains the information he needs.

If there was no other property damaged as a result of the collision, state, "None." Many an unscrupulous individual has tried to tie the old damage to his automobile to a collision that happened in his neighborhood. The person hears of or sees an incident nearby, waits a few days, and then goes down to the police station to claim his vehicle was victimized in the collision. The simple four letter word "none" belies his claim and leaves him open to filing a false report.

Secured Evidence

As the investigating officer is collecting the necessary evidence, he or she follows departmental procedures of identifying that evidence. It is here in this portion of the report that the officer lists what evidence was obtained and the disposition. Evidence includes, but is not restricted to: broken glass, vehicle parts, paint samples, hair samples, clothing samples, blood samples removed from vehicles, chemical samples for intoxication listed by name or case number, and the number of photographs. In short, anything that is taken, preserved, or secured as evidence should be listed. Some examples:

1. Contaminated and uncontaminated paint samples from Vehicle 1.
2. Contaminated and uncontaminated paint samples from Vehicle 2.
3. 26 photographs
4. 5 cc. of blood for chemical analysis for alcohol and/or drugs, retained by A.C. Laboratories. I.D. 57-A-549.
5. Headlamp ring from V-1 found imbedded in the grill of V-2. (Photographed)

If no evidence is taken or preserved, state, "None."

Hit-and-Run

This heading is used only if it is applicable to the collision. When investigating a hit-and-run collision, list in this space every available scrap of information obtained, including vehicle color, vehicle description, driver identification, tail lamp formation, license plate information, decals, interior colors, headlamp configuration, tires, wheel covers, exhaust information (loud, smoking, any notable sounds), special lights in front and rear, if it had a license plate lamp, location of the radio

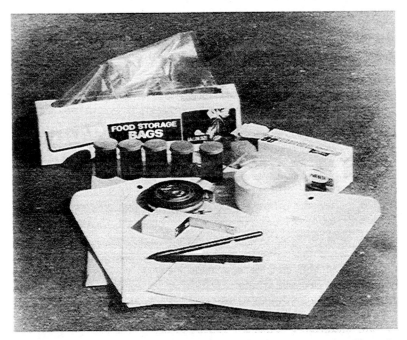

FIGURE 4-1. Items the officer should carry to preserve and obtain evidence include various sizes of envelopes and plastic bags, masking tape to seal envelopes and provide a writing surface, 10 and 50 foot steel tapes, empty 35 mm film cases to preserve and number small pieces of evidence, and chalk to outline the location of the wheels of a collision vehicle at its point of rest and identifying objects on the roadway.

antenna if any was seen, primer spots and color, and so on. Ascertain the direction of travel of a hit-and-run vehicle. If the collision has happened within minutes, perhaps an adjacent unit will be able to intercept the culprit. Finally, obtain the name, address, age, and phone number of the informant, and include that information in this portion of the report as well as on the face page under "witnesses."

Statements

Start with Driver 1 and progress through the statements in logical order: Driver 2, 3, then Witness 1, 2 and so on. Write all the statements in the third person as outlined in Chapter 3. Keep the statements meaningful and comprehensive. If a statement is prepared by the drivers or witnesses, list their names in order and state after the name, "See statement attached." If the officer must prove a violation on the strength of witnesses' statements, he or she must be doubly sure that the information contained in the statements covers the violation in detail. Spell out the violation, who saw it, and what was done. Do not leave the reader of the report guessing as to what would have been said. Remember, the investigative report must stand on its own merits, and it must be complete.

Opinions and Conclusions

P.O.I. (Point of Impact). The point of impact is established by a number of methods and bits of evidence that indicate this spot on the roadway. The most frequently used is the deviation of skid marks, or the beginning of locked wheel skids covered with radiator water and debris such as soil cake and broken glass. The P.O.I. should be located in writing by at least two measurements which pinpoint the exact area of the collision. The P.O.I is another of those measurements which should be taken with a steel tape and measured from permanent points of reference.

Narrative. Once the officer is satisfied that he or she has gathered the pertinent facts in the matter, the officer now combines these facts and relates in narrative form just how he or she believes the collision occurred. This is straightforward reporting. Keep it simple, to the point, and tell the story of how Vehicle 1 met with Vehicle 2. In the narrative portion, give the elements of the vehicle code violation involved and describe how these elements are proven. If the officer cannot prove the elements of the violation which caused the collision, explain here what is missing; for example, "No independent witness." If one of the participants was under the influence of drugs or alcohol and subsequently arrested for driving while intoxicated, this is the portion of the report where the officer offers an opinion as to that sobriety. Try not to be redundant in the narrative portion of the report. The officer need not rewrite all of the measurements, witness statements, and so on. The officer simply brings together all of the facts, blending them into a short but meaningful paragraph or two, showing who did what and to whom, specifically indicating the driver most at fault and why.

Recommendations

This is the last written entry of the investigation and the easiest to complete. Unless there is something which requires follow-up beyond the capabilities of the officer, the word, "None," is all that is required beneath this heading.

If out-of-town, township, county, or state follow-up is required, such as with hit-and-run vehicle information, the notation is indicated here. The officer performing the follow-up and making the contacts to trace the vehicle will complete a supplemental page to be added to the final report.

This is also the portion of the report that involves allied agencies which are requested to be notified or possibly advised to assist. An example of such assistance may be follow-up of a narcotics case. Let us suppose that an officer discovers a broken suitcase full of narcotics during the course of the investigation of a collision. Let us suppose, too, that the department is not equipped to handle the ramifications of the investigation which must follow. The officer, under advisement of his department supervisors, may wish to call upon the officers from the state or federal narcotics bureau to assist. A notation in the recommendations section as to who is to receive a copy of the investigation report and the name of the allied agency is a must. This notation will establish a chain of investigation which is necessary for proper prosecution in court. An experienced officer and his supervisors know the local court system. They may wish to pursue the matter into a federal court, turning the investigation over to federal officers. It is one thing to obtain a conviction in a local court for a narcotics possession charge; it is quite another to break a ring operation that extends well out of the officer's jurisdiction.

Here too is where the officer may advise the department collision review personnel to deliver a copy of this report to the city, township, county, or district attorney. These attorneys are to be advised whenever a complaint is to be filed against the responsible party in the collision. The elements for the violation charged are already enumerated and clarified in the opinions and conclusions section and need not be rewritten here. The officer simply makes the entry, "Deliver a copy of this investigation to the city attorney's office for consideration of filing for prosecution in violation of Section 22350 of the Vehicle Code "Prima Facie Speed" against Mr. Cox, Driver 1."

Factual Diagram

Visual Overlay. Each department has a place in the report for a factual diagram. (See Fig. 4-8 in the sample report at the end of this chapter.) The diagram is simply an overview of the collision scene as observed upon the officer's arrival. The drawing shows the vehicles at their points of rest.

There are a number of excellent plastic drawing guides which may be used to assist the officer in the preparation of the drawing. Some officers employ the use of lettering guides to keep the diagram neat in appearance. A straight edge ruler will suffice in most instances with curves being carefully drawn by freehand sketching.

It is best to attempt to make a diagram to scale to keep the diagram in perspective. Most collisions can be represented on a regular 8½ by 11 inch piece of paper, using the scale of ten feet of roadway represented by one inch in the drawing.

A very good idea used by some departments is to make diagrams of the high-collision intersections within their jurisdiction, and then have copies made of the diagrams. The master diagram is retained for future use. When a collision occurs, the officer simply refers to a diagram file, locates the proper diagram, and draws in the vehicles, indicating the proper distances and noting the evidence. The local streets, roads, or highway departments can be of invaluable assistance in this regard. Their respective engineering departments will already have most of the drawings on file.

All diagrams should bear the words, "Not to Scale." If the officer has prepared the diagram to scale, an attorney may very possibly find something in that diagram which is not exactly correct to use as a defense for the client in question. If any of the distances indicated on the diagram are approximations or measured with anything other than a steel tape, write in the phrase, "Measurements Approximate." This disclaimer is used for the same reason as "Not to Scale." It is next to impossible to draw an exact duplication of any given area of highway, and no two such measurements will ever exactly agree. The careful officer, then, inserts the two disclaimers as a matter of course. Somewhere in the diagram, insert the notation, "Taped," or "Steel Taped," or "Skid marks measured by Steel Tape," or whatever it will take to jog your memory should this case go to civil litigation five years later. Having indicated the critical outline of the intersection or highway on the diagram, the officer should indicate the following: the point of rest of the vehicles, drawing a rough sketch of the skid marks; location of the debris; location of the street lamps and official traffic control devices and signals; location of visual hazards such as bushes, buildings, flashing lights, parked cars, and so on. Be sure to include any lane lines and turn pockets as well as center medians, double yellow lines, and other pockets such as special parking areas.

Indication of Distances.   Having indicated a visual overlay of the collision scene on the diagram, indicate by arrows the critical distances to each item of interest from a fixed reference point such as the prolongation of a curb or berm line. Indicate the lane widths and total width of the road. Indicate the location of the participating vehicles by at least three measurements to permanent points of reference. With the differences between feet and meters, the officer is obligated to specify the mode of measurement used. Remember not to mix meters with feet and inches. It is good to remember that the odometers of most American made automobiles through 1982 will be specified in tenths of a mile. With 5,280 feet in a mile, each tenth is then 528 feet. With back country or super-highway collisions, it is not at all uncommon that the incident occurred some miles and tenths from the nearest crossroad available for reference. The notation for the report and the diagram may well read, "6,336 feet to the north prolongation of the curb line of Forrest Drive." This would indicate one and two-tenths of a mile. Obviously such a measuring device is an approximation and should be noted, "Odometer Reading." The odometer method of measuring is also handy when referring to a collision which happened several tenths of a mile from a state- or county-erected mile post marker. The metric system of measurement is truly much easier with a dekameter being ten meters, a hectometer being one hundred meters, and a kilometer being one thousand meters. The appendix at the end of the book contains a handy reference chart which equates the units of measurement and their counterparts in both systems. (See also the conversion information located in Chapter 9.)

Once your factual diagram includes all the measurements and locations necessary to describe your investigation, affix your signature. If the diagram is prepared by another officer, have that officer affix his or her legible signature and identification number and then the notation, "At the direction of Officer (*your name and I.D.*)." This notation will prevent two officers having to appear on the case. When another officer is acting under your direction, it is construed that you have approved and checked that which has been submitted; in this case, a factual diagram.

Sketch

Some departments require a sketch or drawing on the face page of the report. The sketch is merely a freehand drawing which uses symbols to indicate how a collision occurred. The sketch is not required to be drawn to scale or to show measurements but should be in proper proportion, and reflect the scene of the collision. The sketch shows the point and type of impact through symbols that indicate how the vehicles collided. The sketch is separate from the factual diagram.

To assure uniformity and the proper interpretation of the sketch, the basic sketch symbols shown in Figure 4-2 are used for both reports and investigations. The small circle indicates the initial point of impact.

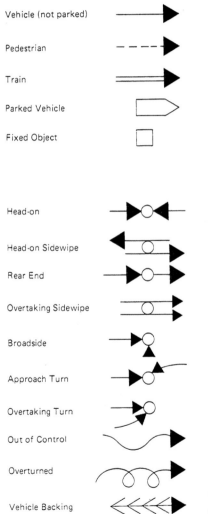

Vehicle (not parked)

Pedestrian

Train

Parked Vehicle

Fixed Object

Head-on

Head-on Sidewipe

Rear End

Overtaking Sidewipe

Broadside

Approach Turn

Overtaking Turn

Out of Control

Overturned

Vehicle Backing

FIGURE 4-2. Basic Symbols for Report and Investigation Demonstrative Sketch

57

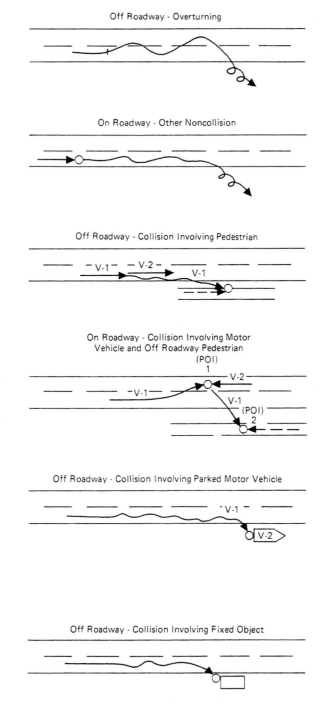

FIGURE 4-3. Examples of Motor Vehicle Traffic Collisions for Demonstrative Sketch

More than one point of impact (P.O.I.) may be shown on the sketch. Where additional points of impact are indicated, number them consecutively beginning with the initial P.O.I

Indicate paths of vehicles before and after points of impact by solid lines even though the vehicles may have been moved prior to the officer's arrival. After points of impact, continue solid lines to the point of rest for each vehicle. Place an arrow head at each P.O.I. indicated on the sketch. Number the solid lines as necessary to identify vehicles.

Indicate paths of pedestrians or animals by dashed lines.

In conclusion, this chapter has outlined a format for a complete and thorough investigation report. Investigative reporting becomes easier with experience. The reasons for the headings and detail also become obvious with experience. It is with a great deal of satisfaction that a department receives congratulatory correspondence on the excellence of its collision reporting and the fine work of an officer. This planned approach to investigations will bring that expectation of excellence into reality. This approach also is sufficiently flexible to allow for the officer's innovative investigative techniques to flourish and grow.

On the following pages, the reader will find a list of common abbreviations used in collision investigation, a sample report (Fig. 4-6), a sample investigation (Fig. 4-7), and a diagram of a sample factual diagram (Fig. 4-8).

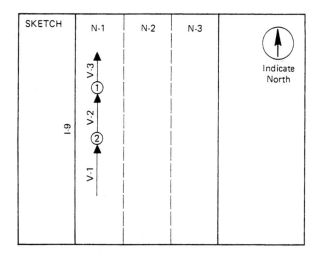

FIGURE 4-4a. Demonstrative sketch and narrative example 1: Property damage collision. Narrative: V-3 was slowing in traffic N/B on I-9 in the N-1 lane when it was struck from behind by V-2. After striking V-3, V-2 was struck from behind by V-1.

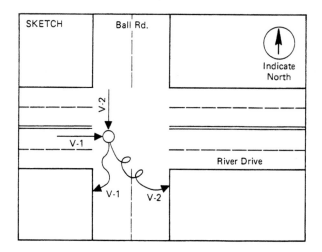

FIGURE 4-4b. Demonstrative sketch and narrative example 2: Property damage collision. Narrative: V-1 was E/B on River Dr. in the E-1 lane and struck V-2 which was S/B on Ball Rd. After impact both vehicles went out of control. V-2 rolled over twice before coming to rest.

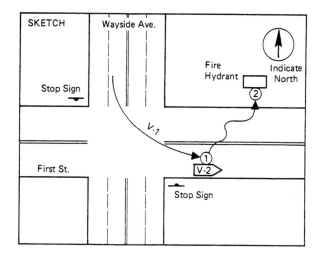

FIGURE 4-4c. Demonstrative sketch and narrative example 3: Collision involving minor injury. Narrative: V-1 was S/B on Wayside Ave. in the S-1 lane and made a left turn on First St. striking V-2 which was parked facing E/B on First St. After impact V-1 went out of control and struck a fire hydrant on the north side of First St.

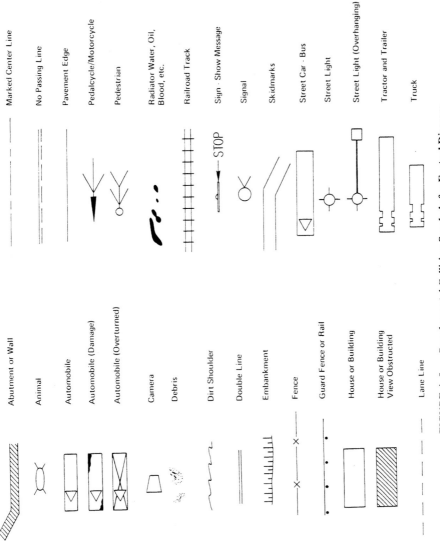

FIGURE 4–5. Supplemental Collision Symbols for Factual Diagram

Abutment or Wall

Animal

Automobile

Automobile (Damage)

Automobile (Overturned)

Camera

Debris

Dirt Shoulder

Double Line

Embankment

Fence

Guard Fence or Rail

House or Building

House or Building View Obstructed

Lane Line

Marked Center Line

No Passing Line

Pavement Edge

Pedalcycle/Motorcycle

Pedestrian

Radiator Water, Oil, Blood, etc.

Railroad Track

Sign - Show Message

Signal

Skidmarks

Street Car - Bus

Street Light

Street Light (Overhanging)

Tractor and Trailer

Truck

STOP

61

TRAFFIC COLLISION REPORT

SPECIAL CONDITIONS	NO. INJURED	H & R FELONY	CITY	JUDICIAL DISTRICT	NUMBER
	0		Symington	Pacific Palisades	81-767
	NO. KILLED	H & R MISD.	COUNTY	REPORTING DISTRICT	BEAT
	0		Crown	470	11

LOCATION

COLLISION OCCURRED ON			MO.	DAY	YR.	TIME (2400)	NCIC NUMBER	OFFICER I.D.
Skyline Drive			07	07	81	2230	9470	4045

AT INTERSECTION WITH — INJURY, FATAL OR TOW AWAY ☐ YES ☒ NO — STATE HWY RELATED ☐ YES ☒ NO

☒ OR 217 FEET XXXX E. Warner Way

PARTY 1

DRIVER ☒ / PEDESTRIAN ☐ / PARKED VEH. ☐ / BICYCLIST ☐ / OTHER ☐

NAME (FIRST, MIDDLE, LAST)	STREET ADDRESS
Dorothy Jean Scott	1743 Myford Circle 369/774-9882

DRIVER'S LICENSE NUMBER	STATE	BIRTHDATE MO. DAY YR.	SEX	RACE	CITY	STATE	PHONE
KD-376591	Minn.	08 19 51	F	----	Wells Lake, Minn. 57978		

VEHICLE YR.	MAKE/MODEL	LICENSE NO.	STATE	OWNER'S NAME ☐ SAME AS DRIVER
'80	Ford Mustang	734 KIG	Minn.	Lawrence Boyd Scott

DIRECTION OF TRAVEL	ON/XXXX (STREET OR HIGHWAY)		OWNER'S ADDRESS ☒ SAME AS DRIVER
W/B	Skyline Drive		

SPEED LIMIT	DISPOSITION OF VEHICLE	☒ BY DRIVER ON ORDERS OF	VEHICLE DAMAGE ☒ MINOR ☐ MOD. ☐ MAJOR ☐ TOTAL	LOCATION	VIOLATION CHARGED
35	Driven away	- - -	EXTENT	Rt. Front	none

PARTY 2

DRIVER ☐ / PEDESTRIAN ☐ / PARKED VEH. ☒ / BICYCLIST ☐ / OTHER ☐

NAME (FIRST, MIDDLE, LAST)	STREET ADDRESS
LEGALLY PARKED	

DRIVER'S LICENSE NUMBER	STATE	BIRTHDATE MO. DAY YR.	SEX	RACE	CITY	STATE	PHONE

VEHICLE YR.	MAKE/MODEL	LICENSE NO.	STATE	OWNER'S NAME ☐ SAME AS DRIVER
'80	Fiat Coupe	178 GGR	Calif.	Kirby James Bettencourt

DIRECTION OF TRAVEL	ON/XXXX (STREET OR HIGHWAY)		OWNER'S ADDRESS ☐ SAME AS DRIVER
N/A	Private driveway at residence		316 Skyline Dr. Symington, Calif.

SPEED LIMIT	DISPOSITION OF VEHICLE	☐ BY DRIVER ON ORDERS OF	VEHICLE DAMAGE ☐ MINOR ☒ MOD. ☐ MAJOR ☐ TOTAL	LOCATION	VIOLATION CHARGED
N/A	left at scene	R.O.	EXTENT	Rt. side	none

PROPERTY

DESCRIPTION OF DAMAGE

Approximately 18 feet of fence and five rose bushes.

OWNER'S NAME	ADDRESS	NOTIFIED
Kirby James Bettencourt	316 Skyline Dr. Symington, Calif. 90013	☒ YES ☐ NO

INJURED/WITNESS

WITNESS ONLY	AGE	SEX	EXTENT OF INJURY				INJURED WAS (Check one)					PARTY NUMBER
			FATAL INJURY	SEVERE WOUND DISTORTED MEMBER	OTHER VISIBLE INJURIES	COMPLAINT OF PAIN	DRIVER	PASS.	PED.	BICYCLIST	OTHER	
☐			☐	☐	☐	☐	☐	☐	☐	☐	☐	
NAME											PHONE	
ADDRESS							TAKEN TO (INJURED ONLY)					
☐			☐	☐	☐	☐	☐	☐	☐	☐	☐	
NAME											PHONE	
ADDRESS							TAKEN TO (INJURED ONLY)					
☐			☐	☐	☐	☐	☐	☐	☐	☐	☐	
NAME											PHONE	
ADDRESS							TAKEN TO (INJURED ONLY)					

SKETCH

Warner Way
316 Skyline
V-2
V-1
N INDICATE NORTH
Skyline Drive

MISCELLANEOUS

VEHICLE TYPE		ROAD TYPE	
PARTY 1		☐ A CONVENTIONAL, ONE WAY	☐ E. OTHER (EXPLAIN IN NARRATIVE)
		☐ B CONVENTIONAL, TWO WAY	
PARTY 2		☐ C EXPRESSWAY	
		☐ D FREEWAY	

USE PREVIOUS EDITIONS UNTIL DEPLETED

13707 —456 500 M - OLP

FIGURE 4-6. Sample Traffic Collision Report

DATE OF COLLISION			TIME (2400)	NCIC NUMBER	OFFICER I.D.	NUMBER	PAGE
MO. 07	DAY 07	YR. 81	2230	9470	4045	81-767	2

COLLISION NARRATIVE

SUMMARY: I received a call of a property damage collision at 2235 hours. I was at I-40 near Riverside Drive. I arrived at 2305 hours. Driver #1, Scott, was westbound on Skyline Drive. As she rounded the curve to the east of Warner Way she states she was momentarily blinded by oncoming headlamps, and was unable to see the curve in the heavy rain. She left the roadway approximately 237 feet east of Warner Way travelling in a north-westerly direction, striking the picket fence, rose bushes and the legally parked Vehicle #2, the Fiat. The rear of the Fiat, Vehicle #2, was approximately 22 feet north of the north prolongation of Skyline Drive and parked in the driveway at 316 Skyline Drive. Driver #1, Scott, states she was travelling at approximately 25 miles per hour as she was entering the area of the curve.

POINT OF IMPACT: The first P.O.I. occurred when Vehicle #1, Ford, struck the fence located approximately six feet north of the north prolongation

PRIMARY COLLISION FACTOR		RIGHT OF WAY CONTROL	1	2	3	4	TYPE OF VEHICLE	1	2	3	4	MOVEMENT PRECEDING COLLISION
	A VC SECTION VIOLATION:	A CONTROLS FUNCTIONING					A PASSENGER CAR (INCLUDES STATION WAGON)					A STOPPED
		B CONTROLS NOT FUNCTIONING	X	X								B PROCEEDING STRAIGHT
X	B OTHER IMPROPER DRIVING*	C CONTROLS OBSCURED					B PASSENGER CAR W/TRAILER					C RAN OFF ROAD
	C OTHER THAN DRIVER*	X D NO CONTROLS PRESENT					C MOTORCYCLE/SCOOTER	X				D MAKING RIGHT TURN
	D UNKNOWN*	TYPE OF COLLISION					D PICKUP OR PANEL TRUCK					E MAKING LEFT TURN
	WEATHER	A HEAD-ON					E PICKUP OR PANEL TRUCK W/TRAILER					F MAKING U TURN
	A CLEAR	B SIDESWIPE					F TRUCK OR TRUCK TRACTOR					G BACKING
	B CLOUDY	C REAR END					G TRUCK OR TRUCK TRACTOR W/TRAILER(S)					H SLOWING — STOPPING
X	C RAINING	D BROADSIDE										I PASSING OTHER VEHICLE
	D SNOWING	X E HIT OBJECT					H SCHOOL BUS					J CHANGING LANES
	E FOG	F OVERTURNED					I OTHER BUS					K PARKING MANEUVER
	F OTHER:	G AUTO/PEDESTRIAN					J EMERGENCY VEHICLE					L ENTERING TRAFFIC FROM SHOULDER, MEDIAN, PARKING STRIP OR PRIVATE DRIVE
	LIGHTING	H OTHER*:					K HWY CONST. EQUIPMENT					
	A DAYLIGHT	MOTOR VEHICLE INVOLVED WITH					L BICYCLE					M OTHER UNSAFE TURNING
	B DUSK — DAWN	A NON-COLLISION					M OTHER VEHICLE					N CROSSED INTO OPPOSING LANE
	C DARK — STREET LIGHTS	B PEDESTRIAN					O MOPED					
X	D DARK — NO STREET LIGHTS	C OTHER MOTOR VEHICLE										O PARKED
	E DARK — STREET LIGHTS NOT FUNCTIONING*	D MOTOR VEHICLE ON OTHER ROADWAY	1	2	3	4	OTHER ASSOCIATED FACTOR (MARK 1 TO 3 ITEMS)					P MERGING
	ROADWAY SURFACE	E PARKED MOTOR VEHICLE					A VC SECTION VIOLATION*					Q TRAVELING WRONG WAY*
	A DRY	F TRAIN										R OTHER*
X	B WET	G BICYCLE					B VC SECTION VIOLATION:					
	C SNOWY — ICY	H ANIMAL:					C VC SECTION VIOLATION:				1 2 3 4	SOBRIETY—DRUG—PHYSICAL (MARK 1 TO 2 ITEMS)
	D SLIPPERY (MUDDY, OILY, ETC.)	I FIXED OBJECT: X Wooden Fence					D VC SECTION VIOLATION:	X				A HAD NOT BEEN DRINKING
	ROADWAY CONDITIONS (MARK 1 TO 3 ITEMS)											B HBD—UNDER INFLUENCE
	A HOLES, DEEP RUTS*	J OTHER OBJECT:					E VISION OBSCUREMENTS:					C HBD—NOT UNDER INFLUENCE*
	B LOOSE MATERIAL ON ROADWAY*						F INATTENTION					D HBD—IMPAIRMENT UNKNOWN*
	C OBSTRUCTION ON ROADWAY*	PEDESTRIAN'S ACTION					G STOP & GO TRAFFIC					E UNDER DRUG INFLUENCE*
	D CONSTRUCTION-REPAIR ZONE	X A NO PEDESTRIAN INVOLVED					H ENTERING/LEAVING RAMP					F IMPAIRMENT—PHYSICAL*
	E REDUCED ROADWAY WIDTH	B CROSSING IN CROSSWALK AT INTERSECTION					I PREVIOUS COLLISION					G IMPAIRMENT NOT KNOWN
	F FLOODED*						J UNFAMILIAR WITH ROAD					H NOT APPLICABLE
	G OTHER:	C CROSSING IN CROSSWALK — NOT AT INTERSECTION					K DEFECTIVE VEHICLE EQUIPMENT:					I SLEEPY/FATIGUED
X	H NO UNUSUAL CONDITIONS	D CROSSING — NOT IN CROSSWALK					L UNINVOLVED VEHICLE					
		E IN ROAD — INCLUDES SHOULDER					M OTHER*:					
		F NOT IN ROAD										
		G APPROACHING/LEAVING SCHOOL BUS					N NONE APPARENT					

INVESTIGATED BY	I.D. NUMBER	INVESTIGATED BY		I.D. NUMBER	REVIEWED BY

*EXPLAIN IN NARRATIVE

FIGURE 4-6. (*cont.*)

SUPPLEMENTAL/NARRATIVE	DATE OF ORIGINAL INCIDENT	TIME (2400)	NCIC NUMBER	OFFICER I.D.	NUMBER	PAGE
(Check one)	MO. 07 DAY 07 YR. 81	2230	9470	4045	81-767	3
☒ NARRATIVE CONTINUATION TRAFFIC COLLISION REPORT	LOCATION/SUBJECT				CITATION NUMBER	
	Skyline Drive				N/A	
☐ SUPPLEMENTAL TRAFFIC COLLISION REPORT					BEAT	
☐ OTHER:	Scott				11	
	CITY/COUNTY				REPORTING DISTRICT	
	Symington, Crown				470	

of Skyline Drive and approximately 217 feet east of Warner Way. The
rose bushes were growing immediately behind the fence. The second P.O.I.
occurred when Vehicle #1, Ford, struck the Fiat, Vehicle #2. Vehicle #2
was struck in the area of the right door by the right front of Vehicle #1.
P.O.I. #2 is approximately 29 feet north of the north prolongation of
Skyline Drive and approximately 163 feet east of Warner Way. The points
of impact are established by tire tracks leaving the roadway, going
through the fence, the rose bushes across the lawn and terminating at
Vehicle #2, the Fiat.

CAUSE: This collision was due in part to Ms. Scott's lack of familiarity
with the road, the heavy rain, and her inattention to the curve warning
sign that preceeds the curve. A check of Vehicle #1, the Ford indicates
that the windshield wipers are in good working order as are the brakes
and the steering.

PREPARED BY					REVIEWED BY			
NAME	I.D. NUMBER	MO.	DAY	YR.	NAME	MO.	DAY	YR.

FIGURE 4-6. (cont.)

SPECIAL CONDITIONS	NO. INJURED	H & R FELONY	CITY		JUDICIAL DISTRICT		NUMBER
	1	☐	Unincorporated		Pacific Palisades		
	NO. KILLED	H & R MISD.	COUNTY	REPORTING DISTRICT		BEAT	81-0736-F
	0	☐	Crown	470		3	

LOCATION

COLLISION OCCURRED ON			MO.	DAY	YR.	TIME (2400)	NCIC NUMBER	OFFICER I.D.
River Road			07	04	81	1810	9470	3783

☐ AT INTERSECTION WITH		STREET ADDRESS	INJURY, FATAL OR TOW AWAY	STATE HWY RELATED
☒ ON 417 FEET/MILES No. or Green Lantern			☒ YES ☐ NO	☐ YES ☒ NO

PARTY 1

NAME (FIRST, MIDDLE, LAST)					STREET ADDRESS		
John Edward Cole							

DRIVER ☒	DRIVER'S LICENSE NUMBER	STATE	MO. BIRTHDATE DAY YR.	SEX	RACE	CITY	STATE	PHONE
PEDESTRIAN ☐	Y054471	Cakif.	05 20 50	M	-			
PARKED VEH. ☐	VEHICLE YR. MAKE/MODEL		LICENSE NO.		STATE	OWNER'S NAME ☐ SAME AS DRIVER		
	'81 Chevrolet		729 XDS		Calif.			
BICYCLIST ☐	DIRECTION OF TRAVEL S/B	ON/ACROSS (STREET OR HIGHWAY) River Road				OWNER'S ADDRESS ☐ SAME AS DRIVER		
OTHER ☐	SPEED LIMIT	DISPOSITION OF VEHICLE Crown County Towing	☐ BY DRIVER	ON ORDERS OF State Police		VEHICLE DAMAGE ☐ MINOR ☐ MOD. ☒ MAJOR ☐ TOTAL	EXTENT LOCATION Front End	VIOLATION CHARGED 23101 VC (DUI Felony)

PARTY 2

NAME (FIRST, MIDDLE, LAST)					STREET ADDRESS		
Solo Vehicle Collision							

DRIVER ☐	DRIVER'S LICENSE NUMBER	STATE	MO. BIRTHDATE DAY YR.	SEX	RACE	CITY	STATE	PHONE
PEDESTRIAN ☐								
PARKED VEH. ☐	VEHICLE YR. MAKE/MODEL		LICENSE NO.		STATE	OWNER'S NAME ☐ SAME AS DRIVER		
BICYCLIST ☐	DIRECTION OF TRAVEL	ON/ACROSS (STREET OR HIGHWAY)				OWNER'S ADDRESS ☐ SAME AS DRIVER		
OTHER ☐	SPEED LIMIT	DISPOSITION OF VEHICLE	☐ BY DRIVER	ON ORDERS OF		VEHICLE DAMAGE ☐ MINOR ☐ MOD. ☐ MAJOR ☐ TOTAL	EXTENT LOCATION	VIOLATION CHARGED

PROPERTY

DESCRIPTION OF DAMAGE		
Sign..."Speed 45 MPH Limit" (Crown Co. Roads Dept. notified 1930 hours)		
OWNER'S NAME Crown County Roads Department	ADDRESS	NOTIFIED ☒ YES ☐ NO

INJURED/WITNESS

WITNESS ONLY	AGE	SEX	FATAL INJURY	SEVERE WOUND DISTORTED MEMBER	OTHER VISIBLE INJURIES	COMPLAINT OF PAIN	DRIVER	PASS.	PED.	BICYCLIST	OTHER	PARTY NUMBER
☐	27	F	☐	☒	☐	☐	☐	☒	☐	☐	☐	In V1

NAME Marilyn Gwynn McMasters (Victim #1)   214/178-9967
ADDRESS 258 Elliott Circle Cambio, Calif. 90083   TAKEN TO (INJURED ONLY) Doctor's Hospital

| ☒ | 43 | M | ☐ | ☐ | ☐ | ☐ | ☐ | ☐ | ☐ | ☐ | ☐ | Wit 1 |

NAME Craig Lincoln Thomas (Witness #1)   214/957-9323
ADDRESS 912 So. Bayshore Drive Miguel Shores, Calif. 90077

| ☐ | | | ☐ | ☐ | ☐ | ☐ | ☐ | ☐ | ☐ | ☐ | |

NAME   PHONE
ADDRESS   TAKEN TO (INJURED ONLY)

SKETCH

River Road

Vehicle #1
Green Lantern

INDICATE NORTH

MISCELLANEOUS

VEHICLE TYPE	ROAD TYPE
PARTY 1	☐ A CONVENTIONAL, ONE WAY ☐ E OTHER (EXPLAIN IN NARRATIVE)
	☒ B CONVENTIONAL, TWO WAY
PARTY 2	☐ C EXPRESSWAY
	☐ D FREEWAY

FIGURE 4-7. Sample Investigation

COLLISION NARRATIVE

NOTIFICATION: Notified of a solo motor vehicle collision with injuries at 1811 hours. Arrived at 1823 hours.

SCENE: River Road is a north/south highway of asphaltic construction with two lanes of travel in either direction separated by double yellow lines. The N-1 lane is 12 feet wide, the N-2 lane is 20 feet wide, the S-1 lane is 12 feet wide, and the S-2 lane is 20 feet wide. An approximate six inch asphaltic curb exists along the periphery of the N-2 and the S-2 lanes. This is an open area void of business or residential districts. A curve exists for southbound traffic, which traverses from south to east in the area of the collision. The curve is posted for 45 MPH. The roadway is clean and unobstructed, the weather is clear and daylight. The sun is to the west and is not a factor in this collision. The roadway is straight and level approaching the curve for both north and southbound traffic.

PRIMARY COLLISION FACTOR		RIGHT OF WAY CONTROL		1	2	3	4	TYPE OF VEHICLE		1	2	3	4	MOVEMENT PRECEDING COLLISION
1	A VC SECTION VIOLATION: 23101 CVC	A CONTROLS FUNCTIONING						A PASSENGER CAR (INCLUDES STATION WAGON)						A STOPPED
	B OTHER IMPROPER DRIVING*	B CONTROLS NOT FUNCTIONING	X					B PASSENGER CAR W/TRAILER						B PROCEEDING STRAIGHT
	C OTHER THAN DRIVER*	C CONTROLS OBSCURED						C MOTORCYCLE/SCOOTER	X					C RAN OFF ROAD
	D UNKNOWN*	X	D NO CONTROLS PRESENT					D PICKUP OR PANEL TRUCK						D MAKING RIGHT TURN
	WEATHER	TYPE OF COLLISION						E PICKUP OR PANEL TRUCK W/TRAILER						E MAKING LEFT TURN
X	A CLEAR	A HEAD-ON						F TRUCK OR TRUCK TRACTOR						F MAKING U TURN
	B CLOUDY	B SIDESWIPE						G TRUCK OR TRUCK TRACTOR W/TRAILER(S)						G BACKING
	C RAINING	C REAR END						H SCHOOL BUS						H SLOWING — STOPPING
	D SNOWING	D BROADSIDE						I OTHER BUS						I PASSING OTHER VEHICLE
	E FOG	E HIT OBJECT						J EMERGENCY VEHICLE						J CHANGING LANES
	F OTHER:	F OVERTURNED						K HWY CONST. EQUIPMENT						K PARKING MANEUVER
		G AUTO/PEDESTRIAN						L BICYCLE						L ENTERING TRAFFIC FROM SHOULDER, MEDIAN, PARKING STRIP OR PRIVATE DRIVE
	LIGHTING	H OTHER*: solo run off road	X					MOTOR VEHICLE INVOLVED WITH						M OTHER UNSAFE TURNING
X	A DAYLIGHT	A NON-COLLISION	X					M OTHER VEHICLE						N CROSSED INTO OPPOSING LANE
	B DUSK — DAWN	B PEDESTRIAN						N PEDESTRIAN					
	C DARK — STREET LIGHTS	C OTHER MOTOR VEHICLE						O MOPED						O PARKED
	D DARK — NO STREET LIGHTS	D MOTOR VEHICLE ON OTHER ROADWAY		1	2	3	4	OTHER ASSOCIATED FACTOR (MARK 1 TO 3 ITEMS)						P MERGING
	E DARK — STREET LIGHTS NOT FUNCTIONING*	E PARKED MOTOR VEHICLE						A VC SECTION VIOLATION:						Q TRAVELING WRONG WAY*
	ROADWAY SURFACE	F TRAIN		X										R OTHER:
X	A DRY	G BICYCLE						B VC SECTION VIOLATION:						
	B WET	H ANIMAL:									1	2	3	4	SOBRIETY—DRUG—PHYSICAL (MARK 1 TO 2 ITEMS)
	C SNOW — ICY							C VC SECTION VIOLATION:						A HAD NOT BEEN DRINKING
	D SLIPPERY (MUDDY, OILY, ETC.)	I FIXED OBJECT:													B HBD— UNDER INFLUENCE
	ROADWAY CONDITIONS (MARK 1 TO 3 ITEMS)							D VC SECTION VIOLATION:	X					C HBD—NOT UNDER INFLUENCE*
	A HOLES, DEEP RUTS*	J OTHER OBJECT:						E VISION OBSCUREMENTS:						D HBD—IMPAIRMENT UNKNOWN*
	B LOOSE MATERIAL ON ROADWAY*														E UNDER DRUG INFLUENCE*
	C OBSTRUCTION ON ROADWAY*							F INATTENTION						F IMPAIRMENT—PHYSICAL*
	D CONSTRUCTION-REPAIR ZONE	PEDESTRIAN'S ACTION						G STOP & GO TRAFFIC						G IMPAIRMENT NOT KNOWN
	E REDUCED ROADWAY WIDTH	A NO PEDESTRIAN INVOLVED	X					H ENTERING/LEAVING RAMP						H NOT APPLICABLE
	F FLOODED*	B CROSSING IN CROSSWALK AT INTERSECTION						I PREVIOUS COLLISION						I SLEEPY/FATIGUED
	G OTHER*							J UNFAMILIAR WITH ROAD						
X	H NO UNUSUAL CONDITIONS	C CROSSING IN CROSSWALK — NOT AT INTERSECTION						K DEFECTIVE VEHICLE EQUIPMENT:						
		D CROSSING — NOT IN CROSSWALK						L UNINVOLVED VEHICLE						
		E IN ROAD — INCLUDES SHOULDER						M OTHER*:						
		F NOT IN ROAD													
		G APPROACHING/LEAVING SCHOOL BUS						N NONE APPARENT						

INVESTIGATED BY		I.D. NUMBER	INVESTIGATED BY		I.D. NUMBER	REVIEWED BY

*EXPLAIN IN NARRATIVE

FIGURE 4-7. (*cont.*)

SUPPLEMENTAL/NARRATIVE	DATE OF ORIGINAL INCIDENT	TIME (2400)	NCIC NUMBER	OFFICER I.D.	NUMBER	PAGE
(Check one)	MO. 07 DAY 04 YR. 81	1811	9470	3783	81-736-F	3
☒ NARRATIVE CONTINUATION TRAFFIC COLLISION REPORT	LOCATION/SUBJECT				CITATION NUMBER	
	River Road				HH36-B44	
☐ SUPPLEMENTAL TRAFFIC COLLISION REPORT					SEAT	
☐ OTHER:	Cole				3	
	CITY/COUNTY				REPORTING DISTRICT	
	Unincorporated Area, Crown County				470	

VEHICLES AND PARTICIPANTS:

Vehicle 1: The Chevrolet was found at rest facing in a westerly direction. The mid-rear of the vehicle was abutted into the street light pole on the east side of Green Lantern Drive. Pole number G-175693. The vehicle was upright on its wheels. All four tires were inflated, the brakes were functional, the speedometer on zero and the bucket front seats were slid completely forward. The hood was buckled and open, grill work was imbedded in the radiator which in turn was into the fan and block. The driver's door was open, the passenger door was wedged closed. The transmission was in fourth gear. The vehicle exhibited major roll over damage.

The vehicle was located with the right side parallel to, and approximately six feet south of the south prolongation of River Drive. The front wheels were on the curb line of Green Lantern Drive. The windshield was shattered but still intact within the molding and heavily starred on the passenger side.

Participants: Driver 1, Cole was located at the passenger door of Vehicle 1 upon my arrival. No observable injuries, no complaints of pain. Passenger Mc Masters was located in the passenger seat of Vehicle 1, pinned between the forward seat and the dashboard. She had an obvious compound fracture of the right femur and complained of chest pains.

PHYSICAL EVIDENCE:

Skidmarks: A centrifugal skidmark exists in the S/B #2 lane of River Road. The skidmark begins 488 feet north of Green Lantern near the line that separates the S/B #1 and #2 lanes. The skidmark arcs west and south for approximately 71 feet and off the roadway 417 feet north of Green Lantern.

Gouge Marks: Gouge Marks begin with the termination of the centrifugal skidmarks at the raised curb, continue on into the dirt in a continuum through the weeds, grass, drainage ditch bank continuing over the west curb of Green Lantern, exitting approximately six feet south of the prolongation of River Road.

Debris: Dirt, grass and weed debris was scattered eastward up to the point of rest of Vehicle 1. Oil and radiator coolant were evident around the area where the vehicle came to rest.

PREPARED BY			REVIEWED BY		
NAME	I.D. NUMBER	MO. DAY YR.	NAME		MO. DAY YR.

FIGURE 4-7. *(cont.)*

SUPPLEMENTAL/NARRATIVE	DATE OF ORIGINAL INCIDENT	TIME (2400)	NCIC NUMBER	OFFICER I.D.	NUMBER	PAGE
(Check one)	MO. 07 DAY 04 YR. 81	1810	9470	3783	81-736-F	4
☒ NARRATIVE CONTINUATION TRAFFIC COLLISION REPORT	LOCATION/SUBJECT				CITATION NUMBER	
☐ SUPPLEMENTAL TRAFFIC COLLISION REPORT	River Road				HH36-B44	
☐ OTHER:	Cole				BEAT 3	
	CITY/COUNTY				REPORTING DISTRICT	
	Unincorporated Area, Crown County				470	

Vehicle Parts: A broken radio antenna was found 54 feet west of the west prolongation of Green Lantern and approximately 33 feet south of River Road. The broken antenna matches the antenna base stub on the Chevrolet.

INJURIES:

Victim 1: Mc Masters. Treated and stabilized at the scene by Paramedics of Station 22, transported to Doctor's Hospital by Curry Ambulance. Diagnosed a broken right femur, two broken ribs, right lung punctured and a greenstick fracture of the left tibia. Condition given as serious and treated by Dr. Hamilton.

INTOXICATION:

Field Sobriety Test: Upon detecting an obvious odor of an alcoholic beverage upon the breath of Driver 1 Cole, and noting the reddened and watery condition of his eyes, a field sobriety test was administered which Cole failed. (See arrest report No. 81-07-15.)

Chemical Test: A Blood Alcohol test was administered by Nurse Irene Murry,32, of Central Forensic Labs. I.D. 81-07-101. The blood test vial was secured in evidence locker three for testing, at 301 Varner St. Symington, CA. Ph: 714/232-4475.

Additional Facts: Driver 1 Cole, restricted to driving only while wearing corrective lenses. No glasses were found at the scene or on his person. He was not wearing contact lenses.

Approximately 20 pictures were taken by Sgt. Alexander I.D. 1645. The photos were taken of the skidmark and continuous path of travel up to the point of rest of Vehicle 1. Each side and the interior of the vehicle was photographed, at the point of rest, and during the time of the intial investigation which concluded at approximately 1930 hours.

Other Property Damage: Sign... Speed Limit 45 MPH.

SECURED EVIDENCE:

1. One roll of film 35mm. Approximately 20 photos.

2. 5cc. of blood for chemical analysis for alcohol and/or drugs, retained by Central Forensic Labs. I.D. 81-07-101.

3. Broken radio antenna found at scene, and antenna stub removed from Vehicle 1.

PREPARED BY				REVIEWED BY		
NAME	I.D. NUMBER	MO. DAY YR.	NAME		MO. DAY YR.

FIGURE 4-7. *(cont.)*

SUPPLEMENTAL/NARRATIVE *(Check one)*	DATE OF ORIGINAL INCIDENT	TIME (2400)	NCIC NUMBER	OFFICER I.O.	NUMBER	PAGE
☒ NARRATIVE CONTINUATION TRAFFIC COLLISION REPORT	MO. 07 DAY 04 YR. 81	1810	9470	3783	81-736-F	5
☐ SUPPLEMENTAL TRAFFIC COLLISION REPORT	LOCATION/SUBJECT River Road				CITATION NUMBER HH36-B44	
☐ OTHER:	Cole				BEAT 3	
	CITY/COUNTY Unincorporated Area, Crown County				REPORTING DISTRICT 470	

STATEMENTS:

Driver 1, Cole: Stated he and Victim 1, Mc Masters were celebrating at a holiday party at the fairgrounds. They were enroute back to the home of Victim 1, southbound on River Road. Just before the curve north of Green Lantern, a large dog darted across the road from right to left in front of them. He swerved to miss the dog and went off the road. Cole estimates his speed between 40 and 50 miles per hour at the time he started the evasive action to miss the dog. He states there were no mechanical defects with the automobile. He claims he had two glasses of beer since noon.

Victim 1, Mc Masters: Due to the injuries sustained, no extensive statements could be obtained. She did verbally identify Driver #1, Cole as the driver of Vehicle #1. She stated they had an argument over his driving and that Cole was driving somewhere between 70 and 80 miles per hour.

Witness 1, Thomas: Stated that he had just rounded the curve going north on River Road when Vehicle 1 literally flew by him going south at 70 plus miles per hour. He saw the cloud of dirt in his rear view mirror and the spinning of the Chevrolet as it left the road. He turned around and returned to help extricate the driver and assist with the passenger. He radioed for assistance on his Citizen's Band radio. He did not observe any large dogs at or near the scene. He further stated that Driver 1 was obviously drunk.

OPINIONS AND CONCLUSIONS:

Driver 1 in the company of Victim 1 was driving southbound on River Road in the S/B #1 lane. Uner the obvious influence of an alcoholic beverage, Driver 1 was operating Vehicle 1 at a rate of speed well in excess of the posted 45 miles per hour.... A 50 foot chord along the centrifugal skidmark was measured. The median was seven inches. Coefficient of friction tests indicate a 72% factor in the immediate area of the centrifugal skidmark. Computations for speed from skidmarks based on the above observations indicates a minimal 76 miles per hour.

Point of Impact: Established as 417 feet north of Green Lantern on the west curb of River Road at the gouge marks indicating the point where Vehicle 1 left the road, and subsequently entered the dirt. Vehicle 1 then struck the drainage ditch, rolled over and backwards to the point of rest

PREPARED BY						REVIEWED BY				
NAME	I.D. NUMBER	MO.	DAY	YR.		NAME		MO.	DAY	YR.

FIGURE 4-7. *(cont.)*

OPINIONS AND CONCLUSIONS: Continued...

Coefficient of friction tests at 25 Miles Per Hour indicate an average test skid length of 29 feet.

$$f = \frac{v^2}{30\ S} \qquad R = \frac{c^2}{8m} + \frac{m}{2} \qquad V = 15\ R\ f$$

$$f = \frac{25^2}{30 \times 29} \qquad R = \frac{50^2}{8 \times 0.583} + \frac{0.583}{2} \qquad V = 15\ s\ 535.967 \times 0.72$$

$$f = \frac{625}{870} \qquad R = \frac{2500}{4.667} + 0.291 \qquad V = 5785.3$$

$f = .72$ or 72% $R = 535.967$ feet   <u>76 Miles per Hour Minimum</u>

Inasmuch as Driver 1, Cole, was under the influence of an intoxicating beverage and driving an automobile at an excessive rate of speed, to wit, a minimal 76 Miles Per Hour in a posted 45 Mile Per Hour zone, and while driving did involve himself in a traffic collision which caused severe injury to another, Driver 1, Cole is charged with Vehicle Code Section 23101...Felony Driving While Intoxicated. Citation Number HH36-B44. Arrest Report Number 81-07-15. Cole booked in Crown County Jail.

RECOMMENDATIONS:

None

PREPARED BY				REVIEWED BY		
NAME	I.D. NUMBER	MO.	DAY	YR.	NAME	MO.	DAY	YR.

FIGURE 4-7. *(cont.)*

70

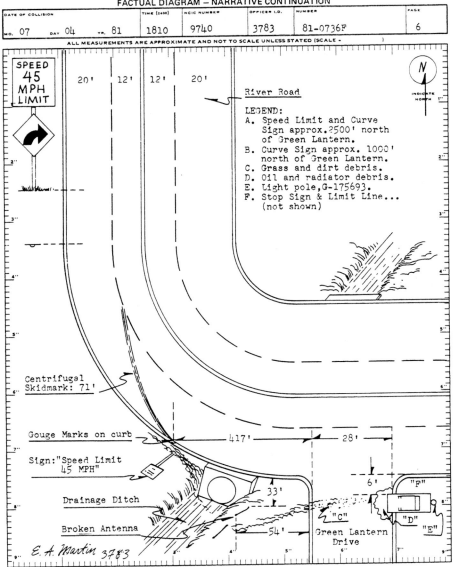

DATE OF COLLISION			TIME (2400)	NCIC NUMBER	OFFICER I.D.	NUMBER	PAGE
MO. 07	DAY 04	YR. 81	1810	9740	3783	81-0736F	6

ALL MEASUREMENTS ARE APPROXIMATE AND NOT TO SCALE UNLESS STATED (SCALE -   )

SPEED
45
MPH
LIMIT

20' 12' 12' 20'

River Road

LEGEND:
A. Speed Limit and Curve
   Sign approx.2500' north
   of Green Lantern.
B. Curve Sign approx. 1000'
   north of Green Lantern.
C. Grass and dirt debris.
D. Oil and radiator debris.
E. Light pole,G-175693.
F. Stop Sign & Limit Line...
   (not shown)

N
INDICATE
NORTH

Centrifugal
Skidmark: 71'

Gouge Marks on curb   417'   28'

Sign:"Speed Limit
45 MPH"   6'   "F"

Drainage Ditch   33'

Broken Antenna   "C"   "D"   "E"
                              54'   Green Lantern
                                       Drive

E. A. Martin 3783

FIGURE 4-8. Factual Diagram–Narrative Continuation

71

COMMON ABBREVIATIONS USED IN COLLISION INVESTIGATION

A.I.	Accident Investigation
Approx.	Approximate
Ave.	Avenue
Blvd.	Boulevard
C.A.	City Attorney
Capt.	Captain
C.H.P.	California Highway Patrol, (substitute relevant state name)
C.I.M.	Collision Investigation Manual
Co.	County
C.R.	County Road
C.S.	City Street
C.V.C.	California Vehicle Code (substitute relevant state name)
D.A.	District Attorney
Dpty.	Deputy
Dpty. Cor.	Deputy Coroner
Dpty. S.O.	Deputy Sheriff
Dr. 1	Driver number one
Dr. Lic.	Driver's License
D.M.V.	Department of Motor Vehicles
E/Curb	East curb (w/curb for west curb, and so on)
Frwy.	Freeway
Hwy.	Highway
Hosp.	Hospital
I-40	Interstate 40 (substitute relevant number)
Inj.	Injury/Injured
Hrs.	Hours
I/O	Investigating Officer
Ln.	Lane
Lt.	Lieutenant
N-1	Northbound number one lane (substitute appropriate number)
N/B	Northbound (s/b for southbound, and so on.)
N-S-E-W	North, South, East, and West
Off.	Officer
P.C.	Penal Code or Probable Cause
P.D.	Police Department
P.O.I.	Point of Impact
P.O.R.	Point of Rest
Rd.	Road
Rdwy.	Roadway
R.O.	Registered Owner
R/O	Reporting Officer

Sgt.	Sergeant
S.P.	State Police
St.	Street
Sta.	Station
S.T.O.	State Traffic Officer
T/C	Traffic collision
Temp.	Temporary
Trlr.	Trailer
Uninc.	Unincorporated
Veh. 1	Vehicle number one
Wit. 1	Witness number one

CONCLUSION

The documentation of collision information is the crux of traffic safety and enforcement programs. The emphasis throughout this text is on thorough collision investigation and recording based on impartial uniformity.

There are four basic reasons why collision investigation and documentation must be accurate, uniform, impartial, and thorough. The finalized reports will provide meaningful data concerning each of the following critical areas.

1. *The Magnitude of the Collision Problem.* Local statistics are compared to other communities of similar structure, past history, and experience throughout the state and the nation. An agency can study one intersection or an entire city and make meaningful decisions based on the priorities.
2. *The Identification of Coincident or Specific Collision Problems.* Well-documented reports highlight specific problems with vehicle design, highway construction, law enforcement deployment, and possible areas that promulgate driver confusion. Countermeasures can then be developed by the various engineers, law enforcement agencies, legislators, driver improvement analysts, and educators.
3. *The Effectiveness of Collision Reduction Programs.* Well-documented reports enumerate the causal relationships involved in collisions and illuminate anticipated as well as unforeseen problems. Creating effective collision reduction programs is then a relatively simple matter of statistical comparison based on the reports.
4. *The Determination of Negligence or Fault.* A completed investigation serves both the courts and the various licensing agencies in identifying negligent drivers and the prevalent collision factors involved.

DISCUSSION QUESTIONS

1. When the physical evidence contradicts the statements of a witness, is it obvious that the witness is not being truthful? Sound travels approxi-

mately 1100 feet per second. Did the witness hear and then see the collision? What is the distance from P.O.I. to the witness?

2. Why do you believe that the "Point of Impact" section is discussed under the section on opinions and conclusions, rather than the section on physical evidence or scene?

3. Why should the factual diagram show the vehicles at their points of rest rather than their points of impact?

4. What questions should be asked of victims and witnesses to a hit-and-run collision? Think in terms of what is out of the ordinary beyond year, make, and model of the vehicle.

5. Discuss the concept that few collisions are accidents, and think in terms of prosecution for the responsible party. How does the judiciary in your area treat driving infractions, property damage collision convictions, and injury and fatal collisions, where a violation of motor vehicle law was involved?

6. If you were the victim of a collision wherein the other party ran a red light and struck your vehicle, how would you react if you later discovered the officer wrote a report rather than an investigation seeking a complaint?

5

Prevalent Collision Factors

THE NECESSITY FOR LEGISLATION

Historical Overview

The Romans documented the first law on the books to govern how two vehicles should pass. Left-to-left was the rule, or more simply stated, drive to the right half of the roadway when passing an oncoming vehicle. That same law was the first statute on the books for the United States. The colonials followed in the footsteps of the Romans and not their British cousins. Imagine the chaos which would result if each state, county, township, or city were given the latitude to select its own interpretation of the basic law. Some areas would drive to the left, others to the right: Bedlam would ensue.

Although a number of cities and eventually states passed legislation concerning the racing of horses within a city's limits, there were no appreciable or enforceable laws governing the speed of vehicles until the advent of the automobile. The cities were to first invoke speed laws. The first speed "cops" of note were mounted on horseback. The horse was soon to be relegated to the stables and replaced by the much faster motorcycle. With the motorcycle and the traffic officer entered a whole new breed of policeman. The traffic specialist was born of necessity. The traffic courts, engineers, and road, street, and highway departments were to follow. Legislation to make driving safer is still fighting a competitive war with collisions and their causes and lags behind the changing times.

Lagging Legislation

An example of lagging legislation is the law which now exists in some states which makes it illegal to wear earphones while driving a vehicle. With the advent of stereophonic sound for automobiles, some enterprising entrepreneurs devised stereophonic headsets. The ability to appreciate the music was no doubt enhanced considerably. Following a number of collisions involving drivers wearing headsets, two major collision factors were discovered. A driver wearing a headset cannot hear external sounds, such as sirens of emergency vehicles crossing intersections in front of the drivers. The second factor was the cord which connected the headphones to the stereo player. The cords were constructed in a spiral much like a telephone cord. The cords became entwined in the steering wheel and the driver's hands. Since the driver's head is attached to the cord by a tight-fitting clamp in the headphones, it is drawn down into the steering wheel as the vehicle is locked in a turning maneuver. After numerous fatalities, the legislators invoked a sanction against a driver wearing headphones while driving. Some states revised the legislation to indicate that the driver could not cover both ears with headphones, which still leaves the problem of the dangling cord.

COLLISION-CAUSING FACTORS

Right-of-Way

Through the early years, speed was the number one collision-causing factor. It was not until the 1960s that a new trend was to take over. Right-of-way violations caught up with and passed speed as the primary collision factor. Right-of-way violations are primarily an urban problem, and difficult to assess until after the collision. Because of the nature of such a violation, and because it is a judgment call, few officers write citations for a right-of-way violation. The officers become weary of losing these cases in traffic court when no collision was involved. The testimony boils down to one word against another, and the case is usually adjudicated in favor of the defendant since, after all, there was no collision. With right-of-way violations leading the nation in collisions, the time has come to train officers who will take a second look at the close calls and near misses and enforce the statutes.

Basic Principles. All of the states and the Uniform Vehicle Code have agreed to the five basic principles of right-of-way:

1. The driver of a vehicle approaching an uncontrolled intersection shall yield the right-of-way to a vehicle which has entered the intersection from a different highway.
2. When two vehicles enter an uncontrolled intersection from different highways at the same time, the driver of the vehicle on the left shall yield the right-of-way to the driver of the vehicle on his right.

3. The driver of a vehicle intending to turn to the left at an intersection or into public or private property, or an alley, shall yield the right-of-way to all vehicles which have approached or are approaching from the opposite direction and which are so close as to constitute a hazard at any time during the turning movement and shall continue to yield the right-of-way to such approaching vehicles until such time as the left turn can be made with reasonable safety. (Most states attach a left turn signal requirement to this statute.)

4. The driver of any vehicle approaching a stop sign at the entrance to, or within, an intersection, shall stop as required and shall then yield the right-of-way to other vehicles which have approached or are approaching so closely from another roadway as to constitute an immediate hazard and shall continue to yield the right-of-way to such approaching vehicles until such time as he can proceed with reasonable safety.

5. The driver of a vehicle about to enter or cross a highway from any public or private property, or from an alley, shall yield the right-of-way to all vehicles approaching on the highway.

It is difficult to imagine that the majority of collisions in the United States occur from violating these five basic statutes.

There are other right-of-way laws which exist in various states such as yielding the right-of-way at yield signs, equestrian crossings, pedestrian crossings, deer crossings. Right-of-way laws governing emergency vehicles apply to all states.

FIGURE 5-1. Although there is no lane to the right, at least two drivers are passing on the right up to the railroad crossing where they will attempt to re-enter the passed traffic in the second lane. There will undoubtedly be a right-of-way violation as they attempt to clear the railroad crossing. What violations of law are applicable to your area?

Speed

The second highest collision-causing factor is speed. The federal government controls the maximum speed law on federally sponsored interstate highways. The legislators of the several states have little to say governing federal control, short of lobbying for a change as the need is seen.

Basic Speed Law. There is, however, a basic speed law within all jurisdictions. Although the wording may vary from state to state the crux of all the basic speed laws may be expressed as follows: No person shall drive a vehicle upon a highway at a speed greater than is reasonable or prudent having due regard for weather, visibility, the traffic on, and the surface and width of, the highway, and in no event at a speed which endangers the safety of persons or property.

The majority of all collisions in which speed was the primary collision factor are a violation of this one statute. Examples are: speeding in the rain; going too fast for the curve; high speeds in a residential district; speeding through a school zone; and speeding into a blind intersection.

In an informal survey conducted by the rangers of Yosemite National Park, it was concluded that the highest percentage of collisions were not only speed-related, solo, run-off-roadway collisions, but involved drivers from flatland states such as Texas, Kansas, Nebraska, and Oklahoma. In percentages, these drivers had the greatest difficulty in negotiating the mountainous roadways, in violation of the *prima facie* speed.

Following Too Closely

Most drivers have been intimidated by the driver who was following immediately to the rear of their car. The errant driver pulls to within a few yards or meters of another driver's rear bumper and literally compresses the slip stream of air between the two vehicles in an attempt to make the other driver pull over. The violator then passes and repeats the violation on the next driver ahead. Nearly every jurisdiction has a law against following too closely, but, as with right-of-way, law enforcement officers seem reluctant to cite for this infraction. The reason again is simple. Each court and jurisdiction has a flexible scale that redefines, "too close," and it becomes a question of interpretation based on two different observations. The driver of a motor vehicle shall not follow another vehicle more closely than is reasonable and prudent, having due regard for the speed of such vehicle and the traffic upon, and the condition of, the roadway.

One rule of thumb for a safe distance between vehicles is one car length for each ten miles per hour of speed. The problem with this gauge is the driver's perception of "car length." A more recent gauge seems far more applicable. It is known as the two second rule. As a driver observes the vehicle ahead pass a fixed object such as a sign, the following vehicle should be far enough to the rear so that at the same speed the rearward driver will pass the same fixed object no sooner than two seconds later.

Rearend collisions which result from this infraction are quite often erroneously recorded as a speeding violation on the part of the rearward driver. Speed is easier to prove, and without an unbiased witness to the act of following too closely, this violation is difficult to establish. Following too closely is still one of the most common causal factors in collisions, even though it is difficult to independently assess and reconstruct. A predominant number of the moving vehicle, rearend collisions that occur upon our highways are a violation of this statute.

Devices and Signs

Traffic control devices and signs seem to account for more than their share of the collision factors. Everyone knows that a vehicle must stop for a red light, and shall proceed on a green. The intent of stop signs is more than evident; yet, too many motorists fail to recognize the inherent dangers in making what is known as a "California Stop." A California Stop is a phrase coined for slowing somewhat, shifting gears, taking a quick glance, and proceeding. The reader will recall that in Chapter 2, the definition of stop included the expression *cessation of movement.*

In Australia, a driver may be suspended from further driving, as well as fined, for running a stop sign in the outback areas. A city stop light is treated with the usual infraction adjudication.

Basic Statute. The basic traffic control signal statute reads as follows: The driver of any vehicle, the person in charge of any animal, any pedestrian, and the motorman of any streetcar, shall obey the instructions of any official traffic signal applicable to him and placed as provided by law, unless otherwise directed by a police traffic officer or when it is necessary for the purpose of avoiding a collision or in case of other emergency, subject to the exemptions granted for emergency vehicles.

Note if you will, that a driver of a vehicle stopped for a red light, for example, has the right to pull through or at least enter an intersection to avoid being struck from the rear by another motorist. This statute would also seem to exempt a driver who is transporting an injured party to a place of emergency medical service. Emergency is the key word for the exemption. Here is where an officer must exercise a great deal of good judgment, for emergency is very often a state-of-mind issue and subject to interpretation. The officer's ability to empathize may be more important than a citation when the violation did not result in a collision.

The red light sections of the various codes vary from state to state. In some states, a driver may turn right at a red light in the absence of other cross traffic. In at least one city and in some states, this maneuver is illegal. The obvious answer to the legality of turning at a red light for the tourist in another state is then, if you are in doubt, do not do it.

As discussed earlier, the right half of the roadway concept is as old as traffic laws in the United States, and is one law on which all states have come to an agreement. This statute has been expanded to become more explicit: Drivers are required to operate their vehicles to the right of center medians, double yellow lines, dividing devices, and so on.

Turning Movements

Most codes agree that: 1) No person shall turn a vehicle from a direct course or move right or left upon a roadway until such movement can be made with reasonable safety, and then only after the giving of an appropriate signal in the manner provided by the code to the driver of any other vehicle that may be affected by the movement. 2) Any signal of intention to turn right or left shall be given continuously during the last 100 feet traveled by the vehicle before turning. (California Vehicle Code Statute 22108 is specifically quoted, as some states differ on the duration of the signal.)

FIGURE 5-2.   Note the vehicle with the high load in the trunk. The load completely obstructs the driver's view through the rear. With no mirror on the right, the driver has no idea of traffic conditions to the right as well as to the rear. Closer examination of the vehicle revealed that the left outside mirror was broken, leaving the driver completely blind to the rear. As the driver changed lanes, without signalling, he narrowly missed the Mercedes-Benz in his blind spot. Given these facts, what violations exist under the laws of your area?

Violations by the drinking driver hold the undisputed record for causing more fatalities than any other violation. It is a sad commentary to note that during the span of the Viet Nam conflict in which approximately 47,000 Americans gave their lives, drinking drivers killed approximately 210,000 Americans. The Viet Nam issue was tragic, highly publicized, and outrageously expensive in human terms. The drinking driver fatalities went unnoticed by most. Approximately fifty percent of all highway fatalities are directly linked to drinking drivers, or drivers under the influence of alcohol and/or drugs. This problem is so vast within the responsibilities of the traffic officer that all of Chapter 6 is devoted to the identification, testing, booking, and procedures of court testimony for this particular crime.

In summary, right-of-way violations account for the greatest number of collisions within the United States. Speeding infractions are the second in terms of primary collision factors. Drivers under the influence of alcohol and/or drugs account for approximately fifty percent of the total of the fatalities. Each state has its own vehicle code or act as well as those legislated and published by the federal government. These codes vary from several hundred to several thousand legislative enactments. What has been outlined here are the few that account for over ninety percent of the collisions. Mechanical malfunctions rarely account for more than five percent of the collisions. The remaining five percent or less of collisions are a series of

FIGURE 5-3. Do you see the violation? Note the heavy smoke coming from the vehicle in the third lane.

isolated events involving the unforeseen, unanticipated, or unlegislated violations, or result from such infractions as U-turns, driving without lights, hitchhiking, and so on.

DISCUSSION QUESTIONS

1. With the aid of the text and the relevant vehicle code, list the primary collision factors prevalent in your city or area, in order of priority.

2. When confronted with a red light and the conflicting orders of a traffic officer directing you to proceed, with which direction are you legally bound, the officer's or the device's?

3. Is it legal to cross a double yellow line to enter a private driveway?

4. In a *prima facie* speed zone posted for 35 M.P.H., is it always a violation to drive at 40 M.P.H.?

5. Upon whom is the burden of proof in an alleged violation of *prima facie* speed; that the circumstances were unsafe?

   The court

   The officer

   The violator

   The collision victim

6. In a rear-end collision where the striking vehicle collides with a vehicle stopped for a red light, what, if any, is the violation? What, if any, is the violation if both vehicles are moving at the time of the rear-end collision?

Driving While Intoxicated

The purpose of this chapter is to acquaint the reader with the drinking driver and to firmly establish the depth of the problem. We will discuss how to identify a drinking driver, provide the necessary tests, effect the arrest, and handle the incarceration. The last step is reporting the arrest and testifying in a court of law.

DEPTH OF THE PROBLEM

Statistics

Alcohol is involved in 50 to 60 percent of the national highway fatalities, causing as many as 30,000 deaths and 800,000 injuries every year. Problem drinkers, not social drinkers, cause at least two-thirds of these deaths. The astonishing truth is that 7 percent of the drivers who cause 50 percent of the Driving While Intoxicated (D.W.I.) deaths can be identified and stopped. These facts are a compilation of figures published by the National Highway Traffic Safety Administration.

History

From the beginning of the horseless carriage's appearance on the highways there has been a linear increase in collisions. Experience shows that in a majority of the fatal and injury collisions, alcohol is the most often noted single contributing factor on the part of the responsible driver. The first substantiative study of note was reported by Dr. H. A. Heise for the *Journal of the American Medical Association* in 1934. In his study, Dr. Heise concluded that although prohibition was legally in effect until December 5, 1933, liquor was accounting for a substantial number of the fatal and injury collisions of the day. Dr. Heise, it may be noted, is also the forerunner of clinical testing for intoxication.

In 1951, Dr. L. Goldberg reported to the First International Conference on Alcohol and Road Traffic. The event was sponsored and hosted by the Swedish government in Stockholm. His subject was the tolerance to alcohol in moderate and heavy drinkers and its significance to alcohol and traffic. For the first time, the alcoholic and drinking driver problems were viewed with global implications and notoriety. Dr. Goldberg's study was extremely important in that it conclusively proved that many persons are adversely affected with respect to driving at blood alcohol concentrations under 0.05 percent, and that all are adversely affected, no matter what their drinking habit, at blood alcohol concentrations of 0.10 percent or higher.

Nine out of ten problem drinkers are not on a skid row but in the general public. This tends to explain why so many of the individuals who end up with collisions or arrests involving alcohol appear on superficial investigation to be solid citizens.

Blood Alcohol Concentrations

Although there are variances among the several states as to the blood alcohol concentrations which comprise a presumptive limit to establish guilt, most states tend to agree with Dr. Goldberg and the American Medical Association: 0.10 percent. At this level, it is held that everyone is sufficiently intoxicated and that driving is definitely impaired. Thousands of studies have been conducted with alcohol and driving reaffirming this level as the absolute cutoff for drinking and driving safely.

There a number of variables in the drinking equation. One is the weight of the drinker. It will take more alcohol to adversely effect the heavier individual. The concentration of alcohol in the beer, liquor, or wine consumed is an obvious factor. One hundred-proof whiskey contains 50 percent alcohol, 80-proof whiskey contains 40 percent alcohol. A twelve ounce can of beer contains approximately the same amount of alcohol as a level ounce of 85-proof whiskey.

Alcohol seems to be absorbed into the system rather rapidly but dissipates rather slowly. Regardless of how much a drinker has consumed, he or she will burn off approximately one drink per hour. Dependent upon the metabolic rate, which may vary slightly, the average person will dissipate about 0.015 percent blood alcohol concentration per hour. This rate varies little in an individual and remains fairly constant. Giving a drunk more coffee has little or no effect on his sobriety; it simply guarantees a wide-awake drunk, with a high anxiety level due to the overdose of caffeine.

With very little in the way of mathematics, a student can readily determine that it will take approximately six ounces of 85-proof whiskey or six twelve-ounce cans of beer in an individual's system to qualify that person to a 0.10 blood alcohol concentration. Persons drinking this heavily know very well what they are doing, and the subsequent intoxication is no accident but an intentional act.

IDENTIFICATION OF THE DRUNKEN DRIVER

Anticipated Behavior

As an observation of over 2,000 drinking drivers arrested and then observed by the author, the following guidelines seem to be the anticipated behavior.

1. At 0.08 to around 0.15 blood alcohol concentration, the person has a diminished sense for, or an appreciation of fear. It appears that the frontal lobes of the brain have become somewhat anesthetized and inhibitions definitely lowered. The frontal lobes of the brain control our social restraints. At this level the driver is evidencing a rather apparent lack of mental control over fear. Without a doubt, this level is the most dangerous of all. This is the high speed and reckless driver.
2. At approximately 0.18 blood alcohol concentration, the driver is developing problems with coordination of walking and is beginning to show the symptoms of a common drunk. Slurred speech and stumbling over curbs are common observations at 0.18 to approximately 0.25. At this level, the driver's vision is narrowed, blurred, and momentary. He or she will have difficulty in visually concentrating on a given object.
3. At approximately 0.30, the subject is beginning to have a hard time hearing as well as seeing.
4. At 0.40, the average person is comotose or more simply stated, out cold.
5. At 0.50, the average person is presumably dead. This is not to say that the figures given will hold true in every case. There have been a number of 0.50 drivers arrested. Not only were they driving a moving automobile, they survived to be re-arrested and re-released.

At approximately 0.15 blood alcohol concentration the drinking driver is obvious to just about any sober witness. The driver's actions are erratic, and he or she begins to bounce the vehicle off curbs and parked cars. This driver slows for the most part and drives with more caution, normally trying to keep the vehicle somewhere inside of the slow lane of traffic. He is doing all in his power to appear as casual as possible. He will drive with the left hand on the wheel, the right draped over the adjacent seat, and even in cold weather, the driver's window will be down to admit as much cold air as possible to keep the driver awake. Turn signals will be ignored or used two miles ahead of the intended turn, depending on his frame of mind. The driver may be driving with parking lights believing his headlamps are on, and cursing the dark streets as he peers over the steering wheel trying to see. For the most part, he will be weaving from side to side, in and out of his lane of traffic. This driver has a tendency to follow too closely in traffic, homing-in on other tail lamps. He very often rear-ends forward traffic involving himself in an unwanted giveaway collision. He will accuse the other driver of stopping abruptly in traffic. Obviously his reaction time and driving skills are greatly depreciated. Higher concentrations of alcohol simply exaggerate the observable symptoms and make the driver much easier to identify.

As previously mentioned, the 0.10 driver is a high speed self-assured individual with lowered inhibitions—the most dangerous driver. The officer who successfully spots and subsequently arrests the driver at 0.10 blood alcohol concentration is truly doing the community a service. Anyone can spot the obvious; it takes a professional officer to locate and arrest the biggest killer of them all, the driver who knows he or she is all right. At high speeds, the 0.10 driver does not just wrinkle fenders in a minor collision, he or she kills and maimes. This driver exhibits a disrespect for other motorists and aggressively takes unwarranted risks. He or she will abruptly change lanes, pass over double yellow lines or on curves, and in general drive like there is no one else on the roadway. The 0.10 driver is also known for sudden changes in mood and temperament. Up to approximately 0.18 blood alcohol concentration, this individual may challenge an officer's patience; if there is a chance to fight, this person is the most likely candidate. An officer must remember this fact when making an arrest and act accordingly.

Patrol Technique

An experienced late-watch officer knows that it is not high speed patrol that nets the drinking drivers but a casual, easy patrolling style. Under ideal conditions the officer will have approximately twenty seconds to view and make a determination on a vehicle in traffic ahead of the patrol unit. This figure is just an average, and represents the actual small corner of time that an officer has to make a determination on a vehicle. Needless to say, most drinking drivers escape detection because of this fact. When vehicles are traveling in a pack, or in the flurry of heavy traffic that occurs when the bars close, an officer has only a few seconds to weed out the worst of the lot to stop for a check of driver sobriety. If by chance the drunk driver is temporarily driving in a straight line, the officer may not give the vehicle a second glance. Upon seeing the patrol unit in the vicinity, the drinking driver will become somewhat hyperactive and the adrenalin in his system will begin to pump. For a short period of time, he or she will be able to drive and act in a more normal manner. Isolating a vehicle operated by a suspected drinking driver is an art. Low and slow patrol driving in and around the business area is a must. Patrol the more frequented roadways, know where the high collision intersections are located, and from time to time, check the back-street drinking drivers. An alcoholic develops a pattern. If a certain course of travel offers the least in the way of cross traffic and police patrol, the alcoholic will be sure to seek it out, and even when the road pattern is way out of his way, he or she will employ this route to avoid detection.

How to effect a traffic stop and the ramifications of officer and violator contact is the subject of Chapter 15. Let us assume now that you have stopped a suspected drinking driver and must develop a plan of action.

Observations of the Driver

Observations for the arrest report are a continuing process. An officer must recall and write not only the driving which came to her attention, but she must also be on the alert for the initial contact. Notice how the drinking driver pulled over to the curb or berm. Some stop at an angle to the curb rather than parallel. Others will drive upon the curb and bounce back down to the shoulder. Still others will scrape their tires on the curb, or park their car so far from the curb that they are stopping in the road.

As you approach, you will notice that most drinking drivers will leave the engine running. Ask the driver first to turn off the ignition. This simple request will save the officer a number of surprises. As you engage the individual in conversation, look at the driver's eyes to see how reddened they are. Casually check the odor on the person's breath. The odor of beer is quite obvious. The odor of mixed drinks upon a person's breath will be a sweeter odor more like perfume. Watch for the driver who has popped a breath mint into his or her mouth just before you stop the car. The sweet odor of the breath mint will soon be gone, and the odor of the alcoholic beverage will begin to override the breath freshener.

Tell the driver why he or she has been stopped, and request the driver's license. Watch closely as the driver searches for a billfold or wallet. Watch the driver dutifully turn the billfold over and over trying to find the right angle of attack to remove the license. Sometimes the drunk will be very careful in finding the license, and then stick her thumb beneath the glassine or plastic window, often ripping the window apart to remove the license. Some will search for a driver's license, spot the license, then take out a credit card or business card without noticing that the license is still in billfold. Make mental notes of all unusual behavior.

Ask the driver to exit the vehicle. If you are standing on the driver's side of the car, use the excuse that you would appreciate the driver stepping out of the car so you need not stand in the traffic lane, and possibly be struck by a passing motorist. Most drinking drivers are eager to oblige. If you are standing on the passenger side, ask the driver to step out so that you will not have to stoop while you continue your conversation. Or say that background noise makes it difficult to hear, or that if he or she steps out, you will be able to monitor your patrol unit outside speaker when you continue your conversation. The list of requests is up to the imagination of the officer. You want the driver out of the vehicle in any event.

Watch how the driver exits the vehicle. Some stumble, hang onto the door frame for support, or walk away leaving the door open into the traffic lane. Shut the door and, if necessary, guide the driver up onto a sidewalk or an area that is flat, clean, and unobstructed. As there are no sidewalks adjacent to our superhighways, the best area for the field sobriety test is in front of the suspect's vehicle. Have the driver leave the lights on to illuminate the shoulder where the test is to be given. Under no circumstance should an officer administer the field sobriety test while standing between the two vehicles. The space between the two cars is forbidden territory. Every month there is another account of an injured officer struck by a drinking driver who rearends a patrol unit pushing it forward and into another violator's vehicle pinning the officer between the bumpers. An experienced officer knows her beat and selects the place for the stop, well lit, with wide shoulders or a parking lot into which the suspect may be directed in order to leave the traffic lanes altogether. Safety first, for the officer and the suspect.

After successfully removing the driver from the vehicle, double check that the engine is off and the transmission of the suspect's vehicle is in neutral with the emergency brake set, or in the "park" position with the brake set. Then the officer is free to continue. It is a good practice to remove the keys to the vehicle. Either give them to the suspect, or place them in a safe place away from other passengers in the vehicle and the suspect, depending on his or her disposition. The easiest method is to have the driver remove and pocket the keys.

Observe the driver walk forward to the front of the vehicle. Is he or she using the fenders for support, or running into the side view mirror? Does the driver lean back on the hood of the car to appear casual as you talk? How does the driver answer your questions? Does he or she make wide sweeping gestures with the hands and arms, or fold arms and lock them across the chest in a manner that looks like someone trying to hold himself together? This study of body language and motion is known as kinesics. There is a great deal of body motion communicated to the observant officer.

The Field Sobriety Tests

1. Modified Position of Attention
2. Heel-to-Toe, Standing and Walking
3. Finger-to-Nose
4. One Foot Balance
5. Alphabet
6. Spelling
7. Finger Counting
8. Lateral Nystagmus

Modified Position of Attention. The officer demonstrates by standing with body erect, heels and toes of the shoes touching, and with arms outstretched to the sides, palms up. Ask the subject to perform this test with head back slightly and eyes shut keeping them closed until you say to open them. As the officer observes the behavior of the person, count the seconds to ten. Do not count out loud, but make a mental note of how long it took for the driver to open his eyes, or start to fall off-balance. Observe the circular arc in the head movement and note how far right or left the head moves from a perpendicular center line. Watch the driver's feet as the driver inches them wider apart into a broader base. Make notes if necessary.

Heel-to-Toe, Standing and Walking. Demonstrate this test by placing one foot directly in front of the other so that the heel of one shoe touches the toe of the other, as if standing on a tightrope. The intoxicated person, standing on flat, level ground with arms outstretched, dips from side to side like a circus performer. This test is accomplished with the eyes open. The officer stands in front of the driver and demonstrates as the driver attempts to duplicate the example demonstrated by the officer. The other foot forward is the second half of the standing test. Hold each test for approximately ten seconds.

Be sure to ask the driver if he or she has any impairment of the hips, legs, or ankles prior to administering the test and placing too much stress on the observed behavior. Ask if the infirmity impairs normal walking or standing. Note the answer and write this into your arrest report. This notation will negate a defense of impairment should the plea be "not guilty."

After this test, ask the individual to attempt to walk an imaginary straight line placing one foot directly in front of the other. The officer again demonstrates the test. It is best to have the individual begin the test from a distance of approximately 15 feet in front of his or her car, and walk towards the headlamp. Tell the suspect to walk eight steps, or any given number, and to turn in any manner that is comfortable and repeat the test returning to the point of origin. During your demonstration, walk the eight steps heel to toe, turn in a military about-face and walk the eight steps back. Do not place your arms in an extended position, but walk at an easy slow pace, counting your steps aloud as you go. As you perform a military about-face, reiterate: "Turn in any manner comfortable to you, and return."

As the driver attempts the test, watch for gaps between the heels and the toes. Observe the tendency to walk duck-footed rather than in a straight line with one foot directly in front of the other. Notice if the arms come up in a balancing act routine as the driver walks the imaginary tight-rope. In particular, be present when the suspect turns around. The suspect will probably attempt to duplicate the military about-face, and odds are very good that he or she will fall off balance to his or her left. Ask the suspect to count out loud as you demonstrated. Watch, too, for the number of steps taken. A number of drinking drivers will continue to walk the total distance to the hood of their car, and use the hood for support as they turn and then start back. Do not insist that the driver perform the test as you explained and demonstrated. The biggest test in all of this is the driver's ability to listen and follow the simple instructions.

Finger-to-Nose. This test is a continuation of the Modified Position of Attention test. The driver stands erect, heels and toes together and arms extended to the side. With eyes closed, the driver attempts to touch the tip of his or her nose with the hand you specify. Again, this test is demonstrated by the officer. The officer does not close his or her eyes, however, for reasons of officer safety.

The officer stands at attention, heels and toes together, extends the arms parallel to the ground, makes a fist of each hand, and extends the index finger. The officer then states, "When I say right hand, you bring your right index finger up to and just touch the tip of your nose. When I say left hand, bring your left hand up and with the tip of your index finger, touch the tip of your nose." The key is *tip to tip:* repeat this phrase as you demonstrate the test.

Now it is the driver's turn for the test. Ask the driver to stand in the attention position, feet together, arms outstretched, index fingers out, then close the eyes. The officer should not just call out right, left, right, left, and so on. The officer should begin with the left, then left, a right, left, right and so on. This diminishes the routineness of the test and forces the driver to listen and think. Watch for false starts. You will state left and the driver will start with the right, stop, hesitate and perhaps continue hoping you do not know your right from your left, or perhaps stop, hold the right in a bent arm position and start with the left as requested.

This test again is a test of the driver's ability to follow simple directions. This is a good test to give when the driver tells you as a defense of poor skills, that he or she has difficulty walking a straight line. The ability to walk a straight line has little to do with the ability to find the nose or recall where it is supposed to be located on the face. Note where the tip of the index finger strikes the face, and make notes if necessary. The nose tip is very susceptible to the effects of alcohol and becomes numb as the blood alcohol concentration increases. Watch how the driver literally depresses the tip of his nose once he or she locates its position.

One Foot Balance. Ask the driver to lift one foot approximately six inches off the ground, point the toe forward, hold the foot off the ground approximately two feet ahead of the other foot as if preparing to take a step, and hold the foot outward for approximately ten seconds.

Again, this test requires the driver to have no infirmities of the hips, legs, or ankles. Demonstrate one foot and then the other. Be prepared to catch the driver if he or she falls or loses balance. Note, too, the kind of shoes worn by the driver. A woman in high heels may wish to remove her shoes prior to the test. A cowboy may want to remove his boots, but, it is not likely. In any event, note the condition of the shoes. Run-down heels on old shoes may not give the driver much on which to stand or balance. Note the shoe construction in your report. A defense attorney may well try to state that a client failed this test because he was, "forced to attempt this test in his old work shoes." Your notation that the arrestee was wearing a sport suit and shirt with seemingly new broad-heeled shoes will prevent the attorney from entering this kind of testimony. If the driver takes off his or her shoes, note this in the report. If the driver insisted upon taking the tests in narrow-heeled shoes, note this in the report as well.

Some officers choose not to administer this test for a good reason. This test may be difficult to replicate in a courtroom in front of a jury while standing on the carpeted floor. The carpet and the backing or carpet cushioning will not offer a stable base on which a good test can be demonstrated. The test was not administered on a thick carpet and sponge backing, but on a solid sidewalk or asphaltic surface. Still, the defense attorney will ask the officer to demonstrate the test. Be prepared for this eventuality if you choose to administer this test, and know what floor surface you will have in a courtroom.

Alphabet. Ask the driver how far he or she went in school. In this day and age, nearly everyone has completed at least eight years of public education. With this background, ask the driver to recall the alphabet and recite it A through Z. Be prepared to note the response. Some will sing-song their way through the alphabet; others will stumble all the way to the letter G. Still, other drivers will continue placing 40 to 50 characters into the 26 letter alphabet. Make notes on a small notepad; or, with a ball point pen, write lightly in the palm of your hand until you can transpose the information onto the report.

Spelling. This test requires no special aptitudes for balance and is much like the Alphabet Test. Ask the driver to spell such things as, "United States" or "California" or "Michigan." Be prepared for the response. An experienced officer has heard some weird responses.

This is a good place to discuss one other observation that is similar to spelling: pronunciation. Pronunciation of everyday words becomes a challenge for an intoxicated person. Slurring is common. Registration may sound like "reg-ē-lation." North Carolina often comes out something like "Norse-care-ina." The simple word south may come out "soused." Note these observations in the report. It is just one more sign of intoxication and one more piece of evidence for a conviction.

Finger Counting. Here, too, is a test that anyone can do as it requires no special skills of even normal balance. The officer demonstrates by holding the right hand open with the palm up. With the right thumb, he or she touches the right index finger and counts aloud, "one." The officer then proceeds leftward, touching the tip of the right thumb to the tip of the next finger and counts, "two." Proceed to the ring finger and count "three," and on to the little finger, counting "four." The process is then reversed from the little finger backwards to the index finger counting aloud: "Four, three, two, one." Demonstrate three rounds then ask the driver to duplicate the counting.

The response might be anything other than what was demonstrated. Some drivers will count to ten or higher; others will miss touching the tip of the thumb to the tip of the finger next in line. Others will start shaking their hand in sweeping motions hoping to disguise the fact that they cannot feel their numbed finger tips touching their thumb, and still others will count to four and forget how to get back to one. Again, make notes that are meaningful; this is all evidence.

Lateral Nystagmus. While standing in front of the driver, hold your right index finger vertically, approximately 12 inches in front of the driver's face. Ask the driver to look at the tip of your finger and, without turning head or body, to follow your finger with his or her eyes. Slowly move your finger to the right or left and observe the driver's eyes tracking your finger movement. As the pupil nears the corner of the eyes, you will notice that an intoxicated person's eyes will begin to bounce in rhythm with his or her heart beat. The eye muscles are weakened by the effects of the alcohol. As a check of the driver's reaction to the test, check the eyes of your partner officer and note the difference. A sober individual can control the movement of the pupils from side to side; an intoxicated individual cannot and develops tunnel vision. The test of Lateral Nystagmus is applicable with drugs as well as alcoholic intoxication.

Other Tests. There are a number of tests officers use which have validity but lack widespread acceptance. One such test is the placing of three or four coins on a sidewalk, and asking the driver to stoop over and pick them up. The problems with the test are obvious. Some people with short fingernails have difficulty in retrieving the coins. Others such as obese persons have problems with their own bulk in attempting to stoop over. Still other people with higher blood alcohol concentrations will stoop over, lose balance, and fall, striking their heads on the concrete sidewalk.

Another test is the hand-clap. Demonstrate by holding your left hand outward from your body about 12 inches, palm up. Place the right hand palm down in the palm of the left hand, as if clapping or applauding. Now, demonstrate turning the right hand over and bringing down the back of the right hand into the palm of the left hand. With wrist action of the right hand, the palm and back of the right hand are alternately brought down into the palm of the left hand. The officer demonstrates slowly stating, "Clap with the palm of the right hand, then the back of the right hand." As the test continues, the clapping and rotating of the right hand is accelerated. As the drunk driver attempts to accelerate the clapping, watch for a lack of coordination. A drunk driver begins to rotate his or her left hand as well, misses hands altogether, or loses track of front and back, resorting to conventional clapping and failing to turn over the right hand.

The tests described here are the standard tests for field sobriety testing. They do not include every test which has been developed. The eight tests described will, however, provide an officer with more than sufficient data to build a successful prosecution. In cases where a driver is obviously intoxicated, the officer may want to abbreviate the testing process. This is often done in cases where the officer is concerned for the safety of the driver. In every case possible, the driver should cover at least four of the tests to give the officer something to talk about in court. If an officer simply states he or she smelled an odor of an alcoholic beverage upon the defendant's breath and noted the defendant's difficulty in walking, the case may well be lost, regardless of intoxication. The defendant does not look the same in the courtroom as he or she did out there on the road. The defendant is now dressed in business attire, sober, and stating that he or she had a couple of social drinks with friends when he or she felt an attack of influenza coming on. The defendant was driving home when he or she was stopped and rudely arrested by the officer. Notwithstanding the results of the subsequent chemical testing of the driver's blood, breath, and urine for blood alcohol concentration, the officer still has a weak case and is subject to criticism for the poor report and disregard for the driver's right to be given a substantial field sobriety test. In short, the officer must observe all the facts and give the driver every opportunity of vindication through testing. The officer must then reduce those facts to writing in the arrest report. A good report stands on its own merits and will save a great deal of unwanted court time.

Satisfied that an individual is under the influence of alcohol or drugs, the officer effects the arrest according to the law. A search of the prisoner is made, the vehicle is checked for evidence of this and other crimes, the vehicle is stored or parked as required, and the driver is taken for chemical testing.

As with skid marks, evidence of the field sobriety and chemical testing is short-lived. This is known as evanescent evidence and must be obtained as soon as practical, and properly recorded and preserved.

Chemical Testing

Breath Test. Normally, the state provides the guidelines for the testing and the types of testing available to the arrestee. The local jurisdictions, city, or district attorneys and the police agencies then must come to grips with the problem of selecting the process that best suits their particular needs and budgets. There are numerous approaches to making determinations as to blood alcohol concentrations. The most popular test is the quantification of the air exchanged in the lungs, or the simple breath test. The arrested party blows into a device for a given period of time. The air blown into the device is trapped in a plastic bag or balloon. The air is then analyzed internally within the device and a determination is completed. The principle behind this test is that the alcohol consumed is exchanged or relieved through the process of breathing. Most jurisdictions require that the test be performed twice and that the results be compared for verification.

Blood Test. The blood test is perhaps the best of the methods used for quantification. A small sample of blood is withdrawn from the arrested party. The blood is then mixed with an anti-coagulant to preserve its validity. A very small portion of the blood taken is actually used in the testing process, leaving a considerable quantity which the defendant's attorney may subpoena and have tested by an independent laboratory. This test is also the least time consuming for the arrested party. The advantage of this test is found in the preservation of physical evidence. The blood remains in solution and may be tested and retested, providing the defendant as well as the police and courts a tangible artifact to be discussed in court. The breath test by comparison offers no more evidence than a piece of paper upon which a number is inscribed either by charting or printing.

Urine Test. The urine test is the third most common form of testing. Again, two samples are normally required. The arrested party is required to void the bladder, wait for twenty to thirty minutes, and void the bladder a second time. The usual problem with this test is the inability of the person to void the bladder the second time. The chemical testing is an analytical process which again isolates the blood alcohol concentration.

USE OF DRUGS WHILE DRIVING

Thus far in our discussion, little has been stated concerning the detection of drugs. With current screening capabilities found in the more sophisticated methodologies, a laboratory has the ability to discern very minute quantities of drugs in both the blood and urine. When opiates are suspected, such as heroin, the urine test may be the test of choice by the officer and the laboratory technician. When barbiturates are known or suspected, the blood test is the best choice. Mind-altering drugs are discernible in the blood test as well. Most of the popular amphetamines can be screened in the urine. The laboratory technician or doctor administering the tests will advise the officer which test to select when drugs are present or suspected.

In addition to chemical tests for the drugs, an officer soon becomes proficient in the observation of physical characteristics apparent in the arrested party. Such observations may include the pinpointed pupils of the eyes in a heroin addict in addition to the "tracks" or needle marks. The mind-altering drugs and amphetamines seem to create a high anxiety level. This is also true of cocaine. A cocaine user will often be compelled to scratch his skin to alleviate the tingling sensation which feels similar to insect bites. Amphetamine users have difficulty standing still. They are constantly moving about, shuffling their feet, talking fast, and making wide sweeping gestures with their hands and arms. The nervousness transcends the normal level of frustration or anxiety experienced in the routine stop. LSD ("Acid") and PCP ("Angel Dust") users are extremely anxious, very paranoid, and very suspicious. The users of these and other mind-altering drugs are extremely dangerous both to themselves and others when driving. Time and distance become distorted, and normal walking for the unintoxicated may seem like a marathon run to the person under the influence or drugs. This observation is noted, for example, in PCP users, and the term "turkey trot" was coined to describe their manner of walk. The movement is a series of fast, jerky, short steps. The solution for handling PCP users is to move, talk, and act very slowly, keeping them as calm as possible. Quick movements by others frighten the user and in his diminished capacity for comprehension he may resort to physical violence. This dimension to the PCP user's personality makes apprehension of the driver extremely hazardous for the officer. The PCP user will feel threatened and fight with amazing strength. Even when injured the user will continue to fight and feel no apparent pain. The user may often find clothing restrictive and appear on the scene with little or nothing on.

The biggest danger is the mixing of alcoholic beverages with any of the drugs. The individual may take a few drinks to relax. The alcohol lowers the social restraints and powers of deductive reasoning. The individual then "pops" a pill or two to relax, sleep, or slip into a state of euphoria. The synergistic effect in the combination is too often deadly, causing the heart to stop and breathing to cease. The anesthetizing devices relax the involuntary muscles of the body, and they stop functioning.

Many people are victimized by well-intentioned doctors who prescribe amphetamines for weight reduction, among other reasons. The recipient becomes hyperactive and literally burns the excess fat in the system. The individual also develops a high degree of irritability and nervousness. This makes driving an automobile in traffic a very difficult process for the individual, and he or she often victimizes others in collisions.

Abnormal behavior is not that difficult to discern. When an officer observes a driving violation and makes the stop, the awareness process is already underway. When alcohol and/or drugs become evident, the officer has few options but to remove this driver from the automobile, and take him or her out of the driving community. The testing for the intoxicant is only one small portion of this process. Unfortunately, many courts rely on the test results to provide the basis for their decisions and place too little value on the driving behavior that initiated the person into the system.

TEST REFUSAL

Having arrested the intoxicated driver and given the field tests, the officer must admonish the individual of the rights and duties under the law of the jurisdiction. In most instances, before chemical testing can be performed, the individual must make a choice of which test he or she prefers. If the driver refuses to take a test, or fails to complete the test that was chosen, and refuses all other tests, his or her driving privilege is normally suspended for a period of time. The suspension privilege is normally controlled by that jurisdiction's department of motor vehicles. A hearing is usually held to give the recalcitrant driver an opportunity to establish a defense for the refusal. Those jurisdictions which impound the individual's driver's license at the time of the refusal appear to have the best system of driving privilege control. When a driver refuses to take a test, the officer simply completes a brief statement of the facts and has the form sent to the appropriate department for suspension action.

Before the officer can elicit information from an arrestee, there is an admonishment given concerning the individual's rights against self-incrimination. If the individual agrees or declines to make a statement or answer questions, the manner of agreement or refusal should be written verbatim in the arrest report. In short, write the answering statement exactly as the arrested party responds. (i.e: "Sure, why not talk about it." "No, I won't talk to anyone 'cept 'n' my tourney.") The manner of reply is, in itself, a statement of evidence for intoxication. Some jurisdictions also have the arrestee sign and date the admonishments. The signature not only shows that he or she was admonished, it also often indicates a degree of sobriety. Few persons are capable of writing when they are intoxicated. The signature itself becomes good evidence.

There is a great deal of case law concerning the dual admonishments of constitutional rights of self-incrimination and the suspension of driver privilege for test refusal. Follow the admonishment process to the letter. To say a drinking driver will comprehend what is being said is also a matter of case law. Most jurisdictions have incorporated a law which makes receiving a driver's license contingent upon the understanding that if the person drives while intoxicated, he or she must submit to a chemical test or have that driving privilege suspended.

INTOXICATION ARREST REPORTS

Like everything else in good police work, a good report makes the case. The intoxicated driver provides the officer with more than enough material to sustain a conviction. If the officer overlooks the evidence and glosses over the facts, the case will most likely be found in the local prosecutor's reject basket. Prosecutors do not like to try half-baked cases any more than an officer who finds he or she must testify in court likes to watch his or her testimony being chewed to pieces by an aggressive defense attorney.

Most departments have a standardized arrest report face page. The face page contains all the data concerning the arrested party, the vehicle, and the associated facts of date, time, and location. The officer then describes the field sobriety test and indicates the manner in which the arrested party responded. There is usually a place in the form for describing the defendant's clothing, the odor upon the breath, the appearance of the eyes, and miscellaneous information.

The portion of the report which makes the case is to be found in the narrative. The following is a guide for writing an intoxication narrative in the chronological order of events:

> Driving observations
>> Moving violations
>> The stop
> Driver contact observations
> Field sobriety test
> Arrest
> Chemical test
> Additional facts

Driving Observations

This should be in a first person narrative of the officer. Give the location, your direction of travel, the violator's direction of travel, the date, time, and anything unusual like the weather or adverse road conditions.

Moving Violations. Specify what drew your attention to the driving of the violator's vehicle. The officer should spell out the reasonable cause for the stop which followed, such as the driver crossing over double yellow lines, unsafe passing, running a stop sign or signal, stopping at a green light, speeding, weaving in and out of the lane, racing, driving on the wrong side of the roadway, driving exceptionally slow so as to block traffic, and so on.

The Stop. Under this heading, list what happened when you activated the emergency lights to effect a stop. Presumably you attempted to stop the violator in a safe area if at all possible. Did he or she continue down the road, oblivious to your presence? Perhaps he or she slowly drove to the right hand curb, drove up on the curb for approximately twenty feet and then, reentering the street, drove out into the traffic lane and cut back to the curb, striking it, and parking the car at an approximate 30° angle across a driveway and sidewalk. Was traffic heavy or light? Were any pedestrians involved, or other vehicles which had to take evasive action when the violator was trying to stop the suspect's car? Was the driving so bad that you had to attempt to stop at any cost to officer safety? Did the driver stop in the number one lane of a major highway without attempting to go to the curb? Did you have to employ the siren, use the high-low beam flashers and spotlights? Did the suspect continue to drive, passing safe well-lit pull-out areas to take you to a darkened and narrow residential street?

Driver Contact Observations

In this category, write a general statement as to the driver's appearance. Include such things as clothing, loose tie, untied shoes, reddened eyes, sweet odor of an alcoholic beverage upon the breath, and overall manner or presence. After you tell the driver why you effected the stop, ask to see a driver's license, and watch as the driver attempts to locate a billfold and retrieve the document. Ask the driver to shut off the engine, set the emergency brake, take the keys out of the ignition, and step out. Write the reactions to this simple four-step process. Note, too, if the driver's window was up or down when you walked up to the car, and if the radio or stereo was playing so loudly that he or she could not have heard the siren. Were rear-view mirrors in such a position as to see the emergency lights in the rear? Write how the driver exited the vehicle—hanging onto the door frame, tripping over the bottom sill of the door, or clinging to the fender—if applicable.

Indicate that a field sobriety test was administered and the driver failed to perform satisfactorily. If your departmental forms do not include a special area to outline the performance of the driver, list each test given in this portion of the report, and explain how the driver performed the test. (i.e: "I explained and demonstrated the heel-to-toe test, eight steps out, turn and eight steps back. Mr. Carr did not once touch heel-to-toe, walked out thirteen steps in a duck-footed manner, and returned in fifteen steps after using his car for support in the turn-around.") It is a good practice to list the tests in the order in which they were given. The experienced officer develops a pattern and writes it in the same rotational order each time. In trial, either the prosecutor or the defense attorney will invariably ask, "Which test did you administer first, second, and so on?"

Before you administer those tests that judge balance, be sure to inquire as to the subject's possible infirmities, such as problems with hips, legs or ankles. Write the response in this portion of your report. List also the level of education if you asked the suspect to recite the alphabet, spell, or count. This may sound a bit ridiculous, but it may well save courtroom embarrassment if the driver has said one thing out on the road, and given a conflicting statement on the witness stand. Good reporting can destroy the credibility of a defendant trapped in perjury.

Arrest

Spell out the specific section of law by number and code for driving under the influence for which the party was arrested. For example: "Mr. Carr was arrested for misdemeanor driving while intoxicated, Section 23102a CVC (California Vehicle Code).

In this portion of the report, also indicate where the driver was incarcerated and where the car is located. If the vehicle was stored or impounded, list the name of the garage and the address. If the vehicle was parked, show where it was parked and that the keys were given to the driver after the car was locked. Most importantly, show that the driver requested the car be parked and not stored or impounded. It is also wise to take anything of value from inside the vehicle and lock it all in the trunk if it meets with the driver's approval. When the vehicle contains obvious valuables, it is undoubtedly best to store or impound the car, completing an inventory and storage report. Some departments rarely store a vehicle, while others make no exceptions and impound all cars in the event of an arrest. Some departments authorize the release of a vehicle at the scene of an arrest to a sober passenger or friend. If a vehicle is released, obtain the name, address, phone number, and relationship to the driver, and note that the release was effected with the driver's permission and upon specific request.

Chemical Test

Note the specifics of the test chosen, the location where the test was conducted, by whom, the tester's title, the date, and the time. If the results are immediately available, such as with a breath test, show the results and underline for ease of identification when reading the report. If the driver refused to take a test, indicate the date and time that the admonishment was given and the circumstances surrounding the refusal. In the event of a refusal, write the specific questions:

Q. "Will you take a breath test?"
A. "No."
Q. "Will you take a blood test?"
A. "I told you no."
Q. "Will you take a urine test?"
A. "No, no, no, a thousand times, no."
Q. "Do you understand that your driving privilege will be suspended?"
A. "Who cares? I don't need a license to drive."

Additional Facts

If your departmental form for arrest does not include a statement check-off list, indicate under this heading any questions you may have asked the driver following his or her admonishment and agreement to talk to you, the officer. For example, you may have asked any of the following questions: How many drinks did you have? What were you drinking? When did you have your first drink? Your last drink? Are you taking and drugs or medication? If so, what kind of drugs? Where were you going? Where are you now? Do you know what time it is? When did you last eat? What did you have to eat? Is there anything wrong with your car? Do you feel ill? How do the drinks you consumed make you feel? If the driver refuses to talk with you, make a note of the refusal statement.

List in this portion any additional charges you may have added as a result of the arrest. For example, you may have discovered an open container of an alcoholic beverage, contraband, or a loaded weapon as the result of the stop. Use this portion of the report to explain how it was observed and the nature of the charges.

Finally, you may have an arrest that arose from the statement of a witness who will be required to appear in court to provide the continuity of events which led up to the arrest of the driver. List any witnesses' statements and all relevant information along with name, address, phone number, and age. Remember, as with the collision investigation, keep witnesse's statements in the third person narrative: "Mrs. McGuire stated that she. . ."

By simply utilizing the format for arrest, you are more likely to get a conviction, a better image for your department, and a high degree of respect from a defense attorney who opposes you in court.

TAKING THE CASE TO COURT

Plea Bargaining

This is the final rung in the arrest ladder of events. The arrestee obtains a defense attorney who makes every effort to have the case mitigated prior to trial. Most jurisdictions allow the prosecutors the latitude to plea bargain those cases on the trial docket. This process was originally designed to allow the prosecutors an opportunity to lighten court overloads in less severe cases. The prosecutor allows the accused an opportunity to plead guilty to a lesser included offense. An original charge of "driving while intoxicated" may be reduced to "reckless driving," or two lesser included offenses, such as speeding and/or running a stop sign. The defense attorney and the client will normally jump at the opportunity to avoid a conviction of driving while intoxicated and take just about anything the prosecutor offers. Obviously this system as employed gives too much power to the office of the prosecutor. A good police agency with officers doing a most commendable job of reporting deserves better than this. Bear in mind that the prosecutors are as reluctant to take cases to court as defense attorneys are reluctant to face the arresting officer. A prosecutor is known by his or her conviction rate. By plea bargaining the case and obtaining a plea of guilty to a lesser included offense, the prosecutor has obtained a conviction and upheld his or her good record. As long as the courts do not monitor the plea bargained cases, this will continue. The real loser in all of this is the community the officer serves.

The Trial

Upon receiving a subpoena to appear in a case involving an intoxicated driver arrest, the officer should make a copy of the arrest report. Since the case will be going to trial some months subsequent to the arrest, the officer should return to the scene of the incident and refresh his or her memory. Check the area to observe what, if any, appreciable changes have occurred in the roadway and the surroundings. Note the changes, and prepare yourself to testify about the differences between then and now. Invariably either the defense attorney or members of the jury will traverse the area and note the differences between what they see and what is described in your testimony. Be prepared to explain early in your testimony that the configuration of the area has changed. This takes the steam out of the defense. If necessary, take pictures to be introduced as evidence. This will solidify your concern for the concepts of fair play. Also, contact the road or streets department and obtain a certified street map of how it looked at the time of the collision, and if necessary, have a subpoena issued for the keeper of those maps to testify in court on the changes and the accuracy of the diagram.

Prepare a neat, hand-drawn diagram to be used in court. This diagram may be prepared on flipchart-size paper or poster board. Make it large enough for the judge and jury to easily see the diagram as you testify. Clearly mark the diagram with the notations, "not to scale" and "all measurements approximate." These disclaimers will save the embarrassment of attack for lack of precision.

The little extras that you, the officer, put into your testimony will help assure a conviction. Pictures and diagrams of the factual data readily assist the jury or judge in reaching a determination. These items break up the monotony of verbal testimony with tangibles which can be seen and scrutinized. Couple good diagrams, photographs, and blood alcohol results with solid, honest testimony.

When the date of the trial arrives, be prompt, look sharp, and be prepared. There is no substitute for a clean, neat uniform and an officer whose bearing and quiet disposition signify that he or she is there to do business. Even the most inexperienced prosecutor should know the ground rules for getting you on the stand and admitting evidence that you will present. Remember, you will present the case for the state, first in order. It is your first impression that will be remembered by the jury. Avoid being overbearing or confident. Keep the testimony simple and avoid jargon language. Sit straight and avoid leaning forward to rest your arms on the railing to the front. You will be excused from the stand soon enough. Give the defense attorney yes and no answers.

Tape recordings made of the defendant while in your custody are extremely advantageous for the prosecutor. If you prepared a tape recording, the prosecutor may wish to save the tape until after the defendant has had an opportunity to testify. The prosecutor can then recall you to the stand to play the recording for the benefit of the jury. The tape is admissible as evidence to ascertain the quality of vocal inflections and clarity of voice. An opportunity to hear a cursing or tongue-tied drunk does wonders for the state's case.

In conclusion, this chapter has presented a methodology for an officer to follow the intoxicated driver from first observation to conviction. The reason for this war on intoxicated drivers is an obvious one. Drinking drivers kill and maim more people than all the murderers since the turn of the century. The conviction of even one intoxicated driver is a victory in the fight for a safe community.

In the pages following, there is a sample arrest and investigation report for the intoxicated driver (Fig. 6-1).

DISCUSSION QUESTIONS

1. Defense attorneys often request a pretrial hearing with a motion to suppress the evidence in drinking- or drug-related crimes. To offset the probability of suppression, what rules must be applied by the officers in your jurisdiction? (Laws of search and seizure of evidence and various exclusionary rules.)

ARREST – INVESTIGATION REPORT

COURT Pac. Palisades	FILE NUMBER 0781-31 M
AREA 470	COLLISION REPORT NUMBER N/A

SUBJ. NO. 1	DATE OF [X] ARREST [ ] REPORT July 4, 1981	TIME OF ARREST/INCIDENT 2330	LOCATION OF ARREST/INCIDENT W/B I-80 at Delaplane

CITATION NUMBER MZ36-C14	OFFENSE(S) CHARGED OR INVESTIGATED 23102a CVC Driving While Intoxicated

NAME (LAST, FIRST, MIDDLE) Murphy, Samuel Cleveland	RESIDENCE ADDRESS 1589 17th St. Symington, CA 90013

RACE Cauc.	SEX M	BIRTHDATE 03-13-47	HAIR Red	EYES Blue	HEIGHT 5-11	WEIGHT 185

DRIVER'S LICENSE NUMBER S 173440	STATE CA	703/773-9136	PLACE OF BIRTH (CITY, STATE, COUNTRY) Tampa Bay, Florida

EMPLOYER City Center Lumber Comp.	ADDRESS 137 Flora Symington, CA 90013

BOOKING, CII, FBI, ETC. NUMBER(S) EE2340-81	WHERE BOOKED/CONFINED Crown County Jail	DATE/TIME BOOKED OR TURNED OVER 0105 07-05-81

JUVENILE NOTIFICATION (WHO, HOW, TIME) N/A	FINGER PRINTED [X] YES [ ] NO

NOTIFYING OFFICIAL N/A	DDL STATUS valid	DATE/TIME DDL CHECK 0110 07-05-81	METHOD OF CHECK [X] TT [ ] MAIL [ ] PHONE

VEHICLE

LICENSE 702 WZK	STATE CA	YEAR 81	VIN'EN NUMBER 7D31F041736	VEHICLE WAS [X] STORED [ ] RECOVERED [ ] IMPOUNDED

YEAR OF VEHICLE 80	MAKE Toyota	BODY STYLE Land Cruiser	COLOR Red/White	CHP 180 SUBMITTED [X] YES [ ] NO

LOCATION OF VEHICLE/RELEASED TO A & M Automotive Towing	ADDRESS 439 Poplar Symington, CA 90013 703/773-9851

NAME OF REGISTERED OWNER	[X] SAME AS DRIVER	ADDRESS	[X] SAME AS DRIVER

NAME OF LEGAL OWNER Crown County Trust & Savings	[ ] SAME AS R/O	ADDRESS 181 Commerce St. Symington, CA 90013

WITNESS

AGE	SEX	NAME	PASSENGER	VICTIM	ADDRESS	PHONE RES./BUS.
		Jack Simson, I.D. 44	[ ]	[ ]	Symington P.D.	BUS. 703/773-9900
		Susan Peterson, R.N.	[ ]	[ ]	C & C Labs 315 No. 10th St. Symington, CA 90013	703/773-9220
30	F	Darlene Anne Murphy	[X]	[ ]	1589 17th St. Symington, CA	703/773-9136

ADMONITION OF RIGHTS

1. YOU HAVE THE RIGHT TO REMAIN SILENT.
2. ANYTHING YOU SAY CAN AND WILL BE USED AGAINST YOU IN A COURT OF LAW.
3. YOU HAVE THE RIGHT TO TALK TO A LAWYER AND HAVE HIM PRESENT WITH YOU WHILE YOU ARE BEING QUESTIONED.
4. IF YOU CANNOT AFFORD TO HIRE A LAWYER, ONE WILL BE APPOINTED TO REPRESENT YOU BEFORE QUESTIONING, IF YOU WISH.

THE ABOVE STATEMENT WAS READ TO THE ARRESTEE BY Officer Jack Simpson	I.D. 44	TIME 2348

DO YOU UNDERSTAND EACH OF THESE RIGHTS I HAVE EXPLAINED TO YOU? [X] YES [ ] NO	HAVING THESE RIGHTS IN MIND, DO YOU WISH TO TALK TO US NOW? [X] YES [ ] NO	SUBJECT'S WAIVER STATEMENT "Sure, why not ..."

MISDEMEANOR INCARCERATION *(To be completed upon a physical arrest for any misdemeanor, pursuant to Penal Code Section 853.6.)*

The person arrested:

1. [ ] was so intoxicated as to be a danger to himself/herself or others.
2. [ ] required medical examination or medical care or was otherwise unable to care for his/her own safety.
3. [X] was charged with one or more of the offenses listed in Section 40302 of the Vehicle Code. *(Note paragraphs five and eight.)*
4. [ ] had one or more outstanding arrest warrants issued.
5. [ ] could not provide satisfactory evidence of personal identification.
6. [ ] if released immediately would jeopardize the prosecution of the offense or offenses for which arrested or the prosecution of any other offenses.
7. [X] would be reasonably likely to continue the offense or offenses, or the safety of persons or property would be imminently endangered if immediately released.
8. [ ] demanded to be taken before a magistrate or refused to sign the citation.
9. [ ] was not released for one or more of the reasons specified above, or

ARRESTING OFFICER (NAME/RANK) Jack Simpson	I.D. NO. 44	SUPERVISOR (NAME/RANK) Charles Alexander, SGT	I.D. NO. 17	DATE 07-05-81

FIGURE 6-1. Sample Intoxication Arrest Report

INTOXICATION INTERROGATION

DO YOU KNOW OF ANYTHING MECHANICALLY WRONG WITH YOUR VEHICLE? DESCRIBE.	ARE YOU SICK OR INJURED? DESCRIBE.
☐ YES ☒ NO	☐ YES ☒ NO "I'm a picture of health..."

ARE YOU DIABETIC OR EPILEPTIC?	DO YOU TAKE INSULIN? (PILLS OR INJECTION)	DO YOU HAVE ANY PHYSICAL DEFECTS? DESCRIBE. (FEET, LEGS, ANKLES OR HIPS)
☐ YES ☒ NO	☐ YES ☒ NO	☒ YES ☐ NO "I gott'a a tennis elbow..." Right

WHEN DID YOU LAST SLEEP?	HOW LONG?	WHEN DID YOU LAST EAT?	DESCRIBE
Last night	8 hours	Dinner tonight	"Steak with all'a trimmings..."

WERE YOU DRIVING THE VEHICLE?	IF NO, WHO?	WHERE DID YOU START DRIVING?	WHERE WERE YOU GOING?
☒ YES ☐ NO ☐ N/A	"Wasn't the 'ol lady"	"The Sands"	"Home"

WHERE ARE YOU NOW?	WHAT HAVE YOU BEEN DRINKING?	HOW MUCH?	TIME STARTED	TIME STOPPED
"13th Street..."	"A little wine with dinner..."	"2 glasses"	"7 PM"	"10 PM"

WHERE WERE YOU DRINKING?	DO YOU FEEL THE EFFECTS OF THE DRINKS? DESCRIBE.
"At the Sands"	☐ YES ☒ NO "Not at all..."

DID YOU BUMP YOUR HEAD?	HAVE YOU BEEN DRINKING SINCE THE ACCIDENT?	WHAT?	HOW MUCH?
☐ YES ☒ NO	☐ YES ☐ NO ☒ N/A	N/A	N/A

ARE YOU UNDER CARE OF DOCTOR OR DENTIST?	IF YES, NAME AND ADDRESS
☐ YES ☒ NO	N/A

HAVE YOU TAKEN ANY MEDICINE OR DRUGS?	IF YES, WHAT	HOW MUCH?	TIME OF LAST DOSAGE
☒ YES ☐ NO	"Just vitamins...multicaps"	1	Breakfast

DO YOU FEEL THE EFFECTS OF THE DRUGS? DESCRIBE.
"Good Heavens...No!"

FIELD SOBRIETY TEST - ALCOHOL/DRUGS

BREATH ODOR OF ALCOHOL		GLASSES/LENSES
☐ STRONG ☒ MOD sweet ☐ WEAK		☐ YES ☒ NO

HEEL TO TOE/WALKING LINE TEST △ L. FOOT ○ R. FOOT

3. Demonstrated 7 steps to left headlamp and back 7 steps. He walked like a tight rope walker, arms out and dipping up and down. Not once touching heel to toe. Took 11 steps; used vehicle for support on turn; came back 14 steps. Steps 6 to 12 inches apart.

ATTITUDE
Cooperative throughout contact

EYES
Reddened and watery

SPEECH Slow, lethargic; difficulty with multi-syllable words.

CLOTHING WORN/CONDITION AND DESCRIPTION Gold metal watch, wedding band.
Grey slacks, whiteshirt open at the neck, new black shoes, grey socks.

DESCRIBE TEST LOCATION, SURFACE, WEATHER AND LIGHTING
Shoulder of I-80 beneath overhead lighting at Delaplane. Clean...Flat.

IDENTIFY AND DESCRIBE EACH TEST GIVEN
1. Modified Position of Attention: Demonstrated...He separated his feet approximately 6 inches, tipped back his head, shut his eyes and started off balance in approximately 3 to 4 seconds, reopening his eyes. Attempted 3 times.

2. Finger to Nose Test: Demonstrated...Right index finger to inside corner of his right eye. Left index finger to mid-left cheek. Right index finger to the bridge of his nose, slid his finger down to the tip of his nose, pressing the tip of his nose flat. "See I found it...I told you I was alright..." Left index finger to mid-bridge of nose with second joint of finger.

4. Alphabet: (B.A. degree in Business Administration) "ABCD...F-H-I-K...M-N-O-P-S-T-Z... This is dumb...who remem'ers the al-a-bet..."

5. Lateral Nystagmus: Distinct bounce to both eyes.

IMPLIED CONSENT 13353 V.C.

YOU ARE REQUIRED BY STATE LAW TO SUBMIT TO A CHEMICAL TEST TO DETERMINE THE ALCOHOLIC CONTENT OF YOUR BLOOD. YOU HAVE A CHOICE OF WHETHER THE TEST IS TO BE OF YOUR BLOOD, BREATH OR URINE. IF YOU REFUSE TO SUBMIT TO A TEST OR FAIL TO COMPLETE A TEST YOUR DRIVING PRIVILEGE WILL BE SUSPENDED FOR A PERIOD OF SIX MONTHS. YOU DO NOT HAVE THE RIGHT TO TALK TO AN ATTORNEY OR TO HAVE AN ATTORNEY PRESENT BEFORE STATING WHETHER YOU WILL SUBMIT TO A TEST, BEFORE DECIDING WHICH TEST TO TAKE, OR DURING THE ADMINISTRATION OF THE TEST CHOSEN. IF YOU ARE INCAPABLE, OR STATE YOU ARE INCAPABLE, OF COMPLETING THE TEST YOU CHOOSE, YOU MUST SUBMIT TO AND COMPLETE ANY OF THE REMAINING TESTS OR TEST.

THE ABOVE STATEMENT WAS READ TO THE ARRESTEE BY: Officer Jack Simpson	I.D. 44	TIME 2345

☒ BLOOD ☐ BREATH ☐ URINE ☐ DL 367 COMPLETED ☐ REFUSED	TIME 07-05-80 1. 0035 2.	I.D. OF SAMPLE 81-1737	RESULTS, IF AVAILABLE N/A	DISPOSITION OF SAMPLE Retained by lab.

LOCATION WHERE TEST CONDUCTED 315 No. 10th St. Symington, CA 90013	NAME AND TITLE OF PERSON GIVING TEST OR TAKING SAMPLE Susan Peterson, R.N.

FIGURE 6-1. *(cont.)*

SUPPLEMENTAL/NARRATIVE	DATE OF ORIGINAL INCIDENT	TIME (24H)	NCIC NUMBER	OFFICER I.D.	NUMBER	PAGE
(Check one)	мо. 07 day 04 yr. 81	2330	9470	44	0781-31M	3

<table>
<tr><td>☐ NARRATIVE CONTINUATION TRAFFIC COLLISION REPORT</td><td colspan="2">LOCATION/SUBJECT
I-80 at Delaplane</td><td>CITATION NUMBER
MZ36-C14</td></tr>
<tr><td>☐ SUPPLEMENTAL TRAFFIC COLLISION REPORT</td><td colspan="2">Murphy</td><td>BEAT
32</td></tr>
<tr><td>☒ OTHER: 23102a CVC
Driving While Intoxicated</td><td>CITY/COUNTY
Symington</td><td>Crown</td><td>REPORTING DISTRICT
470</td></tr>
</table>

DRIVING OBSERVATIONS:

I was W/B on I-80 approximately one mile east of Delaplane. At approximately 2320 hours on 07-04-81, I noticed brake lights on several vehicles ahead and traffic slowed in all lanes. I closed to note a slow moving, red and white Toyota Land Cruiser taking all three W/B lanes in slow arcing movements. The speed of the Toyota ranged from 35 to approximately 50 miles per hour. A light green Chevrolet attempted to pass the Toyota when the Toyota arced into the W/B lane. The Chevrolet was in the W-1. The Toyota increased its speed and swung across the W-3 and into a half straddle position of the W-1 lane, forcing the Chevrolet into the center divider to avoid collision. As the Chevrolet accelerated away in front of the Toyota, the Toyota swung slowly back to the W-2 lane and towards the shoulder on the right aiming directly for a disabled truck-tractor and semi-trailer which was displaying the four-way flashing emergency lights. The Toyota pulled out abruptly just short of another collision. I pulled into a position approximately 50 to 100 feet to the rear of the Toyota and turned on the emergency overhead lights. Traffic to the rear slowed. The Toyota continued to arc through the three lanes with no apparent recognition from the driver. I then applied the white spot lamp and swept the beam through the rear window of the Toyota...still no recognition. I turned on the siren and continued the use of all the lights. Recognition came approximately one quarter mile west of Delaplane and the driver slowed to approximately ten miles per hour and pulled into the W-3 lane. He stuck his left arm out the driver's window and motioned me to pass. Finally the Toyota was brought to a slow stop as the driver drove over the berm on the right shoulder, arced back out into the W-3 lane and stopped with the right front tire abutted into the berm. The vehicle was stopped at an approximately 20° angle to the road.

DRIVER CONTACT OBSERVATIONS:

I met the driver at the open driver's window, and explained the reason for the stop. I asked him to step out and forward. As he attempted to exit the Toyota, he missed the step and fell, breaking his fall when he hooked his right arm through the open window and supported himself with the door. The driver regained his footing, shut the door and walked forward running his right hand along the hood of the vehicle for support.

The driver was identified as Samuel Cleveland Murphy by a valid appearing California driver's license, which he found in his brown billfold. He turned the billfold over in his hands several times, flipping through the plastic windows, passing over his driver's license at least four times before noting its location. In thumbing the driver's license out of the

PREPARED BY				REVIEWED BY		
NAME	I.D. NUMBER	MO. DAY YR.	NAME		MO. DAY YR.
[signature]	44	07 05 81			

FIGURE 6-1. *(cont.)*

SUPPLEMENTAL/NARRATIVE (Check one)	DATE OF ORIGINAL INCIDENT	TIME (2400)	NCIC NUMBER	OFFICER I.D.	NUMBER	PAGE
	MO. 07 DAY 04 YR. 81	2330	9470	44	0781-31M	4
☐ NARRATIVE CONTINUATION TRAFFIC COLLISION REPORT	LOCATION/SUBJECT I-80 at Delaplane				CITATION NUMBER MZ36-C14	
☐ SUPPLEMENTAL TRAFFIC COLLISION REPORT	Murphy				BEAT 32	
☒ OTHER: 23102a CVC Driving While Intoxicated	CITY/COUNTY Symington Crown				REPORTING DISTRICT 470	

holder, he extracted a B of A Mastercharge card and handed it to me as his license. Returning the Mastercharge card, I asked for the driver's license in the adjoining window. He broke the plastic window getting it out with his thumb, and handed it to me upside down. All the time we were talking it was noted that he supported himself against the front bumper of the Toyota and had difficulty with unaided standing.

FIELD SOBRIETY TEST:

See Page 2 for details. Mr. Murphy could not perform satisfactorily.

ARREST:

Mr. Murphy was arrested for violation of Section 23102a CVC, Driving While Intoxicated. The arrest is based on observations of his driving, personal observations of his intoxication, and his inability to perform the Field Sobriety Tests in a satisfactory manner. He was booked in the Crown County Jail following the Chemical Testing.

CHEMICAL TESTING:

See Page 2 for details. Blood test selected and administered at 0035 hours on 07-05-81 by Ms. Susan Peterson, R.N. of C & C Labs. The 5cc sample was retained by the lab for analysis. I.D. 81-1737

ADDITIONAL FACTS:

Darlene Murphy, wife of driver, does not drive and elected to be transported home via Symington Taxi. Driver, Murphy gave her his brown billfold prior to her departure. The Toyota Land Cruiser was stored at A & M Automotive Towing. Storage report completed on the vehicle, release to registered owner or agent.

PREPARED BY					REVIEWED BY		
NAME	I.D. NUMBER	MO.	DAY	YR.	NAME	MO. DAY YR.
	44	07	05	81		

FIGURE 6-1. (cont.)

2. Are violators arrested for driving while intoxicated in your jurisdiction required to submit to a chemical test to determine the blood alcohol concentration in their system? If so, what is the level of presumption of guilt? What is the penalty for refusing to take the test?

3. Does a video or sound tape recording of the police officers conversation with the drinking driver violate the constitutional rights of self-incrimination?

4. Short of involvement in a collision, is there any one observation that could conceivably have more weight in court testimony than another, or would you as a jury member be more inclined to believe an officer who testifies to a number of observations associated with intoxication?

7

Human Factors: Psychological

The human being is the most sophisticated element of the traffic equation. Both pedestrian and driver must be understood in human terms and not solely as a number in a column of statistics. There are a number of limitations which must be considered when discussing people in terms of traffic. Inasmuch as our machines have characteristic limitations that prevent them from going faster or further, our bodies, too, have boundries of adaptation to such factors as stress, vision, hearing, maturity, intellect, attitudes, and learned behavior.

CULTURE

Most countries of the world are now multicultural. The best example of this is the United States. For example, Orange County in California has no less than thirty-two separate languages being spoken in the homes. This represents thirty-two cultures, each with its own philosophies, ideologies, environments, educational standards, and genetic backgrounds. The problem is that there must be only one law. Everyone is expected to act, react, and obey just one set of rules. This problem is not just in California. Illinois, Florida, Texas, and New York are other examples. These myriad cultures and, in particular, the first generation of those cultures to be in this country, are tied to the customs of their ancestors and the dichotomy of cross-cultural acclimation. Societal customs are often in direct conflict with the

107

laws of the United States. There is a great deal of conflict to resolve regarding laws which pertain to driving an automobile. Some countries have few, if any, regulations concerning driving, and so the individual has become accustomed to the idea that the loudest horn and heaviest foot has the right of way. Another culturally-based concept comes from the Orient wherein a driver who simply stops to assist at the scene of a collision involving injury may become responsible for the injured party regardless of who caused the collision. As a consequence, certain drivers coming to the United States from Oriental countries will not stop when they become involved in a collision, regardless of who was at fault. Some misconceptions arise over religious convictions. In certain Arab nations, a drinking driver will be executed for driving while intoxicated, since alcoholic beverages and intoxication are forbidden on religious grounds. Imagine being an officer trying to stop a vehicle driven by someone of this culture when drinking and driving are suspected.

MOOD AND TEMPERAMENT

The various licensing authorities issue a license to anyone passing the driver's test. The driver population is comprised, therefore, of the elderly, the young, the infirm or handicapped, the near-blind, and everyone in between. Unfortunately, the human machine is not completely predictable. The driver going to work in the morning is not the same person that drives home in the evening. Moods and temperaments change on a random basis. Casper Milktoast becomes Leo the Lion behind the wheel of an automobile, asserting his aggression and relieving his frustration at the end of a busy day at work. This phenomenon is equally true for men and women. A 90-pound man or woman behind the wheel of a 3,000-pound automobile is as big as anyone else on the road and will command the same respect.

Collision Candidates

Mood plays a decisive role in collisions that follow a negative interpersonal reaction. The salesman-driver who just lost an important sale is not the same prudent salesman-driver who yesterday made a big sale. The employee-driver who experienced a difficult day with his supervisor is inattentive to his responsibilities as a driver. His mood is one of depression much like the salesman who lost an important sale. Both of these drivers are candidates for a collision. Their vision becomes narrow and fixed, and they will see very little of what is going on around them. Their minds follow the bouncing ball of the day's game, centering around the questions of why they lost. They become very paranoid and ego-centered. In repeated instances they are very remorseful and in severe instances, suicidal.

Suicide Attempts. Although the number of suicides involving fatal collisions will never be known, we are aware that in approximately 50 percent of the fatal collisions investigated, the driver was under the influence of alcohol or drugs. We also know that alcohol and drugs are self-induced and lower inhibitions and social restraints. With an altered state of mind and mood with alcohol, many suicides are reported as traffic collisions. It is very difficult to discern the driver's state-of-mind after the fact in a fatal collision. A number of investigators suspect suicide but are at a loss to record their impressions without factual knowledge or precollision information and state-of-mind conditions.

The Romans observed the effects of alcohol and developed a saying that translated, "In the wine, there is truth." Experienced officers know this observation to be true. A person under the influence of alcohol or drugs tends to reveal mood or temperment in unrestrained speech and actions. An aborted suicide attempt that results in a nonfatal collision can be more easily investigated in terms of statements. The responsible party will usually have a somewhat detached, matter-of-fact disposition that will vacillate between a complete nervous breakdown and normalcy. Statements become important in light of the fact that a suicide attempt, although itself not a crime, is also not investigated as a motor-vehicle collision. The concept of "accident" has been replaced by "intentional act." If others are injured or killed as the result of an intentional act, the penal code applies. The charge could be one of several degrees of murder or manslaughter.

Suicides often leave "hesitation marks" or other signs of a last minute change of mind. Homicide investigators see evidence of this fact in small wrist cuts on "bleeder" suicide attempts who will cut their wrists, but not deep enough to cause traumatic fatal bleeding. Traffic investigators will often find a simular clue in cases where a suicide drives at a high rate of speed into a concrete pillar or over a cliff. At the last moment the driver, depending upon resolve, or lack thereof, may apply the brakes, leaving a short set of locked-wheel skid marks just prior to impact.

When investigating such a premise, attempt to reenact the driver's last day. As an example, one young man had a serious falling-out with his girlfriend at a party in the presence of a number of friends. His ego suffered a major blow since his friends were aware of his inability to maintain his relationship with the woman. He told several of his friends that life was not worth living without her. He left the group, driving to yet another party. At the second function, he appeared to be in a jovial and congenial mood. According to witnesses, he was the life of the party, not at all drunk or depressed, but "alive" and looking better than he had in a long time. At the conclusion of the party, the young man stayed behind to tell everyone good-by. Note that he did not say, "good night" or "see you tomorrow." He said "good-by." Having consumed sufficient alcohol to raise his blood alcohol to a 0.13 percent, the young man left presumably to go home. He entered the freeway at an off-ramp traveling the wrong way, taking traffic head-on, at 60 MPH. Two vehicles successfully evaded collision by swerving out of his way. A third vehicle was not so fortunate. The young man's hesitation was evidenced by last minute swerving with the first two vehicles, and a last minute break application. With the third vehicle, it was a headlamp to headlamp collision. The third vehicle did apply his brakes and was at a near stop. The young man did not apply his brakes, nor did he swerve. He accomplished what he set out to do and put an additional four people in the hospital in critical condition. This story is a common example of vehicular suicide where the responsible party wants to make a statement of anxiety and frustration born of depression. His victim could be anyone; however, he will invariably seek a victim. The investigative clue is the sudden mood-swing from depression to elation.

Angry Drivers. Temperament is a commonplace collision factor evident in a driver's state-of-mind. The suicide had evidenced a marked change of personality from aggression and hostility to one of secret resolve, which was masked behind gregarious behavior. He made a plan and, mentally accepting the plan, he had no more worries. Thus, he could be fun-loving up to the moment of truth. In contrast, when the temper flares in an individual, a common release is to take his frustration to the highway, usually in high speed driving. The result is a second cousin to a suicide attempt. When involved in a collision, the rage-filled driver will usually be angry with the world. Invariably, the temperamental driver finds fault with the other driver and vents an incessant rendering of his or her opinion to the investigator. The collision may not have been intentional, but, then again, maybe it was. Some people fill their need for attention by becoming involved in a collision. The collision is a method of asking for pity; an attention getting device. A number of collisions are actually vehicular assaults acted out in the rage of a temper tantrum.

Attention-Getters. It is not at all uncommon for a child to grow into adulthood handling frustration by breaking things or throwing objects to relieve anxiety. Having established an unchecked pattern of behavior for control of stress, the immature driver gets behind the wheel of a vehicle and vents frustration by speeding, cutting through traffic, and gambling with signals at intersections. When the collision occurs, this driver insists that it is the fault of the other party. This psychological-release mechanism worked as a child and probably went unchecked into adult life. Someone else usually accepted the responsibility for the abnormal behavior. When a person handles stress in this manner as a child and into adulthood, the established modes produce even more frustration and anxiety when the adult society neither accepts nor appreciates this abnormal behavior. Society, in the form of the police and courts, assumes the surrogate role of parent for this person, punishing antisocial or illegal behavior. Too often this person finds the courts unresponsive and repeats the crime again and again until someone pays attention. A number of alcoholics fall into this pattern, complaining that no one is paying attention to them and their needs. In short, neither alcoholics nor the person expressing frustration with a temper tantrum have learned how to deal with adult stress. Their psychological-maturation level is still back in their childhood. They have tempter tantrums and fits of anxiety that are rewarded rather than being punished as unacceptable behavior. The Institute of Transportation Studies of the University of California noted in *The Fundamentals of Traffic Engineering* that impatience, anger, and immaturity along with a negative attitude towards regulation were not at all uncommon expressions with precollision drivers.

Physiological Problems. Mood and temperament changes may be connected to physiological problems. For example, a number of persons suffering from diabetic shock, or low blood-sugar, will evidence a number of the symptoms of an intoxicated driver. The temperament of these persons is also vastly changed, often times from rational to irrational. For this reason, the drinking diabetic is truly a double threat to the safety of the motoring public. When in shock, the diabetic requires immediate medical attention. A number of officers and investigators carry small packets of sugar in the patrol units for just such emergencies.

Officers and investigators also encounter drivers who appear to be suffering from some form of personality change due to epileptic seizures. The epileptic loses touch with reality and has little or no control over the muscular-mechanical skills required to drive a vehicle.

Persons with either of these infirmaties may be licensed to drive under certain conditions, usually with medical certification that the seizures have been under control for a given period of time. It is most tragic when a "closet" diabetic or epileptic has a driver's license because he "forgot" to advise the licensing agency of the problem or overlooked the medical question on the application. Both infirmities can cause acute personality changes during shock or seizure.

ENVIRONMENTAL FACTORS

Human behavior is susceptible to a number of environmental conditions. The atmosphere around us may affect the manner in which we drive. Weather and visibility are the two biggest factors. With reduced visibility, the muscles of the eyes are strained and tire more quickly. There follows an observable psychological change in the driver. Irritability is increased due to the frustration of driving during inclement weather. This is particularly true in urban situations where the stress is compounded by stop-and-go traffic. During inclement weather, the collision rate rises dramatically. The solution to alleviate much of the problem is to shorten driving time and stop more frequently. With an increase in both physical and psychological stress, a driver is far more apt to be involved in a collision when his reaction time is reduced by tension. Under the pressure of driving in bad weather, a driver on a long or protracted journey falls prey to the lulling effects of the slap of the windshield wipers, the rhythm of the rain on the roof of the car, and the broken white lines illuminated by the headlamps. These rhythmic sights and sounds produce a drowsy near-hypnotic state, which is compounded by the desire for rest and relief from the tension and monotony.

Other environmental factors which affect human behavior in driving are the fixed facilities for traffic, signing, signals, street construction, on- and off-ramp design, lane widths, potholes, lane-divider markings, landscaping, and center-divider or median construction, among others. The traffic flow and its characteristics are also environmental and are, for the most part, uncontrollable by an individual driver. To see an example of this, observe the smooth flow of the morning commute, the different personality of the afternoon commute, and then compare your observations with the random self-serving personality of a crowd leaving a sports event. A highway for some becomes a raceway for others, and the aggression expressed in driving by a small minority becomes a battleground of defense for the majority.

One environmental factor often discussed, at times with tongue-in-cheek, is the effect of the full moon. A number of studies have been conducted in mental institutions, prisons, and through related records of crime. There is no scientific data to give the reader causal reasons or motives except for the single recurring factor of the full moon. The studies concur: A full moon will be accompanied by an increase in crime, an increase in hospital admissions, a shortness of temperament, and an increase in collisions. This factor is hardly a defense, but it is nonetheless, a reality.

OTHER PSYCHOLOGICAL FACTORS

Intelligence

The intelligence of the driver can also play a role in collision-free driving. Persons of superior intellect are sometimes found to be inattentive to their driving. A number of theories have been offered in defense of this observation. A person with a superior intellect subconsciously feels that driving time is a loss of time which could be put to better use. Another theory is that the intellectual's brain is engaged in numerous thoughts and activities far removed from the driving process of the here and now. In any event, intellectuals seem to be somewhere else until the reality of a collision or near-miss brings them temporarily back. It is for this same reason that their vision appears to tunnel and they fail to observe the peripheral activity around them. As a consequence they make poor witnesses to events that often occur immediately in front of them. Ironically, some persons of superior intellect, probably because of their gift, become outstanding and trained observers of events. This is true for those persons whose vocation includes a necessity for visual, thought, and action prowess. Most policemen have an above-average I.Q. and are easily trained observers. In conjunction with intellect is a driver's ability to learn. The learning process is primarily one of past experience. The average driver will garner little from the books except the laws and rules of the road. The same individual behind the wheel of an automobile will retain an education based on experience. He will develop skills, habits, and abilities to respond properly to the traffic environment.

Attentiveness

Attentiveness is a psychological factor in driving. Some drivers are very easily distracted by nontraffic events. A vehicle stalled on the side of the roadway is hardly a physical barrier to traffic, but watch as passing traffic will swing wide to avoid the "visual hazard." The attentive driver sees the stalled car and continues without a second thought. The inattentive driver is surprised by the sudden appearance of something out of the ordinary. The same is true for signs in store windows, and so on. Other occupants in the car will distract the driver as well, interrupting his or her attention span to discuss the events taking place ahead. Worry is a prime example of a psychological factor which directly affects attentiveness and driver skills.

Attitude Towards Regulation

Along with cultural influences that affect attitudes is the driver's natural ambivalence towards regulation. Some drivers will adhere religiously to the controls and restraints of the law. Others have no respect for the rules of the road. Many bend the regulations to fit the occasion. Some persons will wait behind a stuck red light even in the prolonged absence of any other traffic. The more disrespectful in this instance are the first to begin blowing their horns to intimidate the individual ahead into crossing the intersection. It is to the credit of the motoring public that most people are susceptible to reasonable regulation and enforcement. It is also true that most drivers will adapt to changing and unusual situations, such as detours and road closures.

Impatience

Perhaps the most noticed driver fault is impatience or anger. Many drivers react to a slow moving vehicle ahead by attempting unsafe passing maneuvers: following too closely, driving off on the shoulders to get around the procrastinator, and if nothing else, relieving their tensions by shaking their fists and "talking" to the slow mover. Some, after passing the recalcitrant slow driver, will vent their frustration by speeding, as if to show the violator a thing or two. The impatience or anger is really a display of immaturity. Taking unnecessary chances is the sort of driving one associates with the young thrill-seekers. In reality, this trait is present in nearly all drivers. Nearly everyone who drives has at one time or another vented his or her anger behind the wheel of an automobile. It is important to remember that behind the wheel of an automobile, we are in a position to intimidate others and, for a change, exert our will or vent our frustrations.

Thoughtless Driving

Much like Dr. Pavlov's dogs who would salivate at the sound of a bell, drivers exhibit a conditioned response. Predictably, most drivers have developed habits which are born of experience. Urbanites who enter a super highway in commuter traffic tend to follow a pattern as if the roadway had ruts which guide the wheels.

Caravan Driving. There is an observation of the processionary caterpillar that comes to mind. One caterpillar will follow directly behind the one ahead. A group of such caterpillars can be formed to walk in a circle, forming a ring. They will continue to walk in this circle even though food is placed in the center of the ring. They continue until some external influence redirects one of them towards the food. In the absence of an outside intervention they will continue until they die of starvation, following in the same path as the one ahead. This is the basis for the observation of conditioned response to driving. People tend to follow the tail lights ahead, anticipating rational behavior in the other driver. The vehicles will string out in a line within the same lane and at a fairly constant speed. There is nothing wrong in this until some external influence interrupts the path. We have all heard of the massive rear-end collisions that have involved as many as 200 vehicles. Driving in this manner reduces the number of decisions of the operator. This is known as caravan driving. Truck drivers have been employing this technique for years. This system reduces driver fatigue, allowing an individual to drive further before the effects of tension and driver fatigue take over. The drivers relieve each other periodically in the lead position and a new driver takes the pole position up front. The new leader then sets the pace and the others fall into position. This trick of the trade is especially helpful when driving in inclement weather; fog is the best example. This system works well, until acted upon or interrupted by the external influence of the impatient driver who causes a collision. The informal and loose association of the caravan has a personality and a character of its own. This camaraderie has been augmented by the advent of radio communications devices allowing the various drivers to communicate. This association has developed the prime example of conditioned response in the motoring community.

Radio Communication. The ability of one motorist to talk with another has been one of the biggest boons to transportation since the advent of the automobile. The transceiver is fast becoming a necessity for anyone who must drive from one urban area to another. This ability has brought the motoring public into a number of associations, both formal and informal, providing much more than just on-the-spot road and weather information. Perhaps the single most important benefit of radio two-way communication in our automobiles has been the relative ease with which a motorist may call for police and emergency services. This, too, has brought about a conditioned response, providing for a greater degree of motorist security.

The nonrhythmic and spontaneous conversations also tend to maintain a higher level of driver awareness, diminishing the effects of fatigue.

Detours. The largest psychological problem involved in the conditioned response phase of motoring is when an external influence changes a driving habit of long-standing. The best example of this is the detour placed by a highway department. For the first few days of the detour, collisions will increase in the area regardless of the signs which forewarn the motorist. The highway department has broken a habit of longstanding and the processionary caterpillar in all of us wants to proceed along the same path we have always taken.

In summary, the human characteristics which comprise our psychological make-up are affected by a number of influences both internal and external. The drivers upon our roadways come from diverse cultures, varied experiential backgrounds, and changing systems of education. All of the drivers, regardless of the thousands of origins and temperaments, must obey one set of driving rules. There are standards for anticipated behavior that must transcend all of the differences in all of the drivers. Collisions occur not by accident but by the failure of one of the participants to recognize the inherent danger in complacency to the law. There are very few real accidents. Most automobile collisions occur not by accident but by the psychological condition of one or all of the participants. Through experience and learning, we must develop an appreciation of the dangers. Through complacency or motivation, some drivers persist until the collision.

DISCUSSION QUESTIONS

1. When is the last time you took a frustration to the highway for resolution? Was it to be alone with your thoughts? Did the driving provide a release or assist in problem-resolution?
2. Do roadside signs really imprint on our consciousness, or do we move very much like the processionary caterpillar? What are the last three speed zones you drove through prior to reading this question? How fast were you going? What signs catch your attention and why?
3. Discuss the possibility that drivers who listen to and use a citizen's band or ham radio are involved in fewer collisions and why. How is the level of alertness arrested when listening to an AM or FM radio station or your car stereo tape player?
4. Have you ever driven faster than the flow of traffic for no particular reason or just to see what the car will do at a higher speed?
5. How do you vent your anger or frustration with the driver who just cut you off in traffic?

8

Human Factors: Physiological

Besides adapting to the psychological factors that operate while we drive, we must also appreciate the physical limitations that nature has genetically given us. Each of us has basically the same equipment. From birth we are aware of our hands and feet, and in time we recognize our ability to see, hear, and use our brain.

There are physical limitations to each of these abilities. It takes a certain amount of time for all of our senses to perform a given task. In this discussion, that task is the art of driving. The reader will undoubtedly make other associations as experience dictates.

VISION

The Snellen Test

Vision is undoubtedly the most important ability since driving depends on our sense of sight. Before an applicant for a driver's license may proceed with any other part of the examination process, there is some form of visual testing to be satisfactorily completed. The usual test is the Snellen Test. The eye chart is hung at certain distances from the applicant who is then asked to read certain lines. This tests a person's ability to read road signs, but it does not test for tunnel vision or visual acuity. The author was witness to an experiment where a man with 20/200 vision, which is legally blind by definition, passed the Snellen Test at a department of motor vehicles. The man is an optometrist and explained what happened in the following manner: The more near-sighted a person becomes, the more the tendency to squint, tunneling vision. The resultant picture is somewhat like the original Kodak pin-hole camera. The eye is focused on one small object at a time. When the test concluded, it was obvious to observers that this effect accounts for the driver who claims, "I just didn't see the other car." An officer should ask the participant drivers at the scene of a collision to read a sign, billboard, or a marquee when hearing a driver make this statement. When a vision problem is suspected, the officer should complete a "request for reexamination" form and have the driver retested by the department of motor vehicles or the licensing agency involved.

Restricted Licenses

Vanity plays a big role in the driver psyche. Some persons, who are not permitted legally to drive an automobile without wearing corrective lenses, will continue to drive with the glasses in the case, or on their kitchen table. When involved in a collision the driver may claim to be wearing contact lenses. The test for this is to have the driver turn in profile. As you look at the profile of the eye, the contact lens will make a shadow ring at the edge of the lens. The officer who has not seen this phenomenon should observe someone who wears contact lenses. Contacts are very easy to see at night. Hold a flashlight approximately chest high in the front of the individual in question. Flash the light skyward with just the soft penumbra, or edge of the light, shining in the subject's eyes. Observe the person again, in profile, as you stand to the side. The shadow will be very evident in the periphery of the lens.

When a driver involved in a collision has the inscription, "Must wear corrective lenses" imprinted on the license, validate that the driver was wearing glasses. In one case, a young man who had a collision in front of his home had to go inside to retrieve his glasses in order to see who or what he struck.

In actuality, most licensing examiners attempt to test to a level of 20/30. Presumably, anyone with vision more restricted will be required to wear glasses while driving. From a very practical standpoint, an officer is more than aware that this is not the case. Eyes, like the rest of our bodies, are subject to change, often within a period of months. Our driving licenses are renewable at rates that vary from one year to four years or more. Sometimes a license need not be renewed at all. This means the driver may never again have his or her vision checked in even the most cursory manner. The officer is shown an unrestricted license presented by a person who cannot even read what it says.

Drivers in Switzerland who are restricted to driving while wearing glasses must by law carry a second pair of glasses in the vehicle at all times.

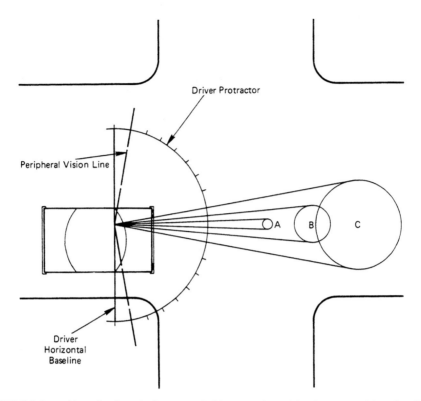

FIGURE 8-1a. Note the three basic cones of vision experienced by the average driver. Best Vision, cone A, is 3°; Clear Vision, cone B, is 10°; Satisfactory Vision, cone C, is 20°. Peripheral Vision, which ranges from 120° to 160°, is shown at 160° on the Driver Protractor. In this case, the driver is visually monitoring all traffic directly ahead and is peripherally aware of potential collision traffic at the intersection.

Physical Limitations of Normal Vision

Let us now discuss those physical limitations of vision found in the average driver. (See Fig. 8-1.)

Best Vision: Occurs within an approximate 3° cone.
Satisfactory Vision: Occurs within an approximate 20° cone.
Peripheral Vision: Varies from 120° to approximately 160°.
Clear Vision: Occurs within an approximate 10° cone.

Tunnel Vision. It is evident from the above that our cone of best vision is only 3°. This is the span of vision for some who suffer from tunnel vision. Tunnel vision is compensated for by turning the head from side to side to see. The cone of clear vision is only 10°. Street signs, signals, and markings are presumably set up to allow

118

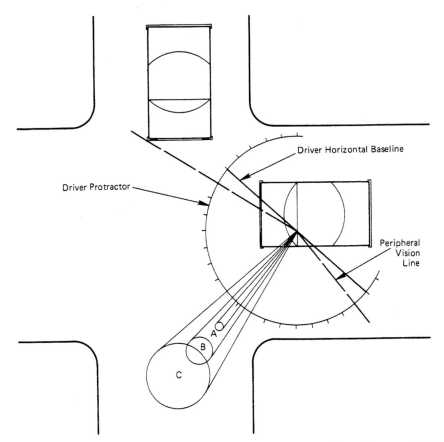

FIGURE 8-1b. When the driver of the automobile diverts his cone of best vision to the left by a mere 50°, the immediate hazard of the vehicle to the right, coming from a driveway, alley, or sidestreet, is outside of the field of peripheral vision.

for this phenomenon so that a person with vision no worse than 20/30 can read the sign within the cone of clear vision.

Satisfactory and Peripheral Vision. Most drivers have a cone of satisfactory vision of approximately 20°. The edges of this cone of satisfactory vision, from approximately 15° to 20°, do not provide the person with clear imagery. As a result, the person is forced to turn the head or eyes slightly to bring the object into focus. This same phenomenon is true of peripheral vision. We are only aware that something is out there and we must turn our head or move our eyes to see what it is. This turning of our heads or moving of the eyes is a time-consuming process. We do not instantaneously see and respond to objects outside of the cone of clear vision. The driver who wears fashion glasses, though operating the car legally, has restricted peripheral vision due to the fancy frames around the lenses.

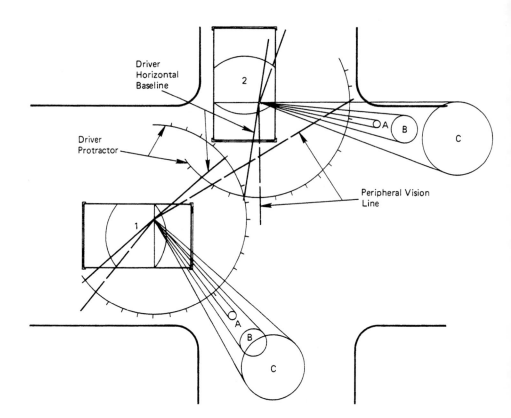

FIGURE 8-1c. When the driver of vehicle 1 diverts his attention to the right by 50°, peripheral obscurity occurs until the conflict vehicle 2 collides with the distracted driver in vehicle 1. As the driver of vehicle 2 enters the through street turning left, his attention is diverted to the most probable conflict from the left, thus, he is normally looking in that direction. The vehicle to the right has the right-of-way; however, vehicle 2 is obviously the first to enter into the intersection. Which driver is most at fault in the event of a collision? Consider a left turning right-of-way violation against driver 2. *Most importantly, note that neither driver's peripheral vision encompasses the other vehicle.* This phenomenon is very common in intersection collisions. Both drivers state that the other had to be traveling fast because they never saw them until the crash. The truth is that neither driver did see the other until the crash.

Some states have legislation which prevents a driver from wearing glasses with temples or supports over one-half inch wide. This law allows for peripheral vision for those persons wearing sunglasses and whose vision is otherwise normal. We have all observed the driver whose lenses look more like the bottom of an ashtray. Do you ever wonder what the driver sees beyond that which is directly in front of the vehicle? As the eyes are turned to the side, the focal length of the lens arrangement changes. This change calls for compensation in the driver, forcing a turn of the head to focus upon the object. That object may be *you* entering from a side street or crossing at a marked crosswalk. To compensate for this shortcoming, most persons with severe vision problems will drive more slowly. This often accounts for the slow moving vehicle collisions.

120

Color Blindness and Monocular Vision

Another problem faced in traffic is color blindness. Some problems can be overcome, such as by remembering that the red light is always supposed to be on the top of the official traffic control signals. The green or "go" light is always supposed to be on the bottom. Problems do occur, however, with curb markings, certain lane linemarkings, and some cautionary signs. Instead of seeing red and green, the individual may observe the markings only in shades of grey.

There are also a number of persons with driver's licenses who are blind in one eye. In short, they are tested and given a license to drive with only monocular vision. These individuals experience problems with depth perception. This complicates passing manuevers, distances to intersections, and high-speed driving. The person with only one good eye adapts or compensates by judging distance by the height of the distant objects, such as telephone poles or the size of an approaching automobile. As an experiment, attempt to judge traffic in this manner on a street corner as a pedestrian. For those with binocular vision you will find this not only difficult but nearly impossible.

Glare Vision and Recovery

The normally sighted person has another limitation which has caused a number of collisions in tunnels and long overpasses during daylight driving. The limitation is known as glare vision and recovery. This same problem occurs at night when faced with bright lights. Going from darkness into light the pupil contracts in approximately three seconds. When going from light into darkness it may take six seconds or more for the pupil to dilate. This problem is greatly enhanced for those who wear corrective lenses and for the elderly. Glasses tend to diffuse the light, slowing pupil recovery. Old age tends to compound our problems with slower muscular response. Genetics may also be a contributing factor in vision although this is still an area for extensive research.

Officers involved in nighttime pursuits may wish to take advantage of the physiological limitations of the glare vision recovery phenomenon. Bright lights directed at the driver of the suspect vehicle will confound his vision. Sweeping a spotlight across the recalcitrant driver's windshield will add to the glare and further tire the driver's eyes. Unable to see, the driver is forced to slow down to a point where the pursuit can be handled at safer speeds to a hopefully uneventful stop in a routine manner. The use of a high intensity light across the windshields and rear view mirrors is a very successful tool at the officer's command.

The Effect of Drugs

Many drugs affect vision and response to the observed signals. When an intoxicated person tries to focus on an object, frequently the muscles of the eyes refuse to cooperate. Alcohol is a central-nervous-system depressant and, by definition, a drug. It has long been known that many illegal compounds, such as LSD and PCP, distort vision. Marijuana also affects visual perception, particularly in the area of depth perception and spacial relationships. A six inch curb may appear to be a foot tall. The person under the influence of drugs may raise his foot way up in the air to accommodate the seemingly high step. Heroin addicts also have vision problems and can become quite lethargic. In contrast, cocaine users become quite hyperactive and, behind the wheel of an automobile, behave more like a 0.10 (blood alcohol concentration) drinking driver. Tranquilizers and a great number of prescribed and over-the-counter drugs give the user a false sense of euphoria and well-being. These drugs, too, distort the vision of the victim, making driving difficult.

Orthokerotology

There is a movement afoot across the United States and Europe to exercise a program of reshaping the lens of the myopic or near-sighted eye through the use of a specially designed contact lens. This process is known as orthokerotology. It has been discovered that by developing a lens that fits over the exterior of the eye, reshaping the natural lens, a temporary transformation takes place. This contact lens presses against the eye and causes a change in the focal length of the eye, bringing it back to a more normal state. When the process was first developed, it was thought that this prosthetic device—which allowed normal vision while worn—would force the eye back into a more perfect shape, or at least the lens portion thereof. It was found that the eye could be reshaped and the focal length returned to normal. The reconditioning process was successful on a temporary basis. Many people seeking employment which required 20/20 vision utilized the process prior to taking the vision examinations. News of the process spread by word of mouth. Airline pilots, police candidates, and others were able to pass their examinations in this manner. But, the process has thus far been *temporary*. The eye appears to return to its original state, and the vision problem is back. In the meantine, however, the examination problem is past and the license renewed or the employment application approved. This process was and is being utilized by drivers who wish to renew their driver's licenses. Again, it is necessary for the traffic officer to *think vision* and set the reexamination process in motion for any driver suspected of not being able to see well enough to drive.

Glaucoma

Glaucoma is a malady that is primarily associated with the elderly. This condition dims vision with a translucent screen in front of the lens of the eye. Unfortunately, many people are not aware of their problem, and as with so many other infirmities, they adjust to the problem in various ways. There is little reason to let this malady go undetected; most optometrists are equipped to detect the problem and institute a treatment program. There is little an officer can do to detect this problem in the field, short of asking the person to read signs, and so on. If the officer notes that the individual has a problem, it is her obligation to institute action to cause retesting. The purpose of retesting is two-fold. The officer is: (1) assisting the individual with the problem, and (2) protecting society, particularly the motoring community.

HEARING

A deficiency in auditory acuity can be enhanced by the use of hearing aids, just as glasses aid the nearsighted. A hearing deficiency is really no major problem to drivers. Most people who suffer from failing auditory response accommodate to the loss. Most drivers are accustomed to not really hearing what is going on around them. The radio or stereo is playing, the air conditioning unit may be going, people are talking, and the normal vehicle sounds tend to drown out external sounds. The following experiment is demonstrated to a number of police cadets. The cadets are placed in a vehicle with the windows down and told to look straight forward. The driver is instructed to proceed at 55 to 60 miles per hour in a rural, open area. A second police unit approaches from the rear with the siren blaring. The cadets are asked to respond when they hear anything unusual. Few cadets note any unusual sounds until the approaching unit is within 50 to 100 feet. Then, blanks are fired from a gun simulating warning shots. Few cadets ever hear the blanks even when the approaching vehicle is passing the unit with the cadets.

It is apparent that drivers rely very little on external sounds to guide their driving habits. A pedestrian on the other hand depends on motoring sounds to gauge the speed of an oncoming vehicle or to second guess the unexpected. Pedestrians rely heavily on sound cues.

Tied to hearing are the semicircular canals. This is one of the three tubular structures in the labyrinth of the ear. They serve as the organ for equilibrium. The semicircular canals control our feelings of stability. A number of physical maladies can upset the canals to a degree, causing feelings of instability. Drugs and alcohol, which depress the central nervous system, also directly affect the stability response. This is why a balance test is given to a suspected intoxicated driver. The loss of the sensation of stability eliminates a driver's awareness of the hazards of potholes, rough roads, sharp curves, bumps, dips, and sudden changes in vehicle direction.

To compensate for the loss of hearing, some states require that a driver maintain no less than two outside mirrors, one on each side of the vehicle. Most new vehicles are now equipped in this fashion.

P.I.E.V. THEORY

What It Is

P.I.E.V. stands for perception, intellection, emotion, and volition. It takes approximately three-quarters of a second for an average person to react to any given situation. This conclusion was based on an experiment using a driving simulator, where a driver was anticipating the unexpected. This conclusion failed to account for the fact that *driving* is not the same as *manipulating a driving simulator.* The only distractions in a simulator are a light bulb and a stop watch. In traffic, there are hours of boredom and moments of panic, and a continuous need for quick decision-making. The necessity for a lane change, stopped traffic ahead, a sudden turning movement, or any one of a thousand situations can be cause for alarm or simply a decision to do nothing. Often, while driving, we make a conscious decision to *continue,* uninterrupted by others. So many times we poise our foot above the brake pedal in preparation for a stop, only to decide that what we observed is no longer a hazard, or will not be a hazard as we enter the area of conflict.

The three-quarters of a second that we called reaction time is actually the muscular-mechanical time involved in moving our feet to the pedals, preparing to move the steering wheel, and repositioning our hands.

There is a much more important phase to all of this, which we have until now neglected. Exactly what goes on inside our nervous system once we are presented with the proper stimuli is explained in the theory of P.I.E.V.[1]

Perception: There is a time element involved in which a driver must visually observe a situation and perceive what is taking place. This is why driver vision is so terribly important. If a driver cannot focus upon an imminent danger confronting the path of travel, the vehicle continues into the area of conflict until perception is possible.

Intellection: The driver must now make conscious decisions based on what is understood from experience and teaching. The brain is at work. Perception and intellection both consume more time as the complexity of the situation is increased.

Emotion: Emotion is a strong surge of feeling marked by an impulse to outward expression. It is manifest by complex time-consuming bodily reactions. Emotions may restrain or adversely effect our actions. In discussing precollision conditions with participants, it is not uncommon to find that there existed a high degree of fear or anger just prior to the collision. Time is lost in overcoming emotional barriers.

Volition: Volition is the termination of uncertainty or reasoning by reaching a decision. More aptly stated, volition is the will to act. Volition is also the last step in the mental decision-making process. Volition is the mental bridge between decision and action.

What is called total P.I.E.V. time may range from one-half second to four seconds, depending on the complexity of the problem confronting the driver. The average time consumed in this process is three-quarters of a second. Thus, we find that there is a total of approximately one and one-half seconds which is consumed from first observation to action. P.I.E.V. time consumes the first three-quarters of a second, and muscular-mechanical reaction time consumes the second

[1] The theory of P.I.E.V. has been observed and studied by a number of prestigious organizations, such as the University of Texas and Massachusetts Institute of Technology. One of the first and perhaps the leading study of this phenomenon was accomplished by the Institute of Transportation Studies at the University of California at Berkeley. This study is reported in *Fundamentals of Traffic Engineering* by Wolfgang S. Homburger and James H. Kell, 9th edition, 1977.

three-quarters of a second. This is only an approximation and may vary slightly with different drivers at different levels of anticipation, skill, and vehicle control familiarity.

Modifying Factors

There are a number of modifying factors involved in P.I.E.V. time. The most common factor is fatigue. Fatigue is induced by a lack of sleep, an overworked mind and body, monotony, travel rhythm, or rarified air when driving in the mountains. An infirmity, deformity, or disability is also directly responsible for slowing one's reaction time as well as P.I.E.V. time. Given sufficient experience, most drivers will accommodate to a disability or infirmity, however, the infirmity tends to raise this driver's anxiety level and the emotional reactions are much more intense. A person living in or with pain tends to be frustrated by the experience and lives with a higher degree of character disorder.

Alcoholic beverages and drugs are well known depressants. The combination of driving and retarded mental alertness increases P.I.E.V. time and reaction time. When intoxication or narcosis reaches certain limits, physical skills deteriorate.

There are a number of additional environmental factors that must be considered. We have previously discussed such things as climate, season, weather, light, altitude, and time of day. These items may all increase P.I.E.V. and reaction time.

In summary, there are a number of physiological factors to be considered. Vision is undoubtedly the most important factor related to driving. Poor vision invariably increases P.I.E.V. time. There is no compensation for the ability to see. Although hearing is important, it is not so much a factor that a driver cannot accommodate and compensate for its loss. Finally, there is the delineation of driver response to situations, a process which is complicated by a number of factors which may produce complex psychological and physiological responses. Courts, investigators, safety coordinators, attorneys, and traffic officers must be aware of these facts, for awareness is the ultimate key to understanding the limitations of the human being.

DISCUSSION QUESTIONS

1. Consider how the wearing of glasses diminishes the total field of vision, with peripheral vision narrowing to the rims of the glasses. What is actually seen beyond the rims of sunglasses? Can one discern color, shapes, and movement?

2. Since most roadside advisory and control signs are designed and placed for drivers with not less than 20/30 vision, how do persons with 20/60 vision or worse manage to drive an automobile without glasses?

3. How much time does it take to look into a rearview mirror, focus on what you see, then refocus on the road in front of you? What other distractions can you think of which require your attention as you are driving?

4. What psychological and physiological factors affecting P.I.E.V. time have you experienced?

9

Collision
Reconstruction

A moving vehicle operating on a roadway must react to the physical laws of natural science. The driver presumably acts according to the laws enacted for prudent collision-free driving. We have learned that the driver is subject to a combination of physiological and psychological factors. The vehicle itself does not have a personality; it is simply a machine of conveyance. Every so often a driver, either by design or lack of volition, propels his vehicle into another vehicle, or into a fixed object, or runs the vehicle off the road. Once the machine is committed to a course of action, there are a number of irreversible physical occurences. This chapter deals with the major facts of physical law and collision reconstruction. The reader will be taken step by step into this most fascinating corner of the traffic officer's responsibilities.

FEET PER SECOND

Since the advent of the first horseless carriage, drivers in the United States have referred to speed in terms of miles per hour. Most other countries of the world refer to speed in terms of kilometers per hour. All express the length of time in one hour. Since miles and kilometers can be easily converted from one to the other, and both are a fixed distance to which all agree, there is really no problem in comprehending the concept of speed in terms of miles per hour or kilometers per hour. In addition, we visually gauge our speed on the car's speedometer, and many drivers can sense speed while passing fixed objects on the side of the roadways.

Early in our school years, we learned that there are 60 seconds in a minute and that there are 60 minutes in an hour. By multiplying 60 by 60 we also know that there are 3,600 seconds in an hour. We have also learned that there are 5,280 feet in one mile. If we divide the 5,280 feet in one mile by the 3,600 seconds in one hour, we derive a figure of 1.47 feet per second. So, at the rate of one mile per hour, we are moving at a rate of 1.47 feet per second. From this we can determine how many feet per second a vehicle was moving when we know the speed of the vehicle in terms of miles per hour. Simply multiply 1.47 by the speed in miles per hour. For example, when a vehicle is moving at a rate of 60 miles per hour, multiply that rate by 1.47 to find that the vehicle is moving at a rate of 88.2 feet per second. At 35 miles per hour times 1.47, we see the vehicle is moving at a rate of 51.45 feet per second. At 90 miles per hour the vehicle is moving at a rate of 132.3 feet per second.

If we develop the mathematics in the metric system, we divide 1000 meters in a kilometer by 3600 seconds in one hour. The result is 0.278 meters per second. At one kilometer per hour, we are moving at a rate of 0.278 meters per second. If we know the speed of a vehicle in terms of K.P.H. we can simply multiply that speed times 0.278 to determine the velocity in terms of meters per second. For example, if a vehicle is moving at 50 K.P.H. we can multiply the speed times 0.278 and determine the velocity to be 13.9 meters per second. At 90 K.P.H. the vehicle is moving at a rate of 25.02 meters per second.

This determination is important for a number of reasons which become apparent in the driver equation. For example, it takes approximately two seconds for a driver to glance upward to a rear view mirror, focus on what he sees, and return his eyes to the front of his vehicle to refocus on what is there. During that simple process of looking behind him, his attention was focused away from the road. If that driver was traveling at a rate of 60 miles per hour or 88.2 feet per second, he went forward 176.4 feet while he was looking behind in the mirror. Similarly, it takes as much as three seconds to find, focus on, check, turn the head, and refocus on the roadway when using an outside mirror which is adjacent to the driver's door. In that length of time, a 60 mile per hour automobile moved forward 264.6 feet. In three seconds a vehicle moving at 90 K.P.H. will move forward 75.06 meters.

We previously noted that P.I.E.V. and reaction time consume approximately one and one-half seconds. At 60 miles per hour, a driver alerted to imminent danger will move forward an additional 132.3 feet in P.I.E.V. and reaction time before any vehicular action is taken, such as applying the brakes or changing the course of travel by turning the steering wheel. At 90 K.P.H., which equals 25.02 meters per second, the P.I.E.V. and reaction time of one and one-half seconds will consume 37.53 meters (25.02 × 1.5 = 37.53).

It is not uncommon for professional race drivers to attain speeds of 200 miles per hour. This equates to 294 feet per second, and with P.I.E.V. and reaction time, 441 feet before the vehicle course is altered in some way. Couple the time factors with the physiological factors of vision and we can see why a drinking driver is involved in so many collisions.

ROLLING FRICTION

Anyone who has ever had the misfortune of necessarily pushing a stalled vehicle by hand knows the resistance which exists between the tires and the roadway. This resistance is a very necessary item in the control of a vehicle. The ability to steer a vehicle depends on this resistance between the tire tread and the surface of the road.

As the vehicle is being propelled upon the roadway, we find it necessary from time to time to alter the course of travel. We accomplish this change in direction by turning the steering wheel which is mechanically or hydraulically connected to the tires on the road. The resistance or friction between the tire and the roadway as the tires changes direction causes the vehicle to deviate from the original line of travel. This concept is known as rolling friction.

Rolling friction and the ability of a driver to alter the path of the vehicle changes with the surface of the roadway. A smooth surface such as glare ice offers less friction between the tire and the surface of the roadway. A brushed concrete roadway offers the greatest amount of friction. The controlled turning of the vehicle obviously can be accomplished with more assurance on the concrete than on the ice. Without rolling friction, a vehicle cannot be turned, controlled, or maintained on the roadway. Hence, rolling friction is necessary to steer a vehicle. As the tire is rotating on its axle, the tread of the tire is on the roadway. The surface of the tire is being worn away by the friction which exists, and in actuality, a small amount of tire tread is left by every tire which passes over the roadway. The greater the amount of friction, the greater the amount of rubber eroded away from the tread. Ice offers little in the way of friction, and as a consequence, steering is nearly impossible. Rolling friction is also required by the drive wheels which propel the vehicle. Without rolling friction the vehicle would not move.

COEFFICIENT OF FRICTION

There are a number of ways to explain the phenomenon of friction as it relates to driving an automobile. We see that rolling friction is necessary to steer or propel a vehicle. Obviously, friction is also necessary for stopping. We know how difficult it is to stop a vehicle on ice or wet pavement; the vehicle just seems to coast with no indication of stopping until the vehicle is brought to rest by running off the roadway or colliding with another object. Conversely, on dry brushed concrete, the same vehicle seems to come to a reasonably quick stop.

Different surfaces offer different amounts of friction. The measurement of these differences is called the coefficient of friction. Technically, coefficient of friction is explained as the *ratio of the friction (retarding) force developed by a skidding wheel and the weight the wheel exerts on the pavement.*

Road Surface Factors

There are a number of road surface factors which affect the coefficient of friction.

1. Surface condition: dry, wet, snow, ice, and so on.
2. Surface construction: type, method, material, texture, and so on.
3. Surface maintenance and contamination by foreign materials.
4. Surface scouring, weathering, time, and age effects.
5. Temperature: ambient, pavement, and tire tread.
6. Effects of traffic.
7. Geometric design features.
8. Acts of nature: washouts, earthquakes, sandstorms, landslides, and so on.

The term *coefficient of friction* has another name which is used on occasion by certain experts: *drag factor*. The meaning of the two expressions is synonymous in this discussion.

The coefficient of friction on any given stretch of roadway is variable. There is no real textbook or graph which can be used to determine the exact coefficient of friction short of an actual test in the field. Coefficient of friction signifies the relationship between the rubber and the road. This number is expressed as a percentage of efficiency.

Computation of Coefficient of Friction

The small letter f is used to denote coefficient of friction. A capital letter S, used in physics formulas, connotes distance in feet. The capital letter V (for our purposes) indicates velocity in miles per hour. The formula for computing coefficient of friction is expressed:

$$f = \frac{V^2}{30\ S}$$

To determine the coefficient of friction in a given area of roadway, the officer drives the patrol vehicle at approximately 30 miles per hour, releases his foot from the accelerator, and lets the vehicle coast slowly down, decelerating to a calibrated 25 miles per hour. At the precise moment the speedometer indicates 25, the officer stands on the brakes, forcing the vehicle to a complete stop. A second officer marks the beginning and end of the skids and the vehicle is driven to the side of the road and parked while the measurements are taken. All four locked-wheel skid marks are measured precisely, and the measurements are recorded. A second set of skid marks is effected just like the first, measured, recorded, and then a third set is laid. The total of all the skid marks is added together, four from the first set, four from the second, and four from the third. The total is then divided by twelve to arrive at an average length of skid mark for any wheel in the three tests. This average skid mark is the S or distance used in the formula. The V is the 25 miles per hour.

As an example, let us suppose that after we performed three skid tests and averaged the skid marks, we find that the answer was a distance of 28 feet. We know the velocity of the test vehicle was 25 miles per hour.

1. $f = \dfrac{V^2}{30\,S}$ The basic formula.

    30 is a constant and does not change.

2. $f = \dfrac{25^2}{30 \times 28}$ Substitution of what is known into the formula.

3. $f = \dfrac{625}{840}$ Velocity is squared, or multiplied by itself.

    The constant 30 is multiplied by the skid distance.

4. $f = .744$ or 74.4%   625 is divided by 840, and the answer is 74.4 percent.

An officer should not attempt to effect test skids at a speed in excess of 40 M.P.H. In like manner, tests should not be conducted at speeds below 25 M.P.H. The 40 M.P.H speed limit for tests is quite adequate for accurate determinations in high-speed collisions and is delineated for purposes of safety. The minimal 25 M.P.H. test speed will most accurately reflect lower speed collisions such as those in residential districts. Therefore, test skids should be run at speeds between 25 to 40 M.P.H. *It is important to remember that when the speed of the collision vehicle is finally determined, the answer will reflect a minimum speed and not an average or maximum.* The process explained herein will result in a fair and impartial *minimum* speed for the collision vehicle. Test skids at higher speeds become very unpredictable in terms of vehicular behavior, particularly on restricted, narrow, or sloping surfaces. Prior to attempting the skid mark test, the officer should scrub the brakes by accelerating to 20 miles per hour or so, and applying the brakes with a full thrust to be sure that all the brakes are in good order and that no unusual conditions exist. The officer should also remember to place everything in the seat of the unit onto the floorboards or in the trunk of the cruiser to prevent being stuck with secondary missiles when the emergency stop is effected in the tests.

The coefficient of friction formula expressed in the metric system is:

$$f = \frac{V^2}{255S}$$

V is the velocity in kilometers per hour
S is the skidmark distance in meters

255 is a constant and does not change
f is the resultant coefficient of friction

SKID MARKS

There are three ways in which an automobile can leave a visible trace of rubber upon the surface of a roadway. The first is the locked-wheel skid mark. This is accomplished by deceleration when the brakes are applied. Another form of locked-wheel skid mark is evidenced when a vehicle is struck and pushed sideways. The effect of both actions decelerates the speed of the vehicle.

The second type is a centrifugal skid mark. The centrifugal skid mark is evidenced by a sudden change in direction when the wheel is turned in an attempt to steer the vehicle. The mark is left when the speed of the vehicle is such that the vehicle cannot follow the direction in which the vehicle was turned.

The third major type of skid mark is one of acceleration. This mark is left when the vehicle drive wheels are rotated faster than the movement of the vehicle. When a sudden acceleration causes the drive wheels to spin, it burns rubber from the tires as the vehicle lurches forward, accelerating to the speed of the spinning wheels.

There are, then, only three: acceleration, deceleration, and centrifugal skid marks. Any other name for skid marks is just a misnomer and another name which denotes one of these three types. There are only three things we can do with a vehicle. We can make it go, we can make it stop, or we can turn it, and each of these maneuvers depend on the action of the rubber meeting the road.

Locked-Wheel Skid Marks

When the brakes of a vehicle are applied with sufficient force to cause skidding, there are several factors evident. First, we are aware that the vehicle weight is shifted forward. The front end of the car lunges downward, the back lifts upward. Secondly, the tires begin the rotate more slowly. The vehicle is moving at one speed, and the wheels are rotating at a progressively slower rate. Lastly, we are aware that the tires have locked and are not rotating at all. We cannot steer the car in this condition, and the vehicle continues to a stop; we hear the squeal of rubber as it is burned from the tread.

Impending Locked-Wheel Skid Mark. As the wheels begin to rotate more slowly and have not yet reached a locked condition, rubber is in fact being erroded from the tread. The rotation of the wheel assures that the burning rubber is taken from the entire periphery and not just any one random spot on the tread. This beginning of a locked-wheel skid mark is known as the impending locked-wheel skid mark. *The most efficient braking occurs during an impending skid mark.* The mark is visible upon the surface of the roadway, and often reveals the tire print of the tread. The tire print is most often visible just as the tire ceases to rotate and locks.

As the tire ceases to rotate, a rubber residue is actually burned from the surface of the tread. This residue of boiling rubber builds in front of the skidding tire, passes beneath the tire, and is left upon the roadway as a locked-wheel skid mark (see Fig. 9-1). As the tire rides upon this burning rubber, the coefficient of friction is decreased. The tire is no longer riding upon the surface of the roadway, but rather on a film of burning rubber. Because of the decreasing coefficient of friction, a series of test skids which also burn rubber from the tires of the test vehicle should be employed. The investigator should not merely estimate the surface characteristics of a roadway.

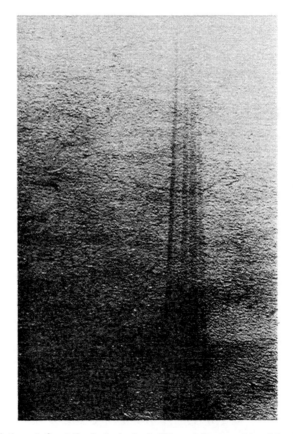

FIGURE 9-1. A front tire locked-wheel skid mark begins with a faint impending mark and darkens up to the point-of-rest. The vehicle leaving this mark was coming towards the viewer. The weight of the vehicle was being transferred from the rear to the front tires.

Measuring Locked-Wheel Skid Marks. Locked-wheel skid marks are measured with a steel tape measure from the beginning of the first shadow of the impending skid mark up to and including the point of impact in a collision.

After measuring all of the skid marks left at the scene of a collision, the *pre-collision* figures are added together and divided by the number of wheels that left skid marks. If only three wheels left skid marks, the total is divided by three. If only two wheels left skid marks, the total is divided by two. Post-collision locked-wheel skid marks, those which are evident after the collision, may be used and computed with the pre-collision skid marks only when the collision vehicle was not accelerated by some outside influence such as another vehicle. For example, if a vehicle collides with a parked car while skidding in a locked-wheel manner and continues to leave locked wheel skid marks after the impact, all of the skid marks can be used to determine minimal speed of the striking vehicle. However, when a vehicle has its brakes applied in a locked-wheel skid and is struck by another vehicle, the second vehicle imparts additional speed to the first vehicle, and the post-collision skid marks will not accurately reflect the pre-collision speed of the first vehicle. In this case, the investigator must use only those skid marks which are evident prior to the collision. A later discussion will treat the determination of total velocities for such a collision.

After arriving at an average length for the skid marks, the number is simply substituted into a formula which gives the officer a minimum speed. That formula is as follows:

$$V = \sqrt{30\,S\,f}$$

V = velocity in terms of miles per hour.
S = the skid distance in feet.
f = coefficient of friction.

Let us assume a skid distance of 110 feet and a coefficient of friction of 70 percent or .70.

1. $V = \sqrt{30\,S\,f}$ Basic formula.
2. $V = \sqrt{30 \times 110 \times .70}$ Substitution of known numbers in the formula.
3. $V = \sqrt{2310}$ We multiplied 30 times 110 times .70 and derived a product of 2310.
4. V = 48 miles per hour minimum.

In the example, 48 is the nearest whole number which multiplied by itself equals 2310. The actual square root of 2310 is 48.062458. For purposes of court testimony and in the interests of fair play, speed is usually rounded off to the lowest whole number, in this case 48.

Let us look at another example. Assume a skid distance average of 230 feet, and a coefficient of friction of 77 percent or .77.

1. $V = \sqrt{30 \, S \, f}$
2. $V = \sqrt{30 \times 230 \times .77}$
3. $V = \sqrt{5315}$
4. $V = 72$ miles per hour minimum

Again, 72 is the nearest whole number which, when multiplied by itself, is most nearly the square root of 5315. 72 times 72 equals 5184. 73 times 73 equals 5329. The speed of the vehicle is then obviously somewhere between 72 and 73 miles per hour, and to be more exact, is most nearly 72.904046 miles per hour. Again, the lower whole number is taken in the interests of fair play.

Let us examine a slower speed and assume a skid distance average of 56 feet and a test coefficient of friction of 66 percent or .66.

1. $V = \sqrt{30 \, S \, f}$
2. $V = \sqrt{30 \times 56 \times .66}$ 30 times 56 times .66 equals 1108.8
3. $V = \sqrt{1108}$
4. $V = 33$ miles per hour minimum

The leading case in the computation of skid marks came about as a result of *People vs. Herman* (City Magistrates' Court of City of New York, Traffic Court) 20 N.Y.S. (2nd) 149 (1940), 174 N.Y. Misc. 235. This court opinion is of particular importance because it sets forth in detail the formulas by which speed is calculated from skid marks and establishes the basis for accepting such physical evidence of speed. Much of what we employ today is a result of the efforts of the New York Criminal Homicide Bureau that developed the case and preserved by measuring and computing the irrefutable evidence. A complete discussion of the formulae for computing skid marks in the metric system can be found at the end of this chapter.

The Side-Skid. There are several other types of locked-wheel skid marks to discuss. The obvious locked-wheel skid mark that occurs after impact is still one of deceleration. This locked-wheel skid mark is often called side-skid or brush-skid. Both of these definitions are simply definitive and may add to the comprehension of what has happened. Upon impact with another vehicle or fixed object, a vehicle is often redirected on another course in a sideways direction. Whether or not the wheels of the vehicle are turning, there is a deceleration taking place as the vehicle is pushed in a direction other than that in which it was traveling. The black skid marks tell the story. The side and brush skid marks are equally as effective as locked-wheels in diminishing the speed of the vehicle. On occasion, a vehicle is sent into a circular spinning path. The skid marks are again very much in evidence. These locked-wheel skid marks are measured just as accurately as the straight line locked-wheel skid marks. A steel tape is employed and the rotation of the marks

FIGURE 9-2. A vehicle left the roadway with the brakes locked, striking the curb, flattening both front tires and subsequently coming to rest in a dirt embankment. The skid marks shown on the sidewalk are excellent examples of blown tire skid marks. How do we know that the driver still had the brakes applied when the vehicle impacted with the dirt bank?

is measured in its entirety, following all the twists and turns, right up to and including the vehicle's point of rest.

The Gap Skid. There is a type of locked-wheel skid mark known as the gap skid. The gap skid is created by a driver who is pumping the brakes of his vehicle. With each application of the brakes the wheels lock and leave an observable locked-wheel skid mark. Then there will be a blank space of approximately 20 to 30 feet or more and another locked-wheel skid mark becomes evident complete with an impending skid mark. This type of skid mark is most often evident when a driver has failing brakes. He applies the brakes and skids, then the brakes fade or fail. He then pumps the brakes by releasing pressure on the pedal and hits the pedal again, and again, and so on. To measure the locked-wheel skid marks, measure only that impending and locked-wheel skid mark which is on the roadway and include that figure in your consideration of the number for the locked-wheel skid formula.

135

Skip Skid. A third type of locked-wheel skid mark is the "Skip Skid." The skip skid is caused by the bouncing of the vehicle, for example, an empty tank truck which bounces over a railroad track in the course of trying to stop. Another example is a vehicle which bounces over a rough or pot-holed road. The wheel in this case remains locked and comes back to earth in approximately five to ten feet. The wheel in this locked position lands on the same portion of the tire that left the roadway and upon the same plane of burning rubber. A skip skid is measured in its entirety, from beginning to end as though it never left the roadway.

Below are three diagrams demonstrating the process by which locked-wheel skid marks are left on a road surface. (Fig. 9-3a, b, and c).

Centrifugal Skid Marks

As previously noted, centrifugal skid marks are left by a vehicle which is being turned in a tighter radius than the forward speed will allow. We have all heard the squeal of tires as a speeding vehicle is turned to make a curve or corner. As the speed of a vehicle is increased, so is the area it takes in which to turn the vehicle. This arc or area is known as the turning radius of the vehicle. At low speeds we can effect a rather tight turn. As our speed increases, we require a broader arc or more room in which to effect the maneuver.

Centripetal and Centrifugal Force. Envision a ball on a rubber band. As we swing the ball in a circle, the rubber band keeps the ball from flying away and out of the restrictive circle. As we increase the speed of the ball, the rubber band stretches and the circle or path taken by the ball becomes larger. Eventually with an increase in speed, the rubber band will break and the ball will orbit into a path of its own, arcing up and away from the center. The rubber band is representative of centripetal force which keeps the ball on a defined path around the center of the circle. Centrifugal force is the force expanded outward and away from the center.

A moving automobile is also subject to the laws of centripetal and centrifugal force. These forces are defined and controlled by the tires which turn the car. Envision a vehicle in a right turn. As a driver, you are aware of the forces at work in the vehicle which tend to throw your weight toward the left side of the passenger compartment. The weight of the vehicle is shifted to the left. In the average front engine automobile, 60 percent of the weight is already up front, coming down on the two front tires. With the weight shift to the left front tire during a right turn, the tire begins to support more weight than any other tire. The weight of the vehicle is brought downward along the sidewall of the outside edge of the tire. The inside of the tire or the side closest to the engine compartment is being relieved of weight as the vehicle begins to roll to the left. The left sidewall of the tire comes in contact with the roadway and rubber is scrubbed from the sidewall. A skid mark is imprinted on the roadway which can be measured precisely. *The centrifugal skid mark leaves the most accurate of all marks from which a determination of speed can be easily developed.*

a. Most front engine vehicles have a weight distribution which approximates 60 percent over the front tires and 40 percent over the rear tires. When the brakes are applied, the weight is transferred forward placing approximately 70 percent to 80 percent over the front tires.

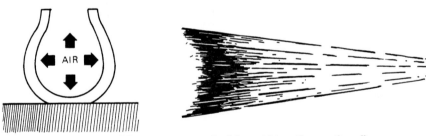

b. The forward weight shift is transmitted downward through the front tire sidewalls. The tread progressively cups upward in the middle as it is compressed. The result leaves a locked-wheel skid mark.

c. The forward moment of force removes much of the weight on the rear tires allowing the tires to balloon. The effect leaves a locked-wheel skid mark that begins quite heavy and is the width of the tread. As the weight continues to shift, the skid mark narrows to a faint, thin line. Air within the rear tire expands. It is to be remembered that once the wheels lock and cease to rotate, there is nothing more a driver can do to slow the vehicle.

FIGURE 9-3. Locked-Wheel Skid Mark Diagrams

The skid mark begins with a thin, apparently solid line and widens as the sidewall comes in contact with the roadway to a width of approximately two to three inches. As successive increments of the sidewall come into contact with the roadway, the pattern of the sidewall is delineated in the skid mark. This identifiable delineation is known as the sidewall striation. In the event of a collision, these

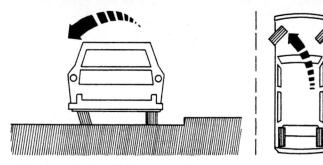

a. The arrows indicate the moment of force placed over the left front tire exhibited in a tight right turn. The weight is shifted left and forward. The weight and subsequent force shifts to the front tire, which is opposite the direction of the turn.

b. Illustrated is a typical example of a solo, run-off-roadway collision wherein a vehicle was traveling too fast to negotiate the right turn. Centrifugal force propelled the vehicle not only out of the lane but also into the opposite lane and off the far side of the roadway. Note identifying heavy lines are with the sidewall striations as the sidewall curls under and comes into contact with the road surface.

FIGURE 9-4.   Centrifugal Skid Mark Diagrams

striations can be measured and matched with the tire leaving the mark. There is little or no speed lost in the centrifugal skid mark. The tire is rotating freely on its axis, and the vehicle is moving.

If the vehicle steering wheel could be held in an exact position and the speed maintained exactly, the vehicle presumably would continue to describe a circle (provided the surface coefficient of friction did not change). There is a method to establish the speed of the vehicle and it is based on the use of two formulas. The first is to determine the radius of the circle. The radius, once known, is inserted into a second formula to develop the velocity in terms of miles per hour.

Formula for Radius. The formula to develop the radius of any circle was developed in early Grecian times. It was discovered that if one only had a straight line that intersected the circle at two points, one could take two measurements that would tell him the radius, or distance from the center of the circle to the circle

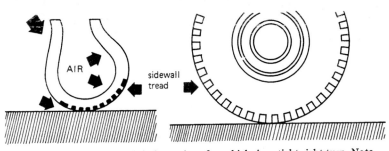

c. Diagrammed above is the left front tire of a vehicle in a tight right turn. Note how the sidewall is curled under as the weight of the vehicle is shifted to the left and downward through the outside of the tire sidewall. In severe turns the sidewall comes into contact with the roadway. The sidewall is scrubbed and scarified in this action, leaving a distinctive series of sidewall pattern marks upon the roadway. These sidewall marks left in a centrifugal skid mark are known as striations.

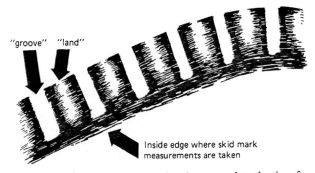

d. The striations can be measured and compared to the tire of a collision vehicle. Measure both the width of the "lands" and the "grooves." This evidence can be extremely valuable in a hit-and-run investigation.

FIGURE 9-4 (cont.)

itself. The straight line can intersect the circle at any given point and does not have to go through the center of the circle. This straight line is called a *chord*. The chord is measured from one point on the circle to the second point on the circle. At a distance of one half of the chord, a second measurement is taken at right angles to the chord up to the circle. This second measurement is called the *median*. With only these two measurements, we can compute the radius of the circle. The formula for radius, once a chord and a median are known, is as follows:

$$R = \frac{C^2}{8\,m} + \frac{m}{2}$$

R is the radius
C is the chord
m is the median

Let us get down to basics and see how this formula works for us. At the scene of a collision an officer observes the telltale centrifugal skid mark. Let us further

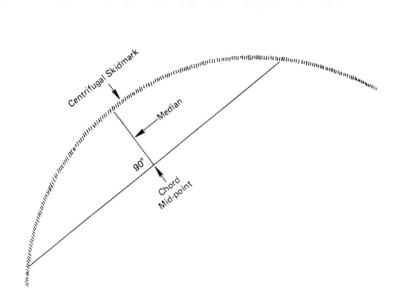

FIGURE 9-5. When evaluating a centrifugal skid mark, the investigator should begin the chord measurement as close as possible to the first visible evidence of the skid mark. For ease in calculation measure either a 50 foot or a 100 foot chord. If the investigator is working in metrics, it would be easier to use a 10, 20 or 30 meter chord. The steel tape measure representing the chord is drawn to the desired length and pulled taut. Measure from the inside of the skid mark where the edge of the skid mark is crisp and well-defined. With the chord tape measure taut and in place the investigator measures from the mid-point of the chord measurement upward to the inside of the skid mark at a 90° angle from the top of the steel chord tape measure. This distance is the median. Having determined a chord and median, the investigator is prepared to make a speed evaluation.

FIGURE 9-6. Two close-up views depicting how a median measurement is taken on a centrifugal skid mark. In this case the median measurement on a 50 foot chord is 28 inches or 2.3 feet. At 70 percent coefficient of friction, this represents 37.9 M.P.H. In a posted 25 M.P.H. residential district, the resultant collision investigation from skid mark analysis was able to determine not only cause but speed in view of conflicting statements.

140

assume this skid mark is approximately 67 feet in length. The officer will locate the beginning of the mark that looks like a pencil-thin line. Using a steel tape measure he will place the end of the tape immediately upon the inside of the line. A partner officer will hold the tape measure as the officer reels off 50 feet of tape. The officer will pull the tape measure taut and place the 50 foot mark on the inside edge of the skid mark. With the tape measure held firmly in place, the officer will return to the 25 foot mark. Using a clipboard or a standard form piece of paper for a straight edge, the officer will place the paper on the steel tape with one edge aligned along the tape with the corner at the 25 foot mark. With a second steel tape, the officer will measure up the straight edge of the paper or clipboard to the inside edge of the skid mark. This second measurement is the median. The 50 feet is the chord.

Let us assume the officer found the median to be 9 inches, or .75 feet. (For the sake of clarity and accuracy, keep everything in terms of feet.)

1. $R = \dfrac{C^2}{8m} + \dfrac{m}{2}$

2. $R = \dfrac{50^2}{8 \times .75} + \dfrac{.75}{2}$

3. $R = \dfrac{2500}{6} + .375$

4. $R = 416.667 + .375$

5. $R = 417.042$ feet

Once the radius is known, the officer is free to run the test skids. Let us assume the test skids indicate a coefficient of friction of 70 percent or .70. The formula for centrifugal skid mark determination, once the radius is known, is as follows:

$$V = \sqrt{15Rf}$$

V = velocity in miles per hour
R = radius
15 = constant
f = coefficient of friction

1. $V = \sqrt{15Rf}$
2. $V = \sqrt{15 \times 417 \times .70}$
3. $V = \sqrt{4378.5}$
4. $V = 66$ miles per hour minimum

The reason that a 50 foot chord is used is that 50 is an easy number to work with; also, there is less room for error in the measurement. Some officers prefer to work with a 100 foot chord, and there is no problem with the mathematics; you will just be working with bigger numbers. Let us suppose that you can only discern 25 feet of centrifugal skid marks, this, too, is acceptable. Shorter centrifugal skid marks are difficult to discern and accurately calculate, however the formula holds true for any length of chord and median relationship. The important reading, the one which requires close scrutiny, is the median. The shorter the chord, the shorter the median, and where the chord is in multiples of feet, the median is usually read in inches and fractions of inches and must be translated to feet. Chords less than 25 feet should not be used because of the difficulty with precise measurements. As a rule, the investigator should work with no less than a 50 foot chord on a centrifugal skidmark.

Let's look at another example from a collision which involves a centrifugal skid mark. These figures are derived from an actual collision involving a driver under the influence of alcohol. He was driving a new imported sports car. He was southbound on a major highway which follows the coastline of southern California. There is a stretch of straight-away that is approximately two miles in length. On the southern end of that straight-away is a left curve which is posted with an advisory sign indicating 40 miles per hour. Shortly after the beginning of the arc of the curve, the sports car left the road, tumbled end-for-end, landed on its wheels, spun around, slid backwards back out onto the roadway, and arced southward again, back into the dirt south of the curve and ultimately some 628 feet from where he originally

FIGURE 9-7. This centrifugal skid mark clearly indicates the striations of the sidewall. See how the skid mark is narrow at the top and widens near the bottom to a width of approximately three inches, indicating that the vehicle traveled in a line towards the viewer.

left the road, coming to rest into a power pole. A 62 foot centrifugal skid mark was found just prior to where the vehicle left the road at point of impact number one (the six inch raised curb). The chord was carefully measured at 50 feet. The median was found to be six and one-half inches. A close-up photograph was taken of the measurement. Satisfied with the accuracy of the chord and median measurements, a series of three test skids were effected. The test skids were laid in the immediate area of the centrifugal mark, at a calibrated 25 miles per hour.

The average length of all the test skid marks was 27 feet. Let us now follow the process through to a conclusion, substituting what we know in the various formulas.

1. $f = \dfrac{V^2}{30\,S}$ Formula to determine coefficient of friction.

2. $f = \dfrac{25^2}{30 \times 27}$ 25 miles per hour was the speed of the test.
30 is a constant times 27 feet, length of the skid mark.

3. $f = \dfrac{625}{810}$ 25 times 25 equals 625.
30 times 27 equals 810.

4. $f = .77$ or 77%   625 divided by 810 equals .77 or 77 percent.

1. $R = \dfrac{C^2}{8m} + \dfrac{m}{2}$ Formula to determine the radius of an arc.

2. $R = \dfrac{50^2}{8 \times 0.54} + \dfrac{0.54}{2}$ The chord is 50 feet in length.
The median is 6.5 inches divided by 12 inches in a foot, or 0.54 feet.

3. $R = \dfrac{2500}{4.32} + \dfrac{0.54}{2}$ 50 times 50 equals 2500.
8 times 0.54 equals 4.32.

4. $R = 578.70 + 0.27$ 2500 divided by 4.32 equals 578.70 and 0.54 divided by 2 equals 0.27.

5. $R = 578.97$ feet   578.70 is added to 0.27. The sum is 578.97 feet.

1. $V = \sqrt{15\,R\,f}$ Formula to determine velocity in miles per hour.

2. $V = \sqrt{15 \times 578.97 \times 0.77}$ 15 is the constant, 578.97 is the radius and 0.77 is the coefficient of friction.

3. $V = \sqrt{6687.10}$ 15 times 578.97 times 0.77 equals 6687.10.

4. $V = 81.77$ or 81 miles per hour minimum.   (The square root of 6687.10 is 81.77469.)

The critical speed of this same curve was taken by measuring the arc of the curve at the point of impact. The chord used again was 50 feet. The median was exactly eight inches. The measurement was taken on the inside of the curve, through the area where the driver left the roadway, to insure a valid result. The critical speed was then computed in the same manner as the centrifugal skid mark, using the same formulae. We know the coefficient of friction is 77 percent.

1. $R = \dfrac{C^2}{8\,m} + \dfrac{m}{2}$ Formula to determine radius of arc.

2. $R = \dfrac{50^2}{8 \times 0.667} + \dfrac{0.667}{2}$ The chord is 50 feet in length.

   The median is 8 inches divided by 12 inches in a foot, or 0.667 feet.

3. $R = \dfrac{2500}{5.336} + \dfrac{0.667}{2}$ 50 times 50 equals 2500.

   8 times 0.667 equals 5.336.

4. $R = 468.515 + 0.333$ 2500 divided by 5.336 equals 468.515 and 0.667 divided by two equals 0.333.

5. $R = 468.848$ feet   468.55 is added to 0.333. The sum is 468.848.

Now we substitute the known quantities into the formula to determine the velocity in miles per hour once the radius and the coefficient of friction are known. This will tell us how fast a vehicle could take this curve without leaving the roadway.

1. $V = \sqrt{15\,R\,f}$ Formula to determine velocity in miles per hour.

2. $V = \sqrt{15 \times 468.848 \times 0.77}$ 15 is the constant, 468.848 is the radius and 0.77 is the coefficient of friction.

3. $V = \sqrt{5415.19}$ 15 times 468.848 times 0.77 equals 5415.19.

4. $V = 73.58$ or 73 miles per hour.   73.58 is the square root of 5415.19.

From our computations it becomes obvious that the drinking driver attempted to negotiate a curve at 81 miles per hour. The maximum speed at which that curve can be taken is the critical speed of approximately 73 miles per hour. Not only was he over the speed limit, he was over the critical speed for the curve and at a speed nearly twice that of the advisory sign.

There is little that an attorney can offer in the way of a defense for such driving. The jury returned a guilty verdict. As an aside, a guilty verdict will do little for the young lady who was riding with the drinking driver; the verdict seems almost hollow.

Acceleration Skid Marks

When a vehicle is accelerated rapidly, the drive wheels overcome the coefficient of friction, or drag factor, and begin to spin. The vehicle begins to move in an attempt to catch up with the rotating tires. Rubber is rapidly eroded from the tread and deposited upon the roadway. The acceleration skid mark continues until the vehicle begins to move at the same rate as the drive tires with the tires no longer overcoming the drag factor of the roadway.

Acceleration skid marks are different from locked-wheel skid marks in both number and shape. There are usually only two wheels driving the vehicle forward. As any vehicle is accelerated forward, the weight of the vehicle is rapidly shifted to

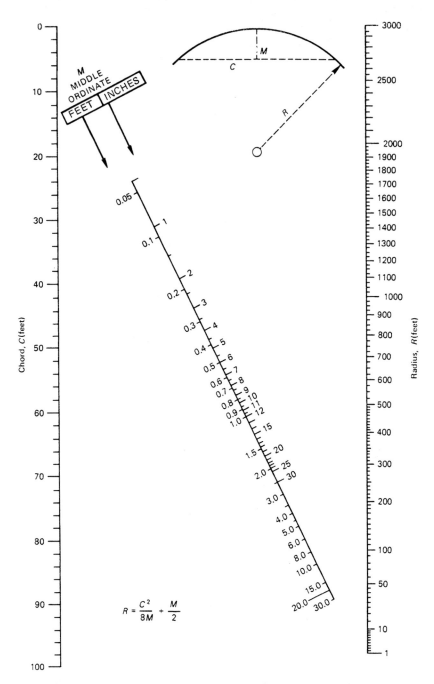

FIGURE 9-8. To determine the approximation of the radius once the chord and median are known, align a straight edge across the page. Affix the straight edge on the appropriate chord and median measurements and read the radius where the straight edge intersects the scale on the right. For example, a 50 foot chord with a seven and one-half inch median indicates a radius of approximately 500 feet.

FIGURE 9-9. Note the uneven left edge to this acceleration skid mark. Note, too, the definition of the tread, which can be measured and compared to the tire of a suspect vehicle leaving the scene of a collision. The tire leaving this mark is worn along the right hand edge.

the rear. The weight comes down on the rear tires and is distributed evenly down the sidewalls of the tires and to the roadway. As always, it is the friction that exists between the tread and the roadway that makes the difference. It is very easy to spin the tires on ice or wet roadways. It is more difficult to spin the tires on dry brushed concrete.

The appearance of the acceleration skid mark is different in that it starts out quite dark with a particularly dark line down each side of the skid mark. As the acceleration skid mark continues, it becomes progressively lighter and narrower as it fades, becoming unobservable (see Fig. 9-10). The path of the skid mark is usually a curving series of arcs. The non-linear path is described because of differences in coefficient of friction between the roadway and the treads of the drive

146

tires. If the right rear drive tire hits an oil slick, the left rear drive tire will turn the vehicle slightly to the right. The right rear drive tire will catch up after leaving the oil slick and after burning the oil residue from its surface. The driver of the vehicle usually compensates for the forced right turn with a left turn of the steering wheel. The result is a snake-like path in many acceleration skids. On a clean surfaced roadway, the acceleration skid mark will be nearly a straight line. The formula for determining speed at the end of an acceleration skid mark is as follows:

$$V = \sqrt{15\ S\ f}$$

V = velocity in miles per hour.
15 = constant.
S = the average of the two skid marks distance in feet.
f = coefficient of friction.

Suppose at the scene of a collision the officer finds two acceleration skid marks. The two marks are measured with a steel tape, added together, and divided by two, to develop an average. Let us assume that the average skid mark is 132 feet in

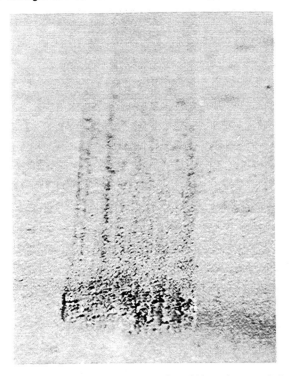

FIGURE 9-10. An example of an acceleration skid mark on asphalt pavement. Note the burning of the surface as the tire was rapidly accelerated. Look at the lines of tread and how the rear of the vehicle moved slightly to the right as it began to accelerate forward.

FIGURE 9-11. A typical acceleration skid mark. The oil residue on the right provides a lower coefficient of friction than the area to the left. The right side rear tire rotates more readily and with less friction than the left. Note how the skid mark curves toward the parked car and then back to the street center. There is little evidence that the left rear tire broke traction.

length. Let us further assume that after laying down three test skids the officer finds a coefficient of friction of 65 percent. We can substitute what we know into the formula and determine the speed at the end of the acceleration skid marks.

1. $V = \sqrt{15\ S\ f}$ Formula for determining velocity in miles per hour from an acceleration skid mark.
2. $V = \sqrt{15 \times 132 \times 0.65}$ 15 is a constant, 132 is the skid distance in feet, and 0.65 is the coefficient of friction.
3. $V = \sqrt{1287}$ 15 times 132 times 0.65 equals 1287.
4. $V = 35.87$ or 35 miles per hour.   (The square root of 1287 is 35.87.)

This is a common residential district acceleration skid mark example. When the speed limit is 25 miles per hour, it is obvious that the driver of the accelerated vehicle is going somewhat over the limit.

A second example of acceleration skid marks is the kind found around high schools and supermarket parking lots. Let us assume the average length of the skid marks was 248 feet. Assume a coefficient of friction of 70 percent.

1. $V = \sqrt{15\ S\ f}$ Acceleration skid mark formula.
2. $V = \sqrt{15 \times 248 \times 0.70}$ 15 is constant, 248 is the skid distance in feet, and 0.70 is the coefficient of friction.
3. $V = \sqrt{2604}$ 15 times 248 times 0.70 equals 2604.
4. $V = 51.02$ or 51 miles per hour.   (The square root of 2604 is 51.02.)

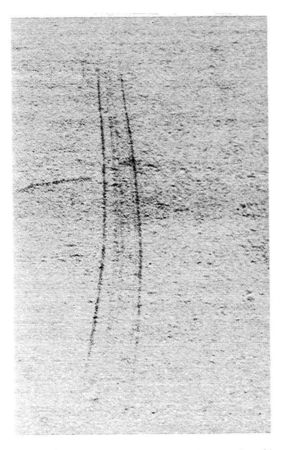

FIGURE 9-12. The driver of this vehicle accelerated to a point of breaking traction after the vehicle was already in motion. The mark fades on both ends. The clue to acceleration and not on-and-off locked-wheel skidding is the snake-like path. A locked-wheel vehicle cannot be steered and follows a path delineated only by gravity.

Recall that these speeds are all minimum. The vehicle was most likely doing something faster than that which is specified in the formula. The reason for this phenomenon is that the vehicle is still accelerating when the drag factor of the roadway is matched by the rotation of the tires, and the skid mark ceases.

For demonstration purposes, not recommended for a roadway, the author has accelerated a vehicle leaving acceleration skid marks, then turned the vehicle sharply so as to leave a centrifugal skid mark and lastly, applied the brakes to skid to a stop. The three skid marks and the formulas were used to test validity when the speed is known. The speed was tested by both radar and a calibrated speedometer, viewed by a passenger witness. The speedometer, the radar, and the formulas concurred in the reconstruction of speed.

As the vehicle's forward motion is equalized with the rapidly rotating tires and the coefficient of friction between the rear tires and the road surface is no longer

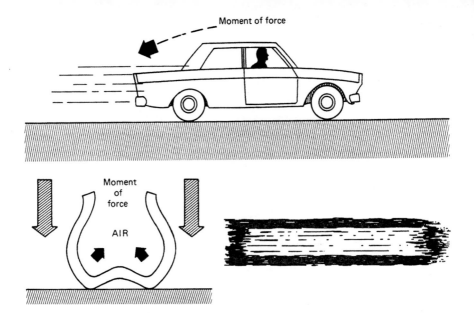

FIGURE 9-13. Acceleration Skid Mark Diagrams. a. During rapid acceleration the weight of the vehicle shifts to the rear tires. b. The downward moment of force on the rear tires causes the disfiguration when the air within the tires is compressed. The rear shock absorbers and rear springs are also compressed.

overcome, the vehicle weight is gradually shifted forward returning the vehicle to normal. The springs and shock absorbers play an important role in this regard, and the skid mark ceases. It is not uncommon for the acceleration skid marks to be a snake-like or curvilinear path as the spinning tires encounter an increased or decreased coefficient of friction on one side of the vehicle or the other.

Square Root Determination

Most officers, investigators, and students have access to a pocket calculator to assist in the calculations, and this is ideal. In court, however, the use of a calculator may be prohibited or impractical. The calculation of square roots, however, is really very easy for anyone who can perform simple addition, subtraction, multiplication, and division.

We have given sufficient examples of the problems involved in square root calculations to know that it is imperative to understand this calculation skill. The symbol of the square root radical over a number simply questions what number multiplied by itself equals the number under the square root symbol: $\sqrt{}$. First, let us look at the easy numbers as an example. $\sqrt{25}$ simply means what number multiplied by itself equals 25. The answer is, of course, 5. $\sqrt{81}$ means what number multiplied by itself equals 81, and the answer is 9. When we must work with three-, four-, and five-digit numbers underneath the square root radical will be explained as follows. Let us start with an easy example:

1. $\sqrt{1444.}$ Problem statement. What is the square root of 1444?

2. $\sqrt{1\,4\,4\,4}$.   Starting with the decimal point underline to the left in groups of two.

3. $\overset{3}{\sqrt{1\,4\,4\,4}}$.   Now ask yourself, what is the largest number multiplied by itself which will be less than 14? The answer is 3. Write 3 above the 14.

4. $\overset{3}{\sqrt{1\,4\,4\,4}}$.   3 time 3 is 9. Write 9 under the 14.
    9
    $\diagup\,5\,4\,4$ Subtract 9 from 14 for a remainder of 5. Bring down the 44, next to the 5.

5. $\overset{3}{\sqrt{1\,4\,4\,4}}$.   Now double the 3 to 6 and write 6 on the step
    9
    $6\diagup\,5\,4\,4$ adjacent to the 544. Put a dash next to the 6 to remind you that you need another number next to it. Now ask yourself 60 *what* will go into 544? 6 times 8 equals 48, let's try an 8.

6. $\overset{3\;\;8\;.}{\sqrt{1\,4\,4\,4}}$.   Place an 8 above the 44. Now multiply 8 times 68,
    9
    $6\,8\diagup\,5\,4\,4$ placing an 8 on the step on the dash next to the 6, to
    $5\,4\,4$ the left of the 544. 8 times 68 equals 544.

To check our work, multiply 38 times 38. The answer is 1444.00.

Let's look at another example, this time one with three digits.

1. $\sqrt{676}$.   Problem statement. What is the square root of 676?

2. $\sqrt{6\,7\,6}$.   Starting with the decimal point, underline to the left in groups of two. In this case, we have one digit, a 6, which stands by itself.

3. $\overset{2}{\sqrt{6\,7\,6}}$.   Now ask yourself what is the largest number which multiplied by itself will go into 6? The answer is 2. Write a 2 above the 6.

4. $\overset{2}{\sqrt{6\,7\,6}}$.   2 times 2 equals 4. Write a 4 under the 6. Subtract 4
    4
    $\diagup\,2$ from 6 for a remainder of 2. Bring down the 76 next to the 2.

5. $\overset{2}{\sqrt{6\,7\,6}}$.   Now, double the 2 to a 4 and write 4 on the step
    4
    $4\diagup\,2\,7\,6$ adjacent to the 276. Put in a dash next to the 4 to remind yourself that you will need another number next to the 4. Now, ask yourself 40 *what* will go into 276? 6 times 4 equals 24, let's try a 6.

6.   Place a 6 above the 76, and another 6 on the dash adjacent to the 4 on the step. Now multiply 6 times 46. The answer is 276.

Now, check the work: 26^2 or 26 times 26 equals 676. One more example:

1. $\sqrt{3306.25}$ Problem statement. What is the square root of 3306.25?

2. $\sqrt{3306.25}$ Starting with the decimal point, underline to the left and right in groups of two.

3.
```
        5  7 . 5
  √3 3 0 6 . 2 5
       2 5
107  ⎛
 _   ⎝ 8 0 6
       7 4 9
1145 ⎛
 _   ⎝ 5 7 2 5
       5 7 2 5
```
Now, ask yourself what is the largest number multiplied by itself that will be less than 33? The answer is 5. Write a 5 above the 33. Five squared, or 5 times 5 is 25. Write 25 beneath the 33. Subtract 25 from 33 for a remainder of 8. Bring down the 06. Double the 5 and write 10 on the step. Put in a dash next to the 10. Now, ask yourself what multiplied by 100 will go into 800, without going over 806? The answer is 7. Write a 7 on the dashed line and another 7 over the 06. 7 times 107 equals 749. Write 749 beneath the 806. When we subtract we find the difference to be 57. We check above the radical and find we now have a 57. Double the 57 and write 114 and a dash on the step. Bring down the 25 from above. Now, ask how many times 11 will go into 57? The answer is 5. Place a decimal point in the answer above the one in the problem. Place a 5 over the 25 and another 5 on the dash adjacent to the 114. Now multiply 5 times 1145. The answer is 5725.

Check the work by multiplying 57.5 times 57.5. The answer is 3306.25.

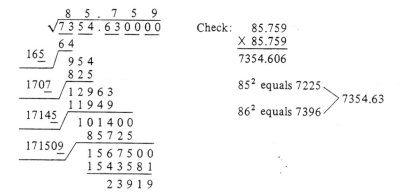

It is doubtful that you as an officer will ever have to carry a square root problem to the extent shown above, as the square root problems deal with velocity in miles per hour and we normally drop the decimal fractions to the right of the decimal point. Suffice it to say in the above problem the violator was traveling at a speed in excess of 85 miles per hour.

To allow an officer the opportunity to obtain a square root or square of any number from 1 to 200, please refer to the tables in the appendix. (A-1). A minimum speed can be quickly read from the tables.

Nomograph. The nomograph is a quick and easy check of calculations. The speed-skid chart can be used to determine a minimal speed for either locked-wheel or centrifugal skid marks.

To use the nomograph (Fig. 9-14) for locked-wheel skid marks, add together the number of feet of skid marks, divide by the number of tires leaving the skid marks, and obtain an average skid distance in feet. Determine the coefficient of friction with test skids. Let us assume an average skid distance of 100 feet. Follow the 100 foot line to the right to where it intersects the 70 percent coefficient of friction diagonal line. At the intersection, follow the vertical lines straight to the bottom of the graph. The speed is approximately 45+ miles per hour according to the chart.

Let us test the validity of the chart against the formula.

1. $V = \sqrt{30\ S\ f}$
2. $V = \sqrt{30 \times 100 \times 0.70}$
3. $V = \sqrt{2100}$
4. $V = 45.8$ miles per hour minimum

If you proceed through the lines and test the answers against the formula, you will notice the same degree of accuracy.

Now let us work on the centrifugal skid marks. The nomograph is based on always using a 50-foot *chord*. Let us assume we obtain a ten-inch median on a 50-foot *chord*, and that the coefficient of friction is 80 percent. Read up the right side of the chart to ten inches or 0.83 feet. Read the chart to the left on the ten-inch median line to where it intersects with the 80 percent coefficient of friction diagonal line. Now, follow the vertical line directly down to the bottom of the chart from the intersection of the two known quantities. The answer, according to the chart, is approximately 66 to 68 miles per hour minimum.

Now, we shall see how the chart compares to the formula.

1. $R = \dfrac{C^2}{8\ m} + \dfrac{m}{2}$

2. $R = \dfrac{50^2}{8 \times 0.83} + \dfrac{0.83}{2}$

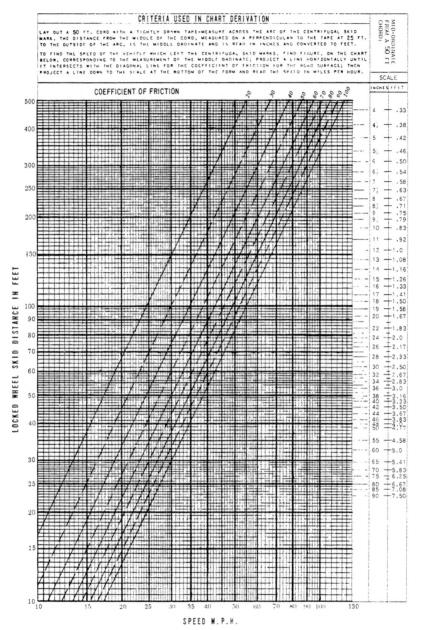

FIGURE 9-14. Skid-Speed Chart

154

3. $R = \dfrac{2500}{6.64} + \dfrac{0.83}{2}$
4. $R = 376.51 + 0.42$
5. $R = 376.93$ feet

1. $V = \sqrt{15\,R\,f}$
2. $V = \sqrt{15 \times 376.93 \times 0.80}$
3. $V = \sqrt{4523.26}$
4. $V = 67.25$ miles per hour minimum.

The chart is right again and will continue to be linear through all the combinations of median measurements and coefficients of friction.

If we have charts and tables from which to work, why do we need to know how to work the formulas? The answer lies in the courtroom. A person testifying as to speed from skid marks is qualifying as an expert in the field. The only charts normally allowed will be those introduced and prepared by the officer. The same is true of a calculator. The officer did not prepare the calculator and cannot testify as to how the answer was derived. An "I don't know" answer will not suffice when testifying as to how the answer was calculated. The court can take judicial notice of the use of a calculator and charts if all parties agree, however, a defense attorney will probably not agree to the use of the aids. It is for this reason that an investigator must be familiar with the various formulas involved. The charts and the tables simply serve to confirm the calculations and renew your own faith in what you are doing. Usually after the officer has demonstrated a proficiency in the mathematics of skid mark calculations, a defense attorney will allow the use of the calculator in the interests of expediting the proceedings.

DEFORMATION DAMAGE

Whenever a vehicle is involved in a collision beyond the tapping of bumpers, there exists some form of deformation to the body. Obviously various automobiles will deform at different rates and in different amounts depending on a number of factors. The factors include such things as the construction of the vehicle, the angle of attack to that vehicle when struck, and the speed and weight of the participating vehicles.

In the many controlled studies of experimental collisions there is a figure which keeps recurring as an average for the deformation. A striking vehicle averages 0.9 inches of deformation per mile per hour. Thus, nine inches of deformation on a striking vehicle is indicative of a speed of approximately ten miles per hour upon impact.

Divide the average deformation by 0.9 to derive the approximate speed. An example would be as follows: Suppose the average deformation is approximately 15 inches. Fifteen divided by 0.9 equals 16.7 miles per hour. Twenty inches of deformation equates to 22.2 miles per hour. Remember, this is only for the striking vehicle. A parked car with twenty inches of deformation does not mean that the parked car was traveling at a rate of 22.2 miles per hour when struck.

Deformation damage reconstruction is only an approximation and is calculated when there is little else to utilize. This process again provides a minimum speed. The best method of deriving deformation damage is to consult the manufacturer of the automobile and obtain the figures for the length or width of the vehicle when new. This can be accomplished through the local new car sales offices as a matter of course. The offices usually maintain a fact sheet on just about every vehicle they have sold. This fact sheet is published by the respective manufacturers. Let us suppose that you find that the vehicle in the collision, when new, was 192 inches in length. You observe the vehicle and see that short of the collision, the vehicle has not been modified. You measure the vehicle after the collision with a steel tape *and measure to a point of the average line of the deformation.* Assume you arrive at a figure of 168 inches. Subtract 168 from 192 and derive 24 inches. Twenty-four divided by 0.9 equals 26.7 miles per hour minimum speed upon impact. Deformation determinations are particularly valid when observing front and rear collisions. The deformation process, although valid as an estimate, provides only minimal speeds when viewing collisions occurring to the sides of a vehicle. An example of this observation is the speeding vehicle that spins out of control and slams into a tree or a power pole, with the side of the vehicle. Depending on the vehicle, a deformation estimation will be quite close up to approximately 25 miles per hour. Beyond that speed, the deformation reading becomes difficult as the vehicle is bent into a horseshoe shape. In the metric system, deformation occurs at an approximate rate of 0.0142 meters per kilometer per hour.

TOTAL VELOCITY

Total velocity is a term applied to the combination of observations which determine the speed of a vehicle. Perhaps the best observation is the vehicle which leaves locked-wheel skid marks and then strikes an object. There was a certain amount of energy absorbed when the wheels locked and the vehicle began to decelerate. The last of the energy was absorbed in the final impact with the object.

An assessment of the skid marks will give us a figure for the miles per hour absorbed in trying to stop prior to the impact. An assessment of the deformation damage will give us the miles per hour upon impact. It would be nice if we could add these two figures together; however, the answer would be erroneous.

Algebraic Formula

Velocities are added algebraically. The formula for algebraic addition is as follows:

$$V_t^2 = V_1^2 + V_2^2 + V_3^2 \text{ and so on}$$

V_t = total velocity.

V_1 is the first determined velocity to add algebraically.

V_2 is the second determined velocity to add algebraically, and so on.

To restate the formula and remove the square from the V_t or total velocity, the formula is rewritten as follows:

$$V_t = \sqrt{V_1^2 + V_2^2 + V_3^2 \ldots} \text{ etc.}$$

In short, what we are doing is to square all the velocities involved, add the squares together, and take the square root of the answer.

Let us take as an example a locked-wheel skid of 82 feet average, a deformation damage of 23 miles per hour, and an after impact side skid of 37 feet, after striking a parked car, with a coefficient of friction of 72 percent. We are now looking at three distinct observations of speed concerning one vehicle. The question: What is the minimum speed for this vehicle? The following is the formula for pre-collision locked-wheel skid mark determination:

1. $V_1 = \sqrt{30 \, S \, f}$
2. $V_1 = \sqrt{30 \times 82 \times 0.72}$
3. $V_1 = \sqrt{1771.2}$
4. V_1 = 42 miles per hour minimum.

V_2 was already determined from deformation to be a minimum of 23 miles per hour. This would equate to approximately 21 inches of deformation.

V_3 is determined again by the locked-wheel skid mark formula.

Here is the formula for post-collision skid mark determination:

1. $V_3 = \sqrt{30 \, S \, f}$
2. $V_3 = \sqrt{30 \times 37 \times 0.72}$
3. $V_3 = \sqrt{799.2}$
4. V_3 = 28 miles per hour minimum.

The formula for total velocity, or combined velocity now that we know the speeds involved, is as follows:

1. $V_t = \sqrt{V_1^2 + V_2^2 + V_3^2}$ Total or combined velocities formula.
2. $V_t = \sqrt{42^2 + 23^2 + 28^2}$ Substitution of known velocities.
3. $V_t = \sqrt{1764 + 529 + 784}$ The known velocities are squared.
4. $V_t = \sqrt{3077}$ The known squares are added together.
5. V_t = 55 miles per hour minimum.   (The square root of 3077 is actually 55.4707.)

If we simply added together the known velocities, we would have arrived at the erroneous figure of 93 miles per hour. The actual speed of 55 miles per hour is a true reflection of the velocity involved. This method is not only mathematically valid but has been proven by observation to be correct.

This same method is employed when a vehicle in locked-wheel skid slides over several significantly different surfaces, altering the coefficient of friction. When a vehicle in a locked-wheel skid lays a portion of those skid marks on the surface of the roadway which may be concrete, then slides over an asphaltic shoulder, and then onto a dirt shoulder, we have three distinct coefficients of friction. A test must be conducted on all three surfaces to ascertain the coefficient of friction for each. The skid marks on each surface are then measured, averaged, and a velocity is computed for that surface. The three velocities are then substituted in the total or combined velocities formula to determine a true velocity. There is nothing exotic nor difficult in the calculations, but the investigator must check and double check the calculations to assure their accuracy, as a mistake can be most embarrassing in court.

VAULTING FORMULA

Every now and then, a vehicle leaves a roadway and vaults into a large ditch or a canyon. The following formula holds true for a ditch or canyon with a slope of approximately 45°. (Most roadbeds are designed with a slope of approximately 45° away and down from the road.)

Refer to Figure 9-15 to ascertain how the various elements are labeled and made reference to in the formula. "S" is, again, the distance in feet, as measured horizontally; "h" is the height from take-off point to landing point as measured vertically;

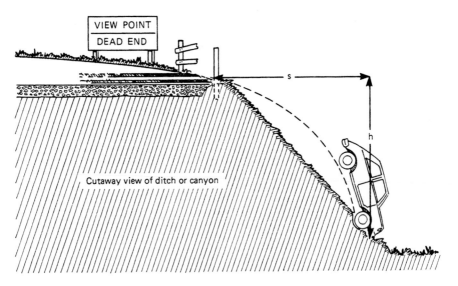

FIGURE 9-15.   Vaulting Speed Determination

and "V" is once again the velocity of the vehicle. The number 2.73 is a constant. The formula for vaulting from a level take-off is:

$$V = \frac{2.73\ S}{\sqrt{h}}$$

Let .us assume that a vehicle leaves the edge of the road and flies outward and down to a point of impact. The officer measures a distance of approximately 75 feet horizontally and a drop of approximately 36 feet vertically.

1. $V = \dfrac{2.73\ S}{\sqrt{h}}$ Vaulting formula

2. $V = \dfrac{2.73 \times 75}{\sqrt{36}}$ Substitution of known quantities

3. $V = \dfrac{204.75}{6}$ 2.73 times 75 equals 204.75
The square root of 36 is 6.

4. $V = 34$ miles per hour minimum   204.75 divided by 6 equals 34.125.

The expression for this formula in the metric system is:

$$V = \frac{7.93\ S}{\sqrt{h}}$$

S is expressed in meters
h is expressed in meters
V is expressed in kilometers per hour

Taking these measurements will give the officer the most difficulty without some help. Few patrol vehicles have the surveying equipment available to assess accurately the horizontal and vertical distance. Local highway departments can be a valuable asset, however. Not only do they have the equipment to make accurate measurements, but they have the staff and the grade schematics to provide the proper figures. An officer or attorney should recruit mathematics teachers and professors from the local high schools, colleges, and universities as well. The teachers can double-check the mathematics and offer other rules of physics and math which may be beneficial in the reconstruction of some of the more spectacular problems which confront the investigator. One such problem is the ballistic flight of a pedestrian struck by a moving automobile. Given the facts of point of impact and point of rest of the pedestrian, plus the variables of height of launch, a qualified instructor in mathematics can easily work out such problems as time of flight and launch speed. These facts will assist the investigator in determining the speed of the vehicle involved in the absence of skid marks. Other areas of interest are the field of kinetic energy, which is the study of an object in motion, measured in terms of foot pounds of energy. These are areas in which the best expert advice, counsel, and testimony may come from your local mathematics or physics professors.

SPECIAL CONDITIONS

The formulas quoted in this chapter have all been repeatedly proven and accepted in courts of law. They are the result of sound mathematics and emperical observation. However, there are certain considerations which must be given to special situations and vehicles.

Truck Tractors and Trailers

The locked-wheels of a truck tractor and semitrailer may leave as many as eighteen skid marks upon a roadway. Dual wheels are to be counted as one skid mark. Dual wheels share one brake drum. When that brake locks, both wheels of the dual arrangement lock and begin to skid together, thus, they are counted as one skid mark. The answer will be correct when the skid marks are all counted, measured, and averaged. Do not be surprised if, when you view the skid marks left by a truck tractor and semitrailer, you cannot find skid marks from the front wheels of the tractor.

Brake Systems. Most tractors are specially rigged by an air valve arrangement which locks the trailer brakes first, the tractor drive wheels second, and the steering wheels last. This system allows for straight line braking. If the tractor brakes are applied first, the weight of the trailer would jackknife the trailer, which would pivot around the tractor. The steering wheels receive only a minimal amount of braking energy so the driver can control the direction of the tractor during the braking process. A number of automobiles are set up in much the same manner. The rear wheels lock first, and then the front wheels lock as the weight is shifted forward. This again allows for more control during the braking process. In the large commercial rigs, this action is controlled by the tractor protection valve. In automobiles, this process is taken care of by a metering valve. The purpose of both systems is the improved control of the vehicle during braking.

There is also the braking system which utilizes a rapid setting and releasing of the brakes. The reader will recall that the most efficient braking is the impending skid mark. By rapidly setting and releasing the brakes, the tire is allowed to rotate slightly and begin a new impending skid. The purpose of this is to rotate the tire slightly to a new surface against the roadway. The burning rubber does not build up beneath the skidding surface of the tread and lower the coefficient of friction. The vehicle will stop in less distance than a vehicle with conventional brakes. The problem develops in the manufacture of a reliable device which will set and release the brakes several hundred times per minute. A number of companies have or are experimenting with such a system with varying degrees of success.

It is to be noted that disc brakes rather than conventional "shoe" brakes are normally utilized on the front wheels of automobiles because of their "no-fade" qualities. When brake shoes become hot, they tend to fade or glaze, reducing the friction between the brake drum and the shoe. In contrast, disc brakes tend not to glaze and hold the tire in a locked position. The heat exchange between the disc pads and the disc itself is more rapidly dispersed than in a conventional shoe and drum arrangement. Both systems will hold and lock a wheel in a locked-wheel skid. The disc brake tends to hold better in prolonged and repeated applications, for example on mountainous roads where the brakes are set and released repeatedly. The disc brake is used on the front wheels primarily because of the weight transfer which comes forward and down over the front wheel.

Motorcycles

Motorcycles offer a special problem in predictability with braking systems (see Fig. 9-16). The front and rear brakes are not set with the same control as in an automobile. The rear brake is activated by a foot pedal. The front brake is controlled by a hand device. Although the rear brake skid mark is usually visible, the front brake may well be adjusted to offer no more than a drag to tire rotation. This

FIGURE 9-16. The rider of this motorcycle ignored the posted and critical speeds for a mountain curve. The rocks caught the rider and the machine.

is particularly true of the off-road motorcycles. If the front wheel is adjusted to a point where braking by locked wheel is accomplished, the motorcycle may pivot upward over the front wheel when the brakes are applied. This will cause the rider to launch. Rear braking with a front wheel drag will assure the rider of more straight line braking. In any event, the brakes of most motorcycles are not as effective as that of the average automobile. When only the rear brake is applied, the braking is about 60 percent as efficient as an automobile. When both brakes are applied, the braking is about 75 percent as efficient. The efficiency of braking systems in motorcycles varies widely. The only test one can use with any degree of accuracy is to test for coefficient of friction using the collision vehicle if possible, or use a similar motorcycle as an option. The question will still remain, however, did the driver of the motorcycle use one or both of his brakes? This is difficult to ascertain in a fatal collision, but if the driver survived, his statements can be most valuable. If the motorcycle is still serviceable, be sure to check the brakes.

Centrifugal skid marks left by a motorcycle can be measured in the same manner as centrifugals left by any other vehicle. The officer must use caution not to confuse centrifugal skid marks with side skids at the scene of a collision. Sidewall striations are still the clue to look for. As the rider lays the motorcycle down, the rear wheel is still engaged with the engine turning or propelling the wheel. The tread is digging against the roadway attempting to propel the vehicle forward. The skid mark is blurred and contains no distinct sidewall striations, which are evident in a centrifugal skid mark.

The surface construction of a roadway may lead persons to believe a defect existed in the vehicle braking system when, in fact, no problem is evident. Nearly every roadway constructed has a crown or high area near the center line. The crown or high area causes water on the roadway to flow towards the curbs and gutters. When a vehicle locks the brakes, it can no longer be steered by the driver. The vehicle is then subject to the laws of gravity which tend to pull the vehicle to the lowest portion of the roadway or towards the curb. This accounts for so many parked cars being struck in and about a collision scene. Simple gravity is in control of a locked-wheel vehicle. The vehicle will tend to take the course or direction it had when the wheels locked, but when the roadway slopes to the side, the vehicle tends to follow the slope or crown to the right hand edge of the roadway.

MEASURING DEVICE ACCURACY

The various measuring devices will vary a great deal from instrument to instrument. Several studies performed by such prestigious institutions as the University of California at Berkeley, Cornell University, and Northwestern University have concluded the following average deviations.

Table 9.1. Errors In Accuracy of Various Measuring Devices

Device	100 feet	10 feet
Pacing	+ or – 6 feet	+ or – 12 inches
100 foot commercial steel tape	+ or – 1 inch	+ or – 1/8th inch
New woven metal steel tape	+ or – 2 inches	+ or – 1/4th inch
Worn woven metal steel tape	+ or – 2 inches	+ or – 1/2 inch
New cloth tape	+ or – 3 inches	+ or – 3/8th inch
Worn cloth tape	+ or – 12 inches	+ or – 1 1/2 inches
Measuring wheel	+ or – 6 inches	+ or – 2 inches (reading factor)

Throughout this text, the author has advocated the use of a steel tape when measuring skid marks. The deviations in this device are minimal by comparison to pacing or using a worn cloth tape measure. A significant problem may occur when using a measuring wheel device. The experiments at the universities are controlled over smooth surfaces that run in a neat, straight line. Unfortunately, our roadways, curves, and most collision scenes do not conform to the sterile setting of scientific environments. A wheeled measuring device can be made to measure around corners simply by a twist of the wrist as it is pushed in front of the investigator. First of all, people do not walk straight, let alone push a measuring wheel straight as the investigator walks, swinging his body. The resultant answers will vary depending on the length of the measurement. A measuring wheel is more than adequate for measuring a long centrifugal skid mark just to indicate the approximate length. However, when it comes time to determine speed from that centrifugal skid mark, a measuring wheel is useless. A good 100 foot commercial grade steel tape has no substitute short of the national standard itself. The tape is also far less expensive to replace.

INVESTIGATOR SAFETY

Safety cannot be overstressed. Do not turn your back to traffic except for brief moments when there is no oncoming traffic. Do not trust warning devices, lights, flares, barricades, or other officers to slow or redirect oncoming traffic. When working a major collision in an intersection, place the traffic control signals on flashing red to stop all traffic, and then, keep a wary eye on traffic to assure compliance. Take nothing for granted in terms of the other driver. When a secondary collision seems imminent, forget the tape measures neatly laid out over the skid marks, forget the cars and units at the scene, and *run* to a position of safety.

SUMMARY OF COLLISION MATHEMATICS

This chapter has dealt with numerous equations and formulas concerning the operation of a motor vehicle. The proofs and derivations of these formulas are to be found in the advanced student appendix to this chapter. The important factor in stopping a vehicle is this: the stopping distance is in direct proportion to the square of the speed. The basic coefficient of friction formula contains all of the elements to demonstrate this fact.

1. $f = \dfrac{V^2}{30\,S}$ Coefficient of friction formula

2. $f \times 30\,S = \dfrac{V^2 \times 30\,S}{30\,S}$ Multiply both sides of the equation by 30 S.

3. $f \times 30\,S = \dfrac{V^2 \times \cancel{30\,S}}{\cancel{30\,S}}$ The 30 S cancels out in the right half of the equation leaving what we see in step 4.

4. $V^2 = 30\,S\,f$ Does this equation look familiar? How about if we eliminate the square of the velocity and place a square root radical over the 30 S f?

5. $V = \sqrt{30\,S\,f}$ The locked-wheel skid mark formula.

Suppose we want to solve the skid distance, knowing the speed and the coefficient of friction. We know that Step 4 is the locked-wheel skid formula and that Step 5 is simply a reinstatement of that formula.

1. $V^2 = 30\,S\,f$ Basic locked-wheel skid mark formula

2. $\dfrac{V^2}{30f} = \dfrac{30\,S\,f}{30f}$ Divide both sides of the equation by 30 f.

3. $\dfrac{V^2}{30f} = \dfrac{\cancel{30}\,S\,\cancel{f}}{\cancel{30f}}$ The 30 f cancels from the right half of the equation.

4. $S = \dfrac{V^2}{30\,f}$ We now have a formula for determining skid distance once velocity and the coefficient of friction are known.

So, no matter how we look at it, stopping distance is directly proportional to the square of the speed. The best example of this observation is the mathematical test. At 10 miles per hour, according to the formula above, we would stop in 4.76 feet. If we square the speed to 100 miles per hour, we find the stopping distance went up to 476.19 feet. We were going 10 times faster and skidded 100 times further. (Computed at 70 percent coefficient of friction.)

We have become very cognizant of the fact that there are only three things a driver can do to an automobile. He can start it by accelerating, change directions by turning, and stop it by applying the brakes or striking an object. We have developed

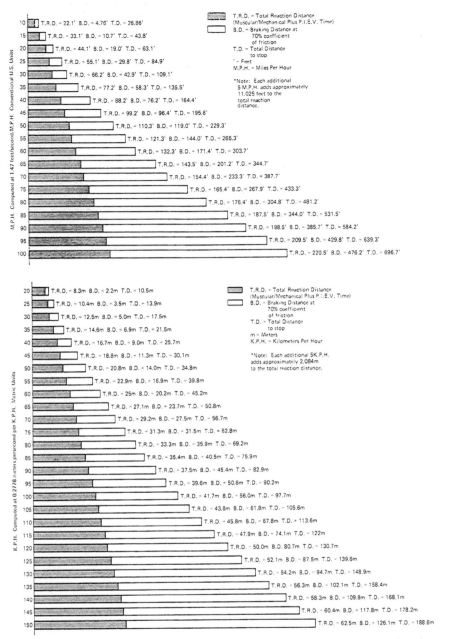

FIGURE 9-17. Total Distance from First Observation to Stop. Flagmen and road construction crews should be aware of the total distance required to stop an automobile from first observation of a hazard. As a minimum standard, the warning signs of construction should be placed at a distance three times that of the total distance required to effect a stop. For example, if the construction area is in a 40 M.P.H. zone, the first warning sign or flagman should be a minimal 493.2 feet prior to the hazard. (164.4 X 3 = 493.2.) This distance buffer will account for those vehicles moving at rates of speed above the posted speed limit and allow drivers time to acclimate prior to slowing or stopping.

165

the formulas to assist in the determination of a speed from skid marks for each of these functions, and learned a bit about how to perform square root calculations without a computer.

A discussion was presented on variables which will affect the coefficient of friction. A good example of this is how the ambient rising temperature will lower the coefficient of friction particularly on an asphaltic roadway. On a very hot day, asphaltic surfaces begin to "bleed" and become spongy. The coefficient of friction takes a respectable dip. For example, on a hot day, a vehicle going 55 miles per hour will skid further than it will in the cool of the evening at the same speed, when the brakes are applied and skidding is induced on this same roadway. This is why test skids should be employed under the same conditions of temperature, and as soon after the collision, as possible.

Determination of Coefficient of Friction Estimation

The following chart will aid in making determinations for coefficient of friction on flat level surfaces. Bear in mind that the chart and estimations should only be used when it is impractical to perform an actual coefficient of friction test. To be absolutely fair, an officer should develop a high and a low speed determination based on the ranges of coefficient of friction indicated in the chart, or develop a speed based on an average or median.

Table 9.2. Estimated Coefficient of Friction

Description of Road Surface	Dry				Wet			
	Less Than 30 MPH		More Than 30 MPH		Less Than 30 MPH		More Than 30 MPH	
	From	To	From	To	From	To	From	To
Concrete								
New, Sharp	.80	1.00	.70	.85	.50	.80	.40	.75
Traveled	.60	.80	.60	.75	.45	.70	.45	.65
Traffic Polished	.55	.75	.50	.65	.45	.65	.45	.60
Asphalt or Tar								
New, Sharp	.80	1.00	.65	.70	.50	.80	.45	.75
Traveled	.60	.80	.55	.70	.45	.70	.40	.65
Gravel								
Packed, Oiled	.55	.85	.50	.80	.40	.80	.40	.60
Loose	.40	.70	.40	.70	.45	.75	.45	.75
Ice								
Smooth	.10	.25	.07	.20	.05	.10	.05	.10
Snow								
Packed	.30	.55	.35	.55	.30	.60	.30	.60

There may be times when it is impractical to perform a coefficient of friction test either because of oncoming driver visibility, road configuration, or lack of proper assistance to close the roadway in question if there are curves or hills.

In such cases, the officer may be forced to not only estimate the coefficient of friction, but also the grade. To determine the grade, a small straight edge with a hole in the center of one end may be employed. The Northwestern Institute for Traffic Engineering has already developed just such a device and incorporated this into their traffic drafting template.

As a general rule, one percent of elevation will add or subtract one percent from the estimate of the flat or level coefficient of friction. Whether the officer adds or subtracts depends on whether the vehicle leaving the skid marks in question was traveling up or down the elevation. Add if the vehicle was going uphill, subtract if the vehicle was going downhill.

A one percent grade means a one foot rise or fall for 100 feet of horizontal distance. The best source of elevation information is the local highway engineering department. Also, a grade or elevation of less than three percent will do little to affect the minimal speed derived from the formulas.

An estimating device available in hardware stores is commercially sold under the brand name of Devil-Level. It is approximately three inches square and one inch thick. The device has a small weighted pointer that indicates degrees and percent of grade. A bumper jack stand laid flat on the road makes a good base on which to place the Devil-Level. Several readings are then taken along the length of the skid marks to determine the average grade.

Another method is to use a blank paper set squarely into a clipboard. A horizontal line is drawn on the paper from top to bottom. The line must be parallel with the side of the paper and the side edges of the clipboard. One officer proceeds 100 feet from the beginning of the skid marks toward the collision. The investigating officer then sights along the edge of the clipboard, fixing and aligning the edge of the clipboard with the head of the other officer. A third officer places a conventional level against the clipboard with the end of the level on the line drawn on the paper. The level "bubble" is centered and the third officer draws a line using the level as a straight edge. The line should begin with the original line drawn on the paper and extend horizontally along the level. The result is a piece of paper 8½″ × 11″ with an angle drawn through the long distance of the paper. This angle represents the grade or elevation of the roadway. The angle can then be measured with a conventional protractor to determine the degree of rise. The degree of rise can be converted to grade percentages.

Another sighting technique which requires very little effort or equipment is to use a clipboard and a 12 inch ruler both of which have holes drilled in the proper places. The holes should be big enough to allow a pencil to pass through (1/4″ to 3/8″); the hole in the clipboard should be as close as possible to the long edge, and as close to the mid-point of this length as possible.

A piece of clean paper is placed squarely in the clipboard with the edge just beneath the hole. The ruler hole is aligned over the clipboard hole and a pencil is dropped into the holes. The pencil serves only as a fulcrum or pivot point for the ruler. A line is then drawn using the ruler as a straight edge which is parallel to the ends of the paper. Now, hold the clipboard and sight along the long edge at the head of an officer 100 feet away. Note that the ruler acts like a "plumb" line and points straight down and at an angle from the first line drawn with the ruler. Holding the ruler in place on its new position, draw another line. The angle formed is the rise or fall in elevation of the road. As before, convert this angle to percent. Use a protractor and measure the degrees.

The conversion from degrees to percent of grade is a trigonometric function of mathematics. For purposes of this text and for ease in determinations, the following chart will facilitate the derivation from degrees to percent of grade. Each 0.5° (one-half degree) equals one percent of elevation, which equates to plus or minus one percent coefficient of friction.

Degrees	Grade %
0.5	1
1.0	2
1.5	3
2.0	4
2.5	5
3.0	6
3.5	7
4.0	8
4.5	9
5.0	10
5.5	11
6.0	12
6.5	13
7.0	14
7.5	15
8.0	16
8.5	17
9.0	18
9.5	19
10.0	20
15	30
20	40
25	50
30	60
35	70
40	80
45	90
50	100
55	110
60	120

A simple device which works well for measuring grade or elevation is a straight and level board, usually a 2 inch by 4 inch by exactly 50 inches in length, or a sturdy piece of "I" beam extruded aluminum which is straight and level and cut to exactly 50 inches in length.

The board or beam is laid on the surface of the roadway. A conventional "bubble-level" is placed atop the beam. The low end of the beam is then lifted to center with the bubble in the level. With a conventional ruler, the investigator measures from the bottom of the beam to the road surface. The inches measured are doubled. The answer is the grade or elevation. For example, if the distance from the bottom of the beam to the road surface is three inches, double the three. The grade is six percent.

The logic in this approach is that 50 inches is half of 100 inches. If we had a beam 100 inches long, we note that it is directly proportional to 100 feet. If the beam is half of 100, or 50, the elevation is also half. Thus, with a 50 inch beam, the elevation reading must be doubled.

Feet per Second to Miles per Hour

We have previously discussed the conversion of miles per hour to feet per second. There are occasions when an investigator may wish to reverse the process and convert the known feet per second to miles per hour. Parking lot, auto-pedestrian, and known time/distance collisions are examples where this conversion may be necessary.

Again, utilizing the known quantities of 5,280 feet in one mile and 3,600 seconds in each hour, we divide 3,600 by 5,280. The answer, or constant, is the decimal 0.68187, or 0.682. To develop miles per hour when the feet per second are known, multiply the feet per second by 0.682. For example, 88 feet per second multiplied by 0.682 equals 60.016 miles per hour.

88	Feet per second	55	F.P.S.
X 0.682	Conversion factor	X 0.682	Constant
60.016	Miles per hour	37.51	M.P.H.

Utilizing the knowns of 1000 meters in one kilometer and 3600 seconds in each hour, we divide 3600 by 1000. The answer or constant for this conversion is 3.6. To develop kilometers per hour when the meters per second are known, multiply the meters per second by 3.6. For example, 25 meters per second X 3.6 = 90 kilometers per hour.

25	Meters per second	30	
X 3.6	Conversion factor	X 3.6	
90	Kilometers per hour	108	

KINETIC ENERGY AND COLLISIONS

It is possible, in the study of collision investigation, that a determination of speed through the use of kinetic energy may be the best possible way to resolve the issue. Kinetic energy is the branch of physics which studies the effect of forces in the production or modification of bodies in motion.

Let us suppose a 3,000 pound vehicle has stopped in mid-intersection and is preparing to make a left turn when it is struck from the side by a 4,000 pound vehicle. Let us further assume the coefficient of friction is 70 percent. The question arises: how fast was the 4,000 pound vehicle (#2) moving when it struck the 3,000 pound vehicle (#1), and pushed it 13 feet?

The formula for converting total energy into miles per hour is:

$$V = 5.5 \sqrt{\frac{K.E.}{W}}$$

3,000		Weight of Vehicle #1
X	.70	Coefficient of friction
2,100		
X	13	The distance Vehicle #1 was moved
27,300		The kinetic energy displaced to Vehicle #1 in terms of foot pounds of energy.

$$4,000 \sqrt{\overset{6.825}{27,300}}$$

The kinetic energy of Vehicle #1 is divided by the weight of Vehicle #2.

$$\sqrt{\overset{2.61}{6.825}} \times 5.5 = 14.35 \ M.P.H.$$

The square root of the kenetic energy divided by the weight of Vehicle #1 is 2.61; 2.61 multiplied by the constant 5.5 equals 14.35 miles per hour upon impact.

The proof of this speed is found in the deformation damage to Vehicle #2. The front end should be deformed to an average depth of 12.9, or approximately 13, inches. (This is also a very good approach to utilize when determing how fast a striking vehicle was moving when it struck a parked car or moveable object of a known or determinable weight.)

SKID MARK APPENDIX

Skid Mark Formulas for Advanced Students

The formulas for speed from skid marks are derived from Newton's Second Law of Motion; definitions can be found in any competently written physics text. The formulas of motion also appear in *The Handbook of Chemistry and Physics* which is updated and published on an annual basis.[1]

The basic premise of formula derivation is: force equals mass multiplied by acceleration ($F = Ma$). Other basic formulas and constants are as follows:

$$a = \frac{V^2}{2S}$$

$$a = \frac{V^2}{R}$$

$$M = \frac{w}{g}$$

$$f = \frac{F}{w}$$

$$F = fw$$

$$g = 32.17 \text{ feet/second}^2$$

$$v = 1.467 \times V$$ (Factor which converts miles per hour to feet per second; for example, 5280 ft/mile ÷ 3600 seconds/hour = 1.467)

a = acceleration
V = velocity in miles per hour or kilometers per hour as applicable
v = velocity in feet per second or meters per second as applicable
M = mass
w = weight
g = gravity
F = force
f = coefficient of friction
R = radius
S = distance

The speed from skid mark formulas have been used and proven in thousands of tests. The examples shown here are for the developmental purposes of the student.

Prove: The locked-wheel skid mark formula: $V = \sqrt{30Sf}$

Given: (a) Newton's Second Law of Motion $F = Ma$
      (b) The formulas for acceleration, mass, coefficient of friction, force, gravity, and velocity.

1. $F = Ma$

2. $fw = \left(\frac{w}{g}\right)\left(\frac{V^2}{2S}\right)$ Substitution of known quantities; that is: $F = fw$, $M = \frac{w}{g}$ and $a = \frac{V^2}{2S}$

3. $f = \frac{V^2}{g(2S)}$ Note that weight cancels out of the formula and is not a factor in speed from skid mark determination.

4. $f = \frac{(1.467\ V^2)^2}{32.17^2(2S)}$ Substitution of known quantities, velocity in feet/ seconds/M.P.H., and gravity.

5. $f = \frac{2.15(V^2)}{64.34(S)}$ Multiplication of givens

[1] Hodgman, C.D., Weast, R.C., and Selby, S.M. *Handbook of Chemistry and Physics*, Chemical Rubber Publishing Co., Cleveland, Ohio, 1980.

6. $f = \dfrac{(1)(V^2)}{(30)(S)}$ Reduction of simplest numbers and terms

7. $f = \dfrac{V^2}{30S}$ Coefficient of friction formula

8. $f(30S) = \dfrac{V^2(\cancel{30S})}{\cancel{30S}}$ Multiply both sides of equation by 30S and cancel.

9. $V^2 = 30Sf$ Remove the square from the velocity by taking the square root of 30Sf.

10. $V = \sqrt{30Sf}$ The locked-wheel skid mark formula

Prove: The centrifugal speed from skid marks formula: $V = \sqrt{15Rf}$

Given: (a) Newton's Second Law of Motion—$F = Ma$
  (b) The formulas for force, mass, acceleration on a curve, gravity, and velocity.

1. $F = Ma$

2. $f\psi = \left(\dfrac{\psi}{g}\right)\left(\dfrac{V^2}{R}\right)$ Substitution of known quantities from basic formulae given.

3. $f = \dfrac{V^2}{gR}$ Note that weight cancels out of the formula and is not a factor in speed from skid mark determination.

4. $f = \dfrac{(1.467\ V^2)^2}{32.17\ R}$ Substitution of known quantities, velocity in feet/seconds/M.P.H., and gravity.

5. $f = \dfrac{2.15\ V^2}{32.17\ R}$ Multiplication of given quantities.

6. $f = \dfrac{V^2}{15\ R}$ Reduction to simplest numbers and terms.

7. $f(15R) = \dfrac{V^2(\cancel{15R})}{\cancel{15R}}$ Multiply both sides of equation by 15R and cancel.

8. $V^2 = 15Rf$ Remove the square from the velocity by taking the square root of 15Rf.

9. $V = \sqrt{15Rf}$ The centrifugal skid mark formula.

Prove: The formula for computing the radius of an arc once the chord and median are known: $R = \dfrac{C^2}{8m} + \dfrac{m}{2}$

Given:

1. $c^2 = a^2 + b^2$ The Pythagorean Theorem for right triangles.

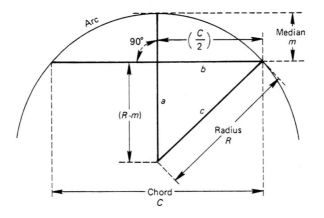

C = Chord   a = R·m
R = Radius   b = C ÷ 2
m = Median   c = R
Pythagorean theorem:
$$c^2 = a^2 + b^2$$

FIGURE 9-18

2. $R^2 = (R-m)^2 + \left(\dfrac{C}{2}\right)^2$ Substitution of known quantities in the Pythagorean Theorem.

3. $R^2 = (R^2 - 2Rm + m^2) + \dfrac{C^2}{4}$ Derived by squaring: multiplying R-m times R-m and $\dfrac{C}{2}$ times $\dfrac{C}{2}$

4. $R^2 - R^2 + 2Rm = \dfrac{C^2}{4} + m^2$ R^2 - 2Rm is taken to the left side of the equation. Note the signs change, and the R^2 is cancelled.

5. $\dfrac{2Rm}{2m} = \dfrac{\frac{C^2}{4}}{2m} + \dfrac{m^2}{2m}$ Divide both sides of the equation by 2m. Note that there exists one "m" remaining following the plus sign.

6. $R = \dfrac{C^2}{8m} + \dfrac{m}{2}$ The formula for determining the radius of an arc once the chord and the median are known.

This derivation was first developed in early Greece and has been a standard proven formula since that time. This formula also appears in standard physics textbooks.

Step 3 of the proof may need explanation for those students not familiar with the multiplication process: $(R - m)^2$ and $\left(\dfrac{C}{2}\right)^2$

$$X \frac{\begin{array}{c} R - m \\ R - m \\ \hline R^2 - Rm \\ - Rm + m^2 \end{array}}{R^2 - 2Rm + m^2} \qquad \frac{C}{2} \cdot \frac{C}{2} = \frac{C^2}{4}$$

Step 4 of the proof may need explanation for those students not familiar with the fact that an expression may be moved from one side of the equation to the other simply by changing the signs of the expression in order to maintain equation equality. Thus, $R^2 - 2Rm$ on the right side of the equation in Step 3 becomes $-R^2 + 2Rm$ when moved to the left side of the equation.

Step 5 of the proof may need explanation for those students not familiar with the division process. The rule is to invert the divisor and multiply.

$$\frac{\frac{C^2}{4}}{2m} = \frac{C^2}{4} \div \frac{2m}{1} = \frac{1}{2m} \times \frac{C^2}{4} = \frac{C^2}{8m}$$

Additionally, as noted in the other proofs, a mathematician may multiply or divide an equation provided the same function is performed equally to both sides of the equation; thus both sides of the equation can be divided by the expression "2m."

There are other ways of expressing the skid mark formulas as follows:

1. $f = \dfrac{V^2}{30S}$ Basic coefficient of friction formula

2. $V = \sqrt{30Sf}$ or $V^2 = 30Sf$ or $V = 5.5\sqrt{Sf}$ Basic locked-wheel, side, or impending skid mark formula

3. $V = \sqrt{15Rf}$ or $V^2 = 15Rf$ or $V = 3.8\sqrt{Rf}$ Basic centrifugal skid mark formula

4. $R = \dfrac{C^2}{8m} + \dfrac{m}{2}$ Basic radius formula with chord and median expressed in like terms

5. $R = \dfrac{3C^2}{2m} + \dfrac{m}{24}$ Basic radius formula with the chord expression in feet and the radius expressed in inches

6. $V = \sqrt{15Sf}$ or $V^2 = 15Sf$ or $V = 3.8\sqrt{Sf}$ Basic acceleration skid mark formula. Note that the acceleration skid mark formula is the same as the locked-wheel formula except for the constant which is half that of capable 4-wheel-locked skid. Acceleration is normally accomplished with only two wheels.

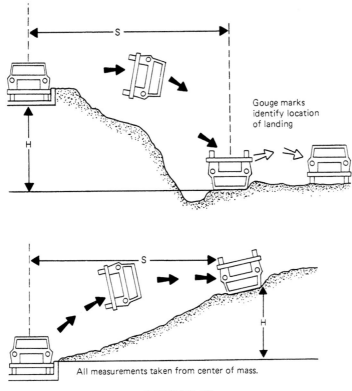

FIGURE 9-19

Speed Determination Formula in Flipped Vehicle Collisions

A formula has been developed that will ascertain the velocity in miles per hour when a flipping action occurs as a result of a side sliding vehicle striking an obstacle such as a curb. The curb or obstacle abruptly stops the side skidding action of the vehicle, and a launch occurs as the vehicle pivots over the curb, lofts into the air, and comes to rest some distance later. As the vehicle comes into contact with the ground, it gouges and scarifies the area of impact. This first landing is usually upside down. The vehicle will then usually continue to roll or slide to a stop.

The speed estimate is based on the horizontal distance, "S," that the center of vehicle mass moves through the air to the point of landing, and the vertical distance between the center of mass on take-off and landing, if any. What happens to the vehicle following the first landing is of no consequence to the determination of speed. S and H are expressed in feet. V is velocity in miles per hour.

175

For landing higher than take-off: $V = \dfrac{3.87S}{\sqrt{S+H}}$
(+H)

For a landing lower than take-off: $V = \dfrac{3.87S}{\sqrt{S-H}}$
(–H)

Skid Mark Conversion Formulas

As previously discussed, the formula for working with locked-wheel skid marks was computed with velocity in miles per hour and distance S was given in feet.

$$V \ M.P.H. = \sqrt{30S \ f}$$

The author has developed the following formula to be used when working locked-wheel skid marks in the metric system. Velocity is expressed in kilometers per hour and distance, S, is given in meters.

Example 1. Given: A locked-wheel skid mark averaging 100 feet or 30.4801 meters at 70 percent coefficient of friction (f).

M.P.H. and FEET	*K.P.H. and METERS*
1. $V = \sqrt{30S \ f}$	A. $V = \sqrt{255Sf}$
2. $V = \sqrt{30(100)(.7)}$	B. $V = \sqrt{255(30.48)(.7)}$
3. $V = \sqrt{2100}$	C. $V = \sqrt{5440.68}$
4. $V = 45.83$ M.P.H. Minimum	D. $V = 73.76$ K.P.H. Minimum

45.83 Miles Per Hour equates to 73.76 Kilometers Per Hour

Example 2. Given: A locked-wheel skid mark averaging 120 feet or 36.576 meters at 82 percent coefficient of friction (f).

M.P.H. and FEET	*K.P.H. and METERS*
1. $V = \sqrt{30 \ Sf}$	A. $V = \sqrt{255 \ Sf}$
2. $V = \sqrt{30(120)(.82)}$	B. $V = \sqrt{255(36.576)(.82)}$
3. $V = \sqrt{2952}$	C. $V = \sqrt{7648}$
4. $V = 54.33$ Miles Per Hour	D. $V = V \ 87.45$ Kilometers Per Hour

54.33 Miles Per Hour equates to 87.45 Kilometers Per Hour

Example 3. Given: A locked-wheel skid mark averaging 45 feet or 13.72 meters at 76 percent coefficient of friction (f).

M.P.H. and FEET	*K.P.H. and METERS*
1. $V = \sqrt{30Sf}$	A. $V = \sqrt{255\ Sf}$
2. $V = \sqrt{30(45)(.76)}$	B. $V = \sqrt{255(13.72)(.76)}$
3. $V = \sqrt{1026}$	C. $V = \sqrt{2658.9}$
4. $V = 32.03$ M.P.H Minimum	D. $V = 51.56$ K.P.H. Minimum

32.03 Miles Per Hour equates to 51.56 Kilometers Per Hour

To compare miles per hour with kilometers per hour check the tables in the back of this book.

Prior work with centrifugal skid marks has made it clear that measurements can be either in feet and inches or meters. Conversions can be made to either system of measurement.

Example 4. Compute the radius of a centrifugal skid mark. Given: A 50 foot chord, a 6 inch or .5 foot median which is 15.24 meters for the chord and 0.1524 meters for the median.

M.P.H. and FEET	*K.P.H. and METERS*
1. $R = \dfrac{C^2}{8m} + \dfrac{m}{2}$	A. $R = \dfrac{C^2}{8m} + \dfrac{m}{2}$
2. $R = \dfrac{50^2}{8(.5)} + \dfrac{.5}{2}$	B. $R = \dfrac{15.24^2}{8(0.1524)} + \dfrac{0.1524}{2}$
3. $R = \dfrac{2500}{4} + .25$	C. $R = \dfrac{232.2576}{1.2192} + 0.0762$
4. $R = 625 + .25$	D. $R = 190.5 + 0.0762$
5. $R = 625.25$ feet	E. $R = 190.5762$ meters

625.25 feet equates to 190.58 meters

The Centrifugal Skid Mark Formula is given as $V = \sqrt{15\ Rf}$ when dealing with miles per hour and a radius expressed in feet. When dealing with meters and kilometers per hour, the formula is $V = \sqrt{128\ Rf}$, as developed by the author.

Example 5. Given: The answers in Example 4 and f = .75, or 75 percent.

M.P.H. and FEET	K.P.H. and METERS
1. $V = \sqrt{15\ Rf}$	A. $V = \sqrt{128\ Rf}$
2. $V = \sqrt{15(625.25)(.75)}$	B. $V = \sqrt{128(190.58)(.75)}$
3. $V = \sqrt{7034.06}$	C. $V = \sqrt{18,295.68}$
4. $V = 83.87$ M.P.H. Minimum	D. $V = 135.26$ K.P.H. Minimum

83.87 Miles Per Hour equates to 135.26 Kilometers Per Hour.

The computation of acceleration skid marks can be accomplished in both feet and metric measurements with resultant answers for velocity in either miles per hour or kilometers per hour.

Example 6. Given: 156 feet of average acceleration skid marks which equals 47.55 meters, and a coefficient of friction of 80 percent.

M.P.H. and FEET	K.P.H. and METERS
1. $V = \sqrt{15\ Sf}$	A. $V = \sqrt{128\ Sf}$
2. $V = \sqrt{15(156)(.80)}$	B. $V = \sqrt{128(47.55)(.80)}$
3. $V = \sqrt{1872}$	C. $V = \sqrt{4869}$
4. $V = 43.27$ M.P.H. Minimum	D. $V = 69.78$ K.P.H. Minimum

43.27 Miles Per Hour equates to 69.78 Kilometers Per Hour

To convert miles per hour to kilometers per hour, multiply miles per hour times 1.60935. To convert kilometers per hour to miles per hour, multiply kilometers per hour times 0.62137.

VELOCITY AT THE MOMENT OF IMPACT

Conservation of Energy

There exists a well established physical law stating that energy can neither be created nor destroyed. Stopping is a good example of how the kinetic energy of a moving vehicle is not destroyed but simply converted and spent in the transfer of heat. The kinetic energy is expended through the heat exchange of the braking system or the combined disfiguration of the vehicle in damage as work was accomplished in conjunction with a slide to a stop as the tires and other vehicle parts were scrubbed along the roadway.

As the energy of the pre-collision vehicles at the microsecond before impact cannot be destroyed, it is converted to work, in this case, damage, as the metal is deformed and the vehicles are displaced from their respective paths of travel to an ultimate point of rest. Energy is also absorbed and converted as the post-collision vehicle collides with other objects and meets surfaces offering varying coefficients of friction.

By compiling the known facts through the use of a simple ratio formula, it is possible to quite accurately establish the speed of the vehicles upon impact. We will be concerned with a number of factors that can be established by on-scene observations and calculations. Careful measurements are the key to greater accuracy, and as a word of caution, a steel tape measure should be used for all measurements when considering reconstruction of a collision. The resultant answers can be only as accurate as the initial measurements used in the formulas.

Moment-of-Force Ratio Formulas

To take the student into the concepts of this method of analysis, we will start first with the comparitively simple rearend or broadside collision wherein the two vehicles remain engaged from the point of impact up to and including the point of rest.

Post-Collision Velocity Determination. As the energy of the striking vehicle cannot be destroyed, it is displaced by the work involved in moving the struck vehicle. Let us assume the weight of the striking vehicle is 3,500 pounds and the weight of the stopped vehicle to be 2,200 pounds. Let us further assume that we know the pre-collision velocity of the striking vehicle to be 40 M.P.H.

We can determine the post-collision velocity in the following formula:

$$V_1 w_1 + V_2 w_2 = V_1' w_1 + V_2' w_2$$

V is the velocity
w is the weight

$$40 \times 3,500 + 0 \times 2,200 = V_1' \times 3,500 + V_2' \times 2,200$$

Because vehicle #2 was stopped, it had no velocity and no moment of force until struck. Following impact, the velocity of both vehicles is the same, or mathematically stated, $V_1' = V_2' = V'$. The velocity of both vehicles moving together is:

$$40 \times 3,500 = V' \times 3,500 + V' \times 2,200 \ (0 \times 2,200 = 0)$$
$$140,000 = V' \ (3,500 + 2,200)$$
$$140,000 = V' \ 5,700$$
$$V' = 24.5 \text{ M.P.H. } (140,000 \div 5,700 = 24.5)$$

As a check of the reconstruction determination, there exists a high probability that skid marks will exist to the point where the struck vehicle comes to rest. At 70 percent coefficient of friction the skid marks would be approximately 28.5 feet in length.

Proof:

1. $S = \dfrac{V^2}{30\,f}$

2. $S = \dfrac{24.5^2}{30 \times 0.70}$

3. $S = \dfrac{600.25}{21}$

4. $S = 28.5$ feet

Pre-collision Velocity Determination. Continue to assume that upon colliding, the vehicles slide to a stop together. A measurement of the post-collision skid marks and a determination of the coefficient of friction are effected. The figures are substituted in the locked-wheel skid mark formula and a post-collision velocity is developed.

If the average post-collision skid mark is 60 feet and the coefficient of friction is 70 percent, the post-collision velocity is 35.5 M.P.H. Pre-collision speed can then be evaluated depending on the speed and weight of the two vehicles.

If the striking vehicle weighs 4,000 pounds and the stopped vehicle 2,800 pounds, we can substitute the knowns into the moment-of-force ratio formula.

1. $V_1 w_1 + V_2 w_2 = V_1' w_1 + V_2' w_2$

2. $V_1 \times 4{,}000 + 0 \times 2{,}800 = 35.5 \times 4{,}000 + 35.5 \times 2{,}800$

3. $V_1 \times 4{,}000 + 0 = 142{,}000 + 99{,}400$

4. $V_1 \times 4{,}000 = 241{,}400$

5. $V_1 = \dfrac{241{,}400}{4{,}000}$

6. $V_1 = 60.35$ M.P.H.

Additionally suppose that the striking vehicle applied the brakes and left an average of 60 feet of locked-wheel skid marks prior to the collision. At 70 percent coefficient of friction, the skid mark is equivalent to 35.5 M.P.H. absorbed prior to the collision.

Proof:

1. $V = \sqrt{30\,S\,f}$

2. $V = \sqrt{30 \times 60 \times 0.70}$

3. $V = \sqrt{1260}$

4. $V = 35.5$ M.P.H.

To determine the velocity of the striking vehicle prior to the initial skid mark, we employ the combined velocity formula. We know that braking accounted for 35.5 M.P.H. We additionally know from the moment-of-force ratio formula the striking vehicle had a pre-collision velocity of 60.35 M.P.H. Substituting the knowns into the total velocity formula, we derive the following conclusion of 70 M.P.H.

1. $V_t = \sqrt{V_1{}^2 + V_2{}^2 \cdots}$
2. $V_t = \sqrt{35.5^2 + 60.35^2}$
3. $V_t = \sqrt{1260 + 3642}$
4. $V_t = \sqrt{4902}$
5. $V_t = 70$ M.P.H.

Auto-Pedestrian Moment-of-Force Transfer. Imagine a 4,200 pound vehicle striking a 160 pound pedestrian. By any stretch of the imagination, the moment of force of the pedestrian can be considered as zero in comparison to the impact vehicle.

In the moment-of-force ratio formula, the velocity of the vehicle and pedestrian are equal upon impact. Assuming we know the post-collision velocity of the pedestrian and vehicle from locked-wheel skid marks to be 50 M.P.H., we can determine what slowing effect the pedestrian had upon the vehicle.

1. $V_1 w_1 + V_2 w_2 = V_1' w_1 + V_2' w_2$ (Upon impact, $V_1' = V_2'$)
2. $50 \times 4{,}200 + 0 \times 160 = V_1' \times 4{,}200 + V_1' \times 160$
3. $210{,}000 = V_1' \, 4{,}360$
4. $V_1' = \dfrac{210{,}000}{4{,}360}$
5. $V_1' = 48.165$

The pedestrian went from essentially a zero velocity to 48.165 M.P.H. The striking vehicle went from 50 M.P.H. down to 48.165 M.P.H., losing 1.83 M.P.H. upon impact with the pedestrian.

VECTOR ANALYSIS

In previous discussion we considered collisions that struck directly from the four sides of a vehicle at 90 degree angles with vehicles that stayed together from point of impact to the point of rest. In the majority of collisions, however, acute and obtuse angles of collision are involved, and the vehicles careen to points of rest disassociated from one another. To evaluate the velocities of the vehicles involved there is a reconstruction process known as vector analysis.

Vehicles in a collision impart their energies and separate for two basic reasons. The first is because of the angle of attack. An acute or oblique angle of collision imparts a rotational displacement and the vehicles separate. Even a sideswipe collision at a 180 degree angle and may or may not impart rotation to one or both vehicles, depending on the amount of deformation caused by the various peripheral items, such as door handles, mirrors, load hooks, fenders, and wide tires, for example.

The second factor that separates vehicles in a collision following maximum deformation is known as the Modulus of Torsional Rigidity. The crumpled metal of the collision vehicles tends to return to its original shape and pre-collision state of stress relief. The Modulus of Torsional Rigidity, or metal memory and elasticity, depends on the structure of the striking vehicles, the depth of the deformation, and the type of material being deformed in the collision. For example, sheet steel has a much better memory and more elasticity than fiberglass; thus steel has a higher "modulus" than fiberglass.

Vector analysis is a graphic representation of pre- and post-collision involvement that visually displays the trigonometric functions of momentum represented in vehicle velocity and weight. Arrows are used to denote both numerical quantity and direction of the moment of force for the vehicle or vehicles involved. The length of the arrow is drawn to a scale representing the velocity of the vehicle times its weight. The direction of the arrow indicates the path of the vehicle.

The student is directed to the progression of vector analysis representation, as shown in the Figures 9-20, a–c. In Figure 9-20, b note the horizontal line represents the product of the velocity times the weight of vehicle 1. Assume a post-collision velocity of 30 M.P.H. and a weight of 2,000 pounds for vehicle 1. The line is drawn to a scale of one inch per the quantity of 50,000. 30 M.P.H times 2,000 pounds equals 60,000; thus the line is 1.2 inches in length along the path shown from point of impact "0".

The progression of the angular line in Figure 9-20, c represents vehicle 2, at 4,500 pounds with a post-collision velocity of 25 M.P.H. The product of 4,500 pounds times 25 M.P.H. equals 112,500. Divided by the scale of 50,000 per inch, the line representing vehicle 2 is 2.25 inches in length and begins at the point of impact "0" in the direction taken from impact. The arrows indicate the paths of the two vehicles from the point of impact "0" outward along the paths taken as a result of the collision.

We now construct a parallelogram around the two vehicle vectors and draw a diagonal line from the point of impact "0" to point "C". The diagonal represents the sum of the moments of force at the instant of impact. A simple measurement of the diagonal line "OC" indicates 3.1 inches. 3.1 inches times the scale of 50,000 indicates a product of 155,000.

As energy can neither be created nor destroyed, the total moment of force following impact, the diagonal line "OC" was identical to the moment of force just prior to impact and on an identical line, "OD", also 3.1 inches in length.

From statements, skid marks, and other bits of physical evidence, we know in this case vehicle 1 was northbound and vehicle 2 was eastbound. We now complete a second parallelogram around the knowns of pre-collision vehicle direction. Measuring the line "OE" we find a distance of 1.9 inches. 1.9 inches times the scale of

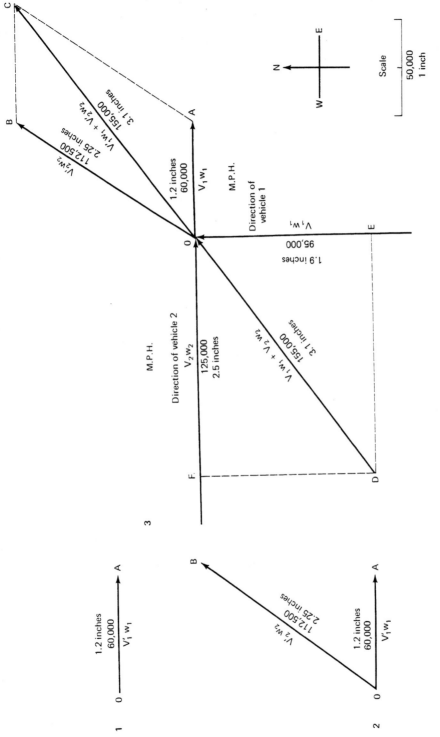

FIGURE 9-20 Progression of Vector Analysis Representation

183

50,000 equals 95,000. Measuring the line "OF" we find 2.5 inches. 2.5 inches times the scale of 50,000 equals 125,000.

Having a product for each of the two lines representing both pre-collision vehicles, we can divide the product by the known vehicle weights and derive the pre-collision speeds. For vehicle 1, the product is 95,000 divided by a weight of 2,000 pounds, which equals a pre-collision velocity of 47.5 M.P.H. For vehicle 2, the product is 125,000 divided by a weight of 4,500 pounds, which equals a pre-collision velocity of 27.8 M.P.H. So, at the moment of impact, vehicle 1 had a velocity of 47.5 M.P.H., vehicle 2 had a velocity of 27.8 M.P.H.

In the event that either or both vehicles left locked-wheel skid marks prior to the collision, these skid marks can be computed in the conventional manner and added to the speeds derived by vector analysis by utilizing the total velocity formula, $V_t = \sqrt{V_1{}^2 \; V_2{}^2} \; \ldots$

Vector Analysis Considerations

The discussion of vector analysis and the resultant reconstruction is dependent upon careful observations at the scene of a collision and should be completed as soon as possible following the collision. Evidence in a collision is of a very evanescent nature and tends to disappear once the roadway is reopened to traffic. We have repeatedly discussed the rotational quality to collision vehicles as they separate. The skid marks and the actual points of rest of the vehicles become fogged with time, memory, various measuing devices and differing opinions. As in the analysis of any important collision, photography plays an important role in identifying the various factors. There are a myriad of factors that can affect the angles taken by the separating vehicles. Fixed objects such as curbs and roadway crowns tend to alter vehicle paths. As the coefficient of friction away from a point of impact is usually the same for both vehicles on the surface of a roadway, it does not become an appreciable factor unless the point of impact and the resultant paths are over two dissimilar surfaces.

Obviously the angle of separation, or deviation, of two striking vehicles is very important in vector analysis. Initial skid marks and gouge marks are the best clues to observe and document. Vector analysis can be greatly affected by a continuum of variables that may be present at a collision involving secondary collisions. Reconstructionists and investigators are cautioned to be precise as possible, use as large a drawing as practical, and keep the scale minimized for increased accuracy. A scale of 10,000 to the inch is far more accurate than the scale of 50,000 used in this text due to space limitations.

Vector analysis and the moment-of-force ratio formula are both equally valid for the metric system and conventional U.S. units of measurement. Both methods of analysis are simple ratio quantities and lend themselves readily to computation.

Although this discussion has used the concepts of the conservation of energy to expand the reader's level of comprehension, the reader will do well to understand that, although the vehicles involved in a collision have kinetic energy, the collisions are explained in terms of momentum and moment of force. Momentum is defined as the quantity of motion in a body as measured by the product of its mass and velocity. Mass is often defined in physics as the quotient of the weight of a body divided by its acceleration due to gravity. As gravity pulls equally upon two vehicles at a collision scene, it is not a determining factor with two colliding vehicles upon a roadway. Thus, we can use vector analysis in consideration of vehicle velocity and weight.

Energy on the other hand, particularly kinetic energy, or the energy of a body in motion, is an expression of the capacity for doing work. In the case of a vehicular collision, the work is in actuality, the capacity for doing damage. Energy is a logarithymic function expressed as half of the mass or weight times velocity squared. Thus, energy cannot be expressed in a straight line vector as it increases by the square and is not a linear function.

The Mechanics of Vector Analysis Observation

It would be advantageous if the investigator had access to surveying equipment that could be utilized to precisely develop the angles of incidence and the deviation from a point-of-impact at a collision scene; it is to be remembered that the resultant answers are no more accurate than the measurements and weights that are plugged into the formula, and if the angles are dramatically in error, so is the resultant answer. The plumb bob of the surveyor's transit can be centered directly over the point of impact and all the angles read directly from the compass rose on the base of the scope.

It is the author's experience that surveying equipment is not always available, nor is there sufficient time to allow for set-up and measurement by the more exotic equipment.

First of all, the point of impact may seem illusive to some observers. There is usually physical evidence that points to where the tires deviated as a result of the collision; however, the tire deviations rarely depict the exact point of impact. The tires are usually protected within wheel wells and fenders, and are located fore and aft of bumpers, which were in fact the points of impact. It is for this reason that, although the skid marks tend to show the general area of the impact, the actual impact occurred forward of the skid mark deviations. By observing the deformation to the respective vehicles, the investigator can determine what parts of the vehicles were first impacted, add the distance from the tire centerline to the front bumper, in the case of a front end impact, and determine how much must be added to the skid mark to fairly represent the actual point of impact. The same measurement process must be accomplished with each of the vehicles involved in the collision.

Having determined what points on the respective vehicles first met in the collision, and having measured the distance from the centerline of the wheels showing deviation skid marks to that point, the investigator can quite accurately assess the actual point of impact on the roadway.

It is from the established point of impact that an investigator must determine the angles of incidence and deviation for the respective vehicles. The angle of incidence, or pre-collision directions can be established from debris, skid marks and statements. The angle of deviation, or post-collision direction, can be established by debris, gouge marks, skid marks, secondary impact marks on fixed objects, vehicle fluids trailed upon the roadway, and other items that indicate the path following inpact.

Flip-chart paper or blank newsprint can be centered over the point of impact. For reference purposes, a straight edge of the paper should be aligned with the roadway, or some identifiable fixed object, or a compass indicating a magnetic north. The angles are then drawn onto the paper with the use of a straight edge, showing and identifying each vehicle's angle of incidence and deviation. A plumber's or carpenter's chalk line is also quite effective as a marking device to indicate the paths of the vehicles to and from the point of impact over the large sheet of paper. A steel tape measure drawn firmly along the various paths can serve as a straight edge from which the lines can be drawn upon the paper.

Once the field paper has been properly marked, the angles can be quickly and easily read with a common protractor. The degrees read from the protractor are recorded, and the various vectors can be reconstructed on graph or diagram paper for the reconstruction report. The field paper should be maintained just as any other piece of secured evidence and filed in the evidence storage or with the original report.

As reconstruction is an estimate based upon mathematics and experience, do not be alarmed if two investigators working the same collision should determine angles of deviation that are not exactly the same. A few degrees of difference between their observations will not appreciably affect the final answer in vector analysis. The difference will probably not lie in their accurate measurements but in a difference of opinion as to the exact angles of deviation, and a disparity of a few miles per hour between two conclusions is rarely an issue.

Another factor that may affect the final answer to some degree is the weight of the vehicles. A vehicle dealer can provide the investigator with the empty curb weight of the respective vehicles. Vehicles in collisions are usually heavier than the dealer information due to fuel in the tank, driver weight, and the weight of the load and other passengers. To be accurate, these items, too, must be taken into consideration to develop a valid answer. A 2,000 pound vehicle carrying four 200 pound men will pose quite a weight difference from the same vehicle being driven by a 100 pound woman and no passengers. Once again, the resultant answers will be only as accurate as the quality of the information entered into the formulas.

MINIMUM SPEED DETERMINATIONS BASED ON
FALLING OBJECTS FROM A MOVING VEHICLE

The author has developed the charts (Figs. 9-21 and 9-22) to assist an investigator with speed determinations of vehicles that are struck at or near a known point of

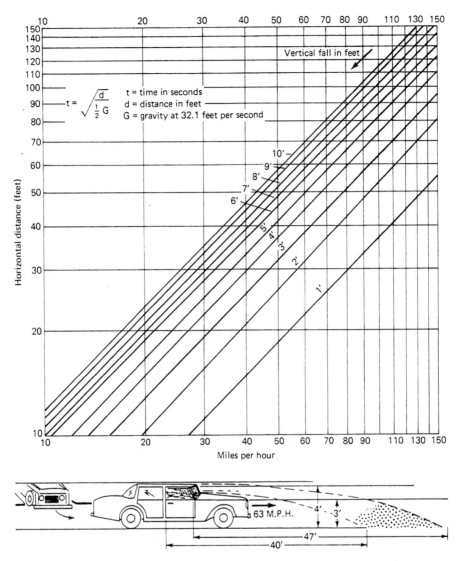

FIGURE 9-21. Minimum Speed Determination Based on Falling Objects from a Moving Vehicle

impact and where side window glass or an object is dislodged and falls to the pavement.

The glass or object must fall uninhibited by any outside force except gravity. As the point of impact is known, and the point of contact with the pavement is also known, the minimum speed of the vehicle losing the glass can be determined. By measuring the height of fall, and the horizontal distance traveled, the charts are interpreted in terms of miles per hour and kilometers per hour.

The horizontal distance from point of impact to point of contact with the road-

187

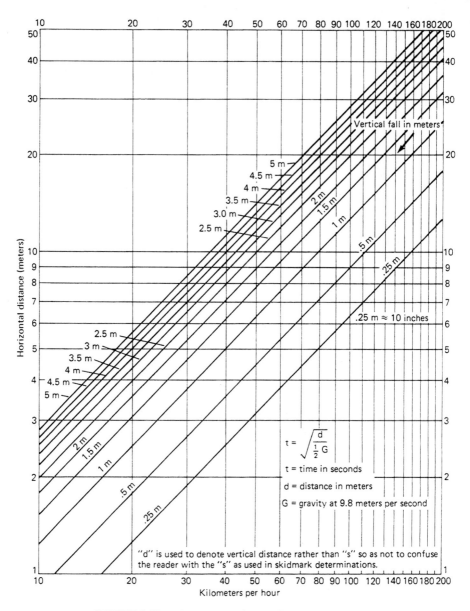

FIGURE 9-22.   Speed Determination from Falling Glass

way is located on the left vertical scale of the chart. The fall distance is read on the diagonal lines. Speed or velocity is read directly beneath the intersection of the two knowns.

For example: An object falling from a height of three feet, moving a horizontal distance of 30 feet from point of impact to point of contact with the roadway, was minimally moving at a rate of 47 miles per hour.

188

An object falling from a height of one meter, moving a horizontal distance of ten meters from point of impact to point of contact with the roadway, was moving at approximately 80 kilometers per hour. These charts are often useful in Auto-Ped collisions where objects are broken and dislodged during impact. Another useful area is the considerations of a broadside or sideswipe type collision.

Windshield glass with its laminated construction does not usually break and fall away like tempered and stressed side window glass. Because tempered side window glass is stressed during the cooling process, it shatters upon impact into kernel-sized pieces. These small pieces fall with relative ease, undisturbed by aerodynamic considerations, and upon striking the pavement, come rather rapidly to rest, caught in the grit of roadway, breaking and shattering even more. The debris of tempered glass is very visible and lends itself readily to night time photography.

An object striking the pavement will usually leave a gouge mark, which can be readily discerned even when peripheral traffic strikes and subsequently moves the object.

SPEED DETERMINATION FROM FALLING GLASS

Assume glass from the door fell a distance of three to four feet from top to bottom of the window. Assume also that the glass from the bottom back of the window strikes the pavement at a distance of 40 feet beyond the point of impact, and that the glass from the upper front corner of the window strikes the roadway 47 feet away from the point of impact. This is a typical-freeway-collision set of circumstances.

By following the three foot line on the chart to the intersection of the 40 foot horizontal index we read down the graph to see the glass was moving at a rate of 63 miles per hour. By following the four foot diagonal line down to where it crosses the 47 foot horizontal index, we read downward to discover this glass also was moving at a rate of 63 miles per hour. In short, when struck and shattered, this glass was attached to a vehicle moving at a rate of 63 miles per hour and fell to earth subject only to the laws of gravity.

When measuring glass debris, measure to the observable peripheries of where the glass struck the pavement, and not to the outer reaches of where the glass is located, which has been subsequently struck and dragged by passing traffic.

DISCUSSION QUESTIONS

1. When trying to determine the coefficient of friction for a roadway, a number of investigators measure only the longest skid left by the test vehicle. Will the resultant coefficient of friction percentage be higher or lower?

2. For low speed collisions, coefficient of friction tests should be run at no less than 25 M.P.H. For high speed collisions the coefficient of friction

tests should be run at 35 or 40 M.P.H. when conditions permit. Discuss the reasons for the different test speeds.

3. Discuss the problems encountered by differing types of terminology when defining skid marks found at a collision scene.

4. Can you convert miles per hour to kilometers per hour?

5. Can you obtain the square root of three and four digit numbers without the aid of a calculator?

6. Why is the formula constant "15" used in the computation of the acceleration skid mark, when "30" is used to compute a locked-wheel skid mark?

7. There are a number of vehicles on the roadway today that are manufactured of a fiberglass rather than a metal exterior. Would you expect that the deformation formula does not apply to such vehicles?

8. It is not uncommon to see an investigator pacing distances or using a wheeled measuring device at the scene of a collision. When would you suppose such measurement methods could be appropriate?

9. Where is the moment of force being exerted as a vehicle makes a tight left turn?

10. There is nothing a driver can do to steer or stop a vehicle once the wheels cease to rotate. Have you ever had the opportunity to witness a collision where the driver could have driven around the area of conflict if he had just let up on the brakes?

The Hydroplaning Phenomenon

Since people decided that the horseless carriage rode better on pneumatic tires, there has been an effort to develop a better tread. We see evidence of this in aggressive sales efforts which use clever or sophisticated advertising, including raised letters on tire sidewalls. The "grappler," the "grabber," the "tracker," the "road handler," the "Indy 500," the "rain tire," the "Daytona," and the "road hugger" are just a few names used over the years. Manufacturers have been extolling the virtues of their tires over the competitors' by claiming *their* tread is more aggressive, modern, or practical. The motoring public shops around, accepts what the auto manufacturers sell them, and often ends up buying whatever is on sale, or whatever seems cosmetically appropriate for their vehicle.

It was not the automotive industry that discovered the real value of tire tread, ironically, but rather the airlines. Studies accomplished by the National Aeronautics and Space Administration taught us the importance of tread.

TIRE TREAD AND PRESSURE

Originally, the aeronautics industry utilized "slicks" or treadless tires. Safety depends not so much in the tread design, but in the depth of the tread. Most states and countries have insisted that tires on all vehicles meet certain tread depth requirements. Motorists ask, "Why all the fuss when we know that a slick tire works better than a treaded tire on brushed concrete which is flat and dry?" Race drivers have known this for years and employ slicks almost exclusively for the race track, when it is dry. The depth of the tire tread experiments began when it was rediscovered that water, unlike air, will not compress beneath the tire. The water must be given a place to escape as it is trapped between the tire and the surface of the asphalt. When the water cannot escape, the tire will ride upon the surface of the water much like a water ski. This phenomenon has been called hydroplaning.

It was further observed that tire pressure played a role in determining when a tire hydroplanes. The tire with more air holds the shape of the tire intact, providing for the widest separation of the tread, and consequently the greatest escape routes for the water.

FACTORS THAT AFFECT HYDROPLANING

Surface Roadway and Runway Considerations

A number of things have been done to alter the surfaces on our airport runways and highways to alleviate the wet weather problems associated with the lower coefficients of friction experienced. Roadways are designed with a crown to force water to run off one side or the other. Concrete surfaces are now poured with a rough brushing as the final step in the process to texture the surface. The brushed surface of a highway accomplishes two things: (1) the individual corners of the brushed surfaces actually "bite" into the surface of the tread, and (2) the recesses of the concrete give the water a run-off area that the tire will not contact.

Old concrete highways and airport runways have most recently undergone a scarifying technique. It has been discovered that when the surface of the roadway is cut by a diamond saw blade, the cuts give a run-off area for the water during inclement weather. To this end, an entire industry has sprung up across the countries of the motoring world that have concrete highways and runways. Cutting machines the width of traffic lanes have been built with saw blades that protrude from the bottom approximately one inch apart. Large tanks of water above the blades spray the cooling liquid onto the blades to prevent them from burning or eroding away as the machine is driven forward. The cuts in the surface of the concrete are only one-eighth to one-fourth of an inch deep, but still do the job most efficiently, allowing water to flow at a sub-surface level below where the rubber meets the road.

Cutting the asphaltic roadways is possible, but not very practical. One problem comes in gumming the saw blades. Another problem is that asphalt congeals in warm weather or under the weight of the vehicles. The cuts fill with the asphalt as it folds and melts into the recesses of the cuts, making the scarifying ineffective. One way to make asphaltic roadways more rain efficient has been the addition of a high grit of crushed gravel to the mix poured over the surface. The high grit increases the coefficient of friction and does allow for small pockets where water can collect. The grit also tends to bite into the rolling tire tread passing over it.

Weather Conditions

An airport landing strip is not that much different from the average roadway. Again, the braking systems worked better with the slicks on dry, asphaltic runways. But both automobiles and airplanes must land on and be operative on concrete and asphalt surfaces in *all* kinds of weather and atmospheric conditions.

When an automobile is driven in inclement weather, not all wheels may lose contact with the roadway and hydroplane at the same time. There are a number of factors which will bear out this observation. First of all, not all drivers will maintain the same tire pressure in all four tires. Secondly, water accumulates near one edge of the lane of travel. Finally, not all the tires on the vehicle will wear evenly, and some tires will have more or less tread than others.

Speed

It has been determined that the speed of the vehicle or airplane was a definite factor in the formula of the hydroplaning phenomenon. The difference is in the speed at which an airplane must come to earth, or a factor called "landing speed." If an airplane attempts to land at a speed below the critical landing speed, the aircraft will nose down and fall to earth. It is not uncommon for airplanes to land, of necessity, at speeds in excess of 100 miles per hour. Tire tread or the lack of tread becomes a decided factor at these speeds on runways that are saturated with rain.

The single biggest factor of traffic collisions during inclement weather is speed *for conditions.* When the tire hydroplanes, it is actually lifted up on the water and no longer has a grip upon the roadway. The action is similar to what happens when a water skier is skimming along the surface of a lake. The water skier skims the surface of the water without difficulty until such time as the speed is lowered. Without sufficient speed, the skier sinks into the water. To be raised from the water, the speed must be increased.

In slow motion photography it has been shown that a tire which is hydroplaning will slow in its rotation and come to a standstill and begin to rotate in the opposite direction as the water splashes upward across the leading edge of the tire. The hydroplaning vehicle or airplane in the meantime is still moving forward unchecked by the action of the tire. As with a locked-wheel skid, it will make little difference what the driver does to the steering wheel of the vehicle while hydroplaning is occurring, for there exists little control. The water striking the side of a hydroplaning wheel will tend to propel the vehicle into a spin and definitely put the vehicle out of control.

FORMULA FOR HYDROPLANING

Through a great deal of observation, notetaking, and mathematics, the following formula was developed:

$$V_{hp} = \sqrt{T.P.} \times 10.34$$

V_{hp} = velocity at which a vehicle will hydroplane in miles per hour.
T.P. = tire pressure (expressed in pounds per square inch).
10.34 is a constant.

This formula holds true whenever the depth of the water exceeds the depth of the tread grooves in the tire. This is an important factor to remember. Any tire can hydroplane whenever it is driven through water which is deeper than the depth of the tread. The speed at which hydroplaning will occur is then a factor determined by tire pressure.

By simply determining the tire pressure, taking the square root of that number, and multiplying the answer by 10.34, we can ascertain the speed at which the tire will hydroplane. Let us assume that a tire has 25 pounds of air. Let us further assume that it is propelled through water which is deeper than the tread of that tire. As previously stated, there is a potential for this tire to hydroplane under these conditions. The square root of 25 is 5. 5 times 10.34 is 51.7. The speed at which hydroplaning will occur is then 51.7 miles per hour. Let us increase the tire pressure to 36 pounds per square inch. The square root of 36 is 6. Six times 10.34 is 62.04. The speed at which hydroplaning will occur is then 62.04 miles per hour. (See Fig. 10-1.)

From this discussion, it is obvious that during inclement weather, it is to our advantage to have the tires on our vehicles pumped to a higher air pressure. Imagine, if you will, the number of vehicles on the roadways riding on soft cushion rides with but 16 pounds per square inch or less in the tires. The square root of 16 is 4. Four times 10.34 is 41.36. The speed at which hydroplaning will occur is then 41.36 miles per hour.

Let us assume for a moment that a right front tire on an automobile has been worn to a point where it has only 1/32 inches of tread. (1/32 inches, tread by the way, is the legal minimum in most states of the United States.) Suppose that this tire is propelled through a pool of standing water adjacent to the right curb that is only 1/8th of an inch deep, a situation that occurs in any measurable rain storm. Let us assume further that the automobile is traveling at a speed of 55 miles per hour, or legal freeway speeds. Let us imagine that this tire has a comfortable 25 pounds per square inch of air. We know from previous mathematics that the tire will hydroplane at 51.07 miles per hour, and hydroplane it will. (See Fig. 10-2.)

The tire rides upon the water, breaking traction with the surface of the roadway. The forward rotation of the tire begins to decelerate almost instantly. Within a

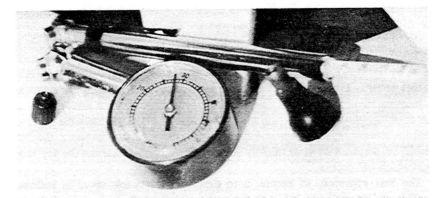

FIGURE 10-1. Shown are the two most common instruments utilized to determine the air pressure of a tire. The "aneroid" type shown with the dial is calibrated in both pounds per square inch and kilograms per square centimeter. As shown, 2 KG/cm² is the equivalent of 28.75 P.S.I. (2.5 KH/cm² equals 35.5 P.S.I.) At 28.75 P.S.I., hydroplaning can occur at 55.44 M.P.H. or 89.22 Kilometers Per Hour. In those areas where the maximum speed limit is 55 M.P.H. or 90 K.P.H., tire pressures on a vehicle should be a minimal 29 P.S.I. or 2 KG per cm² during the wet weather seasons.

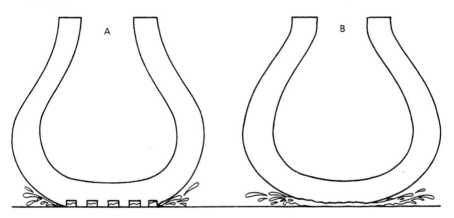

FIGURE 10-2. a. The tire stays on the roadway as the water enters the tread and is given a route of escape. b. The bald tire rides upon the water, hydroplaning. The water, unlike air, will not compress and lifts the tire from the surface of the roadway.

few seconds, a speedometer attached to this tire shows the speed of the tire to be near zero, while the speedometer of the automobile indicates 55 miles per hour. At the end of the puddle or pool of water, the tire is no longer supported by water and meets the surface of the roadway once again. The sudden exposure of roadway surface to the stopped tire causes a sudden gripping action much like braking, but in reverse. The stopped tire must suddenly accelerate to the speed of the vehicle.

This right front braking action tends to pull the vehicle sharply to the right causing the vehicle to pivot around the stopped wheel.

A driver who is not prepared for this phenomenon will probably apply the brakes sharply and broadside to a stop, or spin out of control. In any event, such a driver will most likely end up in a collision. The correct course of action for a driver in this position is to anticipate what is going to happen on seeing the water and slow down, if time permits, prior to entering the water. If time does not permit, the driver should stay away from the brakes when the vehicle enters the water and hold the steering wheel steady and straight. As the wheel exits the water, the driver should be prepared to steer slightly to the left, to compensate for the tug to the right which will occur.

The best approach, of course, is to slow to a reasonable speed in inclement weather and to maintain a higher tire pressure through those seasons of the year when rain is to be anticipated. Expecting the unexpected is a part of modern day driving. The hydroplaning phenomenon occurred and caused very serious injuries in an automobile collision when a swimming pool contractor drained a pool onto a roadway on a dry clear summer day. The water followed the elevations of the roadway for some several blocks and finally drained on the far side of a major roadway. The driver of a station wagon loaded with children coming back from an outing entered the watery area as explained in the example. The tire pressure of the right front tire was a meager 12 pounds per square inch. The tire was nearly bald, the water run-off area was approximately fifty feet wide, and the vehicle's speed was nearly 60 miles per hour. The right front tire hydroplaned in the water and, upon exiting, acted like a pivot point around which the large vehicle rotated prior to slamming into the curb and roadside trees.

The water on the roadway lowers the coefficient of friction to something appreciably less than a dry surface, and skidding becomes an ever present hazard. Couple a lowered coefficient of friction with the hydroplaning phenomenon and the reader can grasp the depth of the problem of driving in inclement weather, and the necessity of driving at lowered speeds.

With a debt of gratitude to the aerospace industry, drivers can now more readily appreciate the necessity for reasonable driving during inclement weather. Pilots have the advantage of grooved tires on their landing gear which spray considerable amounts of water but lets the tires come into contact with the runway, making braking actions possible much sooner than before.

TIRE QUALITY GRADING SYSTEM

The National Highway Traffic Safety Administration, Department of Transportation, requires that all passenger tires manufactured after October 1, 1979 (excluding mud and snow tires and space-saver or temporary-use spare tires) be graded in three areas of performance: treadwear, traction, and temperature resistance.

Treadwear

The treadwear grade is a comparative rating based on the "wear" rate of the tire when tested under controlled conditions on a specified government test course. For example, a tire graded "150" would wear one and a half times as well on this government test course as a tire graded "100."

The problem which arises is that the tire is graded on a standard course under "constant" conditions. The "average" driver is anything but average and the relative actual performance will depart significantly from the norm, due to variations in driving habits, service practices (tire rotation), differences in road characteristics, and climate. Thus, one driver with tires graded at 100 may experience better tire life than a driver whose tires are graded at 150.

Temperature

The temperature grades are A (the highest), B, and C. The grades represent the tire's resistance to the generation of heat and the tire's ability to dissipate heat when tested under controlled conditions on a specified indoor laboratory test wheel. Sustained high temperature can cause the material of the tire to degenerate and reduce tire life. Excessive temperature can lead to sudden tire failure. The grade of C corresponds to a level of performance which all passenger car tires must meet under the Federal Motor Vehicle Safety Standard, Number 109. Grades A and B represent higher levels of performance on the laboratory test wheel than the minimum required by law.

Again, the definition of "average" driver will decidedly affect the tire temperature. Items which alter tire temperatures are high driving speeds, improper tire inflation, excessive loading, skidding, altitude (which affects tire pressure), and brake drag. Any of these conditions in excess will cause heat build-up and possible tire failure.

Traction

The traction grades are A (the highest), B, and C. The grades represent the tire's ability to stop on wet pavement as measured under controlled conditions on specified government test surfaces of asphalt and concrete. A tire marked C may have poor traction performance. A warning is in order according to the testers. The traction grade assigned to the C tire is based on braking traction tests and does not include cornering traction as it affects centrifugal or turning performance.

Tire Grading Summary

It appears that bias ply tires of all sizes have a tread wear rating of 80, a traction rating of B, and a temperature rating of C. Glass belted bias tires of all sizes have a tread wear rating of 100 to 150, a traction rating of A or B, and a temperature rating of C. Glass, fabric, and steel belted radial tires have a substantially better rating in all categories.

Do not be swayed by the traction rating system, as every standard passenger tire will hydroplane when the water depth exceeds the tread depth. Remember that traction grades are based on the wet weather ability of the tread to squeege the water between the tire and the road surface. Tires do wear, and as they wear, the traction rating of the tire decreases. A driver will rarely experience laboratory-like conditions when driving in wet weather. The tire quality grading system is included in this text to develop a more knowledgeable consumer and correct misinformation concerning the various grades of passenger tires.

WET WEATHER DRIVING TIPS

1. Allow more space between your vehicle and the vehicle ahead. Normal driving dictates a two-second cushion between vehicles. Wet weather operation will demand three to four seconds.
2. On multi-laned roadways, travel as much as possible in the lanes near the middle of the roadway. The middle lanes are higher as they comprise the crown of the roadway. The water run-off goes to the lanes on the outside edges.
3. Change lanes only if absolutely necessary and then at reduced speeds. Water will accumulate adjacent to the lane dividing lines. This is particularly true on concrete roadways which are poured in sections one lane at a time. Water will pool at the edge of the adjacent lane line in such instances and may be as much as a half-inch deep. In the rain, it may look level and smooth when in actuality the lane transition from one surface to the other will be quite rough, due to the settling of the heavy concrete slabs.
4. When exiting a major highway, be aware of the change in coefficient of friction. The concrete will provide better drag factors for rolling friction control in steering. The asphaltic ramps will exhibit a coefficient of friction which is much lower. A speed which was safe and reasonable on the freeway is hazardous and unsafe on the asphaltic ramp.
5. The exits from a major highway are natural run-off areas for accumulating water from the highway. At numerous places along a ramp, water will run freely across the entire width of the ramp, not only reducing coefficient of friction, but often deep enough to allow hydroplaning to occur. Slow the vehicle prior to taking the ramp.
6. Although the temptation exists to chase errant drivers who are driving much too fast in the rain, avoid pursuit if at all possible.

In wet weather driving, the probability of hydroplaning is higher for the police officer than for the violator. The police officer must drive faster than the violator to catch and terminate the pursuit. Consequently, the police officer presents a higher risk to himself and others than the violator. By patrolling at a reasonable speed in the center lanes of a multi-laned roadway, the police officer becomes a

FIGURE 10-3. Hydroplaning

pacesetter and controls the flow of traffic during inclement weather in an orderly manner, avoiding the necessity of pursuit driving. Should an errant high speed driver be observed, the officer can radio ahead to another unit or agency to effect the stop.

SUMMARY

The subject of hydroplaning is such a dominant factor in wet weather collisions that this chapter has been devoted to the topic. The dramatic rise in wet weather collisions is a constant reminder that most drivers are either unaware of the inherent dangers or willing to gamble on the probabilities of not being involved in a collision.

The hydroplaning formula was developed through empirical observations of numerous tests by both the public and private sectors concerned with tire manufacture and public safety.

In light rains, every driver has observed the tracks which are left upon the roadway by the forward vehicle. The tracks are no more than the squeegee effect of the tire tread wiping the water from the surface of the roadway. This observation is particularly true in heavy mist and fog. As the moisture on the surface deepens, the tracks and squeegee effect are no longer visible as the water flushes instantly over the marks left by the tire tread. As tire pressure and tread depth decrease with a like increase in water depth, hydroplaning will occur.

An officer or investigator can develop the coefficient of friction for the roadway at the scene of the collision. The process is the same as outlined in Chapter 9. Any testing will have to be at lower speeds because of the very low coefficient of friction. Testing will also have to be accomplished as soon as possible after the collision due to the changing atmospheric conditions. The real problem in reconstructing the collision will arise in determining the distance the collision vehicle skidded prior to the crash. This is an area where witness statements and deformation damage information become critical.

Most wet weather driving collisions occur as a result of violating the basic speed law: too fast for conditions. By using the precepts taught in this text, the investigator can make a very good case in court.

DISCUSSION QUESTIONS

1. When the last rainy season hit your area, do you recall the problem you experienced in driving? Was the problem one of reacclimation to conditions, or a reluctance to accept the slower traffic?

2. What tire pressure do you maintain on your tires? Are all of your tires evenly pressurized, front and rear?

3. Consider the particles of accumulated rubber, dirt, and debris that have accumulated on the highway since the last rain. With the advent of a storm, these particles float to the surface, forming an oil slick residue that is subsequently scrubbed by the passing tires and washed away by the rain. If you rode a motorcycle and found yourself caught in the rain, is there a safer portion of the lane in which to ride? Why would you avoid the middle of a lane?

11

Collision Statistics, Studies, and Solutions

Traffic records are comprised primarily of collision investigations and reports. We will concern ourselves here with the police function and the vital role the reports play in making that function more meaningful.

The National Highway Safety Administration (United States Department of Transportation) estimates that the typical traffic collision has a total cost to society of over $3,000. The total cost to society includes such items as property damage, the costs of collision investigation, and the costs and awards of civil litigations. Considering the large number of collisions which require investigation, in which the damage to the vehicles is only two to three hundred dollars, and the only injury is to the driver's ego, it becomes clear that it is to our benefit to reduce collisions, the tragedy in fatalities and injuries notwithstanding. With inflation climbing on a worldwide basis, it is probable that the $3,000 figure becomes higher every day. The dollars, pounds, marks, guilders, yen, or whatever monetary system is employed cannot pay for the suffering, pain, or death of one individual.

It is the duty of police agencies to reduce collisions in some systematic manner. The hit and miss system of simply sending police officers out into the field will have an effect, but not as much as having a plan and knowledge of where collisions are most likely to occur and why.

The three "E's" of traffic are enforcement, engineering, and education. No one has a greater opportunity to have an impact on the collision problem than the traffic officer. The officer may chose to speak with one violator in terms of education. In another instance the officer may see an engineering problem and suggest a viable solution to collision reduction. In the third capacity the officer may issue citations or effect an in-custody arrest for certain violations.

RECORDING THE COLLISION

In the melee of a serious collision, it is difficult for an officer to grasp or be concerned with the statistical picture. Participants to a collision could not care less that they are a statistic being recorded for posterity by the officer. However, someone does care and someone is reviewing the collision with an eye to cause and prevention. The courts and the attorneys are concerned only after the fact. The engineers are constantly reviewing the causal factors and developing schemes to reduce the number of collisions. In the United States, for example, collisions are being reduced by the placement of international signs and simplified plaques. The standard use of the metric system on a worldwide basis will eventually also be an asset.

FIGURE 11-1.   Not only is the young man sitting in the window of the pick-up a visual hazard, he is risking his life. Sudden braking or a quick turning movement by the driver would undoubtedly throw the young man to the pavement.

The Use of Computers

Collision records are reduced in many instances to microfilm and coded into computers and files which pinpoint problem areas and causal factors. Because the whole recording process begins with the officer, this first step is the most critical. Frequently an officer will write in haste or illegibly or code a collision in error. When the report is processed and information is gleaned for recording into the computer, the error is reiterated and possibly compounded by errors of the computer entry operator. The resultant readout will be necessarily wrong and provide the departmental supervisors with an erroneous reading for consideration. This series of errors has been given the name of "GIGO": "garbage in, garbage out." GIGO is well known throughout the computer industry and has spread its influence over associated customers such as the traffic agencies who demand reliable information based on past experience. The problem of accuracy, legibility, and error-free reporting falls directly on the officer who prepares the initial report.

Computer readouts which provide a historical review of collisions can be extremely beneficial to traffic supervisors. The readouts provide not only the type of collision but location, severity, primary collision factor, time of day, day of week, and severity index, to name just a few of the bits of information available. The supervisor can then deploy the officers to meet the demand in a particular area.

Other Methods

We have thus far discussed the use of computers to keep the records of accumulated history. The majority of police agencies in the world do not have access to such a modern convenience. These departments develop the records and maintain maps to show the collision locations and severity. Some departments use a "pin" map system. One color of pin head indicates a property-damage-only collision, another color indicates injuries, and a third distinctive color is for fatal collisions. As the pins begin to accumulate in a given portion of the map, the police supervisor begins to look for the root of the problem.

RESOLVING THE COLLISION PROBLEM

Be it a pin map or a computer readout which highlights a given problem area, the next step is the same police function of enforcement, education, and engineering. The best approach for the supervisor is to incorporate as much thinking about the resolution of the problem as may be available. The traffic officers working the area are the best source of information as to possible solutions. They are the ones who day in and day out must work the collisions which occur, and they often have a

REPORT OF PRIMARY COLLISION FACTORS FOR ACCIDENTS AND VICTIMS

PRIMARY COLLISION FACTOR	ACCIDENTS					VICTIMS					
	TOTAL	FATAL	INJURY	TOW AWAY	PROP. DAMAGE ONLY DRIVEABLE	TOTAL VICTIMS	TOTAL KILLED	TOTAL INJURED	SEVERE WOUND	OTHER VIS INJ	COMPLAINT OF PAIN
UNKNOWN CAUSE	39	0	12	7	20	19	0	19	2	12	5
DRIVER UNDER INFLU ALCOHOL	87	0	43	23	21	68	0	68	6	45	17
IMPEDING TRAFFIC	0	0	0	0	0	0	0	0	0	0	0
UNSAFE SPEED	180	3	61	49	67	97	3	94	5	43	46
FOLLOWING TOO CLOSELY	6	0	2	2	2	4	0	4	0	3	1
WRONG SIDE OF ROAD	21	1	11	4	5	25	1	24	1	20	3
IMPROPER PASSING	10	0	4	0	6	6	0	6	0	5	1
CHANGING LANE UNSAFELY	30	0	9	5	16	14	0	14	0	9	5
IMPROPER TURNING	69	1	16	16	36	23	1	22	0	14	8
AUTO RIGHT OF WAY	133	1	48	29	55	89	1	88	3	46	39
PEDESTRIAN RIGHT OF WAY	1	0	1	0	0	1	0	1	1	0	0
PEDESTRIAN VIOLATION	7	3	2	1	1	7	3	4	0	2	2
STOP SIGNALS AND SIGNS	26	0	10	7	9	14	0	14	0	5	9
HAZARDOUS PARKING	0	0	0	0	0	0	0	0	0	0	0
LIGHTS	1	0	1	0	0	2	0	2	0	0	2
BRAKES	6	1	1	0	4	2	1	1	0	1	0
OTHER EQUIPMENT	6	0	1	1	4	1	0	1	0	1	0
OTHER HAZARDOUS VIOLATIONS	11	0	6	3	2	8	0	8	0	3	5
OTHER THAN DRIVER	34	1	10	10	13	13	1	12	1	11	0
DRIVER UNDER INFLU DRUGS	4	0	1	1	2	2	0	2	0	1	1
OVER MAXIMUM SPEED	1	0	0	1	0	0	0	0	0	0	0
UNSAFE STARTING/BACKING	19	0	2	3	14	2	0	2	0	1	1
OTHER IMPROPER DRIVING	42	0	18	11	13	23	0	23	1	15	7
PEDESTRIAN UNDER INFLUENCE	0	0	0	0	0	0	0	0	0	0	0
TOTAL	733	11	259	173	290	420	11	409	20	237	152

FIGURE 11-2. Sample Computer Readouts

REPORT OF ACCIDENT LOCATION DETAILS AND INVOLVED PARTY DATA

PRIMARY LOC. REF.

SECONDARY LOC. REF. DIST **DATE** NO. TIME NO. JUR. I.D. NO. WEATHER LIGHTING RD-SUR DIRC. ROAD-COND. MOVEMENT PRE- R-O-W TYPE OF OTHER ASSOC. VEH. INV. PED.

LOC TYPE	REPORT NUMBER	DIRC	DAY	NO. INV.	NO. FAT.	TIME	CODE	INJ.	PRI.COL.FACT. NO.	**VEHICLE-TYPE**	TRAV.	01 / 02 / 03 CEDING COLLISION	CONTROL	COLL.	FACTORS	WITH DRUG/PHYSIC	ACTION

BEAT 0

RT 7

RT 9
NEW SH 8003   19536 01/06/8 1   1555 0   9   055 1 UNSAFE SPEED   DAYLIGHT 1 MOTORCYC/SCOOTER DRY NORM/ EAST / NOT PRES RAN OFF ROAD HIT OBJ FIXED OBJ NOT INV INATTENTION IMPAIR UNK
EAST SUN

LA NATA RD
NEW SH 8014   8976   02/15/8 3   1720 0   9   058 0 UNSAFE SPEED   DAYLIGHT DRY CLEAR NORM/ / NOT PRES SDESWPE OTHER MV NOT INV
EAST FRI   1 CAR/WAGON   WEST   INTO OPPOS. LANE WRNG SIDE RD HBD-NO INF
                                                               2 PICKUP/PANEL TRK EAST   PROCEED STRAIGHT NONE APPARNT HHBD
                                                               3 CAR/WAGON   EAST   PROCEED STRAIGHT NONE APPARNT HHBD

CAMTO VAQUERO
NEW SH 8007   0   02/09/8 1   1500 0   9   055 0 OTHER THAN DRVR DAYLIGHT DRY CLEAR NORM/ / NOT PRES OVRTRND NON-COLL NOT INV
EAST SAT   1 PASS CAR W/TRALR WEST   PROCEED STRAIGHT OTHER EQUIP. HNBD
                                                                                            DEF VEH EQUP

BEAT 1

RT 7

ERT 15
NEW SH 8001   52800 03/02/8 1   0005 0   9   090 2 DRUNK DRIVING   DRK-NO LTS DRY CLOUDY NORM/ / NOT PRES HIT OBJ FIXED OBJ NOT INV
EAST SUN   1 PICKUP/PANEL TRK WEST   RAN OFF ROAD WRNG SIDE RD HBD-UND INF

LA CHICA
NEW SH 8020   10   01/25/8 1   1815 0   9   079 0 IMPROP. TURNING DRK-NO LTS DRY CLEAR NORM/ / NOT PRES HIT OBJ FIXED OBJ NOT INV
EAST FRI   1 CAR/WAGON   EAST   RAN OFF ROAD NONE APPARNT IMPAIR UNK

ELA 15
NEW CT 8016   57024 01/19/8 1   1815 0   9   079 0 IMPROP. TURNING DRK-NO LTS DRY CLEAR NORM/ / NOT PRES HIT OBJ FIXED OBJ NOT INV
EAST SAT   1 CAR/WAGON   WEST   RAN OFF ROAD NONE APPARNT HNBD

SN SINO RD
NEW SH 8008   0   02/09/8 1   2215 0   9   092 0 WRONG SIDE ROAD DAYLIGHT DRY CLEAR NORM/ / NOT PRES HIT OBJ FIXED OBJ NOT INV
EAST SAT   1 CAR/WAGON   WEST   RAN OFF ROAD UNSAFE SPEED HBD-NO INF
                                                                                            UNFAM. ROAD

RT 9
NEW SH 8000   71280 03/01/8 2   1330 0   9   082 1 UNSAFE SPEED   DAYLIGHT DRY CLOUDY NORM/ / CON FUNC OVRTRND NON-COLL NOT INV
EAST SAT   1 MOTORCYC/SCOOTER EAST   INTO OPPOS. LANE NONE APPARNT HNBD
                                                               2 CAR/WAGON   WEST   PROCEED STRAIGHT NONE APPARNT HHBD

FIGURE 11-2. (cont.)

205

feeling or reaction to the problem which cannot be readily translated into words in a collision report. After all, the collision report deals strictly with the facts of each individual case and not the possible changes in the design of the highway which might alleviate the problem altogether. The supervisor should go outside of his department to the engineering staff responsible for the particular highway and encourage the engineering staff to meet with the officers to exchange ideas. This spirit of cooperation not only solves the immediate problem, but serves to build trust between the two groups.

A similar approach is to assign one or two officers to tackle the problem of high collision areas, and to develop a checklist of possible solutions. The officers study one area at a time and develop their recommendations, often with the aid of a staff member from the engineering unit. Their recommendations are then sent upward through channels to the appropriate funding acency for action based on fiscal restraints and budget priorities. This two-pronged attack is quite successful in that both departments are now pushing for resolution to a problem that has been identified, quantified, and justified for consideration. A rating system is developed and the problem areas are given a priority as to the immediacy with which the solution is to be implemented. With patience and supervisory skill, the officers and the engineering staff may be able to motivate the persons responsible for change. The saving of lives and property is far more important than the writing of a few citations, and the time consumed is minimal in comparison to the rewards of success.

Some smaller departments are going to a system of computer time sharing to handle their data. With one small department, the computer technology may be absolutely cost prohibitive. However, if three or four smaller departments all utilize one computer, the cost to each is minimal and well worth the investment. The computer can also be used to handle other police matters that are germane to all, such as the storage of wants and warrants on persons and vehicles.

Traffic Volume Studies

Traffic volume studies are made to obtain factual data concerning the movement of vehicles and persons at selected points on the street or highway system. Volume data is expressed in relation to time. The time base is determined by the type of information desired and the application in which it is to be used.

1. Annual traffic in vehicles per year is used for:
   a. Determining annual travel.
   b. Estimating expected highway user revenue.
   c. Computing collision rates (per million vehicle miles).
   d. Indicating trends in volume, especially on toll facilities.

2. Average Daily Traffic (ADT) or Average Annual Daily Traffic (AADT) in vehicles per day is used for:
   a. Measuring the present demand for service by the street or highway.
   b. Evaluating the present traffic flow with respect to the street.
   c. Developing the major or arterial street system.
   d. Locating areas where new facilities or improvements to existing facilities are needed.
   e. Programming capital improvements.
3. Hourly traffic in vehicles is used for:
   a. Determining length and magnitude of peak periods.
   b. Evaluating capacity deficiencies.
   c. Establishing traffic controls. Volume is usually among the warrants for the:
      (1) Installation of signs, signals, and markings.
      (2) Designation of through streets, one-way streets, unbalanced flow, and traffic routing.
      (3) Prohibition of parking, stopping, and turning.
   d. Geometric design or redesign of streets and intersections.
4. Short term counts, (covering 5, 6, 10, or 15 minute intervals), are usually expanded into hourly flow rates. Such counts are primarily used to analyze:
   a. Maximum flow rates.
   b. Flow variations within peak hours.
   c. Capacity limitations on traffic flow.
   d. Characteristics of peak volumes.
5. Density of traffic in vehicles per mile is obtained by dividing the hourly volume by the average speed. Density may be a better measure of street service than volume since it continues to increase as congestion increases. Volume, on the other hand, reaches a maximum under moderate congestion and then decreases with greater congestion. When a complete blockage occurs, density is at its maximum and volume is zero.

Volume studies are again dependent on the application to which the information is to be used.

1. *Street counts* (total volume without regard to direction) are used in developing daily volumes, preparing traffic flow maps, and so on.
2. *Directional counts* are used for capacity, analysis, determining signal timing, justifying traffic controls, planning improvements, obtaining accumulations of vehicles within a specified area, and so on.
3. *Turning movement or intersection counts* are used in designing channelization, planning turn prohibitions, computing capacity, analyzing high collision intersections, evaluating congestion, and so on.

4. *Classification counts* (which obtain volumes of the various types or classes of vehicles in the traffic stream) are used in establishing structural and geometric design criteria, computing expected highway user revenue, computing capacity (effect of commercial vehicles), determining correction factors for machine counts, and so on.

5. *Occupancy counts* are made to determine the distribution of passengers per vehicle, accumulation of persons within an area, proportion of persons utilizing transit facilities, and so on.

6. *Cordon counts* are made at the perimeter of an enclosed area (shopping center, industrial area, and so on). Vehicles and persons entering and leaving the area during a specified time are counted. This data provides information relative to the accumulation of vehicles or persons within the cordon.

7. *Pedestrian counts* are used in evaluating sidewalk and crosswalk needs, justifying pedestrian signals, timing traffic signals, and so on.

8. *Screen line counts* are classified counts taken at all streets intersecting an imaginary line (screen line) bisecting an area. These counts are used to determine trends, expand origin-destination data, traffic assignment, and so on.

The time and length that a specific location should be counted is also a variable dependent upon the data desired and the application in which the data is to be used. Weekend counts, for example, cover the time period between 1800 hours on a Friday until 0600 hours on Monday morning. Holiday counts are based on the same criteria. When a holiday is coupled with a weekend with the holiday on a Friday, the holiday count begins at 1800 hours on Thursday and ends at 0600 hours on Monday morning.

A 24-hour count normally covers any 24-hour period between noon on Monday until noon on Friday. Traffic on Monday mornings and Friday afternoons usually varies from the norm of any other day. Whenever a specific day count is made, such as for a Tuesday or a Saturday, the counting is performed from midnight to midnight.

Traffic in business or commercial areas is normally counted on a 12-hour shift from 0700 hours to 1900 hours or 7 a.m. to 7 p.m. A 16-hour count covers most of the daily flow of traffic and is run from 6 a.m. to 10 p.m. or 0600 hours to 2200 hours.

Most jurisdictions attempt to obtain a 24-hour count for their arterial streets and highways at least once every four years, or whenever a change of major proportions has altered the traffic flow substantially. The counts on minor streets are repeated only when a change occurs which alters the traffic pattern and flow in some significant manner, such as the addition of a housing tract, a road closure, or a route redesign which forces more or less traffic into or out of the area.

The engineering departments within the police jurisdiction are equipped to provide the police supervisor with any of the foregoing information. Armed with facts, the supervisor and the officers, in conjunction with the engineering staff, are in a position to more properly assess high collision scene areas and offer positive and constructive solutions, most often providing a plan complete with options for the problem resolution.

Spot Speed Studies

Purpose. Speed studies are extremely valuable to the officer and engineer alike. Traffic control planning requires speed distribution information. All vehicles do not travel at the same speed at a location. The amount of dispersion or spread in these speeds affects both capacity and safety. If all vehicles traveled at the same speed, capacity would be at a maximum, and collisions caused by overtaking or passing and rear-end collisions would be eliminated. Spot speed studies are used for these purposes:

1. To establish maximum and minimum speed limits.
2. To determine the need for posting safe speeds at curves.
3. To provide information relative to the proper location of regulatory, warning, and guide signs.
4. To establish lengths of no passing zones.
5. To analyze school zone protection.
6. For collision analysis.
7. To research and analyze capacity in relation to capacity, speed versus volume, speed differential analysis, the influence on speed of roadside obstructions or distractions, and so on.
8. To evaluate the effect of some change in controls or conditions.
9. To analyze geometric design, determining the radius and superelevation of curves, lengths of acceleration and deceleration lanes, and so on.
10. To accumulate data concerning approach speed to high collision areas and scenes of conflict.
11. To study the effects of enforcement.

How to Perform a Spot Speed Study. To effectively perform a spot speed study, the officer should set up as close as practical to the area of immediate traffic conflict. The location should be sufficiently obstructed from the driver's view so as not to cause alarm or to influence the driver's reaction or pattern of driving. The officer will recall that this is not a speed trap to catch errant drivers, but a study to determine speeds at a given location. To this extent, the officer and his equipment should be as inconspicuous as possible. Avoid an accumulation of on-lookers and marked police units.

The easiest device to use in the accumulation of speed data is undoubtedly radar. The results are easily tabulated and quickly recorded, requiring no further mathematics to decipher. In the absence of radar, the officer is bound to accumulate his data on the basis of time versus the measured distance. A stopwatch is used, then started and stopped, as the vehicle being measured crosses a start and finish line.

The distance between the start and finish line is known as the trap distance. The trap distance is usually set up in multiples of 88 feet for ease in deriving the speed, as shown in the following table. Pavement markings are painted or chalked laterally upon the roadway. After the initial marking of the roadway there will be no set-up time required to re-examine the speeds at a later date, as the markings are easily renewed. Since the markings are in place over a period of time, they will have little effect on driver behavior.

Table 11.1. Trap Distance Chart

Average Speed of Traffic Stream	Recommended Trap Length	Conversion Factor (Changing seconds to M.P.H.)
Below 25 M.P.H.	88 ft	60 divided by seconds = M.P.H.
25 to 40 M.P.H.	176 ft	120 divided by seconds = M.P.H.
Over 40 M.P.H.	264 ft	180 divided by seconds = M.P.H.

The disadvantage of this system is the introduction of parallax, or not seeing what you think you see because you are looking at an angle to the line and the vehicle being measured. Error can occur if the person operating the stopwatch does not position himself in the same location for each study made. To correct this parallax problem, some observers use an enoscope or "Flash Box." An enoscope is simply an "L" shaped box open on both ends with a mirror in the apex of the "L" set at a 45° angle. The observer sets an enoscope at each of the two lines and looks directly at the mirror and sees the flash of a vehicle going by. With the flash, the observer starts the stopwatch and turns to look at the enoscope on the finish line. When the vehicle passes over the finish line, the mirror again reflects the passing vehicle, the stopwatch is stopped, and the time recorded.

The advantage of the enoscope is simplicity and minimal cost. There are, of course, other devices which will develop the same information for the observer and provide everything from graphic to digital readouts of the speed. These devices are all valid for the intended purpose and will assist the officer in making determinations as to speed.

The behavior of traffic often gives a good indication of the appropriate speed zone which should apply on a particular highway section. It is generally felt that at least 85 percent of drivers operate at speeds which are reasonable and prudent for conditions. Therefore, the 85th percentile speed of a spot speed distribution is a first approximation of the speed zone which might be imposed. The 85th percentile is often called the "critical speed." The drivers exceeding the 85th percentile are usually considered to be driving faster than is safe under existing conditions. The 85th percentile is the percentage which encompasses 85 percent of the speed observed. The upper 15 percent of the observed speed is probably unsafe. In a like manner, the lower 15 percent of the observed speed is in a like manner probably unsafe. The lower 15th percentile is assuming more importance as the use of minimum speed limits increases. The vehicles traveling below this value tend to obstruct the flow of traffic, thereby creating a collision hazard.

Sample Speed Survey Sheets

Speed limits should be established preferably at or near the 85 percentile speed, which is defined as that speed at or below which 85 percent of the traffic is moving. The 85 percentile speed is often referred to as critical speed. Pace speed is defined as the 10-mile increment of speed containing the largest number of vehicles. The lower limit of the pace is plotted on the Speed Zone Survey Sheets as an aid in determining the proper zone limits. Speed limits higher than the 85 percentile are not generally considered reasonable and safe and limits below the 85 percentile do not facilitate the orderly movement of traffic. Speed limits established on this basis conform to the consensus of those who drive the highway as to what speed is reasonable and safe and are not dependent on the judgment of one or a few individuals.

The basic speed law states that no person shall drive at a speed greater than is reasonable or prudent. The majority of drivers comply with this law and disregard regulations which they consider unreasonable. It is only the top fringe of drivers who are inclined to be reckless and unreliable, or who have faulty judgment and must be controlled by enforcement. Speed limits set at or slightly below the 85 percentile speed provide law enforcement officers with a means of controlling the drivers who will not conform to what the majority considers reasonable and prudent.

Only when roadside development results in traffic conflicts and unusual conditions which are not readily apparent to drivers are speed limits somewhat below the 85 percentile warranted.

CONTRIBUTIVE TRAFFIC PROBLEMS

Congestion

Congestion lowers the speed of traffic on a roadway, increasing density and lowering volume. A study by the California Department of Transportation places the optimum speed for moving the greatest amount of vehicles at 35 miles per hour. On a two lane two-way highway with traffic utilizing both lanes, lane capacity was most efficient at 35 miles per hour with 1500 vehicles per lane per hour passing the observation point. Below 35 miles per hour, the vehicles tended to bunch as demand for highway space tends to exceed capacity and the highway turns into a slow-moving mobile parking lot.

Factors which affect a highway are lane widths (12 feet is optimum) visual hazards such as stalled vehicles, lack of adequate shoulders for emergency stops, high density of wide commercial vehicles, high density of camper vehicles and motor homes, sight distance restrictions (such as undulating roadways or curves), and controlled intersections or traffic collisions that obstruct the normal traffic flow. Given ideal freeway and throughway conditions where multiple lanes exist in each direction, and given marked absence of commercial vehicles, each lane has the capacity for an average of 2,000 passenger vehicles per hour.

Vehicle Parking

There are times when an investigator should consider submitting a proposal to inhibit or restrict parking. Major factors affecting this decision include:

1. Narrow roadway width.
2. Restricted visibility at intersections for pedestrians and drivers.
3. Insufficient shoulder width.
4. Conversion of a parking lane to a through lane or right turn lane.

Narrow streets are commonplace among our older cities, and there are a limited number of parking facilities to accomodate an increasing number of vehicles. Drivers tend to prefer personal transportation over mass transportation. Parking is not only difficult, but dangerous, on narrow streets. Drivers tend to drive adjacent to the parked vehicles, most often of necessity. When a parked vehicle occupant attempts to exit on the street side, he or she is too often an unwitting victim of passing vehicles. As cities are forced to accept more traffic, planners restrict building growth to include more on-site parking, and less on-street parking. A good example of this is the parking in and around an apartment complex.

Street parking at or near intersections creates a visual barricade for both pedestrians and drivers. It is for this reason that bus stands are located on the far side of an intersection.

Frequently a driver is forced to slowly move out into an intersection to see around a truck parked near the corner, only to be involved in a near collision. As the speed limit on the through street increases, the sight-distance should increase in like manner, through restricted curb-side parking.

Many times, the parking lane or shoulder is too narrow to accomodate all vehicles. A passenger vehicle is five to six feet wide. A commercial vehicle, on the other hand, is eight feet wide, with doors and mirrors that extend as much as ten feet. Parking stalls are usually painted at eight feet wide and twenty two to twenty four feet in length. When commercial vehicle operators load or unload, the extra area required may extend to twelve feet. The extra street width required for the commercial vehicles often restricts on-street parking to passenger vehicles only. Investigators should be aware of this width requirement when offering suggestions for pre-collision assessment.

Lastly, an investigator should consider the configuration of the intersection, balancing the Average Daily Traffic (ADT) and right turning movements against the possibility of eliminating parking in favor of gaining an extra lane for through-traffic. An investigator may additionally suggest elimination of some parking slots in favor of a turning lane to accomodate right turning vehicles, thus moving the through traffic in a more expeditious manner. A right turn lane is advantageous where there exists pedestrian cross-traffic. The right turning vehicles are now out of the mainstream of traffic while they wait for a break in pedestrian cross-traffic.

Through-traffic may move in an uninterrupted manner. Remember the basic premise of traffic control is to move traffic, not to restrict and inhibit its free flow. On-street parking is often counterproductive to this goal.

Limited-time parking tends to increase vehicle and pedestrian conflict. The odds of a collision increase in limited-time parking areas as more vehicles and pedestrians are leaving and entering the parking stalls. Limited-time parking should be restricted as much as possible to those areas where it is truly beneficial, around a post office or a utility building, for example. Bear in mind that such parking restrictions are worthless without enforcement, and this drains officer availability. An officer enforcing regulations for overtime parking is not available on in-view patrol and for collision investigation.

REPORTING RATES

In order to express the compiled statistics, the National Transportation Safety Council has developed the following guidelines for standardization of reporting. Fatality rates are to be expressed in terms of 100 million vehicle miles. Total collision rates are reported in terms of one million vehicle miles. Collisions, expressed in terms of population, are reported per 100,000 persons. Drivers involved in collisions are reported in terms of 100,000 drivers. Collisions expressed in terms of registered vehicles are reported in either 10,000 or 100,000 vehicles. If, for example, there are "X" number of collisions, this number is divided by 100,000 to determine the population collision rate. The rate is then expressed as a decimal. This rate gives us a figure which we can compare from year to year to see if our efforts to reduce collisions are working. We are aware that our population is increasing somewhat. If the total number of collisions stays the same, the rate will be lower, indicating a success rate.

Since statistics may vary in some jurisdictions, the national collision and vehicle information statistics indicates certain information to the reader. Most injury collisions occur during the evening peak hours between 3 p.m. to 6 p.m. (1500 to 1800 hours). More collisions occur on Friday since it includes normal weekday travel plus the starting of weekend trips, placing increased demands on the highways. More injury collisions occur in the daytime, and more fatal collisions occur during hours of darkness. This indicates that night collisions are generally more severe. It is generally conceded that the drinking drivers are responsible for this statistic.

THE TRAFFIC ENGINEER

As professionals in traffic management, we should be aware of the traffic engineering profession, how it grew, and what the job entails.

History

Although the first traffic signal was installed as early as 1912, it was almost ten years later when the position of traffic engineer was established in any city. Seattle, Chicago, Pittsburgh, and Philadelphia were among the first to designate traffic engineers.

The traffic engineering functions in the 1920s were more limited in scope than today. The engineer's major function was the management of traffic signals. Most modern techniques for traffic regulation or street and highway planning were still unknown. Traffic signs usually followed local design, since national standards for uniform design and application of traffic control devices had not been adopted.

The Institute of Traffic Engineers, founded in 1930, is the professional society for traffic engineers. Forty years after its inception, the institute had approximately 3,000 members. The institute cooperates with the American Association of State Highway Officials, the American Public Works Administration, the Highway Research Board, and others in developing standards for traffic control devices and in the preparation of manuals, handbooks, and standards of traffic engineering practice.

The Engineer's Profile

A survey of the ITE membership gives an interesting profile of the profession in the United States. Almost three out of four members work for a governmental agency. (2 percent for the federal government, 32 percent for state agencies, 3 percent in county highway departments, and 34 percent in municipal governments.) 13 percent work in consulting engineering firms, 4 percent in colleges and universities, 3 percent in associations, such as auto clubs and safety councils, and 3 percent in industries, manufacturing and supplying traffic engineering hardware. Sixty-seven percent have other degrees. Forty-six percent have done graduate work in traffic engineering. Sixty-five percent of the membership are registered engineers.

The Engineer's Responsibility

The practice of traffic engineering can be divided into five major sections.

1. Studies of traffic characteristics (the science of measuring traffic and travel, and the study of the basic laws relating to traffic flow and generation).
2. Traffic operations (application of this knowledge to operating traffic systems).

214

3. Transportation planning.
4. Geometric design.
5. Administration.

There are seven major areas of study and expertise in the traffic engineering field.

1. Vehicular and human factors.
2. Traffic volumes, speeds, and delays.
3. Traffic stream flow and capacity of streets and intersections.
4. Travel patterns, trip generation factors, origins and destinations.
5. Parking and terminal factors.
6. Mass transit systems.
7. Collisions.

All of this is included for the serious traffic officer or supervisor who wishes to expand an appreciation for the related vocations. It is of benefit to all concerned to know what information is available and who will have the best answers. Obviously, the traffic engineer is best equipped to assist the traffic officer in the resolution of traffic collision problems.

FIGURE 11-3. There exists a visual hazard that distracts passing drivers. Note how wide the pick-up/camper swings to avoid the motorcyclists. Roadside workers are quite common and most drivers take them for granted. It is for this reason that there exists a high incidence of collisions involving department of transportation personnel and vehicles.

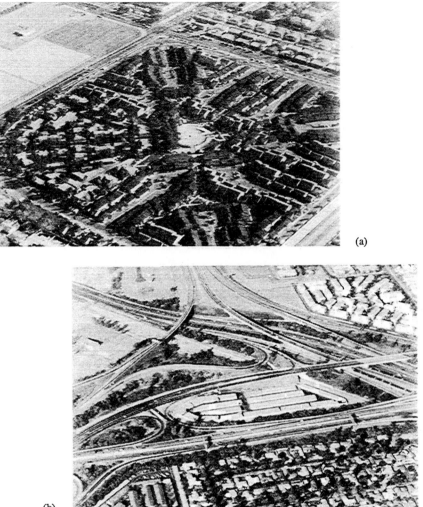

(a)

(b)

FIGURE 11-4.   a. This aerial photograph depicts a combination of street and building designs including single family dwellings and multi-level condominiums built
around small park and recreation areas. Major arterial highways circumscribe the area
with immediate access to industrial and shopping sites. This form of innovative
engineering design gives esthetic as well as practical value to what would otherwise
be just another tract of houses. The use of the cul-de-sac restricts through-traffic for
a higher degree of privacy. b. This aerial photograph depicts the various forms of
transportation design that must be considered. At the top left is an airport taxi strip.
In the center, an industrial area sandwiched between three major highways and a
railroad line. At the bottom left of the photo is an apartment complex with a high
concentration of automobile traffic. The bottom right of the photo shows a com-
pacted grid design residential area. The upper right of the photo shows more com-
pacting and obvious vehicle concentration in yet another apartment complex. All of
these areas have controlled access to the major freeways through arterial highways.

216

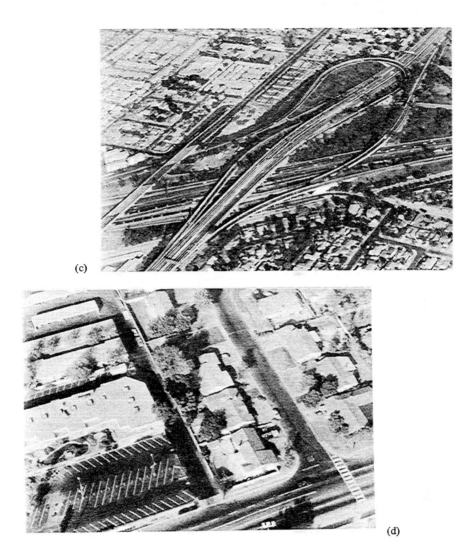

(c)

(d)

FIGURE 11-4 (cont.)
c. Then there exists those designs that seem to defy imagination when a number of major highways cross in an interchange. d. Several innovative engineering ideas are present in this aerial photograph. Note the cross-hatched crosswalk. The wide, broken stripes bordered by the conventional lines provide drivers with a strong visual signal of this school crossing. Note also the reflectorized numbers painted on the roof of the home in this center. The address provides a quick reference to low flying police helicopters. Business establishments should be encouraged to paint the address numbers on their roof tops in those areas where police aircraft are employed. Lastly, observe the parking lot arrangement in the lower left. Traffic is designed to flow in one-way paths to avoid conflict. Collisions and industrial insurance rates are reduced as a result of traffic engineering. e. This is southbound I-5 in San Clemente, California. Note the "Jersey" type barrier in the center median. The base is constructed of concrete and supports an expanded metal fence. The fence serves to effectively block

TRAFFIC EDUCATION

Most experts agree that safe use of streets and highways would be greatly enhanced if all users were made fully safety-conscious. However, there is not a universal agreement on how this can be reached. New drivers can take advantage of driver training programs now available through high schools and private licensed driving schools. Traffic courts sometimes order violators to attend a series of safety lectures. There is, however, no evidence that the general public is beneficially affected by education. This observation is based on studies where saturation campaigns have been waged with death statistics, safety slogans, and driver education campaigns through the various news media. It appears that safety awareness must come through experiential learning rather than a picture and word exposure.

An ironic aspect of the traffic education problem recently revealed in a study by the California Department of Motor Vehicles is that, despite the number of traffic accidents, over 80 percent of all drivers feel they are better than average drivers. Obviously the definition of "better than average" is open to individual interpretation.

Other Methodologies

To fight the problem of rising costs in litigation and damage claims, some insurance carriers, in England for example, are giving their own driving tests. A successful driver earns a lower insurance rate contingent upon an ability to drive with a collision-free experience. Those drivers who receive citations or collisions lose their preferential status and must pay the higher rates. Economics can be a powerful teacher of driver safety, and perhaps it is the only viable means of stressing highway safety.

Japan has invoked yet another means of control which limits the number of drivers. The cost of a driver's license is prohibitive. Only those who can afford to drive are privileged to possess a license.

Driving in any country has become an expensive proposition, and with the increased professionalism of traffic officers, traffic engineers, administrators, and educators, we are entering a new phase of transportation philosophy. Personalized transportation in the form of the automobile may be augmented by more stylized mass transit. Operational costs of the automobile may dictate that the family car be parked at home and reserved for special occasions and not used as the workday transportation vehicle. In the beginning, the automobile was considered a luxury. Perhaps the day is just around the corner when we will agree with our grandparents. There is just so much of our earth which can be converted into highways; there exists just so much steel to convert into automobiles; and there is just so much fuel which can be consumed. These truths are all coming back to haunt the planners, legislators, and engineers. Everyone, including the author, is hoping that someone will invent the panacea of transportation which will not force us to relinquish our mobility nor continue to senselessly exploit our environment and our raw materials.

THE DRIVING EQUATION

There is one area of the Engineering, Education, and Enforcement, The Three "E" concept, that is grossly misunderstood and underrated. For generations, many people have ridiculed, emulated, and admired the rapport between a man and his machine. Engineers, Educators, and Law Enforcement Officers have spent a great deal of effort studying and working in their fields but they have neglected the relationship between the driver and his automobile.

Each driver has passed a written test and a driving test and demonstrated skill in driving and knowledge of both the law and its application. Each driver has in his or her control a vehicle which, like the driver, is an unknown at any given moment.

The driver comprises two entities which must work together—the Psychological and the Physiological. The driver must be both mentally and physically sound to demonstrate the skill and judgment necessary to good driving.

A third element in the equation for good driving is the vehicle. It is often assumed that if a vehicle is on the road, it is "road worthy." This is not always the case as demonstrated by simply viewing the vehicles in any parking lot. Vehicles come in all forms of disrepair and are driven on our highways.

If the driver passes a written test, he or she is thought to possess one of the three elements in the driving equation. The driver knows the basic laws and is mentally qualified to proceed to the next phase of testing, the driving test. Once an examiner is satisfied that an individual can physically handle the test vehicle through a cursory driving test, the driver is given a license to drive. The driver is now legally qualified mentally and physically to drive and has an operator's permit according to the law.

For testing purposes, the driver wisely selects a vehicle which is legally safe. The car he or she drives once a license is obtained may not be as safe. The author recalls one young man who was driving a vehicle on a freeway. The driver was sitting on a wooden box, the steering wheel was a pair of locking pliers, the brakes were inoperable and the vehicle had no lights. The vehicle went to a garage with a tow truck. The young man went home via the hospital emergency room.

There is only so much that can be accomplished through Engineering, Education, and Enforcement, as all three are not at work at all times with every driver or in every place. Not all drivers are equally qualified psychologically and physiologically, and not all drive machines that are equally "road worthy." There is a zone of acceptance which is defined within parameters of acceptable transportation behavior.

To our credit as responsible individuals, most drivers operate within the zone of acceptance most of the time. Few, if any, drivers operate in this preferred area all of the time. Emotional instability caused by a difficult day at the office, personal problems, fatigue, or any number of maladies can affect the driver's psychological quality and quantity, impairing judgment. The physiological aspect can be altered with so common a problem as a tight fitting pair of shoes cramping the driver's feet,

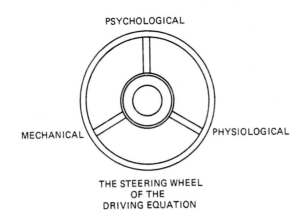

PSYCHOLOGICAL

MECHANICAL

PHYSIOLOGICAL

THE STEERING WHEEL
OF THE
DRIVING EQUATION

FIGURE 11-5. The Steering Wheel of the Driver Equation

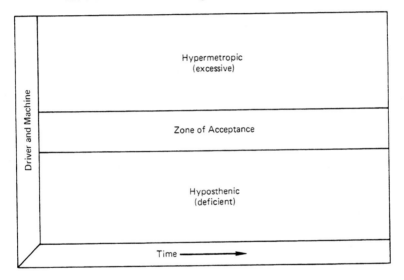

Driver and Machine

Hypermetropic
(excessive)

Zone of Acceptance

Hyposthenic
(deficient)

Time ⟶

FIGURE 11-6. Zone of Acceptance

a couple of drinks, or a doctor's prescription. The mechanical element can be altered when a faulty tire blows at freeway speeds, the brakes fade, or the engine overheats from a lack of water or oil checks and service.

Although there are a number of components that comprise each of the elements of the equation, there are but three basic spokes to the driving wheel. If one spoke fails, the wheel will collapse. The ultimate responsibility for the complete equation lies with the driver.

The three spokes of the true driving equation have little to do with traffic engineers who provide better signs, wider lanes, and the myriad changes in road structures. Nor does law enforcement have any preventive control over fluctuations in personality, how much or little a person drinks, the medications consumed, or the day-to-day mechanical conditions of the vehicle. Education as to the law of driving is also ineffective in reaching the driver experiencing mental depression or fatigue.

The key to safer driving is awareness of the danger of being indifferent to any one aspect of the equation. A driving ethic is needed to reduce collisions. The emphasis must be redirected from the first day of driver's education through driving retirement. The driver must repress the idea of "I" centered driving. For example, at a collision scene a driver is often heard to say, "I had the right-of-way." The "I" is self-oriented. It would have been far more ethical to relinquish the right-of-way and avoid the collision. The psychological spoke of the wheel malfunctioned.

During a bar examination in California, a group of aspiring lawyers were given a test on ethics. A substantial number of these otherwise qualified students failed. The author has often wondered how many vehicles would be on the road if a test of driving ethics were given as a prerequisite to driving.

Safe driving is the sum of each of the elements of the driving equation–the Physiological, the Psychological, and the Mechanical. Collisions occur because of a break-down in one of the three aspects of the driving equation, and all three are driver controlled. The driver cannot abrogate responsibilities to a public entity of the Three "E's" but must look within for causal factors to a collision.

DISCUSSION QUESTIONS

1. Within recollection of most drivers is the advent of lowered speed limits designed to save fuel. With the diminished speeds, we witnessed a dramatic reduction in fatal collisions, a point that traffic administrators attempted to convey to generations of drivers, courts, and legislators. Why do you suppose that fuel and costs and not lives became the final arbiter?

2. A reportable collision is one in which there was an injury or fatality. A non-reportable collision, for national statistical reporting purposes, involves PDO, or property damage only. Which of the two collision categories comprise the greatest annual expense in monetary loss in your area?

3. Of the various types of volume studies, which would be the most valuable to determine traffic around a university? Why?

4. Do collisions in your area tend to follow the pattern of increasing to a peak between 3 P.M. and 6 P.M. on Friday afternoons? Do most of the fatal collisions occur at night?

12

Collecting, Quantifying, and Recording Collision Evidence

It is crucial for the police officer to know what really is evidence, how to preserve evidence, and how to successfully report and record what is observed. There is very little time to analyze the scene before the roadway must be reopened to traffic, which will destroy the skid mark and debris evidence within a matter of hours. The traffic officer must quickly assess the scene and know just what to look for, obtaining facts in a fraction of the time allotted to an officer who is investigating, for example, a homicide. The homicide is spectacular and will be concluded with criminal court action. The traffic officer must see the case through the criminal courts and then be able to testify in civil courts, where the claims run into the millions of dollars. Many civil cases hinge completely on the traffic officer and the observations recorded in the collision report. The rules of evidence for both the homicide and traffic officer remain the same, but it is the traffic officer who must be exceptionally alert, observant, and professional despite the time constraints of the pressures of traffic build-up and the possibilities of additional collisions.

We have discussed skid marks, deformation damage, and collision reconstruction. We have further provided for a most comprehensive reporting format and a methodology for an arrest report. The balance is to be found in the many tidbits of evidence which assist the officer in reaching a conclusion based on evidenciary facts.

Hit and Run Collisions

Evidence of Paint. Most vehicles involved in hit-and-run collisions leave behind something which can be tied to the responsible vehicle. The usual residual is a paint transfer from the striking vehicle left on that which was struck. When a vehicle strikes an object with sufficient force to cause damage, there is usually a deposit of paint which is left behind. The officer is then obligated to discern the evidence and collect the sample. When the paint sample is left on a solid object such as another vehicle, the method is to collect the contaminated paint sample, as well as an uncontaminated paint sample. For example, the officer inspects the struck vehicle and collects the paint sample left by the striking vehicle. The striking vehicle leaves a paint transfer on the struck vehicle. This is accomplished by taking a clean knife blade and scraping the surface of the struck vehicle, removing the paint sample of the striking vehicle. The sample obtained is placed into a clear plastic bag or clean envelope. An uncontaminated sample is then obtained in the same manner from the struck vehicle. The best place to obtain an uncontaminated sample is around the bumper areas or behind the license plates where the striking vehicle could not reach in the collision. When a suspect vehicle is located, the same method is employed. A contaminated paint sample is obtained and an uncontaminated specimen is taken. Then, for one collision between two vehicles, four samples are taken. Each envelope or bag is identified as to what it contains, from which vehicle, the name and identification number of the officer, the time and date, and an identifying notation as to the collision (usually the license plate number of the vehicle).

The paint samples are then submitted to a criminalist's laboratory for analysis. The laboratory will subject the specimens to photo-spectrographic analysis and advise if the paint samples found on the two vehicles match in color and composition.

Broken Glass. Paint is not the only evidence which can be identified in a hit-and-run incident. The striking vehicle often leaves behind a broken headlamp. Headlamp glass found at the scene can be used to match the physical evidence on the responsible vehicle. A piece-by-piece replacement can often be effected. Again, a laboratory facility is very beneficial. Laboratory technicians can often fit the glass found at the scene with a headlamp removed from the suspect vehicle. The manufacturers of headlamps have a distinctive glass and pattern to their product, so even when a suspect removes and destroys a headlamp broken in a collision, the glass found at the scene is still very important. The broken glass can be matched with the other headlamps on the vehicle by both pattern and composition.

Evidence of glass is important in other areas as well: side marker lens glass and taillamp glass also bears a distinctive shape, pattern, and composition. Taillamp glass is one of the best bits of evidence to assist the investigator. Most automobile manufacturers have an identification number which is cast into the glass. This identifier will often tell the investigator the year of the vehicle's manufacture. (For example: SAE A1-252-T-78 identifies a 1978 Dodge Challenger; SAE-TSIR-70-E identifies a 1970 Ford. The manufacturer's "logo" on taillamps is quite common and gives the officer a make on the suspect vehicle. The officer now can determine the make, year of manufacture, and with paint samples or chips left at the scene, the color. An instant appraisal of a collision scene, coupled with a broadcast to adjacent beat units, has netted many a suspect hit-and-run vehicle and driver.

Other Exterior Broken Parts. Among the bits of evidence found at a collision scene is a broken part which is torn from the suspect vehicle in the collision. Auto-pedestrian collisions often tear a vehicle antenna from its mount. The broken radio antenna found at the scene can be easily matched to a suspect vehicle. The same observation is true of bumper guards, trim moldings, license plate frames, rear view mirrors, brackets, door handles, driving lamps, spot lamps, and other external additions to a vehicle. These broken parts will very often have a smear of paint sample of the suspect vehicle, providing color identification.

Amnesia. Auto-pedestrian and hit-and-run collisions are difficult for all too often the surviving victim suffers from retrograde amnesia. The loss of memory renders the victim helpless in recalling the facts of the case. If an investigator can arrange to speak with the victim within a few hours of the incident, the chances of gleaning significant information are good. However, with the passage of time, the victim's conscious memory will fade concerning details of the incident, and a day later, the victim may have no recollection whatsoever. This same phenomenon occurs in many auto collisions as well. It is often difficult to convince the emergency room staff at a hospital that it is imperative that you speak with the victim as soon as possible when the staff is preoccupied with the performance of their life-saving duties. For this reason, the first officer on the scene should attempt to learn as much information as possible from injured victims before the victims are transported from the scene to the hospital. The initial contact with the victims should include an observation of missing buttons, torn clothing, open wounds, and so on, in the event of auto-pedestrian and hit-and-run collisions. In at least one incident, the author was able to identify the color of the hit-and-run vehicle from a paint transfer noted on the belt buckle of the victim. The preservation of the belt buckle became a significant factor as evidence in the prosecution of the responsible driver.

Clothing. When a vehicle strikes a pedestrian, there is often a telltale imprint left on the vehicle. This imprint is in the form of the pattern or weave of the victim's clothing. When a vehicle is waxed, the wax rarely hardens like paint. The wax remains somewhat pliable or malleable. The clothing of the victim-pedestrian will imprint the weave or pattern onto the waxed paint of the vehicle, leaving observable evidence which can be measured, photographed, and compared.

Torn clothing often leaves a bit of evidence on the suspect vehicle. This evidence is more often left in the trim moldings and protrusions beneath the vehicle along the frame cross members, shock absorber mountings, spring bolts, and steering systems.

Blood, Hair, and Skin Samples. The above locations are also good places to locate samples of blood, hair, and skin in those cases where the victim was drawn beneath the suspect vehicle. A suspect may wash and rewax and possibly even repaint her vehicle, but none of these operations will serve to remove the evidence of a victim who passed beneath the vehicle. Again, blood types and clothing can be matched to the victim. The collection of such evidence is best left to the experts in a criminalistics laboratory, who have the proper equipment to preserve the evidence without destroying the product of the investigator's discovery.

Fingerprints. Fingerprints can often play a role in identifying the driver of a suspect vehicle, whether it is a hit-and-run incident or a stolen car or a penal code incident under investigation. An investigator may find the responsible vehicle, but be unable to identify anyone connected with the crime in question. A careful investigation of the vehicle contents may prove as beneficial as a fingerprint "dusting" of the vehicle itself. On one occasion, the author was in pursuit of a felony hit-and-run driver who ditched the automobile behind a service station. He got out of the car and proceeded to walk away. The trail of radiator water led to the automobile, and an observation of a lone male on foot approximately one block away resulted in an inquiry. The male was wearing highly polished black oxford shoes, the type often worn by servicemen. Inside the vehicle, in the fold of the seat cushion was a cigarette lighter bearing the inscription of a ship. A roadside comparison, investigation, and interview led to a tie that convicted the man. The cigarette lighter bore his fingerprints. The victim's testimony—she had observed a lone male driver with glasses and short, blonde hair—was enough to convince the driver, and later his attorney, that there was little left to defend.

There are a number of available tests which can raise fingerprints from paper found in an abandoned vehicle. There are also a number of places in a vehicle where a driver will leave fingerprints that he may neglect to obliterate with even the most careful scrubbing. A qualified lab technician will locate prints quite easily around such items as the rear view mirror (front and back), the dashboard around the radio or stereo controls, from various components, as well as windows, seat control levers and other knobs, and both sides of the glove box lid. The investigator has only to use a little imagination, recalling the sequence of events when a driver enters a vehicle, adjusts the seat, relocates the rear view mirrors, and drives the automobile. The investigator must recall that the simplest scrap of paper, a forgotten match book, a button, or the dirt on the floorboard may be the bit of evidence that makes the case. There is currently a method which can raise latent fingerprints through laser technology. There are many modern methods for gathering evidence and identifying suspects, but it is still the field officer who must put it all together and make the case through initial observations and sound police practices.

Additional Clues

Vehicle Lighting. Broken vehicle lights can tell quite a story for the investigator, especially during hours of darkness and on those occasions when headlamps and tail lamps should be on for visibility during inclement weather.

When a lighted headlamp is broken, there is a rapid oxidation of the filament as the inert gas within the lamp assembly escapes and oxygen is admitted. The oxygen comes into contact with the fragile filament, causing a rapid disintegration and melting. Small globules of filament are all that remain. These globules, resembling small beads, are extremely hot from the rapid melting process and, as they come into contact with the glass mirrored surface at the back of the lamp, will melt the glass and attach to the surface. The result is that the mirrored surface is "peppered" in appearance with what looks like small black beads. Globules are also noted on the posts which supported the filaments.

An unlighted lamp will evidence none of the small beads of filament oxidation. In most cases, pieces of filament will still be intact within the broken lamp housing. The filament will be no more than a small coil of springshaped wire between two supportive posts, or if broken loose upon impact, a "pig-tail" still attached to one post or the other.

The same oxidation phenomenon is observable in tail and brake lamp housings. However, because these are bulbs and not sealed beam headlamp assemblies, there is no mirrored surfaces to show the telltale oxidized beads. There are still the posts which supported the missing filament. These posts will bear the beads which resemble small drops of molten solder. If the broken bulb of the tail or brake lamp was not "on" at the time of the collision, there will be little left again, but the coil of broken filament.

Most headlamps are sealed beam units and manufactured as a Combination Beam #2 or a High Beam #1 lamp. The Combination Beam #2 unit contains two filaments. When the low beam selection is made, only the low beam filament is lighted or energized. When the high beams are selected, both filaments are lighted. In a collision where the Combination Beam #2 assembly is broken when only the low beam was energized, the low beam filament will be oxidized. The high beam filament will be intact, or simply broken. The high beam filament posts will not show the telltale beads of molten tungsten. A High Beam #1 unit contains only one filament which is energized when the high beam light distribution is selected by the driver. The difference between the Combination Beam #2 unit and the High Beam #1 lamp is in the focal arrangement for maximum beam distribution through the lens.

Auxiliary lamps will, of course, provide the investigator with the same observation of oxidation upon breaking. This is good to remember in those cases where a

(a)

(b)

(c)

FIGURE 12-1, a-f. Two views (a. and b.) of a combination 2 lamp taken from a vehicle out of a fatal collision that occurred at 2:00 A.M. The discoloration of the low beam element led to a check of the battery. Because of the low battery, the vehicle had been jump-started moments before. There was insufficient power to ignite the lamps. Not being able to see, the driver drove onto the wrong side of a curve, taking another vehicle head-on. See how the coil of the filament is intact (c.

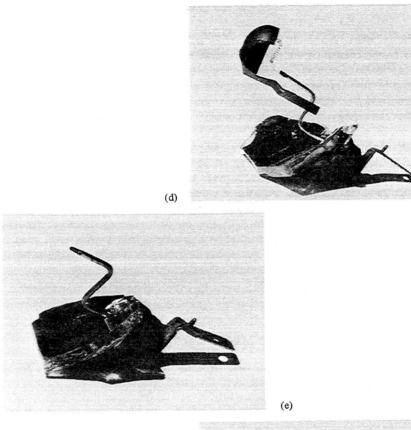

(d)

(e)

(f)

FIGURE 12-1. (*cont.*)
and d.), even though the coil has been bent by the impact of the collision. The lack
of beading on the tip of the coil, even under magnification, is the test. Was this lamp
on or off at the time of impact? e. A high beam 1 lamp that was on at the time of the
collision. f. This combination beam 2 element was lighted at the time of the collision.

229

vehicle collides with a truck, semi-trailer, or trailer which is required to have marker lamps on the corners of the periphery. Most spot lamps are sealed beam units and will oxidize and leave the residue on the mirrored parabola just like a headlamp when it breaks. This observation is of particular importance when reconstructing a collision which involves an emergency vehicle when there may be a question of whether the emergency lights were on or off.

Wheelbase, Track, and Tread Marks. Every automobile or truck manufactured has a distinctive wheelbase, track, and set of treads. There is a unique distance between the two axles front to rear, between the two front tires, between the two rear tires, and that particular tread which is unique to a particular tire manufacturer.

A number of years ago, a sheriff's investigator for the California County of Tulare noted this fact and set about to catalog the wheelbase and track of standard vehicles. Deputy Hank Speers realized that cataloging tire treads would require volumes of pictures and cross references but the track and wheelbase measurements would be distinctive and easy to discern.

Wheelbase is measured from the center line of the front axle to the center line of the rear axle. Track is measured between the center lines of the tires on opposing sides of the vehicle, as between the two front tires for example. By resorting to the manufacturer's specifications which are printed and distributed with each new model, the investigator can determine the specifics of any automobile.

When a hit-and-run collision occurs where skid marks are present or (in case of homicide) where a vehicle was taken into a dirt road area and tire tracks are left, a vehicle type and make can often be determined. Armed with this information, an investigator can readily narrow the investigation and focus on a certain vehicle which may have been seen in the area of the incident.

Track is determined by measuring at a 90° angle to the skid marks or tread print. The measurement is taken from the outside of one mark to the inside of the other for two tires on opposing sides of the vehicle and on the same axle. Each automobile has two track measurements, one for the front wheels and another for the rear wheels. A number of automobiles are manufactured with the rear wheels spaced further apart than the front or vice-versa. Front wheel-locked skid marks are easy to identify and lend themselves readily to accurate track determinations. The reader will recall that the locked front tires leave two distinct lines with each tire as the center of the tire cups upward as the weight is transferred down the tire sidewall and to the surface of the roadway. The rear tires bulge or balloon and leave a narrow skid mark upon locking.

Wheelbase measurements are not as difficult to ascertain from locked-wheel skid marks as it might seem. When a vehicle in a locked-wheel skid strikes another vehicle or object, there is an observable deviation in the skid marks. The deviation alters the path of all four wheels at the same time. The investigator simply has to measure the distance from the front tire to the rear tire deviations to have the wheelbase dimensions. To guarantee the accuracy of the finding, the investigator should measure from front to rear down both sides of the skid marks. When a vehicle slides to a stop, the wheelbase measurement is very much in evidence from the residue of burned rubber deposited on the roadway. The investigator simply measures from the ends of the skid marks, front to rear.

Having ascertained the track and wheelbase measurements, an investigator can simply process this information to match the facts to a vehicle. In very serious cases, it may be helpful to contact the Federal Bureau of Investigation which has now compiled this information for national distribution assistance. In cases where a suspect vehicle is found, it is a good idea to match the track and wheelbase of the suspect vehicle to the evidence found at the scene. The match is one more bit of circumstantial evidence which can be used to solidify a case.

Tread marks assist in the closing of a case. As previously noted, each manufacturer of tires has a distinctive pattern to the tire tread. Tread marks are discernible in the impending portion of the locked-wheel skid mark and occasionally seen in the termination of the skid mark in the deposit of molten rubber. Very good tread marks may be found in loose dirt at the shoulder area of a highway or in the damp mud of a rainy day in the same location. A very short-lived piece of evidence is the pattern the tires will leave upon a damp or dewy asphaltic street or roadway shoulder. The latter has been photographed with success by shooting the picture from a low angle aimed down the roadway from a height of approximately three feet. A legally parked but disabled motorist on the shoulder of a highway in foggy weather was rear-ended by a high speed truck. Having ascertained that the emergency flashers of the automobile were on with the point of rest now out in the middle of a major highway, a "walkdown" was initiated to find the point of impact in this incident. The tire print of the truck was found leading to the point of impact on the asphaltic shoulder. Photographs preserved the tire print evidence found on the fog-dampened asphalt. A tracing copy of the actual tire tread provided an unmistakable match to the photographs.

Centrifugal skid marks will also give the investigator a clue to tread information. The sidewall tread leaves the centrifugal mark. This too is a distinctive pattern. The pattern can be measured and checked very easily against the suspect vehicle. The centrifugal mark is a series of striations which outline the sidewall tread of the responsible vehicle in a continuum of lands and groups as shown in Chapter 9. The investigator can photograph the striations on the roadway surface and then check the suspect vehicle tire for a comparison. A comparison can be effected by physically removing the tire and photographing the tire placed in juxtaposition with the skid mark left on the roadway. Physically removing the tire can be a problem in many cases. Another approach is one developed by the author. Take a plain piece of white stationery or blank report paper that is 8½ by 11 inches. Lay the paper on the sidewall of the tire in question and with a crayon or regular pencil, scrub the crayon or pencil over the paper. The raised portions of the sidewall or tread will outline and become very evident. The investigator then lays the paper adjacent to the skid mark to compare. In the corner of the paper, the investigator identifies the tracing in the same manner as any other bit of evidence. List the name brand of the tire, the size, the serial number, the license number of the vehicle it was on, the date and time the lift was made, and the name and identification of the investigator. The same process can be used to lift the pattern of the width of the tread right around the sidewall on both sides of the tire. In the event of truck tires, simply use a larger piece of paper such as shelf or butcher paper.

A more current technique recently developed by the author is to take a wide piece of tape, such as that found on the back of a bumper sticker, and affix it across the surface of the suspect tire. The tape can be placed across the tire from one side to the other. The tape will lift the dust and dirt residue from the surface of any tire that has been on the road. The resulting "lift" will provide a faithful reproduction of the tire tread and sidewall (see Fig. 12-2). The print is preserved by placing the tape on a clear glassine plastic. An appropriate identification tag is completed and attached. The lift can then be photographed adjacent to the skid-marks and measured for comparison purposes.

Gouge Marks. Gouge marks in the roadway also tell a story. The impacted vehicles in a collision often blow a tire. The deflated tire allows the wheel itself to come into contact with the street. The metal wheel gouges the surface and leaves a distinctive mark. This mark will give a valuable clue as to the direction the vehicle was going at the time the tire deflated. Bear in mind that a tire suffering deflation from impact does not evacuate all of its air in an instant. Like anything in the collision, this process takes a certain amount of time. When you note a gouge mark caused by a wheel, you must realize that the actual point of impact is somewhere to the rear of this mark, depending on the speed of the vehicle with the blown tire. If a striking vehicle was moving at a rate of 60 miles per hour, and if its front tire was blown upon impact, and even if the air could evacuate the tire in one second after impact, the striking vehicle moved 88.2 feet from point of impact to the noted gouge mark. It is to be noted that the air will probably vacate the tire in one to two seconds depending upon the severity of the collision and the method by which the air escapes. When a tire is punctured, the air evacuates much slower than when the bead of the tire is separated from the wheel in a violent rush of compression and resultant escape. There is no real scientific method for determining how fast the air will escape; there is only the observation that such a process takes time. Modifying factors include what kind of damage is done to the tire and how much air was in the tire at the outset of the rapid expulsion process. It would take more time to evacuate the air from a truck or bus tire than a tire from a small sports car.

Gouge marks may be caused by other parts of a damaged vehicle. A vehicle which is rolling over will leave gouge marks caused by any of the many exterior devices attached to a vehicle such as rear view mirrors, door handles, radio antennas, and so on. Gouge marks are also quite common when wheels are extricated and the brake drum housings are exposed to the grinding surface of the roadway. Gouge marks not only give the investigator a clue to vehicle direction following impact, but they often contain some residue which will assist in identification of the vehicle making the marks. The residue may be bits of chrome, grease, oil, or paint.

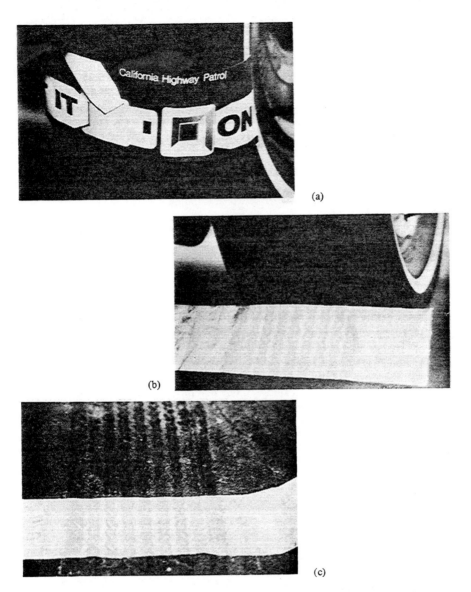

(a)

(b)

(c)

FIGURE 12-2, a–c.   Tire Printing. An investigator may use simple materials at hand, such as a bumper sticker or wide tape, to effect a tire print lift. In this series of photographs the student can see how a simple bumper sticker was applied to the tire of a suspect vehicle, removed, and ultimately compared to the on-scene tire print. The suspect vehicle had been driven through the powdered dust of a spilled load, leaving an observable track. The lift obtained from the suspect vehicle is demonstrably photographed atop the print found at the scene. The irrefutable comparison becomes one more link in the chain of unassailable evidence. Note both the pattern comparison and the worn tread of the tread line, second row from the right.

Radiator Fluid. Radiator fluid is also significant evidence at a collision scene. The fluid leaves a temporary but legible track which leads to the responsible vehicle. In the event of a hit-and-run vehicle which is leaking radiator water or fluid, the investigator has a relatively easy time in following the unmistakable trail to the responsible vehicle, for an engine without coolant will soon stop, leaving the driver stranded. The same is true for tracking a vehicle whose oil pan has been ruptured as a result of a collision. The lack of lubricant will soon render the motor inoperative. When tracking such a vehicle at night, shine the bright lights of the patrol unit as far down the roadway as possible. The low angle of light will reflect from the trail of water or oil and is quite observable to the trailing patrol unit. The viewing of a drop of lubricant or coolant from directly above offers little in the way of a directional clue, but if the investigator selects the patrol unit's high beams and utilizes a spotlight aimed down the roadway as far as possible, the individual drops look like the proverbial dotted line, which is easy to follow.

Brake Fluid. If the trail of liquid is brake fluid the investigator may experience somewhat of a problem. Bear in mind that the getaway driver will probably apply the brakes before making a turn from the straight course. With each application of the brakes, a fresh squirt of brake fluid will be deposited on the roadway and the trail will lead around corners and curves until the brake fluid reservoir is depleted and the vehicle is without brakes on that axle. Without brakes on either the front or rear axle, the driver of the escaping vehicle may be in for a surprise with the next heavy brake application. If the front axle brakes are functional, for example, and the rear brakes are depleted, the vehicle may be set into an unwanted spin and another collision. The same phenomenon may be evidenced if the rear brakes are nonfunctional. A number of surprises await the driver of such a vehicle depending on how well the brakes are adjusted to lock simultaneously. Maladjusted brakes may throw the vehicle into a spin when only one wheel is locked.

PHYSICS OF THE COLLISION

An investigator should be alert to the physics of the collision under investigation. For example, in an instance where the point of impact is known and point of rest is obvious, the investigator should recapitulate the collision with sound logic, asking serious questions with respect to witness statements. Where the struck victim comes to rest is a good place to begin the deductive process. Ask yourself what kind of striking momentum would place the struck vehicle in this position? What outside influence or striking motion was imparted? Was it clockwise or counter-clockwise? This information will afford a clue as to where to anticipate damage on the striking vehicle, or where the striking vehicle was coming from and going at the moment of impact.

Try to imagine what kind of angle was involved. The angle of collision attack may change the complexion of the investigation. One such inquisitive approach proved the responsible driver ran a red light at an intersection rather than attempting a U-turn on a green light as he stated. The collision involved an on-duty emergency vehicle whose emergency lights and siren were operating. The deputy sheriff had crested a rise in the roadway and was proceeding straight through a green light at an intersection. The other driver, at the prompting of his attorney, stated he was making a lawful U-turn, and was beset upon by the speeding unit and could not avoid collision. The angle of attack theory was employed by the author. The point of impact was obvious by the deviation in locked-wheel skid marks. Since the striking vehicle was demolished, a similiar vehicle was located of the same make, model, and year of manufacture, and most importantly, the same steering mechanism. Repeated tests proved that it was impossible to position the striking vehicle over the point of impact while making a lawful or unlawful U-turn. It was further noted that the damage was primarily to the right front fender area of the striking vehicle, and not to the left front nor across the front. The only way the test vehicle could be located over the point of impact was to enter from the intersecting street. Over the objections of the defense attorney, the judge hearing the case was to agree that the responsible driver entered the intersection against the red light. Numerous photographs were taken at each phase of the investigation to substantiate the findings.

In another exemplary reconstruction case, logical physics was to assist in the evaluation. A young lady was returning home from a dance. She stopped at a stop light and waited for the green light before proceeding to make a left turn. The highway she pulled onto has three lanes of travel in each direction. The view to her left is marginally obscured by a concrete bridge and overpass. As her vehicle crossed the southbound lanes to go north, a southbound vehicle was to run the red light at an extreme rate of speed, strike her 280Z Datsun, and cut the vehicle into two pieces. The front portion of the Datsun stayed intact with no appreciable damage to the engine compartment. The lights stayed on. The vehicle severed just behind the driver's door. Following impact, the front portion spun counter-clockwise and literally followed the striking vehicle, a GTO Pontiac, in a southerly direction. The Pontiac came to rest nearly 300 feet south of the collision. The front half of the Datsun came to rest approximately 90 feet south of the point of impact. The rear half of the Datsum pivoted around the blown left rear wheel and came to rest approximately 125 feet east of the point of impact.

The only witness to the incident was a man exiting a restaurant 580 feet south of the intersection. He stated he observed the Datsun making a "U" turn from north to south. The witness stated exactly what he observed and points up the necessity for logical thinking and a knowledge of simple physics. Sound travels at a rate of speed of approximately 1,100 feet per second. He heard the sound of the rending metal, one half second after the fact, looked, and saw the front end of the Datsun in a left turning disposition coming toward his location behind the GTO Pontiac. In excess of 120 Miles Per Hour in a 40 mile per hour zone, the Pontiac, driven by a highly intoxicated driver, had cut through the 280Z Datsun in one-quarter of a second or less, imparting the counter-clockwise movement to the front half, which circled around behind the Pontiac. The action is much like an ax chopping through a block of wood. Anyone who has ever cut wood knows that one piece will invariably fly up into the air in a violent spinning motion.

Once again, the guilty verdict for the felonious driving seems hollow in view of the girl's death. Her vehicle's speedometer was locked on 10 M.P.H. The speedometer of the Pontiac was at zero. At the moment of impact, the transmission of the Pontiac was jammed into the "park" position as evidenced by the photographs showing the lever bent forward into the console. With the speedometer cable attached to the transmission, the gears of the arrangement would be as instantly pulverized as the gears in the balance of the transmission. Occasionally, the speedometer needle will imprint on the face of the dial upon front end impact. It is for this reason that speedometers are taken from the mounts following severe or contestable collisions and examined for telltale scratches or indentations on the dial.

Logical thinking also readily indicates that had the girl been involved in a "U" turn, her vehicle would have been struck on the right side, and not the left. The outstanding series of photographs taken by the police officers of Buena Park, California, made and supported the reconstruction as the criminal phase took over a year to reach superior court. The vehicles had long since been scrapped for salvage; therefore, they were not available for viewing.

The precise measurements and extensive photographic recordation turned an otherwise improbable situation into a solid, irrefutable case for court. Enlargements of the photographs demonstrated such items as the distortion on the clips of the seat belt hook and the violent tearing of the shoulder harness, indicating the belts were in use at the time of the collision. Close-up photographs, taken with a steel tape measure in view, indicated the depth of the deformation damage on the Pontiac at a minimal 36 inches. Scene photos assisted in locating each of the pieces for evaluative reconstruction at actual points of rest, so that a scale diagram depicting various points of rest could be accurately prepared. Individual pictures were taken in a continuous, encompassing movement around the vehicles, showing each vehicle and part from each of the four corners and sides. Photographs were also taken at the night scene, and again in daylight for clarity, so that the evanescent evidence of skid marks, gouge marks, and victim's point of rest, and glass would not be lost to the effects of subsequent traffic.

There is no substitute for solid evidence when reconstructing a collision to demonstrate the various physical laws involved.

TAKING PHOTOGRAPHS

There is so little time to develop all the facets of the collision that an officer must record as much as possible on film in the event of a spectator collision. Once the area is reopened to traffic, skid mark evidence rapidly deteriorates, glass is quickly powdered, and other physical evidence is destroyed and displaced. There is rarely a photo or laboratory unit available to assist so the officer must possess a functional camera for recording evanescent evidence.

Because of the shortcomings of the flash attachments of most cameras, the fol-

FIGURE 12-3. When photographing a collision scene, there are times when the use of available items, such as a pen, clipboard, or ruler, will add immeasurably to the size and perspective, lending credence and meaning to the photograph.

lowing steps should be taken when reconstructing the collision scene in photographs at night. Open the lens, admitting as much light as possible, and obtain a long shot from the point of impact to the point of rest. Then, starting at a point approximately five to ten feet prior to the point of impact, show the contact point with the end of a ruler or tape measure indicating the area. Then proceed to the point of impact and photograph the path taken by each vehicle in a series of photographs taken approximately twenty feet apart up to the point of rest of each of the vehicles. In the event of skid marks prior to the point of impact, shoot the photographs in the same manner. Start from a position approximately five feet beyond where the first skid marks are visible and work your way along the skid marks, taking another picture every twenty feet, roughly seven paces, up to the point of impact.

As much as possible, photograph important bits of evidence with a ruler or tape measure in a position adjacent to the evidence. If a question of distance arises, it can be quickly resolved by the photograph. Whenever possible, try to establish a permanent landmark in the pictures in relationship to the collision evidence. The

237

(a)

(b)

(c)

FIGURE 12-4. This sequence of photos shows the path of the station wagon to point-of-impact with the truck. The station wagon left the roadway, following a path just to the left of the mound of dirt, and struck the truck. Upon impact, the front of the vehicle went down, the rear end up, and pivoted counter-clockwise, coming to rest behind the mound of dirt. The pictures tell a story that would be difficult to express in words.

(d)

(e)

(f)

FIGURE 12–4. (*cont.*)

(a)

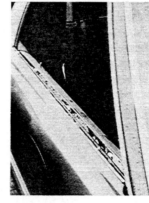

(b)

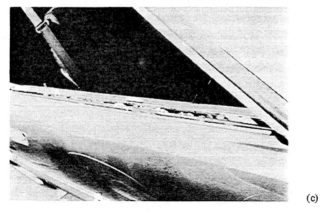

(c)

FIGURE 12-5. This sequence of photographs was taken of a hit-and-run manslaughter vehicle, auto-ped collision. The pens on the hood follow the path of the body. The victim was struck on his left side and slid on his back to impact his head on the windshield molding. The victim's right arm went around and through the door window as the body pivoted clockwise and to the ground.

(d)

(e)

FIGURE 12-5. (*cont.*)

recognizable landmark may assist in reconstructing the collision and refreshing the officer's memory if, and when, the case goes to civil trial five or six years later and the area no longer exists as it did on the collision date in question.

There is usually some form of evidence to be collected at the scene of a collision, such as paint samples, headlamp glass, a piece of vehicle molding, or photographs. Each department has its methods for preserving evidence and minimizing the danger of losing a link in the chain of evidence between the officer, the laboratories, and the court. It is the officer's responsibility to adhere to all the rules for obtaining evidence and to properly identify each item. What the officer sees and collects separates the professional traffic investigator from the amateur.

INTERVIEWING WITNESSES

In previous chapters we discussed how to take statements from witnesses, how to write the information clearly in a report, and how to deal with juveniles. In this section we will discuss how to obtain that information effectively, legally, and expeditiously. Too many investigators jump into the middle of a scene, listen to three or

241

four statements at the same time, listen for a summary that seems to support the evidence, and write an investigative report that states very little of what was said.

One of the leading complaints from persons involved in collisions is that the investigator did not quote accurately what they stated at the time. Too many times people will claim that the statement ascribed to them in the report is not what they said at all, or was taken out of context, or is deliberately misleading. There are some basic guidelines that an officer or investigator can employ that will circumvent the pitfalls of interviews, interrogations, and confessions.

Guidelines for Interviews

Privacy. As previously discussed, the investigator should make every effort to obtain information from witnesses first and participants second. The participants will be all to happy to wait a few minutes when they realize that you are obtaining witness information that will assist in clearing them of responsibility in the incident.

When speaking to an individual concerning observations, do so privately. Take the witness aside, out of hearing range of other witnesses and participants. People expect an investigator to have heard numerous accounts of spectacular incidents and are, therefore, not reluctant to recount possibly unpleasant details during the matter-of-fact conversation with the police officer. If another person is allowed to listen to what is being said to the investigator, it is psychologically unnerving; many important details may be left out if the witness is not assured of privacy.

This rule applies when effecting an arrest interrogation as well. The mere presence of other people in the area is intimidating and destroys communication. There is usually enough psychological pressure on a guilty party for an experienced investigator to bring out the truth in the right setting, without the aid or interference of another person.

Interruptions. The investigator should be free of interruption. Nothing will destroy a communicative relationship faster than a blaring radio in the midst of an interview. A well-meaning but ill-advised third person cutting into the middle of your interview or interrogation will often destroy an individual's willingness to talk. If you are in the field, simply advise your dispatcher that you will be out of service and tell where you will be. If the investigator has a portable radio pack set going, the distraction of listening to the calls raises the anxiety level of the interviewee, cutting short natural responses. There are times when the person being interviewed has the mistaken idea that a pack set radio extender is actually a tape recorder that documents what is being said.

When conducting interviews and interrogations in the office or station, select a room that has no busywork going on at the same time as the interview. Some persons will balk, not only at noise interruptions but at visual images such as a trophy rack full of shooting medals and figurines, a window that looks out on a busy street, or worse yet, the jail. Loose objects on the desk or table in front of the individual also become a source of frustration, not so much for the interviewee but more for the investigator. The individual will fidget with paperclips, pens, pencils, and other objects to relieve tension, much to the frustration of the investigator.

Preparation. A field interview at the scene of a crime or collision requires preparation. The on-scene officer or investigator usually has a fair idea of what happened. A second officer or investigator coming on the scene may not be aware of what is going on. Before the second investigator attempts to take statements, he or she should take a few minutes to speak with the reporting officer to review the pertinent facts. These few moments of preparation will save a great deal of embarrassment in asking the wrong questions of the wrong person. In like manner, the second investigator will be apprised of the right questions to ask of the right persons, especially if an arrest is anticipated. Preparation will also keep the second investigator on the right track and avoid the waste of time that results from unimportant questions.

Attitude. Many an investigator has literally stopped a witness cold with an overbearing or hurried attitude. If an investigator brushes over the highlights of the incident with the individual and promptly cuts the interview short, it is like having tickets to last Sunday's football game. It is all over: you missed the action but you just heard the score. The person is left with a feeling of not having participated even as a spectator.

Even worse is when the investigator conveys the impression that he or she is out to get a confession. When interviewing either a witness or an obviously guilty party, it is best for the investigator to stay neutral in attitude, acting only as a reporter who is seeking the truth. People will quickly sense an overbearing attitude and be repulsed. Just as quickly, they will detect an air of complacency in an investigator who is just going through the motions.

By giving the individual your undivided attention, maintaining eye contact, and displaying an empathetic attitude, the investigator will be able to get the most out of the interview or interrogation. The investigator should demonstrate a genuine feeling for fair play and honesty.

The manner in which an investigator addresses an individual can make or break an interview. If the formalities can be comfortably dismissed so that you and the interviewee are on a first name basis, so much the better, but until that time, the investigator should address the person as Mrs., Mr., Dr., and so on. Professional people, such as doctors and educators will usually prefer you use their title. They will usually tell you during the introduction, "I'm Dr. Walton." So be alert.

Writing Interview Statements

The statement given to an investigator should be written down only after it is given in its entirety. Do not try to write the statement as it is being given for the first time. The interviewee should be allowed to state the facts as perceived; then specific questions should be asked for clarification. Following the response, the investigator can then put the conversation in writing. This approach will save a great deal of time and writing. The investigator can write with more objectivity, clarity, and direction when all the material to be written is known and developed into logical sentences.

After writing the statement, read it back to the interviewee. This has two functions: it insures that what is written is what was said, and you can determine if it makes sense. Many interviews have gone sour when the investigator failed to check the statement with the interviewee. The courtroom is a poor place to discover that information ascribed to a witness in a statement was misquoted, incomplete, and inaccurate due to poor reporting techniques.

When the statement is completed and checked by the interviewee, it is wise to have it signed and dated. First, a signature affixes responsibility for the truth of the statement. Secondly, a signature adds a touch of finality to the interview. As a witness, the individual can go away with a positive feeling of aiding in the investigation. The investigator did not just walk away leaving her dangling without a chance to participate in some way in the process. The investigator satisfied the witness's need for assisting the police. A signed statement has a much higher degree of credibility in everyone's eyes. The signature also cuts down considerably on situations where the person sees the entire collision report and would now like to change the statement to something less incriminating, after discussing the incident with a lawyer or insurance company representatives.

INTERROGATING PARTICIPANTS

So far in this discussion we have centered around the interview with an eye toward completing a statement for the collision report. If during the course of that interview the investigator switches from gathering information about the collision to focusing on a criminal act that has occurred and eliciting information, the interview becomes an interrogation.

When the investigator comes upon the scene of a collision, there is not only the right but the duty to elicit information from the participants and witnesses on the specifics of the collision. When the investigator suspects that one of the participants is under the influence of drugs or alcohol, there is an obvious right and duty to investigate further. Having obtained statements from all concerned about the collision, the investigator will probably have the suspect perform a balance test. Satisfied that the person is under the influence of drugs or alcohol and having focused upon the individual as having committed the crime of driving while intoxicated, the investigator proceeds with an arrest.

Constitutional Rights

The first step in the interrogation phase is the admonishment of the constitutional rights. Thus far in the contact the investigator has ascertained only that the subject had been drinking, took some pills, or smoked a joint or two, and failed a balance test. Before the investigator can proceed with accusatory, self-incriminating questions, the subjects must be advised of their right to remain silent, as any statement made may be used against them as evidence, their right to counsel with a lawyer, and if indigent, their right to a court appointed lawyer.

If the subject agrees to continue the conversation, the investigator can then ask specific questions concerning the intoxication. All the same rules of privacy, lack of interruptions, preparation, and attitude apply. If handled correctly, most people under the influence of alcohol will gladly discuss events leading up to the collision. Drinking and the desire to communicate and socialize seem to go hand-in-hand, even to communicating with the police.

Persons under the influence of drugs can become very paranoid and suspicious and difficult to talk to, while under the influence. Trying to talk to a person under the influence of PCP is nearly impossible, unless the investigator is extremely patient. A person under the influence of PCP may take minutes to answer the simplest of questions. Persons under the influence of "uppers" become very hyperactive. Their voices go up, they are very nervous, and their speech becomes very rapid. Just the opposite is true of opiate and barbiturate users. Cocaine users and those on PCP are switch-hitters, up one instant, down the next, paranoid, and very capable of violence.[1]

Drug users are difficult to interrogate under the best of conditions, even when the investigator has knowledge of what drug was used. Tape recordings of the conversations are invaluable for further interrogations, for court purposes, and most importantly, for further investigations. Drunk drivers will also provide an investigator with an interesting tape recording for court.

The questions on the intoxication arrest form shown in Chapter 6 are an excellent place to begin the interrogation once the subject waives the constitutional rights. The questions are short, easy to understand, and superficially at least, not all that incriminating to an intoxicated mind. The investigator's key is PCP: Patience, Caution, and Perseverance.

Criminal Interrogations

Traffic investigators occassionally become involved in the investigation of criminal matters that are still well within the scope of traffic. Hit-and-run investigations are a prime example. Other examples may be manslaughter, vehicular assault, auto-theft operations, and murder.

All the rules of interview and interrogation discussed thus far apply. There is no way to overemphasize the importance of being prepared for a criminal interrogation.

1. Know all there is to know about the offense.
    a. Legal aspects of the crime.
    b. Date, time, and place of the offense.

[1] Francis E. Camps, ed., *Gradwohl's Legal Medicine* (Chicago, Ill.: John Wright & Sons, Ltd., 1980).

    c. Possible motives for commission of the crime.

    d. Incriminating factors pertaining to the suspect.

  2. Know all there is to know about the suspect.

    a. Relationship to the victim when applicable.

    b. Incriminating facts, witness information, and so on.

    c. Driving record, arrest record, and contact record.

    d. Present state-of-mind, level of cooperativeness, and so on.

  3. Know all there is to know about the victim(s).

    a. The nature of injuries in detail.

    b. Age, sex, marital status, and family responsibilities.

    c. Financial and social circumstances and so on.

The First Meeting. The moment of truth for both the investigator and the suspect is that first face-to-face meeting. First impressions can be most critical and certainly long lasting. Make the introduction sincere; after all, if the suspect is, in fact, the guilty party, the investigator is sincerely glad that it is about over. If it turns out that this is not the responsible party but merely a witness or an innocently implicated person, there is still cause for sincere appreciation for the meeting.

Before beginning the conversation, take just a second or two to study the individual. Look the suspect in the eyes. Do not fidget with your notes or look away. Some of the well-known cliches concerning the eyes are true: "The eyes are the windows to the soul," "The eyes never lie," and so on. Some people have learned to lie and look another in the face, but few can escape a steady gaze.

In their book entitled, *Criminal Interrogation and Confessions,* Fred E. Inbau and John E. Reid discuss and outline twenty-six tactics and techniques for the interrogation of suspects whose guilt is definite or reasonably certain. Their approach is recommended and proven to be sound and effective.

Obtaining a Confession. Obtaining a confession to a traffic-related offense is much easier than trying to delve into sex-related murder, for example. The trick is to advise the suspect of some, but never all, of the incriminating evidence against him or her. Then, get them to admit being at or near the scene of the crime.

Hint that a traffic-related crime is hardly that serious. It is easy to back this up pointing to court decisions. "The courts don't really view traffic-related problems with a great deal of alarm in the belief that the insurance companies will eventually battle it out; it is just that we would like to clear up this matter for the sake of the record. Also, by cooperating with us it will certainly make it easier for you; you can sleep nights knowing that you did the right thing."

Do not make any promises as to what the courts will or will not do. In a system of hit-and-miss justice it is doubtful that an investigator could second guess anything the courts may do. The district attorney or township attorney may mitigate the matter before it ever goes to trial, reducing the charges to some lesser included offense, but do not plan on such actions either. As an investigator, you have no options but to obtain the truth of the matter and present the evidence for the court's consideration. Promises made to a suspect have a way of going sour, so be truthful when a suspect asks about a deal. You will need the concurrence of the prosecuting attorney before any promises can be made.

Above all, be as empathetic as possible with a suspect. Play down the seriousness of the event, agreeing that under the circumstances anyone might have done the same thing, and look for tacit admissions of guilt. If a suspect offers to pay for the damages in a hit-and-run collision, the investigator just heard an admission of guilt. Press the issue; do not let it drop by asking another unrelated question. If the suspect asks about the damages and the cost of repair, try coming back with an unreasonably high figure, just to get a reaction, and then add, "But they would probably settle for a lot less." Continue with follow-up questions in this vein until an admission of guilt is established.

Once an admission of guilt is obtained, put the statement in writing. Have the individual read the statement and sign it. If there are any errors or corrections, be sure to have the suspect initial the corrections. As a word of caution, in a confession statement, use language that reflects the information as given. Do not try to improve the subjects vocabulary by "cleaning-up" the statement. It is difficult to believe that a person with a grammar school education made a statement that sounds like a post-graduate university dissertation. To avoid the accusation that the investigator put words in the suspect's mouth or that the suspect did not read the confession prior to signing, it is a good rule to insert something in the confession that would be known only to the suspect. A statement of where he went to school and the principal's name is a good example. Another idea is to intentionally misspell the name of a city or a friend and have the suspect make a correction in the margin of the confession and sign the correction with his or her initials.

Do not make the error of calling this written interrogation a confession. This is a statement; label it as such. The suspect will have fewer reservations about affixing a signature. The court weight will be the same regardless of the title.

As to witnessing the signature, the investigator should affix his or her name along with another person who witnessed the signing. A second officer or investigator who just happens to be passing through at the precise moment makes a good witness. In a hospital setting, a nurse may be handy or any number of available people, with the possible exception of doctors. Doctors are reluctant to see or hear anything that has a courtroom overtone.

Interrogation Conclusion. There is no law which prevents a person from confessing to a crime or involvement in a criminal act. Everyone wants to be respected and get on with the business of living, unburdened by feelings of guilt. To this end, a well prepared confession statement is a valuable piece of evidence supported by the numerous bits of physical evidence that concludes a case. The art of taking statements, interviewing, and interrogating is best learned from experience and study. There is no substitute for the various techniques outlined. The most important aspects are preparation and attitude; with the proper application of both, an investigator can turn a shaky case into a winner.

CONCLUSION

This chapter has dealt with numerous forms of evidence from physical to circumstantial to the confession. An investigator has merely to keep an open mind and first ask the right questions to gather the physical evidence. With the facts in hand, the investigator should continually try to equate the facts with the various statements, checking one against the other. It may take the work of a math or physics professor from a local college to decipher the actions of the vehicles, objects struck, and the resultant paths of pedestrians. The investigator should be aware of what these people can do to solidify a case.

Lastly, there is the technique of interview and interrogation once the facts come together. Science has yet to decipher such things as motive, anxiety, and heat-of-the-moment passions. This is where the skill of the investigator is really evident and separates the novice from the professional.

DISCUSSION QUESTIONS

1. Where would you anticipate finding fingerprints on a stolen vehicle? What other bits of evidence may be left behind by an auto thief which will lead to an identification?
2. If during an interrogation you were double teamed by two investigators, one the "nice-guy" and the other the "bad-guy", would you be more or less inclined to talk to either one of them?
3. Why do you suppose four paint samples are required in a comparison to determine a match on just two vehicles?
4. Can you obtain a possible year of manufacture on a vehicle by observing the digits imprinted on the tail lamp lens? Is the same true of the headlamp lens?
5. When a front wheel steering vehicle is turned, do the rear wheels follow the same path as the front wheels? If not, why?
6. If following a collision involving hit-and-run, the responsible driver changes tires and puts on wide "slicks", will it change the track measurement or wheelbase length?

Traffic Supervision

There is no call for alarm quite as loud as the cacaphony of traffic for the traffic supervisor. This chapter is intended to simplify the routine responsibilites of the job and allow more time for planning and routine supervision.

DEPLOYMENT OF POLICE OFFICERS

Traffic is somewhat predictable, unlike some other areas of police work. Traffic statistics are helpful in deciding deployment of the police staff. Your department should maintain a beat collision record which is broken down by type of collision, hour of the day, and day of the week. By knowing what shifts will experience the greatest number of collisions and on what days, the supervisor can best deploy the officers to cover anticipated problems.

Knowing Your "Beat"

During briefings, the supervisor can deploy the officers to beats and areas of high collision. It is important to have the officers be particularly alert to the prime factors that cause collisions in a particular situation, such as right-of-way violations, a driver who is intoxicated, and travel over the speed limit. It is not uncommon to have a rookie officer writing parking citations in an area where speeders are going by so fast they nearly singe the decal off the door of the patrol unit. The supervisor may also choose to set up a floating assignment schedule. For example, an afternoon-evening watch may experience a high collision period, during afternoon commute in one area, and in another location when the high school students start their evening of "dragging-the-main." There is no reason why the same officers cannot work both traffic problems. This sort of assignment can solve the problem of response time as the officer is already in the area. Typical Friday assignments in any department tend to lend themselves to this method of deployment. College and high school games tend to deplete the police ranks with the police reserves and regular officers now assigned to traffic control. Once traffic is dispersed from the special event, reassign the units of high collision areas to augment the normally assigned beat officers. The extra units can serve as booking or transportation officers, or if nothing else, assist in keeping the lid on potential problems through exposure.

Investigating Causal Relationships. A collision-based method of deployment solves much of the supervisor's problem. Unlike homicides, robberies, and family feuds, traffic collisions tend to happen in predictable locations. To further the supervisor's cause, it is wise to work on this problem through an assessment of collision factors. Why is this intersection the scene of such carnage? Is it lighting, visibility, sunsets, sunrises, poor construction? Deploy a team of two officers to survey the causal relationships in the collisions, identifying the common denominators. Have them study the intersection, talk to collision participants, and prepare a report to forward through channels. The results of your supervision and interest may well save lives, thousands of dollars in property damage, and a fortune in doctor bills, to say nothing of unmeasured grief and pain. It is one thing to have officers that are experts in emergency medical treatment at collision scenes; it is quite another to have prevented the collision from happening. Instill the concept that safety is everyone's business. Involve the resources of allied agencies such as city streets, county roads, and state highways. Request additional assistance from any other civic or political group available. After identifying the problem through your officers' efforts, it is unimportant who takes the credit for problem resolution if the collision rate drops as a result.

Investigation of causal relationships at high collision scenes has a beneficial effect on the officers as well. First, the officers identify the problem that causes collisions and take appropriate steps to effect a change; secondly, it instills pride in a job well done and sharpens the officer's investigative skills. The officer learns to ask the right questions of participants and witnesses, how to assess the scene, and so on. The officer's investigative report of a collision will reflect a learned and professional approach to traffic. The result is a report which insurance companies, attorneys, and courts can read with assurance and give an eye to unquestioned settlement based on the officer's expertise.

Willingness to Change. The key to deployment is flexibility. Residential area collisions tend to be higher, as a general rule, through the weekday afternoons and evenings. Major highways experience the highest collision rates on Friday and weekend evenings. Deployment based on day-of-the-week factors is also good public relations. Residents have the opportunity to view a unit patrolling their neighborhood, which instills a sense of security. When officers make spot residential contacts, this reinforces the officer's sense of belonging and identifying with an area. Traffic unit patrol also reduces neighborhood crime such as residential burglaries, auto theft, assaults, and so on. The traffic officer's rapport with the residents also engenders a form of camaraderie with those who will provide valuable intelligence reports beneficial to other bureaus within the department or allied agencies. A traffic supervisor cannot afford to make the cellular neighborhood assignments on day watch, Friday afternoon, and weekend evenings.

When the traffic supervisor observes that deployment is based on the premise, "That's the way we've done it for years," start looking at why no changes have been made. The answer to the question might be political ("The Mayor lives out there.") or practical (a high collision area), or just possibly, and most probably, someone made an arbitrary decision some years ago. When first assigned to supervise traffic, remember the lesson of the fox: do a lot of sniffing and listening before you start barking and marking your territory.

The new supervisor in traffic should review the available statistics to appreciate problem areas, what causes the collision, who is involved (such as drinking drivers), when the collisions occur, and what (if anything) is being done to correct the problem. The supervisor should also tour the beats as an observer in a "ride-along" capacity with an experienced traffic officer. As you pass and scrutinize high collision areas, make notes on your observations and the officer's comments. Jot down one-line reminders, then make comprehensive notes and file them in a permanent file in the office. When you have covered all the beats with different officers, you will have not only come to know the problem areas, but you will have gained an insight to the officers with whom you will be working.

Pre-Collision Investigation

Forms. Now, put your notes and observations to work. Start the program of pre-collision investigation involving as many officers as possible, thus making each responsible for the beat. Make a pre-collision investigation reporting format for each officer to follow (see Table 13.1); give officers the latitude to develop suggestions and alternative solutions. This is their program, not yours nor anyone else's at this point. Place reasonable time restraints on submission of the reports. As the reports come in, review them with the officer and compare the findings with your observations and notes. Satisfied that the officer has exhausted all possibilities and sufficiently answered the questions you raise, approve the report.

Officer's Suggestions. The approved report should have a prescribed route that will cut as much of the formal "red-tape" of bureaucracy as possible. Subsequent deployment towards collision factors should follow the officer's prescription. After

Table 13.1. Pre-Collision Investigation and Assessment Forms

Pre-Collision Investigation and Assessment

Location:

History: Time Frame: From _____ To _____

 1. Fatal Collisions: _____

 2. Injury Collisions: _____

 3. Property Damage Collisions: _____

     Collision Totals: _____

Primary Collision Factors: (List 3 most significant)

 1. _____   Number: _____

 2. _____   Number: _____

 3. _____   Number: _____

Types of Collisions: (head-on, rear-end, broadside, etc.,) (List 3 major types)

 1. _____   Number: _____

 2. _____   Number: _____

 3. _____   Number: _____

Time of Day Evaluation:	(24 hour) Number	Driving while Intoxicated
0000 to 0300 hours	_____	Arrested: _____
0300 to 0600 hours	_____	Had Been Drinking, Not Arrested: _____
0600 to 0900 hours	_____	Had Not Been Drinking: _____
0900 to 1200 hours	_____	Impairment Unknown: _____
1200 to 1500 hours	_____	
1500 to 1800 hours	_____	
1800 to 2100 hours	_____	
2100 to 2400 hours	_____	

Routing:

1.

2.

3.

Describe roadway or area of conflict:

Table 13.1. (cont.)

Notes from statements of drivers and witnesses:

Photographs from driver's point of view: Yes _____ No _____ Number _____

Investigator's opinion as to basic causal factor of collisions:

Suggestions for problem resolution:

1.

2.

3.

Recommended approach:

Officer and I.D.	Date	Supervisor's Approval

all, it is the officer's beat. The officer's pre-collision investigation for collision reduction can range from an engineering change to redeployment of officers and increased enforcement. As a supervisor, you are obligated to try the suggestion, knowing that your role as a supervisor requires trust and taking risks. When collisions are reduced in numbers and in severity, the entire evaluation of the pre-collision investigation process must be deemed successful. The department's job is viewed in a new light. Law enforcement, at least in traffic, is now pre-incident-oriented, and much better qualified to handle the post-collision investigations.

Within the scope of this program lies the possibility of redeployment based on the success of the pre-collision investigations and resultant effects. Based on the officer involvement, departmental acceptance, and success, other bureaus might attempt a similar approach with appropriate modifications.

With pre-collision involvement, incidents are minimized and isolated. The officers are now free to handle the isolated incidents as a matter of routine. The supervisor may find it advantageous to change beat lines, boundaries, and responsibilities, deploying the officers to different areas.

Traffic Unit Availability and Control

All of this discussion on deployment is not to say that collisions will be eliminated in any one location. The reduction of incidents of conflict is the goal. Collision elimination is obviously a near impossibility unless the roadway is closed to traffic. The number of collisions experienced in any given area is the criteria for the total number of units assigned to traffic, and there is no magic formula for determining the number of patrol units necessary to cover all the emergencies that could arise. When through collision experience, a supervisor notes the need to request allied agency assistance on a regular basis, it is time to consider redeployment from the less involved beats, or submit a well substantiated proposal for additional units. If your department has a policy of two officers per unit, as with some organizations which double-up on the graveyard watch, it might be helpful to invoke a no-vacation policy for officers while assigned to this watch. A supervisor can then plan on having even numbers of officers regularly assigned to the watch, maximizing the number of available units.

As noted in prior discussions, the day watch will normally experience the fewest collisions. The afternoon watch will cover the highest in number, and the graveyard watch will usually handle the most severe. The optimum facility is the police organization that can draw on officers from other units to handle exigencies such as the increase in collisions which occur on the first few rainy days of the season. Few departments have this luxury, however, and must make do with available personnel usually working on an extended shift or a call-out on overtime. Be apprised; this situation will come to pass sooner or later. There is no real solution short of knowing the priorities of the calls, handling the injury collisions, and relegating "property damage only" collisions to the back-burner, requesting the participants to make "counter-reports" if such is required.

Deployment Techniques. There are a number of deployment techniques for developing traffic unit availability and control. It is not within the realm or intent of this text to attempt an explanation of the many techniques and systems. It is, however, important to stress deployment for the threefold purposes of: (1) officer safety, (2) collision response time, and (3) assistance, if necessary, to reestablish the uninterrupted flow of traffic.

Some departments insist on having two officers in each patrol unit on the road. Other departments insist on two officers in each unit during hours of darkness. Still others double up officers in areas of high crime coupled with collision frequencies. One deployment technique is to establish primary beat boundaries and assign one officer to each beat. An overlap beat is then established which theoretically projects or overlaps half way into the two adjoining beats. This later method has the overlap units providing back-up on stops and collisions for the primary beat units. Thus, three units are available, three officers are utilized, and cover is theoretically close in the event of an emergency. Three officers are covering the same beats that would be assigned to four officers with the advantage of having the third patrol unit available for an extra call if necessary.

Another deployment technique is to assign a number of units to a region or area which encompasses several beats. The regional or area units are then free to roam the entire region. When an injury or special collision call is dispatched, it is radioed simply as a region call without a specific unit assigned. The region units respond to the call, and working as a team, handle the incident. A senior officer or supervisor is usually designated as the team leader and assures the equitable assignment of responsibilities on a rotational basis so that no one officer is stuck with all the paperwork, while another continually handles the traffic control or gathering of evidence. Usually, when left to their own devices, the officers will handle the rotation of responsibilities without supervisorial intervention. The team leader simply has to assure that all the requirements of the investigation are concluded. This is a good method for training new officers and utilizing reserves.

Deployment is a composite of individual departmental needs and depends somewhat on finances for hiring extra officers or purchasing patrol units and support equipment. There is really no program that will cover all exigencies in traffic, but with proper supervisorial planning, problems in deployment can be minimized.

SCHEDULING

Scheduling of available officers assigned to a given watch is not the problem that many supervisors seem to believe. It is well established that Friday afternoons, evenings, and weekend evenings will produce the greatest number of collisions in severity and number. High numbers of collisions are also experienced during weekday afternoons due to commuter traffic.

When an individual agrees to become a police officer, he or she is well aware of the 24-hour, seven day per week employment characteristic. The supervisor's first consideration is the needs of the department. It is obvious that deployment will be the heaviest during those periods when there is the highest probability of collisions. A sample scheduling calendar is shown for clarity of discussion (Fig. 13-1).

The officers' names are written down in the left hand column. It is best to use one calendar for each watch. The supervisor indicates the weekends and holidays

BEAT SCHEDULE WORK SHEET

NUMBER OF REGULAR DAYS OFF __9__
MONTH July ___ 19
PAY PERIOD 7/1 – 7/31

BEAT	OFFICER	SHIFT	LUNCH	1	2	3	4	5	6	7	8	9	10	11	12	13	14	15	16	17	18	19	20	21	22	23	24	25	26	27	28	29	30	31	NO. DAYS OFF
1	ADAMS																						⊠	T										
	BEATTY																						⊠	T										
2	CUMMINS																T																	
	DANIELS															⊠	T							⊠	T									
5	EVANS																T							⊠	T									
	FRANKS															⊠	T							⊠	T									
10	GOEBEL																T								T									
	HOGARD																T							⊠	T									
RLF	LINCOLN															⊠	T							⊠	T									
	MARSH																T								T									
RLF	NORRIS																T								T									
	PETERS																T								T									
	MINIMUM UNITS ASSIGNED			3	3	4	5	5	3	3	3	4	5	5	5	3	3	3	3	4	5	5	3	3	3	3	4	5	5	3	3	3	3	4	

LEGEND:
X = REGULAR DAYS OFF
R = SPECIAL REQUEST DAY OFF
V = VACATION DAY OFF
M = MILITARY LEAVE OF ABSENCE
T = TRAINING DAY (0800 Hours at the Range)

Posted on June 1...Completed June 15

Note the training days and the days off preceding are assigned. All other days are available for officer selection provided the minimum unit coverage is maintained.

FIGURE 13-1. Sample Scheduling Calendar

256

and other days that may contain special events that will require extra officers. Draw a horizontal line beneath the last officer's name. Drop down one space and draw another horizontal line; drop down one more line and draw another. In the space below the last officer's name, write in the words, "minimum deployment." In the next space down simply write in the word "assigned."

The smart supervisor now posts the blank schedule with the notations showing minimum deployment. The schedule is hung on a conspicuous bulletin or watch board with a note to have the officers indicate those days off they prefer. Indicate regular days off in pencil with an "X." If for some reason any of those days are special requests, please indicate with the letter "R." Specify also that partners are to indicate and agree upon the same days off, and to please sign up so that everyone on the watch may enjoy a weekend off. Write in the notation that the sign-up schedule will be taken down on the 15th of the month prior to the month being signed-up.

The officers all know that this is not a haphazard approach, and they know they will have to work with their fellow officers in rearranging days off to accommodate everyone on the shift. The sign-up schedule is posted on the first of each month for the following month. That is to say, July's sign-up is posted on June first, taken down June 15th, formalized by the supervisor, approved by the watch commander if necessary, and posted in its approved form on June 20th. When the schedule is approved, it is wise to give each officer a copy of the completed schedule to take home to post by the kitchen phone or some other convenient place. Encourage the officers to use this calendar as a reminder for court and training days. It will also assist the officers and families in their plans for trips, outings, and so on.

This method relieves the supervisor of being arbitrary with officers on the watch. It also avoids criticism of the supervisor for showing favoritism. The officers know what the required deployment will be on any given day, and that asking for all weekends off is an impossibility when most officers also want a weekend or two to be with their families. Peer pressure is at work, and common sense prevails. The officers themselves devise a schedule with which they can live. In this manner, scheduling becomes quite easy, and the scheduling supervisor can spend less time on this simple and sometimes bothersome monthly task. Vacation days and other extra days can also be worked into the schedule at the time the officer signs for weekend requests. Soldiers on military leave are handled in the same manner.

This technique lends itself well for scheduling regulars and reserve officers alike. The supervisor will have both schedules and know exactly how many officers can be deployed on any given day or for any special event.

Sick leave and injuries are impossible to schedule with the exception of the officer who is out on extended injury or sick leave. When an officer calls in sick, the shift supervisor simply places a red "S" beside the officer's name for the appropriate day. This notation simplifies the bookkeeping and serves as a check for the office staff handling the subsequent paperwork.

There are a number of methods of scheduling that are quite satisfactory for any given department. This discussion is intended only to show an approach. The innovative supervisor will devise modified systems or use an entirely new method, depending on the number of officers and reserves available.

SUPERVISION, THE NUTS AND BOLTS

Anyone in the employment picture can readily relate to the title, "Supervision, The Nuts and Bolts." The "nuts" don't seem to fit anywhere nor with anyone, the bolts fit everywhere and with everyone but can't hold anything together by themselves, and lastly there are those precious few leaders who seem to be able to match the nuts and bolts and put it all together. The descriptive words conjure thoughts of various supervisors we have known and observed, and those who, through intimidation, laxity, or professionalism, have supervised us.

Any number of well-written texts will define different managerial skills or systems, but few offer an assessment scale which can be applied to every day personal affairs, small business operation, or large public agency control. Few texts will offer workable, understandable definitions that apply to leadership and supervision, even though they offer measuring devices by which supervisors can ascertain their individual, categorized styles of management.

Each person placed in a management or supervisorial role sees himself or herself differently depending on experiential background. History is filled with leaders who saw themselves as leaders and became what they envisioned. It was the great poet Robert Burns who penned the lines that summarize the frustrations of how people interact with each other, through near-sighted thinking or myopic philosophies: "The greatest gift the Gods could gi'e us, is to see ourselves as others see us." Supervisors would do well to reflect on the vision of the supervised. The supervised have a surprising acuity, especially police officers whose very lives depend on their ability to "read" people.

HISTORY AND GROWTH OF POLICE SUPERVISION

Historically, management styles have tended to follow the ebb and tide of economics. During times of economic prosperity, management tends to be more democratic, demonstrating a humanistic concern for the employees. During these times it is an employees' market. Usual infractions such as tardiness and minor absenteeism are dealt with lightly. Jobs are plentiful; workers dissatisfied with one job may freely float to another. Children born to parents who frequently change jobs grow up with an "I" centered philosophy. The courts and Police tend to liberalize under pressure to change.

During economic recession or depression we see a reversal of management trends. The job market now favors the employer, who may pick and chose his employees. Employers tend to favor the loyal and hard-working to the vacillating job hunter.

Supervision becomes militaristic, rules more astringent, and very minor infractions result in dismissal. The job now becomes important to the employee who begins to think more of his company's or agency's success and less of his personal ego. Children born to parents coming out of depression economics tend to respect their work, become more company minded and change jobs only of necessity. The courts and police tend to become far more conservative and punishment oriented. The strong-willed, assertive officers in police work tend to promote faster and to higher ranks.

Times, economics, and politics change within decades. The shift is obvious when one views the change from the depression of the 1930's to the 1940's, the war years of the 1940's to the 1950's, the readjustment years of the 1950's to the Viet Nam era and the liberal years of the 1960's. From 1970 to 1980 we witnessed a swing back to conservatism and more saber-rattling, particularly in the Middle East. Each decade has brought a new wave of management techniques, studies, and concepts. The oldest observation of supervision is especially true in our changing times: "The more things change, the more they stay the same."

The premise basic to all supervision, including inter-personal relations is that people do not change. The only thing that changes is technology. Since the first human encountered the second, they found that it was easier to coexist for their mutual benefit–co-existing usually, because of fear of reprisal. Originally, leaders developed through intimidation as noted in Chapter One. With experience and education, leaders developed through superstition, rights of primogeniture, "big-stick" philosophies, fortunes of war, politics, dumb-luck, or manipulation. Each leader in turn, as head of his corner of the world, controlled the populace with some form of police. This brings us full circle to police supervision.

The Roman Caesars utilized police supervisors selected from the centurians. Centurian means "the one hundredth," or the one in a hundred qualified to lead.

Later, city populations experienced a real need for law enforcement. The name "police" comes from the Greek word for city, "polis." They were called "Politia," which appropriately translates "administration."

European nobles entrusted the peacekeeping functions to a person who the British were to later name "sheriff." Sheriff is a blend or words; "Shire" is the territorial division of medieval England and Scotland, which today is called a county. The word "reeve," is from the old Gaelic meaning overseer, steward, or bailiff. Thus, a "shire reeve" was the county authority given the responsibility to oversee the welfare of the county. The student may recall that it was the "High Sheriff of Nottingham," that was the victim of the legendary outlaw, Robin Hood of Sherwood Forest. The sheriff was to become the ultimate administrator of law enforcement within a county.

Police were at first not only peacekeepers but often unscrupulous villains and glorified thieves hiding under the cloak of authority. Modern police departments owe much of their respect from the citizenry to the reforms instituted by Sir Robert Peel (1778-1850). Robert Peel was the English statesman who defined and organized police responsibilities and promotional systems based on capabilities rather than nepotism. The British term "Bobby," given to the newly organized police department, was extracted from Robert "Bobby" Peel's name. The expression "Bobby's Boy," soon gave way to simply Bobby.

With much of western civil service systems coming from England, Rome, or Greece, it is interesting to note that the Chinese were the first recorded culture to utilize a civil service examination system for hiring or promotion. The first system was used for the prestigious position of postman, and was in effect at least a thousand years before the Roman Empire emerged.

Although civil service examinations are predominant in hiring and promotion today, there is little doubt that nepotism, and favoritism, are still alive and well in every facet of any industry, public or private. This is a fact of life, and as such is a commodity which is a condition, not a problem. A condition is something with which we must live; a problem implies a viable solution is possible. Police supervision to the highest levels is no exception to the "condition" observation. A student of human nature will do well to recognize the difference between "condition" and "problem" prior to self-imposing the Don Quixotian task of fighting windmills and "conditions."

CLASSIFICATION AND ASSESSMENT OF ORGANIZATIONAL BEHAVIOR

The Continuum Model

In response to the needs for personal and organizational evaluation, the author has developed a continuum model for the classification and assessment of behavior, decisions, evaluations, and personal or organizational personality (Fig. 13-2).

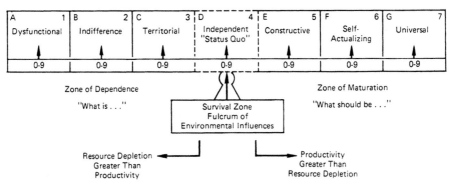

FIGURE 13-2. Continuum Model for Classification and Assessment of Organizational Behavior

LEXICON OF DIMENSIONS

A or 1   *Dysfunctional:* Does not contribute to the development or maintenance of the larger purpose. Not designed for or suited to a particular operation or use. That which causes deterioration of the natural action of a part to the point where the organ, unit, or part malfunctions and will cease to operate unless remedial action is taken.

B or 2   *Indifference:* Absence of compulsion to or toward any given goal. Marked by a lack of interest or concern. Having little importance or significance.

C or 3   *Territorial:* Relates to an assigned or preempted area. (A principle established in 1555 A.D., requiring the inhabitants of a territory to conform to the religion of the local ruler, or to emigrate.) Limited to, or within, the jurisdiction of a particular region.

D or 4   *Independent:* Not requiring nor relying on external influences, nor looking to others for guidance or opinions. One who is satisfied with the existing state of affairs.

E or 5   *Constructive:* Promoting improvement or development. Tendting to build, improve, or advance, resulting in positive conclusions.

F or 6   *Self-Actualizing:* The capability to conceptualize beyond present conditions, then to plan, work, and achieve a higher plateau of understanding by motivating oneself and others.

G or 7   *Universal:* Includes covering all or a whole collective concept without limit or exception. Including, involving, or intended for all, such as a universal law. Applicable to everyone or to all cases such as a universal cure. Common to all within any specific group or field, such as a universal practice.

This continuum model bridges the entire spectrum of human behavior. The open blocks are continuous from end to end, indicating that no one person, problem, idea, or organization is locked into any one category or dimension.

How it Works. The categories involved discern the fundamental dimensions of a series of thus far undescribed traits as used in this context. Organizational development beyond survival depends on how well people recognize their uniqueness and ability to contribute positively beyond maintaining the status quo. Ideas, decisions, conditions, problems, contributions, people, and organizations rise and fall according to where they tend to be on this assessment scale.

The scale shows how an individual, a marriage, a policy, a decision, a condition, or an organizational position falls into one of the two critical zones, dependence or maturation. The dependent zone is expensive as it depletes resources. The zone of maturation is productive as it adds to the resources and subsequent growth.

The uses of the continuum model can be easily understood, taught, and employed. The model can be used for organizational evaluation by subordinates as well as by supervisors as a check and balance. Recall that it is usually the employees who have the real insight. On the other hand, individuals can assess their personal behavior or decisions based on the relevant dimensions.

As most problems have a number of identifiable solutions, each solution for a problem can be tested on the scale and weighed against alternatives. If and when a solution does not fall into the "what should be" side of the scale, the proposed solution should be suspect.

Those decisions and evaluations which fall into the independent dimension are merely sustaining. This dimension comprises the majority of our decisions and maintains the status quo, or sense of business as usual. The other six dimensions identify levels between "what is" and "what should be."

Uses of the Model. The continuum model is helpful for a number of decision-making processes, including the ability to classify the various organizational "needs" as seen by the participants to a planning meeting. The administrator can weigh the "needs" on the scale to see if the "need" is maturation or dependence oriented.

The continuum model is also useful for the selection of personnel for promotion. Prospective candidates for promotion may be asked what they view as the three top needs of their organization. In a roundtable discussion with competing peers, they discuss organizational needs, field questions, and offer possible solutions. The candidates are asked to evaluate one another's contributions to the discussion, according to the continuum scale. Each has a rating chart which numerically quantifies the appraisal of a competitors' observed needs, the discussion skills, and proposed solutions. The results are compiled to establish a list of promotional candidates (see Tables 13.2 and 13.3). To facilitate numerical ratings, the numbers one through seven are substituted for the letters A through G. Each classification is further subdivided, zero through nine. As an example, a constructive idea can then be rated 50 through 59. A territorial needs assessment can be rated 30 through 39. Discussion evaluations (Communication/Interrogation Skills), as any other phase of the process, are rated in the scales 10 through 79.

Competitors in such a promotional system are much more honest in their evaluations than are supervisors, whose evaluations often reflect favoritism. The scores are neither high nor low, but reflective of observed input and responses. An outside non-voting moderator should be in attendance to guarantee the ground rules are consistent and to total the scores of the participants. This process, when explained in advance to the participants, is the best guarantee of impartiality possible, and it engenders individual preparation. The model provides input from the collective wisdom of peers in the promotion selection process. The system further offers the latitude for adjustment to changing times.

The continuum model is, however, most valuable as a decision assessment tool for both short term and long range projections. An administrator can readily evaluate the dimensions of the respective options and develop a plan which offers the greatest productivity for the investment.

Table 13.2. Classification and Assessment of Organizational Behavior Promotional Grading Sheet No. 1

Competitor Number_____

Major Areas of Applicability

1 – 7

1.1–1.9 2.1–2.9 3.1–3.9 4.1–4.9 5.1–5.9 6.1–6.9 7.1–7.9

Name of Rater: _____   Position: _____

Date: _____   Department: _____

Presentation		Communication/Interrogation Skill	
Name	Score	Name	Score
1. _____	_____	1. _____	_____
2. _____	_____	2. _____	_____
3. _____	_____	3. _____	_____
4. _____	_____	4. _____	_____
5. _____	_____	5. _____	_____
6. _____	_____	6. _____	_____
7. _____	_____	7. _____	_____
8. _____	_____	8. _____	_____
9. _____	_____	9. _____	_____
10. _____	_____	10. _____	_____

The primary functions of the continuum model are:

1. to provide a design for individual and organizational growth.
2. to provide for a decision framework.
3. to provide for the continuous process of organizational needs assessment.
4. to provide a method for organizational flexibility to change with the times.

The secondary functions include:

1. to provide for a promotional system from peer groups and the exclusion of nepotism.
2. to provide a process of engendering "reasonableness" in a supervisor.
3. to provide a process for building positive productive thinking into an organization.

Table 13.3. Classification and Assessment of Organizational Behavior Promotional Grading Sheet No. 2

Moderator's Tally of Competitor Grading

Name: (1)	Name: (2)	Name: (3)	Name: (4)	Name: (5)	Name: (6)	Name: (7)	Name: (8)	Name: (9)	Name: (10)
(2) —— ——	(1) —— ——	(1) —— ——	(1) —— ——	(1) —— ——	(1) —— ——	(1) —— ——	(1) —— ——	(1) —— ——	(1) —— ——
(3) —— ——	(3) —— ——	(2) —— ——	(2) —— ——	(2) —— ——	(2) —— ——	(2) —— ——	(2) —— ——	(2) —— ——	(2) —— ——
(4) —— ——	(4) —— ——	(4) —— ——	(3) —— ——	(3) —— ——	(3) —— ——	(3) —— ——	(3) —— ——	(3) —— ——	(3) —— ——
(5) —— ——	(5) —— ——	(5) —— ——	(5) —— ——	(4) —— ——	(4) —— ——	(4) —— ——	(4) —— ——	(4) —— ——	(4) —— ——
(6) —— ——	(6) —— ——	(6) —— ——	(6) —— ——	(6) —— ——	(5) —— ——	(5) —— ——	(5) —— ——	(5) —— ——	(5) —— ——
(7) —— ——	(7) —— ——	(7) —— ——	(7) —— ——	(7) —— ——	(7) —— ——	(6) —— ——	(6) —— ——	(6) —— ——	(6) —— ——
(8) —— ——	(8) —— ——	(8) —— ——	(8) —— ——	(8) —— ——	(8) —— ——	(8) —— ——	(7) —— ——	(7) —— ——	(7) —— ——
(9) —— ——	(9) —— ——	(9) —— ——	(9) —— ——	(9) —— ——	(9) —— ——	(9) —— ——	(9) —— ——	(8) —— ——	(8) —— ——
(10) —— ——	(10) —— ——	(10) —— ——	(10) —— ——	(10) —— ——	(10) —— ——	(10) —— ——	(10) —— ——	(10) —— ——	(9) —— ——
TOTAL P C/I	TOTAL P C/I	TOTAL P C/I	TOTAL P C/I	TOTAL P C/I	TOTAL P C/I	TOTAL P C/I	TOTAL P C/I	TOTAL P C/I	TOTAL P C/I
TOTAL	TOTAL	TOTAL	TOTAL	TOTAL	TOTAL	TOTAL	TOTAL	TOTAL	TOTAL

Rank Order of Competitors (1 through 10)

Leadership and Communication Skills

True leadership is the ability to communicate and teach by word and deed, and having a populace which voluntarily, if not eagerly, emulates and follows the precepts taught. The populace will follow the directions through communicative persuasion provided they are goal-oriented and positively reinforced. The populace may be employees, police officers, club members, a society, city, county, state, or nation.

The Role of the Supervisor. The primary role of any supervisor is to function as a communicator and teacher. Plato observed that to teach was the ultimate goal to which any person could aspire. Insecure supervisors tend to dictate rather than teach, on the premise that an enlightened employee becomes a threat to personal security by aspiring to the supervisor's job. The true leader and supervisor communicates, teaches, and rewards helping subordinates transcend current levels so everyone can move up within the organization.

Too many supervisors and administrators see their role simply in terms of power. *When you must remind an employee that you are the boss, in his or her eyes, you are not.*

The Art of Listening. A true supervisor or administrator is an artist in communication. The individuals who master this skill can, have, and will rule the world or any portion thereof.

The root of good communication is not in speaking, reading, or writing, but in *listening.* Exceptional leaders take the time to listen, evaluate, and then offer suggestions which are constructive and not indifferent, dysfunctional, nor territorial. They hear the answer while discussing the problem and offer a solution based on facts in evidence. Listeners are less likely to be emotionally involved in a problem and far more capable of being objective in their responses and evaluations.

The police supervisor should be an experienced listener by the time he or she attains promotional status. Refer again to the continuum model (Fig. 13-3) and note that the point where environmental and external influences enter the system is in the classification of status quo, the area of business as usual. The police supervisor should be a highly qualified listener to sort out little bits of information from the enormous input that comes to attention under the heading of business as usual. *Listening is an active verb.*

Handling Complaints. The input to a police supervisor comes from both above and below from within the department, especially when someone wants a problem resolved. The supervisor also receives a great deal of input from the external or environmental sources. The external input, especially in the form of an irate citizen, equally requires attention. The taxpaying citizen has a problem which is quite often communicated in an emotional state of anxiety usually about three decibels above a roar. How well the supervisor handles the citizen complaint is truly the benchmark of supervisorial skill as it reflects directly on the department. The crux of handling any of these problems is the ability to listen to what is being communicated, to ask questions as necessary for clarification, and to respond at a level of comprehension understood by the communicator. In most inquiry situations, the persons asking the questions already have the answers; they simply want to vent their frustrations by bending the ear of a police supervisor who will confirm what they already know. Empathetic listening will usually put an end to the complaint. Curt and abrupt interruptions to the communicator will usually result in another complaint against the supervisor. This observation is true for supervisors in any industry, public or private.

In-House Problems. Traditional supervisorial problems with in-house police work centers around such items as schedule adjustments, beat assignments, and other readily resolvable issues. The more unique problems center around officers experiencing a divorce, illness in the family, or problems within the department. The problem of interdepartmental relations is perhaps the most challenging.

Employees are still men and women subject to the emotional and physical laws of attraction. Experience tells us that this attraction between the sexes holds true for both male and female uniformed personnel as well as dispatchers, clerks, and anyone else in and around the department. Some of the problems which arise may require a supervisor's understanding of human psychology and an ability to do counseling when work performance and the department itself are affected by employee behavior. According to the L.A.P.D. and the California Highway Patrol academies, the police profession has one of the highest divorce rates of all categories of employments. This has a great deal to do with the high degree of job stress which accompanies an officer or investigator on every call or traffic stop. The reasons for stress are most likely based on two salient points. The first is the officer's observations of the proximity and finality of death. The officer with any experience has witnessed some form of violent death, and realizes the aftermath in a subconscious knowledge that life itself is suspended by a very thin and tenuous thread. This thread can be cut in a second in a high-speed pursuit collision or the lucky shot from some scared teenager during a liquor store holdup. The next call, the next stop, might well be the officer's last.

The second reason for stress is poor or non-existent supervision on the job. The officer lacks a supportive framework. Neither the courts nor their supervisors guarantee unconditional support. A captain in a large police organization once stated, "If you're right, I'll be behind you all the way, but if you're wrong I'll bury you." This is obviously not very comforting to an officer. An officer needs support and understanding when he was wrong but thought he was right. The supervisor we remember is the one who was supportive of the officer and minimized an infraction of the rules while taking steps to see that the officer does not reinvolve the department in a repeat performance of the infraction. You can be sure that there exists a communication between the supervisor and the officer: The supportive supervisor is the one who listened, asked questions, and made a decision, working *with* and not *on* the employee.

Guidelines for the Traffic Supervisor

A supervisor who has grown through the ranks is usually experienced in dealing with the public and has learned to cope competently with the most serious issues that arise. That same supervisor may not know how to supervise and evaluate experienced traffic officers and investigators. Motorcycle officers seem to develop their own subculture, investigators another, and car-cops yet another. To facilitate the work of the fledgling supervisor in this area, the author offers the following "Three A's" for consideration.

Accountability. Hold an officer responsible for his beat. Ask yourself: Does the officer know what is happening on the beat? What is the collision picture? When do the collisions occur? What is the quality of the collision reports? Who is involved in the collisions: drunks, commuters, tourists, locals? What is the officer doing about the problem to have an impact on the number of collisions? Has the officer submitted any suggestions to offer engineering changes to reduce collisions?

Availability. Is the officer available for calls, or out of the high collision area of the beat during times of highest collision anticipation? How many calls are missed and why? Which calls were missed or unanswered? Check the officer's citations. Look at the time of issuance and the location of the stop to see when and where an officer is working the beat or adjoining beat. It may well be that the officer has located a "berrypatch" or "hole", is writing quantity rather than quality, and is unavailable when his presence is required to reduce collisions where it really matters, on the beat.

Activity. How many citations does the officer write? How many verbal and or written warnings are made? How many abandoned vehicles are checked? How many motorist services are made? How many stolen vehicles are recovered? How many other non-traffic related crimes are turned as a result of traffic stops? What is the total number of collisions worked and of what severity? How many parking citations were issued, where and for what infraction? What is the total enforcement contact number in relationship to the total number of hours worked? Is the officer writing one ticket per hour, or three to four per day in a month averaging 164 working hours? Is the officer writing citations and collisions at the same rate as others who have worked this same beat in the past? Every supervisor knows any given area, and approximately what number of citations will be judiciously generated by the officers previously assigned any given beat. An officer who writes more or less than a reasonable figure calls for supervisorial inquiry.

Look also at the violation and the location on the officer's citation. Was the violation worthy of a citation or should it have been a written or verbal warning? Look too, for patterns: some officers cite men and warn women or vice versa for the same offense. Other officers look for and cite tourists and out of state vehicles. In short, just like working traffic, look for that which is out of the ordinary. Be aware, too, that some officers stop writing citations when the sun goes down, and although they are out there somewhere, they are not making traffic stops. Collisions and violations do not cease simply because of the hour of day or night.

There are different reasons why various departments issue citations. The reason may differ from one city's police department to the next, or from one watch commander and the next within the same department. As a supervisor, you must translate these differences to the officers, giving reasonable direction in every instance. Avoid the expression, "Because I say so." Make it a point to know the watch commander's expectations and be able to convey those expectations into reasonable terms the officers will understand. If, as a supervisor, you are aware of the "Three A's," your officers and supervisors alike will know that your concern is for the best interests of your community, the department, and the officers.

The Importance of Teaching. There is but one cardinal rule to effective police and traffic leadership: *Be available.* A supervisor who is in the office is hardly effective in the field. There is no substitute for an on-the-scene supervisor. This individual is present when the officer needs assistance, and is not in the office doing paperwork that should and can be handled by someone assigned to the administrative function.

There is a very wise, tried, and true adage that states, "The job of police work is out there where the rubber meets the road." Few collisions or crimes can be solved, investigated, or prevented from a position behind a desk in the station. Too many supervisors bury themselves into the niche of administrative functions when they are promoted, leaving the officers to handle their own problems.

The most effective supervisor is a teacher. The most effective learning comes from the experienced supervisor who is present, on the scene, and offering assistance to the officers as needed. This premise is basic to all police work. Supervisors assign new recruits to work with a break-in officer. After a period of time, they are free to work on their own, and to grow, but young officers mature and continually learn with the help of a concerned supervisor.

The teacher concept should never be forgotten. Teaching should be a consistent theme throughout all the ranks in a healthy department. There should be a sharing of experiences, ideas, and methodologies that work, preventing the subordinate from having to reinvent the wheel to solve a particular problem. In a healthy department, the supervisor is available to meet with the subordinate, to listen, and offer suggestions that will help the officer mature.

Handling Questions From Officers. When an officer asks "Why?" the answer, too often, is "It's in the book." This is not an appropriate nor acceptable response. The supervisor should answer the question, and give the officer the source to review. Otherwise, the supervisor will soon find that no one asks questions for two reasons. First, no one wishes to appear stupid; why ask a question if the supervisor's response is going to be "It's in the book." Secondly, communication has failed, and will continue to fail, because the supervisor has closed the door to communication. The supervisor's stock answer—"It's in the book"—is unresponsive and one-way. The supervisor is neither listening nor teaching.

Supervisors often forget that subordinates occasionally ask a question or make a statement in the presence of others in order to open a meaningful conversation. By keeping the question simple, the subordinate is giving the supervisor an opportunity to respond in a thoughtful and intelligent manner. If an ego-centered supervisor answers the subordinate with something like "Why do you ask such a stupid question?" while still in the presence of others, the supervisor can be sure that the officer or subordinate will not ask any more questions. Communication dies between a supervisor and a subordinate when the subordinate is belittled in front of his peers. This kind of behavior breeds mistrust; future communication is now ruled out.

DISCUSSION QUESTIONS

1. Discuss the predictability of traffic collisions in your area or near your home. Is police coverage adequate? What can be done from a supervisor's point of view to reduce the number of collisions in this area?

2. What is the effect of citizen group complaints on deployment and scheduling in your area? Do the police supervisors seem responsive and empathetic? What is the attitude of the officers?

3. Does it appear that there exists a camaraderie and unity of purpose between the local streets and roads departments with the police in your area, or are the two entities working seemingly at odds with one another?

4. Discuss "ego-centered" versus "other-centered" supervisors. as their talents apply to public service, and in particular, the police profession.

5. Utilizing the continuum model, how do you rate your local police department, policies where you work or attend school, and the advisability of your last important decision?

6. Discuss various supervisors and their negative or positive impact on your life, your work, or your education.

14

Management of
Unusual Collisions

EXAMPLES OF UNUSUAL TRAFFIC OCCURRENCES

Spilled Loads

Collisions involving spilled loads are, without a doubt, the most hazardous to the officer. Such collisions are becoming more prevalent and deserve special consideration. The prevailing winds in the northern hemisphere are predominantly out of the west; for this reason, the officer should consider working from the west side of a spilled load collision for driver extrication to avoid inhaling toxic fumes.

First Steps. In a typical collision as diagrammed (Fig. 14-1), the officer's pre-investigation evaluation should include a call for assistance to reroute all north-bound traffic. If the officer allowed traffic to continue in the N-1 lane, a passing motorist might drop a lighted cigarette or a car might backfire or cause a spark which could easily ignite the ground level vapors. As quickly as possible after clearing victims, the officer should obtain a shovel and start building a series of dirt dams to protect the storm drain. If gasoline, oil, acid, solvents, or many commercial chemicals enter the storm drain system, a number of dangerous situations can arise such as explosions which can occur miles from the scene, death of fish and wildlife, contamination of water systems, and neutralization of sewage disposal plants.

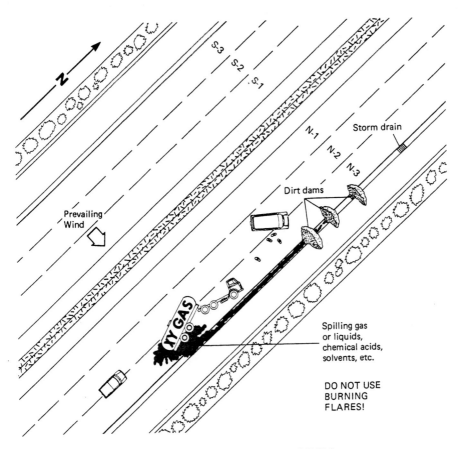

FIGURE 14-1. Spilled Load Collision

Determining the Nature of the Load. The officer should determine the nature of the spilled load as quickly as possible. Placards on the vehicle may be a clue but are often misleading. One available source of information is the driver's bill of lading located in the cab of the truck tractor. *If the spilled load is containerized, the best information as to the nature of the chemicals involved is the placard on the container.*

Spilled loads involving nuclear material are not uncommon when you consider the thousands of shipments to and from hospitals, universities, commercial enterprises, and military bases. Most shipments are well protected in sealed, spillproof containers; others are not so guarded. Downed aircraft are an excellent example. The tremendous impact of an airline collision will unleash the best of containers. The officer should also be aware that nuclear containers may well be part of a mixed load hauled by a common carrier.

Gaseous products are common materials hauled in tankers on our highways. Besides butane, the dangerous items being transported are ammonia, liquid oxygen

271

(L.O.X.), liquid natural gas (L.N.G.), and chlorine. Each of these gases is extremely dangerous either for its explosive capability or fatal toxicity. Numerous non-toxic, normally stable, products become killers when exposed to a firefighter's vigorous hose during scene washdown.

Not to be forgotten, in the realm of bizarre is the grocery truck. There are a wealth of toxic mixtures carried as a cargo. Suppose a number of soft drink cases are broken, spilling that liquid refreshment and saturating the load. In that same van will undoubtedly be a box or two of powdered pool chlorine. The combination of soft drinks and harmless powdered pool chlorine releases a deadly green cloud of chlorine gas and a 300° F chemical fire. Cleaning agents are another similar example. Scouring powders contain chlorine in a relatively harmless form until mixed with window cleaner liquids which contain ammonia. The effective combination is a killer. Look around a supermarket and note the potential hazards. How many items made of plastic or styrofoam do you find on the toy and home products counters? When burned, plastics and styrofoam produce a fatally toxic gas. If these materials are confined in an enclosed semi-trailer and there is heat from malfunctioning or over used brakes, there is often an exceptionally dangerous fire.

Handling Dangerous Chemicals in a Spilled Load

Numerous collision fatalities are attributed to farm chemicals, fertilizers, and defoliants. The ammonia and nitrate family of chemicals and combinations of sodium are quite common. The trigger to an explosion might well be something as simple as the addition of water as firefighters attempt to knock down a blaze. Recall that fertilizer nitrates leveled a Texas harbor. Parathyon is a deadly killer which has claimed a number of policemen, firemen, farmers, and truckers.

The cloud of smoke from a truck fire is a big clue. Avoid the smoke, stay upwind, and know that if you go in for a rescue you are risking your life. Unfortunately, there may not always be a cloud or odor to warn of danger. A number of spills may offer no more than visual impression that something is leaking or spilling. Some industrial cleaning agents, such as trichlorethylene or perchlorethylene may easily go unnoticed. In fact, some people believe these solvents have a rather pleasant perfume-type odor. The silent toxic fumes of these agents contain carcinogens which attack the lungs, and cause cancer or other respiratory diseases. The best approach to a spilled load or truck fire is one of caution; avoid lighting flares, reroute traffic, and call for assistance. If the officer has reason to believe that there is toxic gas escaping, a downward perimeter of at least 1,000 feet should be established and evacuated. As a guide, the average city block is approximately 400 feet. Three city blocks should, therefore, be the minimum cutoff. After establishing a downwind perimeter, circle around to a full 1,000 feet in all directions to account for shifting winds. The 1,000 foot clearance is a minimum. Chlorine gas is perhaps the most dangerous. Because of the vast quantities shipped, coupled with the violently toxic and deadly vapors, a chlorine gas spill may require a 2,000 foot perimeter. Given possible crosswind, fog, or inversion layer conditions where the gas does not

FIGURE 14-2.   Occupational Safety Pearl of Wisdom: One picture is worth a thousand words.

rise, it may be necessary to evacuate up to a mile away, especially in railroad tank car collisions.

To aid law enforcement personnel who must work with the many chemicals under transport, the chemical industries have established a 24 hour-a-day, nationwide phone number to provide immediate assistance. This emergency organization is known as Chemtrec. The toll-free phone number is **Area Code 800/424-9300.** When working a nuclear spill, emergency assistance will be provided by the military and specified nuclear regulatory agencies. The key to handling such incidents is containment and perimeter control. In the event of aircraft disasters involving nuclear products, clear the area to a diameter of 2,000 feet. Notify all responding agencies as to the nature of the spill or hazard and maintain the integrity of the perimeter.

FIGURE 14-3. Spilled loads may be toxic.

This includes the media, residents, and commercial vehicles. Responsible agencies may want to screen all persons coming out of the area. The screen may include decontamination by shower and a complete change of clothing.

When advising Chemtrec or any agency of a spill, obtain as much information as possible concerning the unknown substance. To reiterate an important point, package labels are the best source for chemical information. The driver's bill of lading is the second choice. The bill of lading rarely has information on chemical characteristics listed on the label.

During a truck collision when smoke is coming out from around the closed door or tailgate, *do not open the door.* An officer will be exposed to unknown danger and will, at the same time, permit fresh air into the oxygen-starved interior. Only firefighters wearing fresh air packs can enter the vehicle without fear of poisonous

274

gas exposure to obtain information; they will also have equipment to smother the fire. The officer's primary responsibility is evaluating the problem and performing emergency first aid, providing responding agencies with as much information as possible, and keeping the area secure. Many poisonous chemicals are carried by exterminators. These chemicals are extremely toxic, even in small quantities. In one case, an exterminating company employee "borrowed" a small jar full of a brown oil-like substance. The mason jar was capped and placed in the back seat of his vehicle. On the away home, the employee was involved in a serious injury collision. The driver was extricated from his vehicle and taken to a local hospital. The officer handling the collision completed a storage report on the wrecked vehicle and took inventory of the vehicle contents. The broken jar on the back floorboard did not alarm anyone at the scene. Soon after, the assisting officers became violently ill. The investigating officer is now retired with painful and permanent lung damage. The others who assisted in extricating the driver all suffered problems and lost time due to the compound. The lesson to be learned is this: First, if you do not know what it is, stay away from it. Secondly, if exposed to an unknown chemical, have a firefighter, wearing a breathing apparatus, seal a sample of that chemical for analysis if reasonable and possible. Finally, seek medical attention. It is still better to be safe than sorry. The police profession needs you on the job, not as an incapacitated example, but as a live and healthy officer.

Emergency Railway Warning

When a collision or other disaster blocks a railroad track, officers, fire fighting personnel, and investigators are often confronted with the emergency warning of railway engineers and conductors of oncoming trains. The rail conflict may result from natural disasters, a structural fire, or traffic collision.

The first officer on the scene should assess the situation, provide life-saving attention, and make arrangements as quickly as possible to stop oncoming trains. The fastest on-scene notification is effected by electrically connecting the two rails. This is accomplished by attaching the portable battery jumper cables taken from the patrol unit. The jumper cables are clipped together to form one long electrical wire. The clips on the ends of the jumper cables are attached to the wires on either side of the track.

During the construction of the track, the parallel rails are usually laid in a staggered position so that train wheels will not simultaneously pass over a rail connection on both sides of a track. As each rail union is bolted into place, a heavy gauge wire is connected around the junction plate to insure an electrical as well as a mechanical connection between the individual pieces of track. A low voltage current flows through each of the two rails and controls the track signals. By connecting the jumper cables from one track to the other, the electrical circuit is diverted in front of an oncoming train. The circuit will cause the railroad signals to change, warning the engineer.

The clear-track green lights will turn to closed-track red indicators when the tracks are electrically tied together. The red light indicator is not only evident to the engineer and conductor of the train, but to the dispatcher as well. The red lights along the track ahead of the train close a sensing device on the control panel in the railroad dispatch center, alerting the railroad dispatcher and controller. Closing the circuit instantly notifies the dispatcher who in turn notifies the engineer via radio communications of a problem ahead.

Once the officer "shorts" the rails, the next step is to notify the police dispatcher of the nature of the problem and arrange for notification of the railroad control center. The control center can then radio the staff of the train and apprise them of the emergency, its nature, and exact location.

As a necessary adjunct to shorting the tracks, warning officers should be immediately routed to locations of three to four miles on either side of the emergency incident. The warning officers should also establish the jumper cable track connections to the rails and observe that the track signals turn red. Secondly, the warning officers should establish no less than three pyramids of lighted flares in the middle of the track right of way. The lighted pyramids or stacks of flares should be set at a distance of approximately a city block apart. The stacks should be established on a straight stretch of track that will allow early visual observation by the engineer. Having seen three stacks of flares, the engineer should see the warning officer as the fourth warning. The officer should stand in the middle of the track with a flare and slowly arc the flare in a side-to-side motion. As the train approaches, the motion is continued by the officer who steps out of the way when the train is close enough to threaten his safety. The warning officer may also use the emergency lights on the patrol unit to warn the engineer on the oncoming train. The patrol unit should not be stopped or parked on the tracks. It may take several miles to stop a fast moving freight or commute train, and it will take most of the lead distance to effect a braking action. A local switch engine may be stopped by laying a three stack flare pattern closer to the incident.

The beat officer should know what type of rail traffic is to be anticipated. The on-scene officer may wish to establish warnings for both local and through rail traffic in the event of multiple tracks, depending on the nature of the emergency.

As a word of caution, the officers should be aware that nothing is truly official until word is received that oncoming rail traffic has successfully been stopped. Do not depend on any one signal, warning device, controller, dispatcher, or officer to notify the railroad engineer and conductor. Be prepared to immediately evacuate the area of the scene in the event attempts to stop an oncoming train have failed.

Collisions Involving Animals

A number of rural collisions involve animals including cattle, horses, deer, dogs, and cats. An inexperienced officer may be overeager to dispatch the injured animal. The use of a handgun for this purpose is occasionally the only option available, but usually there is a better way. Before an officer shoots an animal, there are some primary responsibilities. First, notify the local animal control personnel to see if they will handle the animal. They have the facilities for disposal and removal of the carcass. *If* no animal control personnel are available, and *if* the animal's owner requests your assistance, and *if* your department allows the humane taking of an animal's life, *then* proceed with caution.

Smaller animals should be taken to a safe location off the pavement and into a dirt or grassy area. This can be accomplished with a small length of rope or a belt put into a loop and placed over the animal's head. Do not attempt to carry the animal and do not allow any part of your body near a wounded animal's head. A wounded animal will often bite anyone coming within range, and that anyone includes owners and children. Shooting an injured animal has, on several occasions, taken an officer's or a bystander's life when the bullet ricocheted from the animal's skull or a hard object beneath the animal.

Vehicle Arson

The use of arson to destroy an automobile is employed to cover a vehicle theft, to defraud an insurance company, to surreptitiously cover another crime, or to vent displeasure with a manufacturer or dealer. Arson is a penal code crime, and not a collision.

Identification of Arson. The identification of most arson cases is not at all difficult for the officer and is a subject for further inquiry when a question exists. Most vehicle arson involves the use of an accelerant such as gasoline. The arsonist will usually pour sufficient accelerant into the vehicle to guarantee ignition and total involvement. When the accelerant burns, the abnormal heat causes the roof to buckle downward or cave in as the roof metal loses its temper. This phenomenon is readily observable whether the accelerant is used in the front, rear, or over the entire interior.

An officer should observe the condition of seat cushion springs. When an accelerant is used, the intense heat will again remove the temper from the metal and the springs will collapse. A normal fire does not develop sufficient heat for this to occur, and the springs will be in place and functional, even when the upholstery is burned away.

The presence of an unusual odor such as cleaning fluid, lighter fluid, kerosene, or oil requires investigation. Look, too, for spot burns on the upholstery in places where the fire should not have been in evidence. An engine wiring fire does not burn holes in the back seat cushion, for example.

If the engine compartment is involved when you arrive at the scene of a car fire, do not attempt to open the hood until you are ready to fight the fire. Effect an evaluation, call for the appropriate fire fighting agencies, effect first aid, and clear the immediate scene. Lastly, and then only when armed with capable equipment, extinguish the fire.

Fire and Burn Prevention. In the event of a front-end collision, it is not un-common for the collapsing metal to tear into the electrical circuits, creating fire-causing shorts. As a safety measure, remove the cables from the batteries of collision vehicles as soon as possible. Even when fire is not evident, the hook-up by the tow truck may torque the twisted metal into cutting through the insulation of a "hot" wire. Bear in mind that most front engine vehicles cradle the battery near the front grill in one corner of the engine compartment. In this position, the battery is very vulnerable to a front-end collision. The acid spray of a shattered battery is also a factor to be reckoned with at a collision scene. Battery acid sprays forward and onto the struck vehicle. Many an officer has come away with a uniform that makes him look like a fugitive from a moth convention, after brushing against an acid-sprayed vehicle or component parts. The chemical acid burns are quite painful to a careless officer.

Fire Rescue Operations. Fire rescue operations out of a burning vehicle are diffi-cult. If the collision did not seal the doors of the vehicle, making entry difficult, the heat which is conducted through the metal will often expand the door, making entry next to impossible. The windshield, however, affords as large an opening as a door; if the windshield opening cannot be used, try a side window.

Breaking a window to effect a rescue can be a difficult task. There are a number of ways to get the rescuer inside a locked vehicle. When the victim is trapped in the front seat, there are several approaches. First, wear gloves if you have them handy; if not, do not stop to look for them when seconds count. Using a large lock blade knife or a military "K" bar type hunting knife, insert the point under the windshield weather-stripping, starting at the upper midpoint of the windshield. With one hand on the knife handle and the other on the back of the blade, draw the knife towards you and follow down the edge of the windshield. Go quickly to the other side of the car and start again at the midpoint of the windshield and draw the knife again through the weather-stripping rubber, towards you and down. Now, using a tire iron, jackstand, crowbar, the knife, or anything else available, pry the windshield away from its moorings at the top mid-point, the weakest portion of the windshield. The windshield will break, but will remain in one or two big pieces which can be thrown aside in order to gain entry. This method alleviates the problem of extri-cating the occupant over broken glass. Also, if the occupant is trapped behind a collapsed steering wheel, the rescuer is in a position to pry the wheel upward and take the weight off the victim. The prying can be done with a jackstand, crowbar, or if present, a tow truck hook. Entry to a vehicle can be accomplished in a short period of time using this method.

Some departments carry "Slim-Jim" door openers to allow entry to a locked vehicle. When a person is trapped in a vehicle and the doors are locked, this is a good tool. However, with burning vehicles this takes time, and the doors, handles, and all metal will be hot, so be careful. Entry can also be effected by smashing a window on the side opposite the victim. This can be accomplished with the solid butt stroke of a police baton, jackstand, crowbar, tire iron, or a fire extinguisher. A baseball bat type swing will rarely break a car window; a butt stroke will. Another method of breaking windows is to carry an inexpensive spring loaded center punch of a type used in metal work. By cocking the punch and holding the point to the glass in the lower ledge or corner of a door window, the glass will shatter when the punch is released.

There is obviously no way that an officer or rescuer can predict or train for all possibilities which can occur in a collision setting. It is important to think about the possible situations that could occur and work out solutions through the planning process. For example, there are a limited number of ways to enter a vehicle; think about the ways you would choose under various circumstances.

Plan for collisions which might occur, including where such collisions are most likely to happen and why. The minutes you save because of preplanning may very well save a life, possibly even your own.

USE OF FLARES AND CONES

The paramount rule stressed throughout this text is *Never turn your back to moving traffic.* Do not trust drivers to drive in a safe and prudent manner, believing they will see and respond as you, the officer, would anticipate or direct.

As previously noted, drivers respond better to flares interspersed with cones. The cones provide a visual barrier of height. As a matter of course, each patrol unit should and can easily carry eight to ten 12 to 18 inch cones in the trunk of the unit. The reflectorized cones, or cones which have a reflectorized sleeve, will provide the best visibility.

When laying a flare and cone pattern, follow these simple guidelines:

1. *Walk facing traffic* as you lay out the flare and cone pattern.
2. Lay the pattern in such a manner that on-coming traffic has a logical path to travel.
3. Taper the pattern, creating a path for lateral compression that is gradual and obvious, not just for the officer, but for approaching drivers.
4. Avoid a pattern which instantly cuts off a lane of travel, particularly at intersections where turning vehicles become a factor.

A good flare and cone pattern takes care of traffic around the scene, relieving a traffic control officer from the duty of flagging traffic. The traffic officer can lay the pattern and then return to the scene to assist in vehicle removal, storage, and scene management.

FIGURE 14-4. The flare arrangement shown is known as "pyramiding." In this instance three 30 minute flares are arranged to provide one and a half hours of uninterrupted and trouble-free traffic control. This method frees an officer from flare maintenance and replacement.

STARTING STALLED VEHICLES

There are numerous occasions when an officer finds drivers who are disabled on the shoulder of a highway. In a number of cases, the battery of the disabled vehicle has such a low charge that it will not start the engine. In most instances a jump start from the patrol unit is all that is needed to get a disabled vehicle on its way.

Jumper cables are usually too short to reach between the batteries of two cars facing in the same direction, parked one behind the other, and it is impractical to turn the patrol car around on a freeway to face into the disabled vehicle. It is also impractical and unsafe to pull alongside the disabled vehicle. Faced with an impossible situation, the officer usually calls for a tow truck to bring out a portable battery to effect a jump-start.

Each moment that a disabled vehicle sits on the side of a freeway increases the probability of a collision. The following method can eliminate the necessity of waiting for a tow truck.

Take the battery jumper cables and clip two ends together, forming one long cable. Then drive the patrol unit forward until it touches the bumper of the disabled vehicle. This provides a common electrical ground between the two vehicles.

Then, attach the extended jumper cable between the "hot" posts of the two batteries. Have the driver start the disabled vehicle.

In those cases where the bumpers are shrouded in plastics, a common ground can be effected by laying the jack stand across any bare metal contacts between the patrol unit and the trunk area of the disabled vehicle. The common ground is the necessary contact.

When jump starting another vehicle be extremely careful not to cause any sparks over the tops of the batteries. The hydrogen gas which escapes from a battery will explode as the sparks are generated. The explosion will split the battery, spray the acid, and cause a fire.

DOWNED POWER LINES AND POLES

Collision vehicles occasionally strike power poles and cause live wires to fall in and around the immediate scene. When a hot wire falls on an occupied vehicle, rescue operations are difficult. Remember that the vehicle itself is insulated from the ground by the rubber tires, and the occupants in the vehicle are in little danger of electrocution.

The first rule for the investigator is to isolate the area from well intentioned but unwary citizens who may attempt to open the doors of the car to effect a rescue. As they touch the vehicle, they become a short to ground and may be electrocuted.

The best source of immediate assistance will be the local fire fighters. They have ropes and safety devices which can cut and pull the dangerous wires out of the way so that a safe rescue can be effected. Until rescue units arrive, encourage the vehicle occupants to stay inside; they should not attempt to escape except in the event of a fire. If a fire ensues, have the occupants open the doors and jump clear so that their bodies do not touch the ground and the vehicle at the same time. If there are no gasoline spills and the occupants are in no immediate danger, poles and lines can be pulled off of a vehicle by attaching the rope to the patrol car and dragging the pole and lines to the side of the roadway.

When calling for the fire department rescue units, the officer should also have the dispatcher immediately notify the local power company. To facilitate the needs of the power company, the officer should give the dispatcher the number on the pole. The pole number will provide the power company with information concerning needed repair items, transformers, cross arms, insulators, wire size, and so on.

If an accident involving power lines occurs in the rain, the officer must be doubly alert as anything wet will conduct electricity. Even in dry weather, the rescuer may be standing on a freshly watered lawn and be electrocuted. The key once again is to think safety first and keep others away from the downed lines. The lines may go dead for a few moments, and then an automatic device will close the circuit once again, and the lines will be fully charged. This process will be repeated several times before the high voltage lines are rendered safe. In any event, consider any downed line to be hot unless you have positive proof to the contrary. Even when a line switch is opened, the line may be fed from another source.

CONCLUSION

This chapter has dealt with safety and awareness. There is no possible way to deal with each unusual incident which could and has occurred. It is anticipated, however, that students will grasp the enormity of an officer's responsibilities to self and others and think through the consequences of all possible actions. When the odds favor a successful rescue, there is little to do but make an educated and thoughtful attempt. It is the author's personal experience that officers will continue to effect rescues in the teeth of very poor odds. Some will pay the ultimate price, others will survive, and still others will be successful. There are times when, for whatever reason, officers are prone to try.

DISCUSSION QUESTIONS

1. Do gasoline and propane fumes tend to rise or flow at ground level? How will these spills affect an officer's response to clearing an area?
2. What is the best source of information concerning the contents of a hazardous spill from an overturned truck?
   a. The truck placards
   b. The shipping papers
   c. The container labels
   d. The driver
3. What agency in your area has the responsibility for the investigation of vehicle arson? Is it viewed as a police or fire department responsibility?
4. The battery in an automobile generates hydrogen gas as it is being charged. What engine-compartment fire hazards exist because of this phenomenon?
5. Does your local police department carry warning cones in the trunks of the units? How about your fire department and ambulance services?

Traffic Enforcement Techniques

INTRODUCTION

This chapter is designed to expose students to enforcement tactics and instill an appreciation of safety techniques. Most police departments have developed training programs utilizing the experiences of its force. There is no substitute for on-the-job training and experience. Classroom texts and instruction can only instill a deep sense of awareness and uncover a student's potential.

The techniques presented in this chapter have been selected because they represent the various tested methodologies employed by most departments. Positive discussion of these techniques is encouraged.

OMNIPRESENCE

Perhaps the biggest single factor in traffic control is the visible police unit on patrol. The unit that is carefully hidden behind a blind intersection may be initiating activity by writing a large number of tickets; however, he is not contributing to collision prevention quite like the unit that is cruising through the high collision areas, looking for the primary collision factor violations.

There are a number of identifiable factors involved in the psychology of successful police patrol which are particularly true of traffic enforcement. First, we assume that because an individual has a driver's license that he has passed an examination with the licensing agency and therefore knows the basic laws of driving and believes that the laws are for the good of everyone. Secondly, a driver has the subliminal feeling that the moment he or she breaks the law that the officer will be there to observe the violation and take appropriate action. Lastly, the driver believes that when arrested or apprehended there will be a judicial sanction of a fine, a sentence to traffic school, or for the more serious offenses, a term in jail. In previous chapters we have dealt with the psychological factors involved that make traffic enforcement possible through awareness. In this discussion, we will be concerned with what the traffic officer can do to perpetuate the driver's feeling of an officer's omnipresence on the road.

ROAD PATROL

Two Types of Officers

A supervisor can readily discern the difference between a successful officer and a mediocre officer who is simply putting in time during the line-up or briefing. When an all-points bulletin is read, the mediocre officer is not paying attention and will probably not record the information. When the officers leave the briefing and get into their units, the mediocre officer is busy lining up the first coffee stop while the successful officer is checking his equipment, first-aid kit, shotgun, tires, and vehicle log.

When the officers leave the yard of the station the two officers and their units may look alike in nearly every respect, but there is a vast difference in the quality of road patrol which will follow. The successful officer will follow the cardinal rule of sweeping the beat, that is, he drives the length of the major highway or primary streets within the beat to insure that there are no disabled motorists in need of attention and that there are no surprises which have been unreported, such as malfunctioning signal lights. The successful officer is not in a hurry, but cruising in the slow lane, allowing other traffic to pass, and noticing what is new on the beat today; road construction, lane closures, and visual hazards. The mediocre officer, meanwhile, is probably finishing his second cup of coffee.

He is running late, so he beelines to an intersection on the backside of a residential tract where there is a stop sign that most residents roll through in a California stop. Although there have been no collisions at this intersection, the mediocre officer still writes three or four citations per day at this intersection to keep his activity "count" acceptable. Because he is so far out of position, when a collision call is received he has to drive in a manner well over his capabilities. He finds out too late that the street department closed two of the three lanes on a major highway to work on a sewer pipe, and he is stuck in impassable traffic. He now has to rely on his fellow officers to cover for him again.

The successful, omnipresent officer stops for a coffee break on his beat and knows what there is to know about the area. He notices the delivery trucks stopped in the alley and is well aware of the lane closures. When the collision call is broadcast, he goes immediately to assist, probably knowing that the primary unit will be late and he will be stuck taking his report.

This is not an uncommon scenario but an everyday occurrence. There are some officers who seem always to be in the thick of things and others who are always spectators, according to some supervisors.

Patrol Techniques

High Visibility. When the officer is visible and on patrol, drivers are on their best behavior, and collisions are minimized. The best patrol techniques are to drive at or below the speed limit to best observe all that is going on around the unit. Secondly, make turns and scout the side streets as well as the main highways. There is little to be gained in driving for great distances with the same vehicles in front and behind the unit. In moving with the platoon of traffic, the officer simply becomes just another driver. By turning out of the traffic, the officer will be looking at a new group of vehicles, who will be looking at the officer as well. Once again, the object of patrol is *visibility*. The presence of a marked patrol unit will engender safer driving and will reduce collisions. It is logical to assume that most drivers violate the precepts of the law when there is a reasonable expectation that there is little or no patrol in the area. It is for this reason that intoxicated drivers will attempt to negotiate the backstreets avoiding certain detection, only to become involved in a collision on unfamiliar roads.

By all means, the officer should obey the law and set the example for others to emulate. The officer who makes the illegal "U" turn, runs the stop sign, or intentionally speeds for no apparent reason runs the risk of irritating the motoring public, engendering complaints, and most importantly, becoming an unwitting participant in a preventable collision.

Fixed Post Observation. Depending upon policies of the department, there may be incidents where fixed post observations may be desirable. There was one freeway incident where motorists were passing stop-and-go traffic which was lined up in the daily commute to go off at a downtown ramp. When the passing vehicles approached the ramp, some would suddenly attempt to enter the exit lane. The collision rate was extremely high. A motor officer stationed himself in the gore point of the ramp and began to issue citations to the violators. It was not long before the press picked up the story, praising the officer's efforts. It seems that any number of people who lawfully exited were becoming increasingly frustrated by those who did not, and when they observed the violators being stopped, they were impressed. The positive press was worth a thousand citations for any other infraction, as it reaffirmed driver faith in the certainty of apprehension. The officer was not on patrol, but he was certainly visible. As the bulk of the traffic at this location was commuter traffic, the message of enforcement stuck. The collisions dramatically dropped, as did the need for the officer's presence. Other instances of fixed post enforcement may be equally as valid, such as with speeders going through a construction zone or shoulder passers at the scene of a collision, interfering with rescue units. Note that fixed post enforcement should be allowed only on a temporary basis, as it drains officer strength needed for emergency response. Fixed post enforcement or traffic control takes the officer out of the picture and effectively drains response and assistance capabilities.

Rolling Fixed Post. There is a patrol procedure which calls for "rolling fixed post." One example of a rolling fixed post is the use of marked patrol units, usually motorcycles, along parade routes or on V.I.P. escorts. Another example is a unit assigned to follow school buses to insure that motorists stop for the flashing red lights when students are being picked up or dropped off. Again, these assignments are temporary in nature.

Special Events. When there is a recurring event that requires control and enforcement capabilities, the supervisor will have to specifically schedule coverage. An example of such a requirement is a county fair, race track season, regular sporting events, and so on.

High-speed Patrol. There are some officers who patrol at a rate of speed faster than the flow of traffic, or over the speed limits. The idea behind this procedure is that the officer is constantly looking at traffic as he or she overtakes the vehicles ahead. Now, let's look at the pitfalls of this patrol methodology. First of all, without the use of the emergency equipment, it is illegal. Secondly, the officer fails to see what is going on around the unit in, on, or with adjacent vehicles, because of the limitations of narrowing peripheral vision at the higher speeds. Lastly, and most importantly, high speed driving is dangerous. Collisions at high speeds increase in severity and tend to be more spectacular in nature. Other drivers do not anticipate that a patrol unit not running with emergency equipment is speeding, or a danger to them. A sudden but legal lane change from a vehicle ahead is all that it takes to set up a patrol unit collision.

Operating Emergency Equipment. When operating the emergency equipment on the patrol unit, you are committed to operation in the fast lane only. If you attempt to pass yielding traffic to the right, the yielding driver may lawfully collide with the patrol unit and state that he was pulling to the right as required by the law, and he is right. Save the emergency operation equipment for those moments when it is actually needed—to clear an intersection, for example—and drive at or near the speed limits so that you may see and be seen. Remember that the emergency equipment was designed to allow certain exemptions from the law, but it still does not exempt the officer from sensibly exercising responsible driving techniques. In the event of a collision, the burden of proof lies with the driver of the emergency equipment to prove that the lights and siren were functioning; this is especially true in civil litigation.

There are a number of police academies which teach a hands-on course in driving skills for recruits and cadets. There is no substitute for a professionally-prepared course in emergency vehicle operations, and no officer should be assigned to traffic enforcement without the benefit of such a program.

PURSUIT DRIVING

Pursuit driving is the crux of emergency vehicle operations and demands the most in driving skills. Before entering a pursuit to apprehend a violator, the officer has to mentally weigh the odds of successful apprehension. In the event of a collision, odds are very high that someone is going to be hurt. When a pursuit begins to enter an area of high traffic density, the officer will have to answer some very heavy questions.

1. What is the reason for the pursuit?
2. Is the pursued person wanted for anything more than speeding?
3. What is the risk to others?
4. What is the risk to the officer?
5. If the pursuit were terminated, is it likely that the offender would slow down to a more reasonable speed?
6. If the officer can identify the driver and has a "make" on the plate and vehicle description, is there any reason why the officer cannot file a criminal complaint and bring in the violator at a later time on a warrant?

It may very well be that the officer chooses to discontinue the pursuit after thinking it out rationally. There will be times, however, when the officer must continue the pursuit, such as when chasing a fleeing felon. In these instances, the officer is often left with no option. There are a number of items in the officer's favor, however. The officer knows his or her beat, including every little pot hole in the road, and the speed at which a curve can be successfully handled. The violator is usually not aware of the idiosyncrasies of the roadway and has had few opportunities to test the capabilities of his vehicle. Additionally, the violater usually is not a professional driver; the officer drives for a living. The violator will invariably make, wide turns and gamble with passing maneuvers, whereas the officer has emergency equipment to forewarn motorists of his presence. Lastly, the officer is driving a vehicle that is mechanically sound, in comparison to the average violator's street machine.

Guidelines for Pursuit Driving

If during a pursuit the officer loses sight of the violator at an intersection and wonders if the vehicle went right or left, bet on a right turn. Left turns are too time-consuming and difficult to handle, especially at high speeds and at night.

Avoid all the pitfalls of normal driving while in a pursuit; do not overdrive the ca-

FIGURE 15-1. This tire was on the right, front wheel of a patrol unit in pursuit of a speeder when the sidewall separated from tread. Even though this tire "quit" in a curve, there was fortunately no collision. Slowing to a stop from 100+ MPH without crashing is a tribute to the skill of the officer.

pabilities of the vehicle nor forget your ability to respond to changes in the traffic pattern in front of you. Do not follow too close behind the pursued unit. Fluctuate the siren for the best effect rather than a steady drone. Keep dispatch informed as to your location, speed, direction, vehicle information, occupant information, and information of other units with you in the pursuit, and have dispatch notify the shift supervisor. Limit the number of units in a pursuit to no more than three as more than three is an invitation to disaster. The use of motorcycle units in a car pursuit also increases danger. The primary unit in the pursuit is always in charge until relieved by another unit, and whenever possible, the use of an aircraft should be employed. When the aircraft comes into play and spots the violator, the pursuing units can back-off and let the aircraft observer follow the violator. The violator will most often slow down and eventually stop, not realizing that the police units fell back because he is still under surveillance from the air.

Legal Intervention or "Ramming." Under some circumstances, it may be advisable to "ram" the violator, pinning the violator's vehicle to a pole, guard rail, or off the roadway into a ditch or open area. This is known as "legal intervention" and should be initiated only when legal grounds exist and with supervisorial approval. If legal intervention is the only alternative left to the pursuer, it should not be accomplished at speeds in excess of 25 to 30 miles per hour. Consider trying to strike the

288

violator's vehicle at an angle so as to offset the rear wheels, thereby setting up a spinout and a safe stop. Legal intervention is particularly effective in turns and on tight curves in the roadway. Circumstances will dictate the method and the place to the officer who knows the beat.

Shootouts. When a pursuit turns into a shooting match, the officer will again have the advantage if he keeps his head about him, recalling that the shotgun is the most effective weapon. A shotgun blast will shatter a rear window on a vehicle, whereas a bullet from a handgun will probably ricochet. The shotgun will also flatten tires, particularly on a glancing shot off the pavement. The pellets will flatten upon impact with the pavement and enter the tires, cutting through like sharpened saucers; a bullet will probably miss completely. The words of caution about shooting cannot be overemphasized. The fleeing felon has nothing to lose and will shoot at anything in his way. The officer is still duty-bound with legal and moral obligations to shoot only when it is safe to do so without endangering the lives of others.

Roadblocks. Roadblocks are an effective tool for terminating a pursuit, if properly applied with forethought and when officer safety permits. The author recalls one instance when we had a very reliable tip of a large shipment of narcotics that was being hauled in a one-and-a-half ton, covered truck. The shipment was to take place at night and was reportedly guarded by men inside the truck with automatic weapons. Knowing the freeway route to be taken, we established a dummy construction zone, shutting down the freeway and routing all traffic down a wide off-ramp. When the suspected truck was spotted, the officers, with the patrol units hidden out of sight, located themselves in and around heavy construction equipment. They all carried shotguns. When the truck came down the ramp, the equipment was moved immediately in front of, to the sides, and in behind the truck. The occupants surrendered without an incident and were completely surprised by what they thought was a genuine construction project.

In another incident on a back country road with only one lane in each direction, two officers, aware that a murder and bank robbery suspect was being pursued their way, set up another kind of roadblock. They located themselves on the pursuit side of a curve and laid out a flare pattern across the roadway as the pursuit closed in on them. They also advised the pursuing units to back-off the pursuit when they came abreast of the flares. The violator simply observed two officers standing by a flare pattern and passed the officers and their units. As he rounded the curve he was looking at two spare tires laying directly in front of him. He struck the two spare tires, went out of control, and crashed. The pursuit was terminated. The officers had taken the spare tires out of their units and laid them in the lane of travel. The lower speed required by the curve simply caused the suspect to spinout into the ditch where apprehension was easily effected. No one was hurt, and not a shot was fired. The trick is to reduce the speed of the pursuit to a point where it can be controlled.

Different jurisdictions, states, counties, and departments all have different legal requirements placed on them concerning the use of legal intervention. Prior to employing any technique, the officer must know the legal ramifications and then work the plan only with supervisorial approval.

THE TRAFFIC STOP AND APPROACH

Police officers are usually depicted approaching the violator at the driver's door. This is the most dangerous approach an officer can make to a violator.

The Right-Hand Side Approach

The safest method for all concerned is for the officer to approach the violator's car from the right hand side, or at the passenger's door. There are several important reasons for this approach. First, the driver is looking for the officer to approach from the left. If the driver intends to shoot the officer, he can have his left hand on the door handle and his right hand on the gun. At the propitious moment, he flings the door open and begins to shoot. If the officer approaches from the right side in a cautious manner, he will observe the driver and hopefully the weapon. It is very difficult for the driver to shoot back over his right shoulder or get into a position of safety for himself once the element of surprise is gone and the officer begins to shoot back. Secondly, an officer on the right side of the violator's car is less likely to be struck by passing traffic. Third, the officer can see into the glove box of the automobile as the driver goes into this compartment for the vehicle registration or for a weapon. Fourth, the driver is thrown off-balance when the officer is to the right. The driver must stretch across the front seat to roll down the window or open the door. If the driver opens the door, so much the better for the officer, as any offensive weapons can more easily be detected. Fifth, should an altercation occur, the officer is very nicely protected by the violator's vehicle and can quickly and easily return to the patrol unit to make use of the radio or obtain his shotgun while the violator is still trying to figure out a way to exit the right side of his car and still retain offense without being shot.

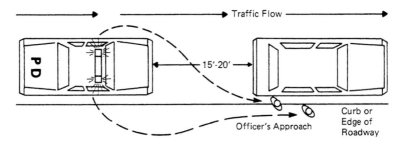

FIGURE 15-2. **Parking Directly to Rear—The Right Side Approach**

Some departments still utilize the left hand approach and compound the problem by setting up a collision situation by offsetting the patrol vehicle to the rear and to the left of the violator's vehicle. Passing traffic has less room in which to manuever on the roadway and a violator assailant has a bigger and better target to shoot. Compounding the problem of the left hand approach is the fact that the officer must constantly divide his or her attention between the violator and approaching traffic. The only time an officer should be on the left side of a violator's vehicle is to insure the violator's safe egress or entrance to the vehicle, if the officer feels it is necessary.

Progression of the Traffic Stop

The progression of the stop will usually proceed as follows. The officer will observe a violation and make an effort to quickly and safely get in behind the violator's vehicle. Next the officer will pick a safe place for the stop, off the roadway and into a parking lot, if possible. The emergency lights will be activated and the violator will pull to the curb. If a parking lot is available, the officer will address the violator over the public address speaker to please pull into the parking lot, or he or she will motion the violator into the off-highway area.

Whether curbside or in a parking lot, the officer will check the rearview mirror for approaching traffic prior to opening the door and stepping out. Satisfied that it is clear, the officer will step forward to the violator's vehicle, keeping an eye on the occupants of the vehicle. The officer will place a hand on the trunk to be sure that it is secure and that no one is inside, and walk to the right side of the car, slowly proceeding up to, but stopping short of, the passenger door. The officer will check the placement of the hands of the vehicle's occupants and ask the right front passenger or driver to roll down the passenger window. The business of the stop is then conducted in a normal manner. The only time the officer is in the traffic lane is to exit and re-enter the patrol unit.

Ideally, the officer would exit and re-enter the patrol unit from the right side; however, this is very impractical. The idea is to minimize the officer's time and exposure in the traffic lane or between the vehicles and provide for a maximum of officer security. In a two officer unit, the partner officer takes a position to the right and off set from the contact officer, so as to be in a position to triangulate and provide cover for the contact officer if necessary.

TRAFFIC BREAKS

There is a technique used by traffic officers to develop a break in traffic known as a traffic break, or "Round Robin." The purpose is two-fold: to slow traffic coming into a collision scene, and to develop a traffic free space in order to remove an object from the roadway.

When an officer comes upon, or is dispatched to, an object in the roadway or a spilled load, other officers are called on to run a roadblock that slows or stops traffic coming into the area of conflict. The break gives the responding officer an opportunity to remove the hazard without having to dodge high speed vehicles skidding into the scene.

To run a traffic break, assisting officers will enter the flow of traffic at a distance well in advance of the danger area, accelerate to the speed of existing vehicles, and then apply the emergency lights as the police units are cautiously slowed and swept across all the lanes.

Traffic is slowed in this manner as the officers in the "break" units radio ahead to the officer at the scene, advising of the make and color of the last car in front of the break units.

When the officer at the scene observes the last car pass the area of conflict, the hazard can be removed. The "break" units continue to slow traffic until they receive an "all-clear" from the unit at the scene. Upon hearing the "all-clear," the break officers will accelerate to the speed limit, pull to the slow lane, and turn the emergency lights off. The officers then continue to the problem area to provide any further assistance that may be required.

When running a break, an officer should not attempt to pursue a passing vehicle that slips through. If the officer accelerates to catch the nonobservant driver, the pack of cars built up behind the unit will also accelerate. Everyone will now be coming into the scene at a high rate of speed. The scene officer will be greatly endangered in the middle of a freeway, believing the break is in effect when in fact a "break" officer is chasing a recalcitrant driver and bearing down at a high rate of speed.

If a vehicle slips by, simply radio ahead to let the scene officer know about the make, model, and color of the vehicle. The scene officer will be looking for the vehicle. Through all of this, the scene officer should have the radio speaker on the "outside" position to be able to monitor traffic from the "break" units. Needless to say, radio communication is imperative between the "break" and "scene" units. Other radio traffic should be minimized or stopped completely to avoid the obvious problems of officer safety. Another officer initiating radio traffic could very easily override the conversation between the units endangering the scene officer.

"Round Robin" Technique

"Round Robin" usually infers a group of units which enter well in advance of a spectacular collision scene, in spaced progression, solely to slow traffic into platoons. As the units near the collision scene and slowing traffic, they pull off the freeway at the nearest ramp and go back to the starting point to pick up another platoon of traffic. The object of this system is to slow the traffic coming into the scene area, preventing a series of rear-end collisions. The benefits of this method of traffic control become very obvious when a collision scene is around a curve or over the crest of a hill. A unit responding to a collision should use the technique of slowing traffic coming into the area of collision conflict. A reduced speed arrival starts a natural break and increases awareness for other drivers.

Another use for Round Robin is the platooning of traffic through fog, heavy rain, or other natural disasters that impair traffic flow. Massive collisions have occurred in heavy fog or blinding snow blizzards. The techniques of Round Robin can, and do, aid in the prevention of such collisions; however there is little anyone can do to prevent the recalcitrant driving that is a catalyst for these disasters.

THE POLICE RADIO

The radio is the primary link with the dispatcher and provides that immediate tie to the world of emergency services. The codes provided with this text are the standard references, however, some departments do use other systems. Some utilize a plain language approach, while others utilize only parts of one of the codes.

In the event of an emergency, it is quite common for officers to forget the correct code. In this case, use plain language or anything else it takes to get the message across to the dispatcher or other units. The codes are not designed to confuse or confound a listening public, but to provide brevity to a radio transmission. An officer on the job for any length of time is very familiar with the problem of having to transmit a message while another officer ties up the air time with trivial matters. Unnecessary time spent in radio conversation in police work does more than waste money. In one case, an officer had stopped four men in a new, expensive automobile for speeding. None of the occupants looked as if he belonged in such a car. During the course of the traffic stop the officer became curious about the ownership of the vehicle in view of conflicting stories from the occupants. He ran a check on the vehicle identification number and a vehicle owner check on the plate. While waiting for a response from dispatch, he proceeded with the citation. An adjacent beat unit came on the air and proceeded to arrange a meet with another unit for a lunch break. They carried on a rather extensive conversation, trying to find a place mutually agreeable and close to the two beats. Their conversation and the casual approach to the use of the radio covered the "stolen" information that was transmitted from the dispatcher. The dispatcher, unable to raise a reply from the unit on the stop, had to clear the air to raise the unit. The two units were unable to read the dispatcher and continued their cross-talk. They covered the one and only transmission of the unit on the stop when he advised 10-35, back-up needed. Two precious minutes were lost before the "talkers" could both comprehend that one of their fellow officers was in trouble. When help arrived, the officer was completely surrounded by a hostile crowd. He had effected an arrest on the driver, had the suspect in custody in the patrol unit, and was in physical combat with the other three suspects. The crowd had opened the patrol unit, extricated the driver, and led him into a housing project where they were in the midst of cutting off his handcuffs when they were captured. The arresting officer had to be taken to the hospital emergency room for treatment and observation.

There is no excuse for lengthy conversations on a police radio network. The message is simple: *use the codes, and minimize unnecessary radio traffic.*

FIGURE 15-3. An officer who knows the beat will know what effect, if any, will be present for radio transmissions when in the area of high-voltage lines. An emergency transmission can be completely blocked by electrical arcing or magnetic hysteresis when the transmitter is keyed in immediate proximity to the lines. The extent of the problem will be in proportion to the humidity. Fog and rain will increase the probability of interference.

Phonetic Alphabet

The Phonetic Alphabet (Table 15.1) is extremely useful in spelling difficult names of people and streets, and assists the dispatchers and the officers in clarifying mispronounced or misunderstood directions. Radio reception, voice inflections, interference, and varying distances from the microphone often lead to problems for the receiver of the message. For example, even a simple name like Clark, can sound like Park, Bark, Lark and so on. To clarify, the sender transmits phonetically, "*C*harlie, *L*ima, *A*lpha, *R*omeo, *K*ilo." It is imperative that an officer memorize and become completely familiar with the phonetic alphabet used by the department.

The use of the police radio network has confused many recruits until they become familiar with the various codes and the phonetic alphabet used by their department. It is not unusual to hear a recruit stutter and stammer on the radio, burning precious air time attempting to recall the correct code. Here are the predominant codes in use throughout the United States, and two of the common phonetic alphabets. The International Phonetic Alphabet is preferred by the major departments, but some utilize an older and somewhat easier Police or Departmental Phonetic Alphabet. Both systems clarify a radio transmission so that the receiver of a message will obtain an actual spelling of the word, street, or name in question.

294

Table 15.1 Radio Phonetic Alphabet

International	Departmental	International	Departmental
Alpha	Adam	November	Nora
Bravo	Boy	Oscar	Ocean
Charlie	Charles	Papa	Paul
Delta	David	Quebec	Queen
Echo	Edward	Romeo	Robert
Foxtrot	Frank	Sierra	Sam
Golf	George	Tango	Tom
Hotel	Henry	Uniform	Union
India	Ida	Victor	Victor
Juliette	John	Whiskey	William
Kilo	King	Xray	Xray
Lima	Lincoln	Yankee	Yellow
Mike	Mary	Zulu	Zebra

Aural Brevity Codes

Codes 901 through 999, as listed, are known as the Nine Code. Codes 10-1 through 10-98, as listed, are known as Ten Codes. Codes 11-10 through 11-99, as listed, are known as Eleven Codes.

901	Traffic collision, unknown if injury
901-K	Ambulance dispatched
901-N	Ambulance needed
901-Y	Is ambulance needed?
901-T	Injury traffic collision
902	Accident, non-traffic
902-H	Enroute to the hospital
902-M	Medical aid
902-T	Non-injury traffic collision
903	Plane Crash
903-L	Low flying plane
904	Fire
904-A	Fire Alarm
904-B	Boat fire
904-C	Car fire
904-G	Grass fire
904-I	Incendiary or illegal fire
904-M	Trash fire
904-S	Structural fire
905	Animal information
905-B	Animal bite

905–D	Dead animal
905–H	Animal in heat
905–I	Animal injured
905–R	Rabies suspect
905–L	Loose stock
905–N	Animal noise
905–S	Stray animal (dog, cat)
906	Rescue
906–N	Rescue unit needed
906–K	Rescue unit dispatched
907–N	Paramedic team needed
907–Y	Is paramedic team needed?
909	Traffic information
909–C	Traffic congestion/control
909–F	Traffic flares needed
909–T	Traffic hazard
910	Can handle call
911–B	Contact the officer
912	Are we clear to/for _____?
913	Are you clear to/for _____?
914–A	Attempt suicide
914–C	Coroner needed
914–D	Doctor needed
914–H	Heart attack
914–S	Suicide
917–A	Abandoned vehicle
918	Mental case
918–V	Violent mental case
919	Keep the peace
920–A	Missing adult (18 years or older)
920–C	Missing child (13 years or under)
920–J	Missing juvenile (14 to 17 years)
920–F	Found child
921	Prowler
922	Peddling illegally
924	Station detail
924–D	Station detail/desk
924–F	Food to prisoners
924–R	Return to station to file
925	Suspicious person
925–C	Suspicious person in car
925–V	Suspicious vehicle
926	Tow truck needed
926–A	Tow truck dispatched

927	Unknown trouble
927-D	Investigate dead body
928	Found property
928-B	Found bicycle
929	Investigate person down
930	See the man
931	See the woman
932	Open door
933	Open window
949	Gasoline spill
950	Burning permit
951	Need fire investigator
952	Report on conditions
953	Check smoke
954	Off the air at the scene
955	Fire under control
959	Assignment unfinished but available for dispatch to another assignment
957	Fire out on arrival
960	Car stop, request follow-up
960-X	Car stop, expedite follow-up, dangerous suspects
961	Car stop, no follow-up required
962	Subject armed and dangerous, are you clear to copy?
965	Tab for intelligence unit, perform complete field interrogation
966	Sniper activity
967	Outlaw motorcycle movement
968	Request record check of a person
970	Illegal surfing
971	Boat over
972	Boat speeding
973	Swimmer on boat
974	Boat adrift
975	Wreckage adrift
976	Oil slick
977	Check mooring line
978	Vessel aground
979	Vessel sinking
980	Radioactive materials present or involved
981	Need radiological monitoring team
982	Bomb threat at _____
983	Explosion at _____

995	Riot or major disturbance
997	Officer needs assistance from own agency only, urgent
998	Officer involved in gun battle
999	Officer needs help, any units respond, *EMERGENCY*
10-1	Reception Poor
10-2	Reception Good
10-3	Change channels
10-4	Message received
10-5	Relay message
10-6	Busy, stand-by
10-7	Out of service
10-8	In service
10-9	Repeat the message
10-10	Off duty
10-11	Identify the frequency
10-12	Computer delay
10-13	Advise of road or weather conditions
10-14	Provide escort
10-15	Prisoner in custody
10-17	Relay papers, supplies, and so on
10-19	Return or report to _____
10-20	Location requested
10-21	Telephone _____
10-22	Cancel or disregard
10-23	Stand-by
10-29	Check for wanted (person, vehicle, or object)
10-30	Improper radio traffic
10-35	Officer requires back-up, respond Code 2, suspect present
10-36	Confidential information
10-36A	Confidential information, suspect possibly armed
10-36F	Confidential information, possible felony wants
10-36M	Confidential information, possible misdemeanor wants
10-37	What time is it?
10-39	Message or item delivered
10-97	Arrived at the scene
10-98	Assignment completed

11–10	Take a report
11–12	Loose stock
11–24	Abandoned vehicle
11–25	Traffic hazard (vehicle or object)
11–27	Driver's license check, driver held
11–28	Registration check, driver held
11–41	Ambulance required
11–42	Paramedic required
11–44	Possible fatality
11–48	Provide transportation (person)
11–66	Defective signal lights
11–78	Paramedic dispatched
11–79	Collision - Ambulance rolling
11–80	Collision - Major injury
11–81	Collision - Minor injury
11–82	Collision - Property damage
11–83	Collision - No details
11–84	Direct traffic
11–85	Tow truck required
11–86	Bomb threat
11–87	Bomb found
11–98	Meet _____
11–99	Officer requires help, *EMERGENCY*
Code 1	Routine, take this call next
Code 2	Urgent, expedite, but obey all traffic laws. No red light and siren
Code 3	Emergency, proceed immediately, use red light and siren
Code 4	No further assistance required
Code 4-A	No further assistance required, suspect at large in the area
Code 5	Stake-out. Other units avoid the area unless called for assistance
Code 6	Out for investigation
Code 7	Out of service to eat
Code 8	Fire box pulled
Code 9	Jail break
Code 12	Patrol your assigned area and report the extent of disaster damage
Code 13	Activate major disaster plan or perform major disaster duties
Code 14	Resume normal operations (used only in conjunction with Codes 12 and 13)
Code 20	Notify the news media

Code 33   Clear radio channels for emergency traffic
Code 99   Emergency situation. Emergency button in
                 mobile unit has been depressed. No voice
                 contact.

Standardization of Descriptions

There are other radio and teletype rules to follow that tend to standardize descriptions and speed the process of police identifications.

VEHICLES

1. Year
2. Make
3. Model
4. Color
5. License/VIN
6. Unusual markings

PERSONS

1. Name
2. Race
3. Sex
4. Age/Date of Birth
5. Height
6. Weight
7. Hair
8. Eyes
9. Complexion
10. Physical marks, (scars, limp, and so on)
11. Clothing (head to foot)
    a. Hat/cap
    b. Shirt/tie
    c. Coat
    d. Trousers
    e. Socks
    f. Shoes
    g. Unusual items
       1. Rings
       2. Belt/Buckle
       3. Patches

CONCLUSION

The primary goal of traffic enforcement is to observe the collision-causing violations and take immediate, safe, and appropriate action. To withhold action is a sign to other motorists that the law is selective as well as hit-and-miss. When immediate action is taken while in view of other motorists, the concepts of law enforcement are upheld and reaffirmed. In this way, the officer continues to be of service to the public and to his department.

DISCUSSION QUESTIONS

1. Discuss the advantages and disadvantages of various approaches to a vehicle stop for enforcement action.
2. How do you view the necessity for, and the use of, emergency equipment on police vehicles?
3. How do you view vehicle pursuits chasing a speeder? Should the same rules apply to the pursuit of an auto thief, or fleeing felon?
4. Depending on how you view question 3, consider where you would draw the line: who should be chased, and what effect would laws have if a violator were allowed to continue regardless of the infraction? Is it possible that no one would stop if action was contemplated and not enforced?

16

Specialization in Traffic Management

The day may well be upon us when more political and police organizations will see the wisdom in training and maintaining a department which handles traffic exclusively and other crimes only incidentally to the traffic function. A number of cities, states, and countries have already made this approach. Some even include civilian traffic investigators. There are a number of very good reasons for this consideration, which will be discussed in this chapter. Traffic is a specialized industry within the broad definition of the police role. There is obviously more to traffic management than the safe and efficient control of a collision scene. There are numerous other specialties that complete and compliment the picture, some capably performed by one officer, others requiring a bureau of specialists.

AUTO THEFT

Most departments of any size have an assigned auto theft team whose entire purpose is the early detection and apprehension of gang or ring operations. The stolen auto business represents the single largest monetary loss of all crimes. Although the actual count varies slightly over the many areas of the United States, the average figure is one stolen auto per every twelve seconds.

Auto Theft Methods

There are two ways a vehicle may be entered into the police system as stolen. The first is the usual theft from a curbside location. The thief sees an automobile parked in front of a home or in a parking lot and takes the vehicle. Often the keys are left in the ignition switch; more often the vehicle is simply "hot-wired." The victim reports the loss and the police take a report.

The second method involving stolen vehicle reporting is through misappropriation or embezzlement. This method involves the unlawful appropriation of the vehicle by the "trusted" employee or vehicle lessee in a rental arrangement. The police do not normally take embezzlement reports until advised to do so by the local township or district attorney's office. The business operator must first go to the local prosecutor, obtain a criminal complaint for embezzlement and then present this complaint to the police for enforcement action. There is also a usual time delay prescribed by law which allows the trusted employee or lessee to rectify the "misunderstanding," and return the vehicle. This time delay is usually a period of five days, exclusive of weekends and holidays.

Police Action on Auto Thefts

Once a stolen vehicle report is entered into the police system, a teletype entry is made which lists the pertinent facts concerning the vehicle, year, make, model, license, Vehicle Identification Number, (VIN), owner information, along with a case number and the agency identifier information. This police teletype entry places the stolen vehicle into the local, state, and national Crime Information Center computers. Every law enforcement agency in every corner of the United States and Canada can now identify the stolen vehicle based on a "hit" from the National Crime Information Center, as well as any of the several local files and computer references which are maintained.

In addition to the embezzlement delay of the mandatory five days, some departments—especially in high crime areas—have been known to delay the entering of the stolen information into the computer for a period of approximately three days, depending on local policy. The extra time allows the reporting party an opportunity to find his own car. Sometimes, when the vehicle is reported to have been taken while parked in front of a bar or night club, an individual has actually forgotten where the vehicle was parked, which bar was being patronized, and which friend borrowed the vehicle to take someone home. This person often recollects where the car was parked a day later. Many so-called "stolen" vehicles are located the day after the reported incident. By entering the vehicle as stolen at the time of the report, the departmental crime statistics are raised, and a false statistic is created when no crime occurred.

On the other hand, if no report is taken, and the vehicle was actually stolen, an officer who sees or stops the vehicle has no way of knowing the nature of the incident. To offset this possibility, some departments maintain a temporary local file of reported stolen cars, and dispatchers broadcast the stolen vehicle report as a "tentative" stolen car. In this case, when an officer sees and stops the tentative stolen vehicle, the driver had better have a good reason for being in possession of the vehicle. If, after a period of two to three days, the vehicle is not found by the owner, a teletype is prepared and the crime entry is completed. Confirmation that the vehicle is still outstanding requires only a phone call to the registered owner.

Auto Thieves' Ploys

Car Stripping. Thieves stealing vehicles, for the most part, are stealing for short term transportation. The vehicle is usually found abandoned at or near the thief's destination. The more serious thieves steal vehicles for the stripping racket. They take bucket seats, tires, hub caps, batteries, engines, transmissions, radios, and other component parts such as fenders and bumpers. These thieves know the problems they encounter if found in possession of identifiable serialized parts which can be tied to the theft; therefore, they want nothing to do with the vehicle itself. Their sales outlet is usually through "swap meets" and "flea markets." The more sophisticated thieves steal "to order" and sell the products directly to a customer. The stripped "hulks" are usually towed away to a drop location once the stripping operation is complete. Officers seeing a fairly new vehicle under tow should take the time to look at the towed vehicle. Thieves will not leave new tires and hub caps on the stripped vehicle. The tires will be old and worn. Hub caps will be cheap or missing. A quick look inside and a VIN check on the vehicle will confirm the rest of the story. This same observation holds true for vehicles parked in lightly traveled residential and industrial areas where little police patrol is likely during the hours of darkness. Thieves, like all of us, tend to develop habits, such as selecting "safe" drop spots. They can often be apprehended or followed by keeping an eye on their drop spots when they dispose of the stripped hulk.

VIN Switch Racket. An older ploy in the auto theft business is the Vehicle Identification Number (VIN) switch racket. Older cars, trucks, farming equipment, and most commercial equipment have a VIN tag that identifies the sequential serial number for the particular vehicle. The thief obtains a VIN plate from a wrecked or salvaged vehicle and installs the salvaged VIN plate onto the stolen vehicle. There are several clues for the police officer observing this gimmick. The "cold" VIN plate will be fastened with the wrong type of "blind" rivets; the VIN plate may have a paint transfer on its face that does not match the color of the car in question; or the plate may be attached with glue. Often, in removing the "cold" VIN plate, the thief will bend the plate or elongate the two fastening holes. To test for the glue fastening, simply insert your fingernail behind the plate and pull. A glued plate will often fall free of the door post with little effort.

With the advent of mounting VIN numbers into a recess in the left front dashboard on automobiles, thieves have been at work developing techniques to circumvent the identification process. It has been discovered that thieves are using a tape writer with blackened tape and locating the tape over the top of the "hot" VIN. A simple test for tape is to run your fingernail across the numbers; if they indent as the tape is depressed, check further. A slick, glossy VIN surface is another clue. Another feature to observe is the specific manufacturers "logo" or symbol on the VIN number. Tape writing machines cannot reproduce the distinctive symbols.

Along with the dashboard VIN is the Federal Identification Sticker which is distinctively displayed on the vehicle doorpost. The factory VIN is reproduced on the sticker or plaque as well and thwarts circumvention due to its construction. Another place to look for a VIN is inside the glove box. Many manufacturers reproduce the VIN on the plaque that tells the owner about the proper air pressure to be maintained in the tires. The glove box is another logical place to locate other evidence of vehicle ownership and VIN information. When looking for vehicle ownership and VIN information, do not overlook insurance documents, rental agreements, and contracts for service, as well as the regular papers of registration. Other numbers and identifying bits of information can be developed through secret information known only on an as-needed basis to auto theft officers and certain individuals in the insurance and auto manufacturing business. When a gang or ring operation is suspected, or involved, an officer should contact the various state and federal agencies which specialize in auto theft investigations. These investigators can readily make a proper identification of the vehicle certificates of ownership and suspect, not forgetting that there are federal violations often involving federal fugitives and federal crimes.

As previously noted, the VIN is the best source of information concerning a vehicle. Most auto thieves possess a set of "cold" plates to attach to a stolen vehicle. Cold plates are usually obtained from wrecked and abandoned vehicles. An officer spotting loose plates in a vehicle should inquire how the driver came into possession of the plates, then check and compare the VIN and the rightful ownership of the plates. The driver may be part of a gang operation involved in auto theft.

Salvage Reconstruction Rackets. More sophisticated auto theft operations include a salvage reconstruction racket, where an expensive auto is stolen-to-order for a customer. The VIN information from a wrecked vehicle is carefully removed from the wreck and reapplied to the stolen car. When the switch is complete, the thief takes the registration documents of the wrecked auto to the local department of motor vehicles and applies for the licensing of a salvaged wreck. In most states, the applicant is referred to a state police agency auto theft specialist or VIN officer who can verify the authenticity of the VIN and the documentation. This double-check reduces the incidence of this form of auto theft.

VIN Alteration. Another gimmick is the alteration of the VIN itself. Current state of the art by manufacturers makes this very difficult as the dyes necessary to make the smooth obliteration and restamping of the numbers are difficult to obtain. Some VIN alterations are still attempted, especially on motorcycles, farming equipment, and heavy construction vehicles. The officer should look for grinding marks and an uneven surface on the "boss," or raised metal area where the numbers are stamped. The "boss" is cast flat and even by the manufacturer and will not evidence grinding marks or a wavy surface. Another trick is to cut the VIN "boss" from a wreck, and then carefully weld it over, or in place of a "hot" VIN. Weld marks around a VIN "boss" should be immediately suspect. To off-set the VIN plate switch and the "boss" overlay, manufacturers will often restamp the VIN number into the metal near the VIN plate. If the two numbers do not match, number for number, there is a problem Also, there is a way to identify a vehicle known only to the auto theft specialists who can develop a true VIN number in the event of a question.

Some motorcycle manufacturers have a "cross-hatching" series of raised lines on the "boss." The VIN is then stamped through the cross-hatching. When the thief attempts to alter the numbers, he will disturb the pattern of the lines and make the overstamp very obvious.

Some gang operations drive over state and international borders. This, of course, is a violation of federal statues and punishable by federal prison sentences. The risks are apparently worthwhile to some thieves. Thousands of stolen vehicles have made their way out of the United States in "containerized shipping cases" by air or sea, while others are simply driven over international borders, depending on the ultimate destination and the needs of the customer. Stolen heavy equipment and farming vehicles often leave the United States in just such a manner.

The need for awareness in officers is acute, since it will probably be the street cop and traffic officer that trips the ring operation through a routine stop. For the traffic officer, the last word in vehicle theft control and recovery is *"Check that VIN."*

COMMERCIAL VEHICLE LAW ENFORCEMENT

The officer who specializes in commercial enforcement is an expert in laws regarding loading, weight, height, width, binding, covering, and mechanics of commercial vehicles.

Most states employ civilian specialists to check trucks and buses at the various scale facilities and garages. The enforcement arm, or commercial officer, must be attuned to the work and knowledge of the civilian mechanics and specialists. The officer must also know the pertinent laws governing how objects and people are to be legally transported for hire. There are several volumes of federal statutes alone that cover the interstate transportation of goods, products, and people. There are numerous restrictions, for example, on the commercial hauling of explosives. Routes are specified by various state police agencies and departments of transportation. Rest stops are governed by local and state fire marshalls. Load restrictions are prescribed by state and federal statutes which require that the vehicles be inspected and approved with the proper placarding, and that vehicle operation be under the scrutiny of any and all law enforcement agencies along the route. These restrictions are further controlled by written permits applicable for only a specified period of time, over certain routes, and indicated by maps which the driver must carry in addition to his required log book and shipping papers.

The commercial officer is also an expert in collision reconstruction. The officer will make mechanical determinations as to brake, steering, compressor, and other component part malfunctions. This officer will also be the one to follow the matter through the court system to prosecution of a responsible party. Although oriented to commercial vehicles, these officers are invaluable when it comes to making mechanical determinations in collisions of all descriptions. Because of the wide range of knowledge required, this position usually befalls the older and more experienced officer who must additionally be trained in this field of expertise.

Specialties within this field are the school bus, tow truck, ambulance, and armored car certification officers. Each speciality requires specific knowledge that is, for the most part, irrelevant to the officer on the street, but indispensible for the continued safe use of the highways.

With commercial vehicle collisions on the rise, it is extremely important that we establish a classification of officer that can cope with the enormity of the problem. Without commercial enforcement, our highways would be bedlam: overweight vehicles would soon chop our highways to pieces, each ambulance company might be

FIGURE 16-1. Commercially oriented officers would note no less than two violations with this load. First, the load is not blocked to prevent shifting. Secondly, the single cable tie-down is insufficient to hold the load in an emergency situation. Close examination of the cable revealed frayed and broken strands where the cable was drawn over the rear of the trailer. An emergency stop would roll the load forward over the unprotected cab.

operating its own distinctive siren and using unqualified and unlicensed drivers and attendants; tow trucks could scavange tow calls and drop the vehicles in unprotected areas with no security for the vehicles; armored cars could run with red lights and sirens between their pick-ups; school bus operators could pick and choose their stops, vehicle colors, lighting arrangements, and they could hire unqualified drivers. In short, commercial enforcement is necessary for the good of all, preserving and promiting safe, economical, and rapid transportation for everyone.

PUBLIC RELATIONS

In traffic-related public relations, the officer is faced with a very real challenge. Most adults are drivers who consider themselves better than average in driver-related skills. Giving a talk about bad check artists from a police officer's point of view is relatively easy, for few in the audience are experts in the field. A safe driving lecture must be something more, for most adult audiences tend to tune out the speaker. Most will also have been involved in a collision at some time and can recall how the situation was handled by the officer on the scene.

We do not know just what impact driver education has on drivers. Some officers are skilled in communication and leave a lasting impression on an audience, while other officers delivering the same message will put the audience to sleep, or leave them feeling indifferent. There is a special skill in relating to a group of drivers, and it is not true, as some claim, that young officers relate best to young drivers, or senior officers are best equipped to talk to older groups concerning safe driving. Quite often, just the opposite is true.

The most successful public relations presentations are those which intersperse a touch of humor with the reality of a spectacular collision. Drinking driver presentations are appreciated when discussed in terms of proximity (an incident close to home), time (a recent occurrence), and economics (hospital costs, court fines, insurance premiums, automotive repairs, doctor bills, and morticians fees.)

A successful public affairs presentation is honest. If an officer erred in judgment, follow the dictates of supervisors as to what is to be said on the subject, but above all else, do not stretch the truth. If an incident is under investigation, say so. Do not minimize the gravity of the findings. More than one department's credibility has come under heavy fire when a public affairs officer was less than truthful when dealing with the press and public.

Sometimes a public relations officer must deal with an irate citizen, following what is otherwise a very favorable presentation. The officer must listen patiently as people vent their displeasure over the "unjust" citations they received. This public airing usually occurs when the officer or program chairman asks if there are any questions from the audience. One individual will usually become a self-appointed spokesperson; the time allotted for questions becomes a vendetta forum to relate how an officer cited them for speeding and the judge agreed because the officer and the judge are golfing buddies, and this made their quota of tickets. The public relations officer must have patience and must take the time to respond sensibly. As an outsider, the public relations officer was not present during the time of the citation and trial, and therefore cannot respond on this matter. Do not take sides in the issue. The judge heard the case and decided the officer was correct; the officer was simply doing the job for which he or she is being paid, a job which is often distasteful. Usually this kind of response will endear the department to almost everyone present. Do not try to argue with a loud or boisterous individual. A public affairs presentation is not, nor should it be, a public debate or shouting match. A good method of showing concern is to ask the individual to stay after the meeting to continue the discussion so as not to cut short the time for others who would like to ask questions. As in all police work, courtesy is the key. The public relations officer is very visible, representing the entire police department. For obvious reasons this officer must know and understand the operations of the entire department, as well as trends and public opinion.

STATISTICIAN

Someone must maintain the records of the collisions and satisfy the criteria for identifying trouble or "hot-spots." The statistician also shares responsibility for reporting the collisions, injuries, and fatalities to the statisticians at the county, state, and federal levels. Concomitant with this role is the sale and distribution of collision investigation reports to interested parties, such as participants, attorneys, insurance companies, district attorney's offices, and allied agencies. The statistician and the public relations officer are both responsible for keeping the press informed about trends, spectacular collisions, victim information, and other items of general interest.

The statistician may also be known as the accident investigator or A.I. officer. Peripheral duties include reviewing collision reports for clarity, completeness, and prosecution, as well as providing any follow-up work that may be required.

The statistician may also prepare departmental graphic representations which show the rise and fall of crime, collisions, budget items, or expenditures. When the chief has a council meeting to attend, it is most beneficial to have someone in the department who can graphically display budget items in terms of cost effectiveness. This is particularly true in traffic related areas where portions of court revenues are returned for the police budget. The statistical officer should have a knowledge of mathematics in order to develop meaningful comparisons; he or she must be able to display one item against another without confusion.

COURT LIAISON

Within each department an officer must be assigned to maintain a liaison with the courts. This officer has a responsibility to the department to insure that cases are properly filed and followed through to conclusion in the court process. The court liaison officer insures that officers within the department receive a subpoena if their presence is required for the ajudication of a matter before the court, as well as call off the officers whose cases have been ajudicated prior to the trial date.

The court liaison officer also reviews arrest reports for clarity, completeness, and follow-up before taking a case to court for the filing of criminal complaints and obtaining warrants. This officer has an extremely responsible position and must be very knowledgeable in current laws as well as the policies of the particular department and the courts. This officer is the center of the entire process of criminal prosecution, as he or she must bring the arresting officer, the evidence, and the reports together before the prosecutors and the courts.

In light of the volume of activity generated in traffic-related matters, the court liaison officer must develop systems of control to insure the orderly processing of subpoenas, prosecution guides, call-offs, evidence, lab reports, and ajudications. In addition, the follow-up procedures must be checked for completeness. As an example, if pictures were taken at the collision scene, it will be of little benefit if the pictures are not ready when the trial date rolls around. This function requires a very orderly and experienced officer, capable of working under pressure and maintaining a rapport with the courts and prosecutors. This officer can make or break a departmental reputation, with the officers, the courts, and the public.

COLLISION INVESTIGATION EXPERT

In addition to all of the peripheral duties which grow out of traffic management is the need for the collision investigation expert. The development of this individual is the specific intent of this text. There is a strong need for officers who are more than reporters of facts. The collision investigation field desperately needs men and women who can take the facts to a logical conclusion. There is a large and ready market for the skill of investigating all facets of the driving equation, whether it is a poorly designed gas tank location, a faulty tire, a drinking driver, or a recapitulation of collision reconstruction which allows a judge and jury to reach an informed conclusion.

Employment in the Field

There is now, and always will be, a ready employment for the trained individual who will take the time to study physics, mathematics, psychology, chemistry, and sociology. More schools specializing in the police sciences are realizing this and attempting to locate teachers for this career. Insurance companies employ many reconstruction experts to assist in their determinations, and there are an increasing number of private investigators who make independent studies. Attorneys and courts employ specialists who have been trained in this field to assist them in preparation of their cases and providing expert testimony, ranging from product liability to degrees of driver involvement with a collision in litigation.

Additionally, there is a vast industry specializing in the auto-driver equation. The automotive industry is seeking qualified and experienced personnel who can accurately assess collisions and work in the many projects of testing and design of a better product.

Finally, there are numerous governmental agencies and private industries directly involved in the driving-safety project including military authorities, city planners, overseas organizations, truck and bus firms, and numerous safety councils and administrations. Employment prospects are many and varied for the traffic officer who understands the world of traffic and is willing to make the sacrifice of study and personal involvement. The work of traffic requires a firm commitment.

CONCLUSION

> "Man changes? Nay. . . . .
> Naught, but his technology."

Historically, people of societies do not change, but simply alter their technology to meet current needs. We cannot be so naive as to believe that future generations will be dependent upon fossil fuel engines to power their transportation vehicles. Future generations of vehicles will undoubtedly enjoy an alternate power plant, whether it is electricity or artifically manufactured propellants.

As demonstrated in Chapter 9, there are only three things which can be accomplished with any earthbound vehicle. It can accelerate, turn, and decelerate. All earthbound vehicles are, and will for all time be tied to the roadways by the physical laws of gravity, and without exception, the precepts of every chapter in this text will stand the test of changing technology. Traffic management and collision investigation is truly a discipline which is coming of age.

Projects for Traffic Education

INTRODUCTION

Because the reading of literature gives us only one side of traffic education, the author has developed two projects. The on-site exercises are designed to expand the student's appreciation through personal involvement of the actual problems present in traffic management.

The first project is designed to encourage teamwork in a low-speed vehicle and pedestrian environment, while developing a parking lot program of self-maintaining traffic control and safety. The second project requires individual effort in compiling, recording, and presenting intersection or highway data with an eye to collision reduction. Both projects are designed to give students a valuable learning experience that transcends the classroom.

PROJECT #1

Project #1 has been selected to:

1. teach the student the concepts of teamwork required in collision investigation.
2. build confidence in applying skills learned in the classroom.

3. allow the student to equate to a non-collision situation while working with the problem of moving traffic.
4. provide an on-site experience of working the traffic equation for education, engineering, and enforcement.

Scene

The scene may be a shopping center, hospital, public facility, or commercial project that demonstrates a potential conflict for auto-pedestrian parking lot conflict.

Time

During the first two weeks of the class, the instructor will poll the class and assign teams of four to six students who will work together on the project. The students will meet with their respective teams, select a location and team leader whose responsibility will be to make the observation assignments and coordinate the compilation of the final report.

Purpose

The purpose of the assignment is to have the students prepare a traffic report to present to the instructor for grading and to the facility management for apprisal of possible deficiencies with positive suggestions.

The overall purpose of the project is to develop two major considerations: (1) What is and (2) What should be.

The Report

The students will mark a sidewalk or pedestrian crossing area with two chalk lines 50 feet apart. With the aid of a stop watch or sweep second hand the students will observe pedestrian walking rates and categorize these rates over a one hour observation time frame. The pedestrian categories should minimally range as follows: the elderly, children, and all others. The students may wish to develop special categories for infirmed persons who walk with the aid of crutches, a cane, or an obvious limp, for example.

The object is to develop an understanding of how long it takes various categories of pedestrians to cross an area 50 feet in width in terms of meters or feet per second. These observations should be taken through an area void of display windows and doors which will attract pedestrian attention and slow or marginally alter the walking rates. Two separate traps should be studied.

The students should be alert to areas of conflict between pedestrians and passing or parking automobiles, especially those of "through" traffic. If, for example, it takes a pedestrian 12 seconds to walk 50 feet, you divide 50 by 12 to ascertain a walking rate of 4.17 feet per second. Note: Students who are making observations of pedestrians should be as inconspicuous as possible so that pedestrians are not watching the observers rather than traffic.

The students will also measure vehicle speeds through the parking lot of the selected locations. Be particularly alert to higher speeds of traffic in and around areas of high pedestrian traffic; look for areas of conflict. As with the pedestrian walking rates, vehicle rates should be measured over a minimal one hour time frame through a given area, and at a time of high density. For the report, list the high and low speeds (disregard stopping vehicles) and ascertain the average speed through the area. For vehicles, use a 100 foot "trap" length and, as before, use a stop watch to gauge the time it takes for the vehicle to go from one chalk mark to the other. If a vehicle travels through the 100 foot area in four seconds, the vehicle is moving at a rate of 25 feet per second. To convert feet per second to miles per hour, multiply the feet per second times the factor 0.682. In this case, 25 × 0.682 = 17 miles per hour.

Lastly, prepare a diagram of the parking lot under observation. Diagram the entrances and exits. Note areas of conflict for traffic coming into and leaving the parking lot from the main street. Look for and diagram the traffic patterns once traffic has entered the parking area. Be particularly mindful of areas of conflict, such as vehicles backing out of parking stalls; backing conflicts comprise the vast majority of parking lot collisions.

To round out the report, logically list a "What is" section supported by team observations and conclude with a "What should be" section to reduce vehicle and pedestrian conflicts. The final report is to be submitted bearing the names of the team members and the particulars of where, when, and how the report was compiled.

Forms are attached to aid the team members in making and recording their observations (Tables 17.1 and 17.2; Fig. 17-1).

PROJECT #2

Project #2: The student is required to select an intersection or length of roadway that has historically proven to be a high collision area. This study is proposed to:

1. acquaint the student with available record keeping agencies in the traffic equation.
2. provide an opportunity for the student to provide input to effect possible changes.
3. provide experience in thinking traffic and safety.
4. demonstrate those skills learned in the classroom.

Table 17.1. Pedestrian Walking Rate Study Worksheet

Location:_____

Date:_____ Time:_____

Recorded By:_____

Trap Length:_____ Other:_____ (Indicate Length)

Location of Trap:_____

Seconds to Traverse Trap

Elderly	Children	All Others	Special Study

| Average Feet/Sec. | Average Feet/Sec. | Average Feet/Sec. | Average Feet/Sec. |

Scene

The scene may be an intersection or length of roadway selected by the individual student as a high collision or high risk area.

Student's Assignment

During the first two weeks of the class, the instructor will advise the students of this individual assignment and what is expected for the completion of a satisfactory

315

Table 17.2. Vehicle Velocity Rate Worksheet

Location:_____

Date:_____Time:_____

Recorded By:_____

Trap Length:_____ Other:_____ (Indicate Length)

Location of Traps:_____

Seconds to Traverse Trap

Trap #1	Trap #2

Average Feet/Second	Average Feet/Second
F.P.S. × 0.682 = _____ M.P.H.	F.P.S. × 0.682 = _____ M.P.H.

Highest Speed M.P.H	Lowest Speed M.P.H	Highest Speed M.P.H.	Lowest Speed M.P.H.

report for grading and transmittal to the appropriate agencies for consideration. As drivers, we have all experienced a situation in some location where we feel changes could be effected that would reduce the probability of a collision. The solution, among others, might be the addition of a stop sign, restripping a center line, rezoning a speed limit, or restricting traffic with appropriate turn lanes.

316

FIGURE 17-1. Factual Diagram

The Report

After selecting an area for consideration, contact the local agency which maintains records of traffic collisions and obtain the vital statistics. Compile the statistics as to severity, time of day, and day of week, and make notes about the common

317

primary collision factors, such as right-of-way, speed, driving while intoxicated, and so on.

Armed with the historical facts, visit the area, measure the road scene, observe traffic, and, in general, develop a pattern for traffic, noting the near collisions and what causes the conflict. Ask yourself these questions: Is there a vision problem? What does this area look like from the driver's point of view? What is the effect of side traffic which is uncontrolled? Has recent commercial development made the existing speed zoning impractical? Is road side parking a factor in collisions?

If necessary, develop speed information on traffic through the area. If auto-pedestrian factors are present, determine where the auto comes into view for the pedestrian, and vice versa. When does a driver first notice the pedestrian? Knowing pedestrian walking rates, is there a possibility that the pedestrian is in an irreversible situation and doomed to a point of no return from certain positions in a crosswalk? It may be that the vehicle traveling at a given rate in terms of feet per second may be closing in on a pedestrian too quickly to effect an escape.

As with the Project #1, the investigator has to consider two major points: (1) What is and (2) What should be.

Two diagrams will be required in most projects (Fig. 17.1), the first to show present conditions, the second to demonstrate the proposed changes. Pedestrian and Vehicle Rate Worksheets will complete the study (Tables 17.1 and 17.2).

The final report should be complete, neat in appearance, and present a logical order to be forwarded to the appropriate agencies as suggestions for improvement and collision reduction, following the instructor's grading.

Appendixes

Squares and Square Roots

$\sqrt{N^2}$ N	N^2	$\sqrt{N^2}$ N	N^2	$\sqrt{N^2}$ N	N^2	$\sqrt{N^2}$ N	N^2
1	1	51	2,601	101	10,201	151	22,801
2	4	52	2,704	102	10,404	152	23,104
3	9	53	2,809	103	10,609	153	23,409
4	16	54	2,916	104	10,816	154	23,716
5	25	55	3,025	105	11,025	155	24,025
6	36	56	3,136	106	11,236	156	24,336
7	49	57	3,249	107	11,449	157	24,649
8	64	58	3,364	108	11,664	158	24,964
9	81	59	3,481	109	11,881	159	25,281
10	100	60	3,600	110	12,100	160	25,600
11	121	61	3,721	111	12,321	161	25,921
12	144	62	3,844	112	12,544	162	26,244
13	169	63	3,969	113	12,769	163	26,569
14	196	64	4,096	114	12,996	164	26,896
15	225	65	4,225	115	13,225	165	27,225
16	256	66	4,356	116	13,456	166	27,556

Squares and Square Roots

$\sqrt{N^2}$ N	N^2	$\sqrt{N^2}$ N	N^2	$\sqrt{N^2}$ N	N^2	$\sqrt{N^2}$ N	N^2
17	289	67	4,489	117	13,689	167	27,889
18	324	68	4,624	118	13,924	168	28,224
19	361	69	4,761	119	14,161	169	28,561
20	400	70	4,900	120	14,400	170	28,900
21	441	71	5,041	121	14,641	171	29,241
22	484	72	5,184	122	14,884	172	29,584
23	529	73	5,329	123	15,129	173	29,929
24	576	74	5,476	124	15,376	174	30,276
25	625	75	5,625	125	15,625	175	30,625
26	676	76	5,776	126	15,876	176	30,976
27	729	77	5,929	127	16,129	177	31,329
28	784	78	6,084	128	16,384	178	31,684
29	841	79	6,241	129	16,641	179	32,041
30	900	80	6,400	130	16,900	180	32,400
31	961	81	6,561	131	17,161	181	32,761
32	1,024	82	6,724	132	17,424	182	33,124
33	1,089	83	6,889	133	17,689	183	33,489
34	1,156	84	7,056	134	17,956	184	33,586
35	1,225	85	7,225	135	18,225	185	34,225
36	1,296	86	7,396	136	18,496	186	34,596
37	1,369	87	7,569	137	18,769	187	34,969
38	1,444	88	7,744	138	19,044	188	35,334
39	1,521	89	7,921	139	19,321	189	35,721
40	1,600	90	8,100	140	19,600	190	36,100
41	1,681	91	8,281	141	19,881	191	36,481
42	1,764	92	8,464	142	20,164	192	36,864
43	1,849	93	8,649	143	20,449	193	37,249
44	1,936	94	8,836	144	20,736	194	37,636
45	2,025	95	9,025	145	21,025	195	38,025
46	2,116	96	9,216	146	21,316	196	38,416
47	2,209	97	9,409	147	21,609	197	38,809
48	2,304	98	9.604	148	21,904	198	39,204
49	2,401	99	9,801	149	22,201	199	39,601
50	2,500	100	10,000	150	22,500	200	40,000

APPENDIX 2

Comparison of Meters and Customary Units of Feet

Feet	Meters	Meters	Feet	Feet	Meters	Meters	Feet
1	0.304801	1	3.28083	51	15.544851	51	167.32233
2	0.609601	2	6.56167	52	15.849652	52	170.60316
3	0.914402	3	9.84250	53	16.154453	53	173.88399
4	1.219202	4	13.12333	54	16.459254	54	177.16482
5	1.524003	5	16.40417	55	16.764055	55	180.44565
6	1.828804	6	19.68500	56	17.068856	56	183.72648
7	2.133604	7	22.96583	57	17.373657	57	187.00731
8	2.438405	8	26.24667	58	17.678458	58	190.28814
9	2.743205	9	29.52750	59	17.983259	59	193.56897
10	3.04801	10	32.8083	60	18.28806	60	196.8498
11	3.352811	11	36.08913	61	18.592861	61	200.13063
12	3.657611	12	39.36996	62	18.897662	62	203.41146
13	3.962412	13	42.65079	63	19.202463	63	206.69229
14	4.267212	14	45.93162	64	19.507264	64	209.97312
15	4.572013	15	49.21245	65	19.812065	65	213.25395
16	4.876814	16	52.49328	66	20.116866	66	216.53478
17	5.181614	17	55.77411	67	20.421667	67	219.81561
18	5.486415	18	59.05494	68	20.726468	68	223.09644
19	5.791215	19	62.33577	69	21.031269	69	226.37727
20	6.096016	20	65.6167	70	21.33607	70	229.6581
21	6.400821	21	68.89743	71	21.640871	71	232.93893
22	6.705622	22	72.17826	72	21.945672	72	236.21976
23	7.010423	23	75.45909	73	22.250473	73	239.50059
24	7.315224	24	78.73992	74	22.555274	74	242.78142
25	7.620025	25	82.02075	75	22.860075	75	246.06225
26	7.924826	26	85.30158	76	23.164876	76	249.34308
27	8.229627	27	88.58241	77	23.469677	77	252.62391
28	8.534428	28	91.86324	78	23.774478	78	255.90474
29	8.839229	29	95.14407	79	24.079279	79	259.18557
30	9.14403	30	98.4249	80	24.38408	80	262.4664
31	9.448831	31	101.70573	81	24.688881	81	265.74723
32	9.753632	32	104.98656	82	24.993682	82	269.02806
33	10.058433	33	108.26739	83	25.298483	83	272.30889
34	10.363234	34	111.54822	84	25.603284	84	275.58972
35	10.668035	35	114.82905	85	25.908085	85	278.87055
36	10.972836	36	118.10988	86	26.212886	86	282.15138
37	11.277637	37	121.39071	87	26.517687	87	285.43221
38	11.582438	38	124.67154	88	26.822488	88	288.71304
39	11.887239	39	127.95237	89	27.127289	89	291.99387
40	12.19204	40	131.2332	90	27.43209	90	295.2747

Comparison of Meters and Customary Units of Feet

Feet	Meters	Meters	Feet	Feet	Meters	Meters	Feet
41	12.496841	41	134.51403	91	27.736891	91	298.55553
42	12.801642	42	137.79486	92	28.041692	92	301.83636
43	13.106443	43	141.07569	93	28.346493	93	305.11719
44	13.411244	44	144.35652	94	28.651294	94	308.39802
45	13.716045	45	147.63735	95	28.956095	95	311.67885
46	14.020846	46	150.91818	96	29.260896	96	314.95968
47	14.325647	47	154.19901	97	29.565697	97	318.24051
48	14.630448	48	157.47984	98	29.870498	98	321.52134
49	14.935249	49	160.76067	99	30.175299	99	324.80217
50	15.24002	50	164.0415	100	30.4801	100	328.083

APPENDIX 3

Comparison of Inches and Meters

Inches	Meters
1	0.0254
2	0.0508
3	0.0762
4	0.1016
5	0.127
6	0.1524
7	0.1778
8	0.2032
9	0.2286
10	0.254
11	0.2794
12	0.3048

APPENDIX 4

Comparison of Miles Per Hour to Kilometers Per Hour

M.P.H.	K.P.H.	K.P.H.	M.P.H.	M.P.H.	K.P.H.	K.P.H.	M.P.H.
1	1.60935	1	0.62137	51	82.07685	51	31.68987
2	3.2187	2	1.24274	52	83.6862	52	32.31124
3	4.82805	3	1.86411	53	85.29555	53	32.93261
4	6.4374	4	2.48548	54	86.9049	54	33.55398
5	8.04675	5	3.10685	55	88.51425	55	34.17535
6	9.6561	6	3.72822	56	90.1236	56	34.79672
7	11.26545	7	4.34959	57	91.73295	57	35.41809
8	12.8748	8	4.97096	58	93.3423	58	36.03946
9	14.48415	9	5.59233	59	94.95165	59	36.66083
10	16.0935	10	6.2137	60	96.561	60	37.2822
11	17.70285	11	6.83507	61	98.17035	61	37.90357
12	19.3122	12	7.45644	62	99.7797	62	38.52494
13	20.92155	13	8.07781	63	101.38905	63	39.14631
14	22.5309	14	8.69918	64	102.9984	64	39.76768
15	24.7496	15	9.32055	65	104.60775	65	40.38905
16	25.7496	16	9.94192	66	106.2171	66	41.01042
17	27.35895	17	10.56329	67	107.82645	67	41.63179
18	28.9683	18	11.18466	68	109.4358	68	42.25316
19	30.57765	19	11.80603	69	111.04515	69	42.87453
20	32.187	20	12.4274	70	112.6545	70	43.4959
21	33.79635	21	13.04877	71	114.26385	71	44.11727
22	35.4057	22	13.67014	72	115.8732	72	44.73864
23	37.01505	23	14.29151	73	117.48255	73	45.36001
24	38.6244	24	14.91288	74	119.0919	74	45.98138
25	40.23375	25	15.53425	75	120.70125	75	46.60275
26	41.8431	26	16.15562	76	122.3106	76	47.22412
27	43.45245	27	16.77699	77	123.91995	77	47.84549
28	45.0618	28	17.39836	78	125.5293	78	48.46686
29	46.67155	29	18.01973	79	127.13865	79	49.08823
30	48.2805	30	18.6411	80	128.748	80	49.7096
31	49.88985	31	19.26247	81	130.35735	81	50.33097
32	51.4992	32	19.88384	82	131.9667	82	50.95234
33	53.10855	33	20.50521	83	133.57605	83	51.57371
34	54.7179	34	21.12658	84	135.1854	84	52.19508
35	56.32725	35	21.74795	85	136.79475	85	52.81645
36	57.9366	36	22.36932	86	138.4041	86	53.43782
37	59.54595	37	22.99069	87	140.01345	87	54.05919
38	61.1553	38	23.61206	88	141.6228	88	54.68056
39	62.76465	39	24.23343	89	143.23215	89	55.30193
40	64.374	40	24.8548	90	144.8415	90	55.9233

Comparison of Miles Per Hour to Kilometers Per Hour

M.P.H.	K.P.H.	K.P.H.	M.P.H.	M.P.H.	K.P.H.	K.P.H.	M.P.H.
41	65.98335	41	25.47617	91	146.45085	91	56.54467
42	67.5927	42	26.09754	92	148.0602	92	57.16604
43	69.20205	43	26.71891	93	149.66955	93	57.78741
44	70.8114	44	27.34028	94	151.2789	94	58.40878
45	72.42075	45	27.96165	95	152.88825	95	59.03015
46	74.0301	46	28.58302	96	154.4976	96	59.65152
47	75.63945	47	29.20439	97	156.10695	97	60.27289
48	77.2488	48	29.82576	98	157.7163	98	60.89426
49	78.85815	49	30.44713	99	159.32565	99	61.51563
50	80.4675	50	31.0685	100	160.935	100	62.137

Bibliography

Baker, J. Stannard. *Traffic Accident Investigation Manual for Police.* Evanston, Illinois: The Traffic Institute, Northwestern University, 1975.

Broom, Leonard, and Selznick, Philip. *Sociology* 6th edition. New York: Harper and Row, 1977.

Blanchard, Kenneth H., and Hersey, Paul. *Management of Organizational Behavior: Utilizing Human Resources.* Englewood Cliffs, New Jersey: Prentice-Hall, 1972.

California Highway Patrol. *Collision Investigation Manual.* Sacramento: 1980.

Drew, Donald R. *Traffic Flow Theory and Control.* New York: McGraw-Hill, 1968.

Eldridge, John A. *College Physics.* 3rd edition. New York: John Wiley, 1947.

Hand, Bruce A. *Traffic Investigation and Control.* Columbus, Ohio: Chas. E. Merrill, 1980.

Homburger, Wolfgang S., and Kell, James H. *Fundamentals of Traffic Engineering.* 9th edition. Berkeley: Institute of Transportation Studies, University of California, 1977.

Iannone, N.F. *Supervision of Police Personnel.* 2nd edition. Englewood Cliffs, New Jersey: Prentice-Hall, 1975.

Inbau, Fred E., and Reid, John E. *Criminal Interrogation and Confessions.* Baltimore: Williams and Wilkins, 1967.

Krauskopf, Konrad Bates. *Fundamentals of Physical Science.* 5th edition. New York: McGraw-Hill, 1965.

McGregor, Douglas. *The Human Side of Enterprise.* New York: McGraw-Hill, 1960.

National Safety Council. *Public Safety Memo 28.* Reprint. Washington, D.C., October 1948.

325

Ross, Murray G. *Community Organization, Theory and Practice.* 2nd edition. New York: Harper and Row, 1967.

Sharkansky, Ira. *Public Administration, Policy Making in Government Agencies.* 4th edition. Chicago: Rand McNally, 1978.

York, Kenneth J. (I.T. Corporation). *Hazardous Materials Spills.* Unpublished. Los Angeles, California: 1980.

Zimbardo, M.L. *Psychology and Life.* 10th edition. Fair Lawn, New Jersey; Scott, Foresman, 1978.

Index